FICTION
WITHOUT
HUMANITY

Person, Animal, Thing
in Early Enlightenment
Literature and Culture

Lynn Festa

PENN

UNIVERSITY OF PENNSYLVANIA PRESS

PHILADELPHIA

Published by
University of Pennsylvania Press
Philadelphia, Pennsylvania 19104-4112
www.upenn.edu/pennpress

Printed in the United States of America on acid-free paper
1 3 5 7 9 10 8 6 4 2

Library of Congress Cataloging-in-Publication Data

Names: Festa, Lynn M., author.
Title: Fiction without humanity : person, animal, thing in early
Enlightenment literature and culture / Lynn Festa.
Description: 1st edition. | Philadelphia : University of Pennsylvania
Press, [2019] | Includes bibliographical references and index.
Identifiers: LCCN 2018054071 | ISBN 978-0-8122-5131-9 (hardcover)
Subjects: LCSH: English prose literature—18th century—History
and criticism. | English prose literature—17th century—History and
criticism. | Philosophical anthropology—Europe—History. | Fictions,
Theory of. | Enlightenment—Europe. | Anthropomorphism in
literature. | Humanity in literature.
Classification: LCC PR769 .F47 2019 | DDC 828/.508—dc23
LC record available at https://lccn.loc.gov/2018054071

FICTION
WITHOUT
HUMANITY

CONTENTS

Color plates follow page 66

Introduction

The Enlightenment is often celebrated as the era in which modern theories of human rights and humanitarian sensibility took shape. These discourses appeal to the self-evident nature of humanity, yet "the human" is a strangely elusive category in the literary, philosophical, scientific, and political writings of the period. "Wherein then, would I gladly know, consists the precise and *unmovable Boundaries* of that *Species* [of man]?" the philosopher John Locke writes in 1690. " 'Tis plain, if we examine, that there is *no* such thing *made by Nature*, and established by Her amongst Men."[1] This book analyzes late seventeenth- and early eighteenth-century efforts to delineate these boundaries, by focusing on the shifting terms in which human difference from other creatures and inanimate things was expressed during the period. Although modern thought generally appeals to an abstract model of humanity grounded in its distinction from—indeed, its opposition to—animals and things, writers during this period describe a subject neither anterior to nor aloof from its objects and struggle to define the traits that distinguish humans from animals. What happens to our understanding of Enlightenment humanity when we recognize that person and thing, human and animal, are intertwined rather than opposed?

Fiction Without Humanity takes seriously the profound incertitude writers, artists, and philosophers expressed about what and who counted as human, arguing that humanity was treated not as a known quantity to be mimetically represented but as something that had to be defined and produced through literature and works of art. The title of the book is thus not mere melodrama. Literature and art, I argue, often worked without a positive, stable concept of humanity as an organizing rubric; indeed, many of the works analyzed below—still life and trompe l'oeil paintings, scientific treatises, riddles, and fables—do not feature human figures at all. The argument of the book is contained in the seeming contradiction offered by its title: it is by reading fiction without humanity (that is, by reading literary texts and artworks that do not feature human figures and by reading without treating humanity as an established rubric) that we can trace early elaborations of Enlightenment conceptions of the human. Rather than starting from a presumptive (human) subject and adding predicates or appealing to preestablished binaries of person and thing, human and animal, I show how writers use anthropomorphized animals and personified things to investigate humanity's own creaturely and thinglike nature, offering estranging descriptions of the world from perspectives that are not (necessarily) lodged in human beings. I argue that literature and works of art produce the category of humanity not only thematically (by testing the traits associated with the human) and formally (through innovations in narrative point of view, voice, characterization, description, and plotting that create and police the boundaries between human, animal, and thing) but also performatively (by eliciting reactions and practices that marked the beholder or reader as human). Enlightenment concepts of the human were created by *fiction*, understood not only as the stories writers told about the nature of humanity but also in its etymological sense of "making."

The difficulty of defining the nature of humanity is not, of course, unique to the seventeenth and eighteenth centuries—the Cynic Diogenes reportedly debunked Plato's (ironic) definition of man as a featherless biped by flinging a plucked rooster into the school, crying "Here is Plato's Man"[2]—but it is a matter of renewed urgency during a period in which changing social, political, and economic structures thrust person and thing, human and animal, into unprecedented relations that threatened to collapse the differences between them. Notwithstanding persistent religious faith in humankind's spiritual being, humanity teeters between animal and machine in much philosophical thought of the period, dominated on the one hand by its own internal mechanicity (the unthinking automatism of the body) and on the other by mechanisms of its own fabrication (of the state, of the economy, of the social order). In the late seventeenth century, political theorists bent on charting the emergence of civil society from a brutish state of nature advanced models of sovereignty that extended the powers of a Leviathan state over the bare life of its subjects, while materialist thought shattered the privileged status of man as a creature made in god's image, suggesting that humans were molded of the same base matter as animals and inanimate things. Instruments such as the microscope revealed that the human body was teeming with nonhuman life, and philosophers and scientists, in investigating the mechanisms governing a clockwork universe, spurred on technological advances that increasingly incorporated the laboring body into manufacturing machinery. The development of new systems of finance, credit, and banking in the 1690s and the subsequent revolution in habits of consumption fostered by a burgeoning market economy redefined the relation of person to property, while the great taxonomical projects of the Enlightenment strove to place human beings in relation to animals and plants on the tabula of natural history. Even as the diverse populations encountered by European merchants, sailors, soldiers, and scientists fractured assumptions about anthropological uniformity, global commerce and conquest fostered brutal oppression on a hitherto unthinkable scale, as the expansion of the slave trade reduced millions of human beings to the status of property, traded as commodities and treated like beasts. The discourses of inalienable human rights and humanitarian sensibility, with their appeal to a self-evident class of "humanity," thus blossomed at a moment in which philosophical, political, scientific, and literary discourses and practices struggled to determine where humanity ended and things and animals began.

Writers as diverse as Karl Marx, Jacob Burckhardt, Michel Foucault, Jacques Derrida, Giorgio Agamben, and Bruno Latour have stressed the dissevering of humanity from "'nonhumanity'—things, or objects, or beasts" (the phrase is Latour's) as an essential aspect of modern thought.[3] Georg Lukács tells us that the novel emerges out of "the mutually alien worlds of subject and object."[4] This book traces the various ways in which these worlds are *not* mutually alien in late seventeenth- and early eighteenth-century literature and culture. Although things have (until recently) been slighted in literary histories that emphasize the free-standing, self-proprietary individual, the liberal rights-bearing subject, and the psychological self, it is things—worn objects, props, tools, land, personal possessions—that make human identities visible during the period. And although modern accounts of lyric, of the novel, and of theatrical character often conceive of human singularity in lofty, quasi-immaterial terms (language, biography, consciousness, free will), writers were deeply interested in the passions and necessities that bind human to animal. This book thus joins the body of recent work that has questioned the nature of the individual whose emergence has been so central to eighteenth-century literary history.

Even as writers and artists endeavor to articulate the nature of human difference, they recognize that personal and collective identities are inescapably constituted through the things humans possess and in relation to the animal life over which they seek to hold sway. The silk-clad preening beau, the political economist Bernard Mandeville sardonically observes, is "beholden . . . to . . . a dying Worm," while Jonathan Swift's nymph, pluck-ing out a crystal eye and peeling off her mouse-skin eyebrows, dismantles a body pieced together out of artificial parts (some filched from animals).[5] The close relation of persons and things calls into question the conventional understanding of identity as the manifestation of an interior life and psycho-logical depth that individuals de facto possess, while the permeable threshold between human and animal challenges accounts of a self-proprietary reason-ing subject able to soar above its bodily imperatives. Although, as Cary Wolfe has contended, "there is no longer any good reason to take . . . for granted that the theoretical, ethical, and political question of the subject is automati-cally coterminous with the species distinction between *Homo sapiens* and everything else," much of the history of the correlation of subjectivity and humanity has yet to be written.[6] In what follows, I question this presumed human monopoly on subjectivity, in part by reinstating the nonhuman ele-ments or forces that reside within or behind the model of humanity to which the Enlightenment appeals. My focus on humanity is thus not simply a his-tory of the sovereign subject writ large.

Until the late eighteenth century, the term *humanity* was principally (though not always) used to refer to benevolence in one's relations to others. Inasmuch as the status of individuals was defined by corporate identities involving property, rank, gender, religion, nation, occupation, and what we would now call race, humanity was not a significant social or political cate-gory until well into the eighteenth century.[7] Indeed, as Raymond Williams notes, "The use of humanity to indicate, neutrally, a set of human character-istics or attributes is not really common, in its most abstract sense, before the eighteenth century, though thereafter it is very common indeed."[8] This book endeavors to chart the emergence of humanity as an independent category to which writers systematically appeal.

The positive content of the category of humanity was much disputed, as philosophers, theologians, and natural historians sought to secure the thresh-old between human and animal, on the one hand, and to grapple with dis-tinctions of so-called variety internal to the species, on the other. Writers feverishly scrabble for a shared trait or evasive feature—reason, speech, laugh-ter, tool use—that will serve as a gatekeeper to the class of the human, yet the chosen criteria muster categories that tend to be either overly inclusive (Diogenes's plucked rooster) or not inclusive enough (omitting prelinguistic infants because they do not speak, for example). Enumerative definitions—the "featherless biped" and its ilk—reel individual cases in and out of the circle of humanity in a dangerous game of classificatory hokeypokey, while the quest for a lowest common denominator reduces humanity to a poor, bare, forked creature or, worse, dead-ends in a tautology—humanity is what makes humans human—that reveals a void at the heart of this powerful abstraction. Materializing as a kind of remainder, as what is left after qualities are subtracted out, humanity resides less in a perdurable essence shared by all human beings than in the figures and tropes that sanction action in its name. "There are men," as the French rhetorician César Chesneau Dumarsais pointed out in his 1730 *Treatise on Tropes*, "but *humanity* does not exist; that is, there is no being that is *humanity*."[9] The absence of a paradigmatic figure—a "being that is *humanity*"—means that the abstract singularity of humanity depends on the representative powers of fiction to give it form. That is why my project is necessarily, though not exclusively, a literary one.

Indeed, many philosophers point out that *humanity* is an empty word. "To have names that would express the essence of substances," Étienne Bonnot de Condillac sneers (in a passage that found an afterlife in the *Encyclopédie*), philosophers infatuated with models of abstract logic "invented the words 'corporeity,' 'animality,' 'humanity' to designate the essences of 'body,' 'animal,' and 'man.' Once these terms have become familiar to them, it is very difficult to persuade them that they are empty of sense."[10] Ossified into self-explanatory concepts, these words operate at best as a kind of unifying fiction and at worst as a seemingly stable placeholder that disguises the absence of a definition. Habituated to the tautological logic that creates such terms, people cease to recognize their vacuity, even as these abstractions come to wield real power in the world. It is in order to breach the tautology of such circular definitions, I argue, that late seventeenth- and eighteenth-century writers and artists enfold the nonhuman into their accounts of the human.

The Enlightenment emergence of "humanity" to designate the commonality of species has been considered as one element in a much broader set of shifts: epistemological (as in the invention of "man" in Michel Foucault's *Order of Things*), natural historical (the classification of *Homo sapiens*, for example, in Linnaean taxonomies), political (in discourses surrounding human rights), philosophical (the countless essays on human nature, human knowledge, human understanding) and literary (the celebration of humanity as benevolence in the culture of sensibility). It is a commonplace that, as one essay collection puts it, "the eighteenth century in Europe was a great age for talk about 'humanity' . . . [as] many sought to understand the world around them by an increasingly intensive focus upon the nature, history and ontological condition of their species."[11] In eighteenth-century studies, questions about the nature of humanity (or "man") have been addressed in terms of the epistemological shift away from a divinely ordered worldview (the great studies of the Enlightenment by Ernst Cassirer, Peter Gay, Foucault, and others) or through work on the way global encounters recast the terms of anthropology (Daniel Carey, Felicity Nussbaum, Anthony Pagden, and Chad Wellmon). The Enlightenment concept of humanity, critics note, "is best understood not as a shared intellectual supposition, . . . but as a field of conflict in which competing visions of human life and political organization were mobilized."[12] My argument traces the ways these "competing visions" embraced the nonhuman as well as the human, for humanity arrived in this "field of conflict" flanked by animals, machines, and all manner of things. This book analyzes the roles played by this entourage.

Many of the theorists who have influenced recent work on the question of the human—Hannah Arendt, Jacques Derrida, Gilles Deleuze, Félix Guattari, Michel Foucault, Barbara Johnson, Donna Haraway, Bruno Latour, Michel Serres, Jane Bennett, Karen Barad, Giorgio Agamben, Jacques Rancière, and Cary Wolfe—have taken the Enlightenment as a foundational moment, variously drawing on Descartes, Spinoza, Leibniz, Hobbes, Locke, Kant, Rousseau, and the American and French revolutionaries, among others. These theories tend to emphasize philosophy, political theory, and the natural and social sciences. *Fiction Without Humanity* focuses on an array of literary and artistic genres in order to address the way humanity emerges not from formal definitions but through the performative interpellation of readers and viewers by fictions: writers and artists *produce* humanity by requiring their readers or beholders to enact qualities that define them as such.

Both things and animals have attracted considerable interest in eighteenth-century studies of late.[13] Building on earlier waves of scholarship on the consumption of goods, possessive individualism, and materialist philosophy, recent work has tackled the way literature represents the complex imbrication of persons and things during the eighteenth century. What defines the threshold between person and thing? How does the distribution of things (property) govern personhood, and what titles do things acquire independent of their owners? What are the ethical, legal, and political consequences of the materialist understanding of humans as mere matter? What kinds of tropes—metonymy, metaphor, anthropomorphism, personification—are suitable for interpreting the literary work of things? Recent scholarship in animal studies has reanimated the vast hitherto-disregarded bestiary within eighteenth-century literature. What traits—reason, language, sensibility, sociability—cleave living beings into separate species? How do writers grapple with an animal nature that is seemingly intrinsic to human being? Under what circumstances do we glimpse the animal "as such," liberated from what Laurie Shannon calls its "yoke of human symbolic service"?[14] Conversely, how do literary and rhetorical figures give expression to animal life and help elaborate human political and social communities? The focus of much of this scholarship has been on reinstating the figure of the animal or the agency of things rather than on the conception of humanity wrought from the encounters between them.

Discussions of "humanity" in eighteenth-century studies, meanwhile, have often focused on the sentimental recognition of a common human nature in acts of sympathetic fellowship toward suffering objects. (I told a portion of this story myself in *Sentimental Figures of Empire in Eighteenth-Century Britain and France*.)[15] In this account, "humanity" is summoned into existence to describe those who cannot find personhood through a title to things—to property, to institutions, to power to enforce their rights—but who are still not to be classed as animals. The assumption that human rights are eternal and self-evident or that humanitarian sensibility is automatic and irresistible is undermined by the fact that the entity said to bear rights or incite sympathy has to be called into being: a subject (humanity) needs to be constructed to which the predicate of rights—those rights that Hannah Arendt famously attributes to those who are "nothing but human"[16]—may be attached. Here I trace an earlier chapter of that history, before the ascendancy of the novel, illusionistic theater, moral sense philosophy, and the culture of sensibility anchored human particularity in the feeling, psychological self, and thus before sympathy and benevolence become entrenched as the privileged signifiers of human nature and the principal means of acknowledging the humanity of others.

Rather than grounding human difference in emotional kinship or psychological particularity, *Fiction Without Humanity* focuses on decidedly unsentimental experiments with the perspectives of nonhuman creatures and things in late seventeenth- and early eighteenth-century literature, science, and the arts. I explore an array of literary, scientific, artistic, and philosophical devices—the riddle, the fable, the microscope, the artifice of perspective in painting, and the abstract "bird's-eye view"—that invite identification with viewpoints that cannot quite be attached to a human vantage. The baleful glare of things in trompe l'oeil, the impersonal exactitude of geometric perspective, the monstrous insects peering up at the lens of a microscope, the estranging self-descriptions of mysterious riddle-creatures, the zoomorphic world of the fable—all escape what might be termed a human point of view. Circuited through such devices as the camera obscura or the microscope, through the speculative eye-view of animals or objects, and even through the virtual prospect of no one at all, the viewpoints presented in the works examined in the first four chapters of this book are subjective (individuated) but not necessarily attributable to the kind of particularity we associate with human psychology. When seventeenth-century natural historians speculate about what a bird sees or fables offer moral lessons in zoomorphic forms, they invite the reader to court nonhuman points of view not to produce sympathy with the other or to proffer a likeness with which to identify but to incite acts of self-differentiation that *create* humanity. By conscripting readers into particular ways of seeing and then inviting them to distance themselves from or reflexively critique these points of view, these texts bring to light the fact that we, not only as individual subjects but also as members of a species, *have a point of view*. The provisional occupation of these nonhuman viewpoints, that is, creates a greater awareness of what a human viewpoint might be. In my fifth and final chapter, I show how these experiments with estranging nonhuman perspectives shape the representation of individual human consciousness. Focusing on Daniel Defoe's *Robinson Crusoe*, I trace the ways the novel's realism issues from its alignment with a distinctively anthropocentric framework.

Although the works of literature and art that I examine below may not posit a consistent definition of humanity, they *elicit* it through capacities solicited and put into practice by reading. These texts operate as machines for extracting performances of human abilities; they demand not absorption but critical distance (the trompe l'oeil); not recognition but analytical estrangement (the microscope); not acquiescence but an answer (the riddle); not just identification with characters but also differentiation from them (fable). When a reader solves a riddle by deciphering the defamiliarizing self-descriptions of its speaker, projects herself into the rescaled world opened up by a scientific device, grasps the trickery of a trompe l'oeil, or extracts a lesson from the zoomorphic figures of a fable, she performs what Enlightenment writers understood to be distinctly human capacities to use language, to reason, to see through deceit, to alter one's given nature. The ability to abstract—to detach oneself from the referential, to play with the tools of representation, to entertain the virtual (adopting perspectives that are not one's own)—becomes one of the signal traits of humanity in these works. These texts demand that we *use* our minds; they *make* us enact the qualities that make us human.[17] In the texts I examine, humanity is constituted as a process, reinvented (often as an assumption) each time it is invoked.

Although this book offers a genealogy of a lofty abstraction—the "humanity" in whose name so many claimed to speak by the end of the eighteenth century—the chapters themselves are devoted to the "low" genres normally slighted in literary histories: the riddle, the fable, the still life, the trompe l'oeil, the experiment, and the novel. (While the novel is now canonical, it too was considered a lesser form in the eighteenth century.) Each of the chapters addresses a specific nexus of human, animal, and thing: the relation taken by humans and animals to the work of art (Chapter 1); the distance between species created by the instrumental or prosthetic augmentation of bodily powers (Chapter 2); the human capacity to recognize anthropomorphic likeness in the nonhuman forms of riddle creatures (Chapter 3); the zoomorphic representations of human political communities in fable (Chapter 4); and the human capacity to tailor the material world to its creaturely needs (Chapter 5). Each chapter likewise focuses on what was understood to be a distinctively human trait—deceit (Chapter 1), toolmaking (Chapter 2), language (Chapter 3), educability (Chapter 4), the capacity to inhabit a virtual point of view (Chapter 5)—and each addresses a formal technique that interpellates its beholder or reader as human: perspective (Chapter 1), experimental practice (Chapter 2), the enigma (Chapter 3), the example (Chapter 4), and description (Chapter 5).

I look at the human in relation to *both* things and animals rather than focusing on one or the other. Curiously, thing theory and animal studies, two of the main approaches to what recent work calls "the question of the human," have had little to say to one another. Thingness—just flesh or mere bodily mechanism as opposed to soul or reason, for example—is central to the difference between human and animal, while questions of animation and life reside at the heart of the distinction of humans and things. Indeed, the terms of one binary are often used to uphold the other in Enlightenment texts, which distinguish humans and animals through the relation each takes to things, such as tools or works of art, and sort machines from animals through their responsiveness to humans in a kind of early modern Turing test.[18]

Although nonhumanity is (by definition) the opposite of humanity, its various forms—the machine and the divine as well as the animal and the

thing that are my focus below—each cast in relief a different aspect of the
human in sometimes incompatible ways. Whereas thing theory, for example, often emphasizes the irreducible alterity of the thing—the way it
exceeds subject-object relations (utility, meaning, value)—animal studies
sees animality as a difference always already within—what is "there before
me, there next to me, there in front of me" (in Derrida's formulation).[19]
My approach seeks to recognize the plurality of the configurations into
which human beings are enfolded. If, as Thomas Hobbes writes in the
opening lines of *De cive*, "Man is a God to man, *and* Man is a wolf to
Man," humanity defined in relation to the divine differs substantially from
humanity distinguished from beasts.[20] Efforts to pin down human distinction through binary oppositions lead not only to the predictable insight
that each side of the dyad contains traces of its other but also to the revelation that the difference one seeks to discover has been outsourced to a
device that is proper to neither. Thus the extrication of humanity from its
constitutive animality in Hobbes's *Leviathan* takes a circuit through the
monstrous figure of its titular sovereign, a nonhuman mechanism fashioned
by and out of humankind.

In asking how these different constellations define the human, I hope
to cast in relief the default versions of unmarked identity (mostly white,
European, Christian, masculine) that otherwise hold unacknowledged sway
over efforts to theorize the nonhuman. For things and animals (real and
fictive) do not solicit all humans equally. Like the famous "talking book,"
which refuses to address the African in the slave narrative, the material
artifacts or cultural "works" that purportedly build a common human
world discriminate, while the animals that serve as ostensibly generic
human avatars in fables, children's stories, and modern advertising arrive
laden with cultural baggage.[21] Although the performative dimension of my
argument leaves the category of humanity open, the fictions of the human
described in this book are not empowering for all. By analyzing the mechanisms through which these fictions are elaborated, however, we may obtain
a cannier sense of why "humanity" can both supply the grounds for the
emancipatory reclamation of revolutionary rights and serve as an instrument to legitimate oppressive hierarchies. Inasmuch as humanity remains
inextricably bound to the multifarious forms of nonhuman being against
which it defines itself, it supplies the tools both for imagining more inclusive polities and for generating exclusionary orders that enable some to
claim to be more human than others.

Humanity's Mobile Devices

The twinned terms—subject and object, human and animal, person and thing—glide off the tongue, yet these seeming binaries are not analogous. Nor do they form perfect antitheses. All subjects are also objects, but persons are not things; and if all humans are also animals, the distinctions between them carry significant political and ethical freight. It is in part due to the difficulty of disaggregating these terms that one concept of choice in recent scholarship has been the "person," a fictive unit that, for philosophers and political theorists such as Locke and Hobbes, bestows continuity and stability on the discontinuous consciousness of the empirical self and anchors the legal and political identity of the civil subject. Yet the person is not necessarily human in seventeenth- and eighteenth-century thought: the category includes such nonhuman entities as corporations and excludes human beings— the enslaved, the poor, minors, and women under coverture—in certain contexts. Rather than treating the division of person and thing, human and animal, as self-evident, I trace the shifting terms on which they are both conjoined and dissevered. The trouble created by their confusion may be glimpsed both in the pejorative connotations of such terms as *idolatry, fetishism, reification, objectification*, and in the more colloquial condemnation of "using people" or "treating them like animals or things" as a violation of the Kantian categorical imperative. The mistaking of a human for a thing or an animal comes to be seen as a category error of the highest order by the end of the century.

Although I argue that person and thing, human and animal, are intertwined, my point is not that they should be conflated; rather, my point is that efforts to theorize humanity emerge precisely out of moments of their conflation. Jean de La Bruyère's startled realization that the savage animals crouched in a country field, "black, livid, sun-burnt," have a "human face," like Gulliver's horrified discovery of "a perfect human Figure" in the visage of a Yahoo, prompts the reader to reappraise the criteria for human distinction.[22] We seek to define category boundaries *after* they have been violated. The chapters of the book thus revolve around moments in which the literal as well as metaphorical borders between human, animal, or thing are blurred (as work of art passes for living thing, as parasite burrows into host, as the nonhuman creatures of riddle and fable don anthropomorphic guises). The definitions wrung from such moments of confusion often offer not strict predicates but mechanisms for establishing differences that point to the fragility of the categories they attempt to stabilize. What determines the order of things often proves to be less a fixed essence than the point of view from which one sees.

Chapter 1, "Bird's-Eye View," traces the relation between the abstracted top-down viewpoint we associate with the expression and two early views from the eyes of a bird: speculative scientific accounts of what a bird really sees and the view of the birds who pecked at Zeuxis's painted grapes in an enduringly popular classical anecdote. Early writers use stories about art's capacity to deceive other creatures to interrogate the standards of realism, asking what in the work of art compels the eye. Is resemblance the true source of an image's allure? How can we know what the eye—of a human no less than a bird—actually sees? Drawing on contemporary discussions of optics, perspective, and the efflorescence of Northern European art, I conjoin anecdotes of animals tricked by art with descriptions of human encounters with seventeenth-century trompe l'oeil paintings. Locating the difference between humans and animals in the capacity to appreciate the deceptive nature of the work of art, early writers—natural historians and optical theorists as well as art historians—speculate about what seduces the avian as opposed to the human eye. Writers and painters locate the illusionistic power of painting not simply in mimetic exactitude but in the manipulation of perspective. The enchantment of the trompe l'oeil issues not from the beholder's total absorption in the illusion but from the heightened awareness it offers of the activity of seeing and of our ability to adopt a perspective on the world that is not our own. Centuries before Jacques Lacan and Martin Heidegger, writers claim that humans alone are able to detect and remain inexhaustibly interested in a fiction.

Chapter 2 turns from art's endeavor to represent the empirical world to the New Science's interest in the capacity of technology to transform it. Focusing on Robert Hooke, curator of experiments at the Royal Society and author of the 1665 *Micrographia*, a dazzling compendium of images of the microscopic world, "Lousy Bodies" examines the relationship between Hooke's recognition of the insufficiency of the human senses—our lousy bodies in the modern colloquial sense—and his faith in the ability of instruments to supplement these organic defects. If Hooke's prosthetically enhanced body (the microscope and other *"helps of Art, and Experience"*)[23] blurs the line between human and thing, it simultaneously makes possible the progression of collective knowledge that Hooke identifies as the distinctive dispensation of humanity as a toolmaking and tool-using animal. Material things—what Hannah Arendt calls "works"—store the accumulated knowledge of humankind and make that knowledge available to future generations.[24]

Hooke celebrates his capacity to manipulate the microscopic world, exalting his mastery of the clockwork mechanisms that make things and other creatures tick. Because the microscopic world unearthed by Hooke's devices bears little resemblance to the world encountered by the naked eye, and because the subvisible eludes even his instrumentally enhanced senses, Hooke grounds his claims about the truth of his microscopic observations not in verisimilitude but in operability: whether things work. He adopts mediating points of view in order to see relations between interlocking parts that will allow him to manipulate the tiny machines of nature. His famous anthropomorphic allegory of the louse invites the reader to dabble in the perspective of vermin, revealing the alien worlds nourished by and within our bodies, and obliging us to demonstrate a uniquely human capacity to apprehend the world from a point of view not our own. If the microscope's revelation of a human body teeming with other creatures blurs the borders between human and animal, the parasite's exploitation of its host, by undermining the threshold of the individual body, makes the louse into the Janus face of the instrumentally dependent scientist. Even as the parasite calls attention to what Robert Markley wittily terms "our eukaryotic provincialism"—our inability to recognize our coevolution with the archaea in our guts—so too does the scientific device that supplements the senses reveal our dependency, individual and collective, on the human knowledge harbored in things.[25]

Turning from scientific instrument to literary device, Chapter 3, "Anthropomorphic Things," focuses on a minor genre that enjoyed renewed popularity in the early eighteenth century: the riddle. Offering an estranging self-description from the point of view of an unidentified object or creature, the riddle presents an "it" made an "I," soliciting our highest cognitive skills as humans in its demand that we use language to see what is not explicitly there (the disguised identity of the riddle creature). Drawing on both eighteenth-century and modern discussions of anthropomorphism and personification, I analyze the complexities of the riddle's extension of speech and subjectivity (if not psychology) to a nonhuman entity in order to ask what precisely is animated by these two tropes. The riddle toys with anthropomorphism, lending human features and behaviors to nonhuman entities and unveiling the entangled relations of an ostensibly sovereign humanity with things and other creatures, but it also uses personification to reveal the non-

or extra-human agencies (linguistic, bodily, systemic) that refuse anthropo-morphic domestication. I argue that the shifting representation of the non-human in the riddle affords a glimpse of what Lorraine Daston calls the "morphos" of anthropomorphism—the shape of the nonhuman that helps define the *anthropos*.[26]

Chapter 4, "Flea, Fly, Fable," focuses on two of the most trivial creatures featured in seventeenth- and eighteenth-century fables—the flea and the fly—to think about how fables wring human value even from the seemingly worthless lives of vermin. If the purpose of the fable, as one seventeenth-century writer would have it, is "to make Men lesser Beasts," why pursue this end by depicting them as animals?[27] I examine how the thematic concerns and pedagogical aims of the fable are enacted through its form: the figures of personification and anthropomorphism it employs and the reading practices it institutes. Inasmuch as the reader must determine what is added to (or subtracted from) the human to make an anthropomorphic animal, the fable produces critical reflexivity about the intrinsic bestiality from which human-ity as a "political animal" ceaselessly seeks to separate itself.

As these summaries suggest, the works analyzed in the first four chapters do not prize verisimilitude. Even the tale of Zeuxis's grapes, that Ur-narrative of mimetic exactitude, is more tool of critique than realist ideal. Those works that seem most to celebrate illusionism, such as the trompe l'oeil, embrace mimetic protocols to drag them into the abyss, their mesmerizing effect resid-ing not in the exact replication of an external reality but in the disclosure of painting's irreality. Lifelikeness crumbles before the hallucinatory hyperreal-ism of the trompe l'oeil, while the magnified artifacts and insects in the *Micrographia* bear scant resemblance to what is seen by the naked eye. Indeed, what is so arresting about Hooke's text is not its empirical description of objects but its delirious estrangement of the commonplace: the wild pers-pectival distortions that attend our encounter with the microscopic world. In upending our familiar accounts of things, Hooke's *Micrographia* is closer to the riddle than to empiricism's version of nature.

Abstracting us from our normative stances, the works considered in the first four chapters invite the reader to dwell in another's skin, to imagine what it might be like to be another creature, reconstructing a bird's-eye view, adopting the moral viewpoint of wolves. The trickery of trompe l'oeil, the bricoleur's mechanical know-how, the riddle's defamiliarizing insights, the fable's "*raison du plus fort*"—all toy with perspective, dislodging humanity from its place as the cynosure of the world. Even the hyperrealism of the trompe l'oeil uses its eerie lifelikeness to expose the labor of illusionism—the work involved in making the represented world accord with a point of view identified with and scaled to a particular eye, an eye that may (but need not) be human. Because these devices jar the processes of normative perception, they enable us to ask how artistic and literary forms consolidate—or undermine—the viewpoint from which an image or description seems "real." The realism of the New Science and Northern European painting issues not only from their investment in the concrete particularity of the material world but also from their manipulation of perspective so as to confirm the "truth" or authority of a particular point of view.

In the final chapter of the book, I bring these questions of realism and estranged perspective to bear on the novel. What happens when we consider the novel's celebrated investment in individual particularity and empirical description in light of these nonrealist experiments with nonhuman points of view? Like the artifice of trompe l'oeil, Hooke's optical prostheses, the riddle's linguistic trickery, and the fable's zoomorphic allegory, the novel is a device, a means of experimenting with an eye-view. It offers a record of the world from a perspective not necessarily anchored in a particular subject and under no particular obligation to be human. Like perspective in painting, the microscope, the riddle, and the fable, the novel rescales and repartitions objects, redistributes power, and makes new aspects of familiar objects visible. In the process, it constitutes its reader in relation to the rules by which the world it depicts can be made intelligible. As John Frow has argued, "The binding-in of the reading or viewing or speaking subject occurs above all in its slotting into these positions which constitute it as a subject in the very process of making sense. And, conversely, 'sense' is 'made' within a textual circuit articulating positions through processes of identification."[28] Is our apprehension that a text or a work of art is realistic merely the confirmation that it conforms to a "human" way of seeing the world? Or, conversely, is it the work of realism precisely to orient the world around a gaze designated as human? Nowhere are these questions more powerfully raised than in the novel. It is for this reason that the book concludes with a chapter on *Robinson Crusoe*.

It may be somewhat surprising to conclude an argument that explores nonhuman or impersonal perspectives with a chapter on a first-person novel often celebrated as a literary monument to modern individualism and humanist—indeed, imperialist—values. It may also seem counterintuitive to end a book that resolutely focuses on estranging, nonverisimilitudinous representations with a novel traditionally singled out as a locus classicus of formal realism. But since my argument seeks (among other things) to question accounts of eighteenth-century literary history that correlate the emergence of the presumptively human individual with the rise of the novel, it seems important to consider not only the canonical outliers and rogue philosophies that would self-evidently depart from this master narrative but also the figures most associated with it.

"Crusoe's Island of Misfit Things" argues that Defoe's novel, notwithstanding its first-person narrator, borrows from not-entirely-human perspectives in order to wrest the represented world into coherent, unified form. I contend that novelistic description entails much more than the mimetic rendering of an ostensibly preexisting reality; it involves the laborious fitting of objects to forms—skins to bodies, parts to wholes, words to things—in order to create a provisional unity out of the irremediably heterogeneous elements that make up the world of the novel. Focusing on the errant trait or detail that disrupts the fit of word to thing, individual to category, animal skin to human body, the chapter examines the way Crusoe, as the novel's first-person narrator, uses description to give shape and delineated form to subjects and objects (human, animal, and thing), and to articulate divisions between them. Although the novel as a genre is usually associated with psychological depth, what knits the world of Defoe's novel together is not the transparent depiction of inwardness (Crusoe's "self") but his subjective perception of objects: our sense, so to speak, of his eye-view. The novel strives to anchor its formal unity in the singularity of this point of view. Novelistic realism depends less on the mimetically exact representation of subjects and objects than on the tailoring of the depicted world to a distinctively human eye.

By placing the novel in the genealogy offered in the first four chapters, I argue that these experiments in nonhuman perspective serve as a testing ground for novelistic techniques for the representation of consciousness. Montaigne's contention that "there is more difference between a given man and a given man than between a given animal and a given man" suggests that the novel's foray into an individual human mind involves a parallel leap.[29] Even as the speculative reconstruction of the eye-view of a bird, a louse, a candlestick, or a wolf takes us beyond our ken, offering views of the world that are empirically impossible, so too does the novel, for it pitches us into another person's mind, operating as a kind of extended virtual-reality machine that gives us a front-row seat before a spectacle we can never actually experience: what another human being perceives, a character's inner life made impossibly transparent to narration. As Dorrit Cohn observes, "The special life-likeness of narrative fiction . . . depends on what writers and readers know least in life: how another mind thinks, another body feels."[30] The point at which the novel's psychological realism is most consummately realized is also the point at greatest distance from our experiences in real life. It is on these terms that the novel may be understood as an inheritor of the estranging virtual vantage points offered by the bird's-eye view, the microscope, the riddle, and the fable.

Indeed, what is at stake in *Robinson Crusoe*'s manipulation of perspective is less the reader's ability to see the world through the protagonist's eyes than the novel's capacity to represent the world without us. As Crusoe's encounter with the solitary footprint in the sand shows, the world continues to record the impress of other beings even when we are not there. In affording an impossible glimpse of what we cannot know—what the world is like in our absence—the novel allows us to imagine the world without planting ourselves at its center. On these terms, I argue, it is an extension rather than a reversal of the nonhuman perspectives described in the first four chapters of the book. Inasmuch as the signal trait of the human is the capacity to see the world from a point of view not one's own, this book makes an argument, counter-intuitive though it may seem, for a model of humanity that is not entirely anthropocentric.

A few remarks about what I am and am not trying to argue in this book are perhaps necessary. As the chapter summaries indicate, this study takes its examples primarily but not exclusively from Great Britain in the second half of the seventeenth century and the first decades of the eighteenth. Writers in other times and places have asked the same questions and have sometimes arrived at the same answers given below. (To take only my favorite example, the discussion in Chapter 1 of the birds that pecked at Zeuxis's painted grapes finds a twentieth-century counterpart in experiments on avian art appreciation, which show that pigeons trained to peck at a Monet or a Picasso can learn to distinguish impressionist from cubist art.)[31] I am neither trying to argue that other times and other cultures did not have a concept of humanity nor that the early Enlightenment "invented" the human. As Siep Stuurman's magisterial 2017 *The Invention of Humanity* shows, the notion of a common humanity has existed across millennia and in every major world tradition.[32]

Although I have endeavored throughout to anchor my claims in histori-cal particulars by showing, for example, how Hooke participated in the

broader culture of the Royal Society or by pointing to the expedience of
fable's indirection in the politically volatile decades following the English
Civil War, this is not principally a historical argument. The generic organization of the chapters means that I range across periods and geographies. Chapter 1, for instance, traces the anecdote of Zeuxis and Parrhasius from Pliny to
Lacan, ranging from classical antiquity to the end of the eighteenth century
and embracing French and British texts as well as Northern European works
of art, while my discussion of the fable draws on pan-European sources from
Aesop to Rousseau. Other chapters are more narrowly organized around a
single author (Robert Hooke), a single form (the riddle), or even a single text
(*Robinson Crusoe*), although there too I range widely. The transhistorical and
transcultural popularity of still life, fable, and riddle defeat strict adherence
to conventional periodization, while natural history, trompe l'oeil, and the
novel all belong to pan-European scientific, artistic, and literary traditions
that defy the specificity of national histories.

     In placing *Robinson Crusoe* in relation to such a smorgasbord of genres,
I am not trying to argue that the novel is the misbegotten love child of the
fable and the riddle. Rather, I am trying to see what elements of the novel
spring to unexpected life when it is inserted in a genealogy that registers a
wider range of works than are generally included in literary histories. By
incorporating late seventeenth-century visual culture—still life and trompe
l'oeil painting, scientific plates—into my argument, I endeavor to show how
the empiricism of Northern European art and the New Science contribute to
novelistic realism not only through their verisimilar representations of the
referential world but also through their manipulation of perspective. Devot-
ing two chapters to art and science has left rather less room for the strictly
literary, and, with the exception of *Robinson Crusoe*, the selection below is
not especially canonical. There are many works that I would have liked to
discuss in greater detail. A book treating of humans, animals, and things
embraces even the proverbial kitchen sink, however, and although such texts
as Aphra Behn's *Oroonoko*, Alexander Pope's *Rape of the Lock*, or Swift's
Gulliver's Travels (to name only a handful of the most obvious literary examples) all beg for consideration, additional chapters would have made an
already long book interminable. It is my hope that the approaches outlined
here will open up new angles on these works.

     Although I discuss (for example) the theological implications of Hooke's
scientific undertakings in Chapter 2, I have devoted less attention to religion
than I might have wished. There was, of course, one very simple answer to

the question of the human during the period: man is made in God's image. Yet this response opens up some of the same circular issues with defining humanity that my authors seek to circumvent by focusing on the *distinction* of humans from animals and things (rather than humanity's likeness to a specific template): for what, after all, is God's image? "The human shape," as one eighteenth-century commentator puts it, "is no more a true representation of God than the shape of any other animal, nay, than a clod of earth or any other inanimate thing."[33] The anterior power of divine artifice nevertheless haunts all the texts under discussion here; indeed, the difficulty in sustaining explanations without God as a motivating force necessitates recourse to the personifications and anthropomorphisms that populate the chapters below.

The argument in this book is resolutely humanist (and not only because many of the writers in it are fundamentally committed to human exceptionalism). While I endeavor to register the agency and interests of animals and things throughout, readers hoping to find an Enlightenment successor to the human-animal "cosmopolity" that Laurie Shannon identifies in some Renaissance texts or an eighteenth-century anticipation of a Latourian Parliament of Things may be disappointed.[34] The writers analyzed below were not penning posthuman manifestos. The fables, experiments, riddles, and works of art invite readers to enact capacities—solving a puzzle, extracting a moral, seeing through deception—designed to create and secure human difference. While their authors sometimes recognize "humanity" as a fiction, more often they treat it as a real thing. The theoretical question of whether humanity is recognized as fictive or real was, moreover, often a moot point in practice, inasmuch as the line between person and thing, human and animal, cut through the lives and bodies of enslaved Africans and colonized populations, of metropolitan workers, women, and the poor. While the texts I consider below are often fanciful, dabbling in the consciousness of nonhuman creatures and inanimate things, the abstract category they construct cannot be neatly dissevered from the fate of actual human beings.

I emphasize relations between human and nonhuman rather than enshrining things or animals at an epicenter from which humanity has been conveniently dislodged. Calls for "a more object-oriented democracy in which subaltern things will be liberated from the humanist rule of subject-centered discourse," Frank Trentmann observes, at times fail to recognize that "giving things greater voice can have troubling outcomes."[35] Although we do not live in a zero-sum world, in which granting trees standing means that humans will be felled like logs and shipped like lumber, attention to the nonhuman may compound the disenfranchisement of more vulnerable human communities. "Too often what passes for a wider concern inclusive of the environment," Theodore Walker contends, "is in fact a white racially gerrymandered concern which reaches out to include plants and animals while continuing to exclude black and colored peoples."[36] Eighteenth-century pleas for the humane treatment of animals often surface in disconcerting proximity to discussions of the slave trade. For those "who have labored so hard to rescue or protect the human from dehumanization or objectifica-tion," Richard Grusin justly observes, "the nonhuman turn" in academic studies "can seem repressive, reactionary, or worse."[37] Laudable efforts to provincialize humanity sometimes slight the uneven effects of these redistri-butions of power on different individuals and groups. The ease with which one relinquishes human privilege or disavows anthropocentric dominion may depend on whether one is held in another human's thrall. Joseph Addison's depiction of human kinship with the worm as a token of humanity's place in the "middle Space between the Animal and Intellectual Nature" stands in stark contrast to Olaudah Equiano's despairing identification with "the meanest worm on the earth."[38]

Yet elective identification with the nonhuman may not simply reflect abjection; it may also serve as a means of escaping the categories that lock subjects in place. To be relegated to the status of an animal or treated like a thing is to be disbarred from the privileges accorded humanity, to be sure, but the language of animality or thinghood that expresses the dehumanization of the oppressed may be appropriated as a form of resistance—a challenge to hegemonic discourses that arrogate the right to say who and what counts as a subject. Given that people "go about being human in radically different ways,"[39] identification with the nonhuman may preserve modes of being or action for those whose lives are not registered as meaningful or valuable in the master narratives or dominant practices of a given historical moment. It is telling in this regard that the genres treated below are all considered "low" in hierarchies of the arts. The still-life or trompe l'oeil artist paints the hum-ble bywork rather than the splendors of human history; the "menial" scien-tific practitioner plays second fiddle to the natural philosopher; the writer barred from neoclassical genres takes up the novel. The fable and the riddle are the recourse of those who must tell the truth slant. "In the slave," Hegel observes of Aesop, "prose begins."[40] Composed by the underdogs of history, these texts ventriloquize animals and things to summon humanity to answer to a nonhuman tribunal, describing the injustices to which they have been subjected in deflected form.

By reinstating the nonhuman forces that reside within or behind the models of humanity to which the Enlightenment appeals, the texts discussed in the chapters below question the presumption that we know what humanity is. They present estranging nonhuman perspectives that offer no set likeness or designated template of "man" with which the reader might identify. Perhaps most crucially, they do not produce humanity through mimesis. Instead, they solicit the performance of human traits—the capacity to reason, to abstract, to delight in fiction, to entertain virtual perspectives—*making* their readers or beholders human, *producing* subjects, rather than reproducing a preestablished line between species. What matters is less how these fictions represent human beings (indeed, many do not represent human figures at all) than how they interpellate the reader through the demands made by their form. Perverse though it may sound, the realization of the abstract fiction that is humanity depends on the absence of the human from the fictions that create it.

If literature and the arts become so central to the fabrication of the human, it is in part because early philosophers and political thinkers often treat the category as indeterminate or formally empty. Yet even as they scoff at the absurdity of such chimerical entities as "humanity," they acknowledge that, as Dumarsais argues, "men realize [*réalisent*] their abstractions; they speak of them in imitation of the way they speak of real objects."[41] In the final section of this introduction, I examine the uses to which these "realized" abstractions are put, showing how the vacuity of the abstract category "humanity," which so vexed philosophers, becomes its greatest asset in Enlightenment and modern discussions of human rights. The fictions that make up humanity bestow real power on the fiction that *is* humanity, as a seemingly empty abstraction comes to serve first as the vessel for human distinction and then as an engine for revolutionary claims to human rights.

A Brief History of "Humanity"

Easily invoked but hard to define, the word *humanity* produces almost comically circular entries in dictionaries from the period. Ephraim Chambers's 1728 *Cyclopaedia*, for example, informs us that "humanity" is "the Nature of Man, or that which denominates him *human*."[42] Although such tautological formulations suggest self-evidence—the immediate intuition that *this* is a human being rather than a laborious deduction—they often amount to little more than a paraphrase of Justice Potter Stewart's definition of pornography: "I know humanity when I see it." Such definitions beg the question they purport to answer, alternately affirming the existence of an abstract human nature without specifying its properties or positing the empirical existence of humanity without designating the principle of inclusion that constitutes the set. Thus Samuel Johnson's 1755 *Dictionary of the English Language* juxtaposes the abstract essence from which the class of humanity is to be deduced ("1. The nature of man") with the communal referent from which that essence is inductively derived ("2. Humankind; the collective body of mankind").[43] Whereas the first of Johnson's entries points to the criteria for designating certain creatures as human (albeit without specifying what the criteria might be), the second treats that collective as already established. Each entry on its own verges on tautology: together, they point to a fundamental conundrum that haunts all attempts to corral the heterogeneity of humankind into a unified form. How can the empirical diversity of humanity be reduced to a singular essence? And how do we know who is human in the first place?

Late seventeenth- and eighteenth-century attempts to elaborate a positive definition of humanity shadow forth a strangely elusive category. Although human beings, in the singular and the plural, have referents (real entities in the world to which they refer), there is no paradigmatic figure that is "humanity." What Derrida remarks of the animal also holds for the human: if "there is no Animal in the general singular, separated from man by a single, indivisible limit," nor is there a human in the general singular, which means in turn that humanity (like the more commonly used "man" or "mankind") is not indexed to a particular referent and cannot be represented mimetically.[44] What, after all, is "the human" to which humanity refers? There is no humanity degree zero, no substrate to which qualities may be attached. The term is little more than a catachresis, a "figurative substitute . . . for a literal term that does not exist," its abstract singularity dependent on the rhetorical powers of language to give it form.[45] Often derided by Enlightenment philosophers as a fatuous abstraction—a placeholder designed to disguise ignorance of the essence—humanity, I argue, requires an assist from literature to acquire the rhetorical muscle that will give it force in the world.

The failure of definitions of humanity grounded in attributed content—*what one is*—compels seventeenth- and eighteenth-century writers alternately to punt (falling back on "humanity makes humans human"); to offer differential negative definitions (humans are not animals, not things, not gods); or to attend to capacities either grounded in potential or performance (what one could do) or exercised in relations (the uses to which a human may be rightfully put). Although some writers argue over whether laughter, reason, speech, or tears should be the species' definitive traits, and others litigate the margins by disputing the admission of specific individuals or groups into the class of humankind, it is, I will argue, as much the formal structure of these definitions as their specific content that constrains efforts to convert the abstraction into a universal category, able to embrace all who belong to the species. Indeed, the loose definition of "humanity"—its frequent lack of philosophical rigor—becomes both its greatest demerit and its strongest asset in theoretical discussions of human rights.

Seventeenth- and eighteenth-century philosophers were keenly aware of the strange referential status—and potential vacuity—of abstractions such as humanity, man, mankind. As Hobbes puts it in his 1640 *Elements of Law*,

> This universality of one name to many things, hath been the cause
> that men . . . do seriously contend, that besides Peter and John, and
> all the rest of the men that are, have been, or shall be in the world,
> there is yet somewhat else that we call man, (viz.) man in general,
> deceiving themselves by taking the universal, or general appellation,
> for the thing it signifieth. For if one should desire the painter to
> make him the picture of a man, which is as much to say, of a man
> in general; he meaneth no more, but that the painter shall choose
> what man he pleaseth to draw, which must needs be some of them
> that are, have been, or may be, none of which are universal. . . . It
> is plain therefore, that there is nothing universal but names; which
> are therefore also called indefinite; because we limit them not ourselves, but leave them to be applied by the hearer.[46]

Left to the discrimination of the hearer, "man" in Hobbes's account is the object of ongoing negotiation: "We limit them not ourselves, but leave them to be applied by the hearer." The individual that Hobbes's painter "pleaseth to draw" is, so to speak, one man's man—a particular instance singled out as a representative example and thus an arbitrary template: *this* or *that* man, past, present, or future ("some of them that are, have been, or may be"). The universal "man," unlike Peter or John, is an appellation that exists only in language, and it produces a kind of ghost: that "somewhat else that we call man" designed to give, as it were, substance to an abstraction, binding the category together.

That Hobbes's painter must have recourse to a specific example to represent the universal category of "man" is a reflection of the limited capacities of the human mind. Unlike God, we can imagine neither all possible instantiations of humankind nor a human without qualities.[47] "Peter and John" (occasionally joined by James and even Elizabeth, Mary, and Jane) serve as epitomes of an elusive universal, but they are also, at the same time, the individuals from whom the abstract category is derived. In Locke's *Essay Concerning Human Understanding*, for example, children arrive at the abstract category of "man" through empirical experience with particular men and women. Having encountered individuals (their nurse, their mother), children come to "frame an *Idea*, which they find those many Particulars do partake in" to which they give "the name *Man* . . . Wherein they make nothing new, but only leave out of the complex *Idea* they had of *Peter* and *James, Mary* and *Jane*, that which is peculiar to each, and retain only what is common to them all."[48] Distilling a lowest common denominator of traits shared by all encountered instances of "man," Locke's child sorts incidental from essential attributes to create a general idea, unifying these particulars through "a relation, that by the mind of Man is added to them" (3.3.§11, 414). Inasmuch as this "relation," like Hobbes's "somewhat else that we call man," issues from the mind, the general ideas devised by the child "belong not to the real existence of Things; but are *the Invention and Creatures of the Understanding*" (3.3.§11, 414). The abstract idea of humanity is a fiction.

To be sure, such fictions act on the world. Although Locke dismisses such words as "*Animalitas, Humanitas*" as absurdities by which philosophers "pretend to signify the real Essences of those Substances, whereof they knew they had no *Ideas*" (3.8.§2, 475), he notes that we treat such terms as if they were true. The real (ontological) essence of things may escape human understanding, but nominal essences (the cluster of known traits used to classify an object) call the shots, serving as "the measures of Names, and the boundaries of Species" by which members of a class are identified (3.3.§14, 416). Thus in Locke's account, "to be a *Man*, or of the Species *Man*, and to have a right to the name *Man*, is the same thing" (3.3.§12, 415). Indeed, for Locke, humanity's capacity to abstract an idea of its own kind becomes, with some circularity, a mark of its existence: "The power of *Abstracting* is not at all in them [beasts]," Locke insists. "The having of general *Ideas,* is that which puts a perfect distinction betwixt Man and Brutes" (2.11.§10, 159). It is not simply language but the conversion of signs into vehicles for abstractions that signifies human difference. Here the very ability to conceive of "humanity" is a token of being human.

In his 1710 *Treatise Concerning the Principles of Human Knowledge*, Bishop George Berkeley takes issue both with Locke's selection of abstract thought as a definitively human ability and with his contention that the human imagination can hold abstractions (ideas stripped of particularizing traits) in its gyre. "The idea of man that I frame to myself," Berkeley contends, "must be either of a white, or a black, or a tawny, a straight, or a crooked . . . man. I cannot by any effort of thought conceive the abstract idea."[49] Even as the mind cannot imagine a block without extension, neither can it envision a human without shape, gender, color, and other particularizing traits. The mind adds attributes that establish a normative template that curtails the capaciousness of an ostensibly all-embracing category. On these terms, as Rosi Braidotti has argued, "The human . . . is neither an ideal nor an objective statistical average or middle ground. It rather spells out a systematized standard of recognizability—of Sameness—by . . . transposing a specific mode of being into a generalized standard."[50] Abstractions are not the benign vehicle of a generic concept but the site on which a contested norm is naturalized, as the prototype silently, even insidiously, shapes the class.

The abstraction becomes, in effect, the measure of man. Because knowledge is, for Locke, "nothing but *the perception of the connexion and agreement, or disagreement and repugnancy of any of our Ideas*," we have difficulty conceiving of things on heaven and earth that escape our ideas' narrow bounds (4.1.§2, 525). We endeavor to coax all things into the constructs available to receive them. Thus we cannot conceive that a changeling is "something between a Man and a Beast," Locke notes, because of our "false Supposition, that these two Names, *Man* and *Beast*, stand for distinct Species so set out by real Essences, that there can come no other Species between them" (4.4.§13, 569). The ossified abstraction, like the checkbox on a census or the door of a restroom, offers a restricted menu of possible identifications, with little room for ambiguity or mixture.

That said, Locke's general idea of man is repeatedly driven onto the rocks of particular examples, for the derivation of general ideas from the shared qualities of John, Peter, Elizabeth, and Jane binds his abstractions to their empirical origins. Not all instances cleave to their archetypes. Whereas a triangle, Locke notes, must by definition have three sides, creatures may not seamlessly fit into their procrustean class. The epitome spawns the exception, inevitably and relentlessly. "Shall the want of a Nose, or a Neck," he inquires, "make a *Monster*, and put such Issue out of the rank of Men?" (4.4.§16, 572). How can one know what traits are essential? What if Locke's child, having only encountered Europeans, mistakenly adds whiteness to the category of humanity (3.8.§1, 474; 4.7.§16, 606–7)? It is for this reason that Locke devotes considerable energy to various borderline cases that deviate from the general idea, as he feverishly adds and subtracts traits in a series of thought experiments that reel individual creatures—the monstrous birth, the changeling, the drill—in and out of the class of humanity. "Where now," Locke asks, "shall be the just measure; which the utmost Bounds of that Shape, that carries with it a rational Soul?" (4.4.§16, 572).

Locke struggles to align the person or the self with the outward form of the human being. Since the atoms of living bodies are in continual flux, identity cannot be grounded in substance, while the continuity and sameness of the person as "this present thinking thing" issues from a unified consciousness created through attribution: "That with which the *consciousness* of this present thinking thing can join it self," Locke states, "makes the same *Person*, and is one *self* with it" (2.27.§17, 341). Yet nothing guarantees that this personal identity need be human, as Locke shows through a series of fanciful thought experiments in which consciousness decamps from the body of Heliogabalus to take up residence in a hog or follows a little finger that has been amputated (2.27.§6, 332). However inadequate outward form might be as an index of the consciousness lodged within, morphology governs in practice: " 'Tis not the *Idea* of a thinking or rational Being alone, that makes the *Idea* of a *Man* in most People[']s Sense; but of a Body so and so shaped joined to it" (2.27.§8, 335). A parrot capable of rational speech, Locke points out, would not be a human in parrot form, but a rational parrot: " 'Tis the Shape, as the leading Quality, that seems more to determine that Species, than a Faculty of Reasoning, which appears not at first, and in some never" (3.11.§20, 519). Humanity on these terms involves a kind of anthropomorphism, grounded in the perception or projection of outward likeness. Yet this outward form of man need not be aligned with a subjectivity or consciousness one would designate as human, Locke acknowledges, "it being one thing to be the same *Substance*, another the same *Man*, and a third the same *Person*" (2.27.§7, 332). Indeed, we are all anthropomorphic riddles to ourselves, seeking or finding our likeness in a chimerical version of humanity, using fictions to fill in the blanks.[51]

Empirical observation thus affords at best partial knowledge of the nature of humankind. In his 1746 *Essay on the Origin of Human Knowledge*, Condillac follows Locke in affirming that categories constructed inductively from resemblances do not furnish an exhaustive account. Philosophical accounts of things—water, human being, substance—"will always be unsound, owing to our own inability to know essences, an inability the philosophers do not suspect, because they have a prior commitment to the abstractions which they realize [*réalisent*] and afterwards take to be the very essence of things."[52] Having pledged allegiance to these abstractions, Condillac's philosopher "realizes" them in the strong sense of making them real. While for Condillac as for Locke the idea of "humanity" emerges from the particularized form of Peter, Paul, or Mary, we quickly forget the concept's empirical origins. Once sensations—"different modifications" understood as "belonging to our being"—are transcribed into ideas, we preserve them in our minds as if they are distinct from these sensory impressions (1.5.§6, 94). The mind "regards them as something by continuing to attribute to them the same reality it first perceived them to have, even though that reality can no longer belong to them" (1.5.§6, 94). Thus philosophers, Condillac writes, "have realized all their abstractions, or have regarded them as beings that had real existence independent of that of the things," allowing them to take on a life of their own (1.5.§5, 93). First in thought and then in practice, abstractions come to possess real powers. We bow in obeisance to the idols we have made. It is this unthinking fidelity to ossified fictions that Locke, Condillac, and others denounce.

Etymologically, humanity is derived from the classical Latin term *humanitas*, a term that, Locke notes, did not refer to a specific entity; it "stood not for the abstract Essence of any Substance; but was the abstract Name of a Mode, in its concrete *Humanus*, not *Homo*" (3.8.§2, 475). *Humanity* thus understood is a qualifier that designates a subset of mankind, distinguishing *homo barbarus* from *homo humanus* in the Ciceronian contrast between "savagery and a life refined by humanity."[53] The defining traits of humanity in this context are lodged not in the biological category but in forms of life created and preserved by the polis, through which distinctively human capacities for action, speech, and thought are passed down across generations.[54] Inasmuch as this model sunders the properly "human" from the species "homo," it institutes hierarchies that restrict the universality of the category. Some are more human than others.

The lack of a clear referent—the human—to stabilize the abstraction humanity has important consequences for Enlightenment political thinkers, who sought to use the category to create a more inclusive polity—and at times invoked its purported universality to arrogate the right to speak for all. Notwithstanding the philosophical dismissal of humanity as a vacuous, elusive abstraction, later writers strive to "realize" the conception in political terms. Yet who is part of humanity and who could speak on its behalf? What prerogatives and obligations would accompany membership in this newly significant class? The cumbersome doubling of the rights-bearing individual in the *Declaration of the Rights of Man and of the Citizen* underscores the novelty of this insistence upon the political importance of humanity. Before 1789, as Susan Maslan observes, "humanity had never been the subject of rights: rights were distributed on the basis of social class, of religion, of community."[55] Enlightenment efforts to ground political being in the humanity of the person reverse the historical basis of rights in the personhood possessed by (some) human beings.

For the Enlightenment inherits not only the Roman division of humanity into *barbarus* and *humanus*, but also the sorting of humankind into persons, those "politically qualified" beings possessed of rights, titles, and duties, on the one hand, and the mere human or *homo*, lacking the civil and juridical protections afforded to subjects under the state, on the other. In Hannah Arendt's influential analysis of this model, the rights-bearing "person" is recognized as the sole unit of political agency, with the human as its disempowered leftover. "Without his *persona*," Arendt writes, "there would be an individual without rights and duties, perhaps a 'natural man'—that is, a human being or *homo* in the original meaning of the word, indicating someone outside the range of the law and the body politic of the citizens, as for instance a slave—but certainly a politically irrelevant being."[56] Those lacking the predicates of nationality, citizenship, property, and legal status, as Arendt argued of the plight of stateless refugees in post–World War I Europe, become the defenseless bearers of human rights, reduced to "the abstract nakedness of being nothing but human."[57] On these terms, humanity is less a species category than a mode of political nonbeing that exposes its bereft subjects to a nasty and brutish Hobbesian world.

This sharp division between the "person" and the human is a common feature in seventeenth- and eighteenth-century political thought, where status is determined by rank, family, gender, and property, not species. The constitutive element of the commonwealth in Hobbes's *Leviathan*, for example, is not the human being but the person, the representative civil subject to which deeds or words are attributed.[58] Writing in the wake of the English civil war, Hobbes uses the artificial monstrosity of his titular sovereign to wrest mankind from the animality of the state of nature, instituting a political order through human covenant. The Leviathan makes humans, not beasts; it is what humans make because they are not beasts. Yet for Hobbes, as for others, the human and the person are not neatly aligned even after humankind's emergence from the state of nature: some humans (madmen, minors, women under coverture, the enslaved) are not persons, and some persons (churches, corporations, the monarchy) are not human. It is the fundamental and enduring noncongruence of these two categories that makes the Enlightenment attempt to found rights claims on human being such a radical and unprecedented move.

This lack of convergence between the human and the (political) person only becomes an explicit, widespread object of concern later in the eighteenth century, and it does so not through species membership or even *humanitas* in the sense of the arts of civility and civilization, but through another sense of the term *humanity*, referring to the benevolence and compassion believed to express a "humane" disposition. Feeling, not reason, is increasingly singled out as the defining trait for humanity, as the rank-inflected language of "Gentleness, Courtesie, Affability, also Humane Learning" in seventeenth-century dictionaries is gradually supplanted by the vocabulary of benevolence and sympathy favored by moral sense philosophers and celebrated by the culture of sensibility.[59]

Sensibility and sympathy furnish an unstable basis for categorical definitions of species, however, as I have argued more extensively elsewhere.[60] The spontaneous outpouring of feeling said to justify the claim that compassion is intrinsic to humanity pertains to the feeling subject rather than the object of feeling; the ad hoc rather than categorical operation of sympathy only selectively acknowledges others (and only inasmuch as they suffer). Enthusiastic claims that "pity and kindness towards our Brethren have a long time, passed under the name of Humanity, as properties essential to, and not without Violence to be separated from humane Nature" skirt the question of who will count as "our Brethren."[61] Worse, the humanity conferred upon these brethren by sentimental feeling is only as enduring as the recognition of the metropolitan subject who bestows it, while those who do not feel or excite humanity (as benevolence) may be exiled from humanity (as a class) alto-gether.[62] On these terms, it is not that "we" have feelings for others because they are human; rather, those for whom we have feelings come to be consid-ered as such.

The ease with which sympathy traverses and even erases species bound-aries further challenges efforts to render humanity as fellow-feeling coexten-sive with the human race.[63] Indeed, rather than being a distinctively human trait, sensibility may be understood as the manifestation of a common crea-turely nature anterior to distinctions of kind. Thus Tobias Menely has recently found in sensibility—the "prelinguistic semiosis humans share with other animals"—a (human) "responsiveness, within a symbolic domain defined by representation and reflexivity, to a prior [animal] voice, a voice not necessarily human."[64] Sensibility on these terms is less an expression of humanity than the recognition of a shared creaturely nature that defeats any attempt to create a bright line between human and animal.

Because this book largely centers on a period *before* the ascendency of the culture of sensibility, I turn away from narratives that derive humanity from sympathetic feeling to focus on texts that derive humanity from the *enactment* of capacities (reason, speech, tool use) that distinguish humans from other creatures. My argument thus departs both from the sentimental understanding of humanity that has largely held sway over eighteenth-century literary studies and from influential accounts that ground the emer-gence of human rights in the sympathetic recognition of the suffering of hitherto disenfranchised populations.[65] While these accounts justly locate one impetus for human rights in the sense of commonality fostered by sensibility, the self-evident humanity they affirm depends on the recognition of sympa-thetic likeness as the basis of species identification—an account that implic-itly elevates the sympathizing subject as the template for all humankind. By contrast, the fictions without humanity analyzed in the book withhold a human image with which to identify, inviting readers to perform capacities that distinguish them from other creatures. Because there is no master tem-plate, these fictions keep the category of humanity open. (If we turn to "humanity" for a guarantee of "what" we are, we are doomed to find the same fixed likeness again and again.)

In the remainder of this introduction, I explore the implications of this conception of humanity for modern discussions of human rights and cri-tiques thereof. Although the chapters below only lightly touch on Enlighten-ment debates about rights—I hope to pursue these questions in future work—it is important to understand how eighteenth-century conceptions of humanity shape modern discussions of human rights in order to grasp the revisionary possibilities of the fictions without humanity analyzed below. Inasmuch as the "processual" model of humanity I argue for in this book avoids elevating a singular template to be imitated, it unsettles the restrictive conception of the human that bedevils human rights discourse to this day: its endorsement of a culturally specific model of what constitutes human thriving, its tacit authorization of one community as arbiters of the standards by which others live, its recapitulation of Western imperial values in a more palatable key, and its prioritizing of the needs of humanity over other forms of life.[66] Because the works of art and literature analyzed below invite the reader to identify with nonhuman and even impersonal perspectives, they resist the consolidation of a singular (anthropocentric) point of view and thus forestall the installation of a master template of the human against which all are to be measured. In suggesting that humanity is constituted *through* relations to others (rather than being an essence that is simply possessed), these texts make the interests and needs of other living creatures and even things intrinsic to human flourishing. In the next few pages, then, I consider how this alternative conception of humanity may help answer some of the charges levelled against modern human rights. Readers who are principally interested in the eighteenth-century contexts of my argument may wish, however, to skip straight to Chapter 1.

If human rights continue to be a central object of contention to this day, it is in part because of the immense political power that Enlightenment thinkers came to lodge in "humanity." The struggle to designate what constitutes the human has high stakes, because a fixed (as opposed to a processual) account of humanity does not just stipulate who counts and who does not; it also indicates that one party has arrogated the right to designate what humanity is and to speak exclusively in its name. While humanity "as a practical definition of all presently living human beings" may be "neutral and politically blind," as Reinhart Koselleck contends, it becomes a powerful instrument in Enlightenment political struggles precisely because the "initially unpolitical meaning of the word *Menschheit* . . . facilitated the claim to that greatest possible universality which, as justification of political critique and political action could no longer be outbid."[67] ("Whoever invokes humanity," in Karl Schmitt's succinct summation, "wants to cheat.")[68] To speak for humanity is to speak for all; to oppose those who speak in the name of humanity is to declare oneself the enemy of humankind. Only the fact that humanity squirms out of definitional grasp helps prevent it from falling definitively into the hands of any one party.

It is in part for this reason that the processual model of humanity outlined in the chapters below is so significant. By refusing to offer—and calling into question—fixed definitions of humanity, these texts leave room for those hitherto excluded from its purview to claim their rightful share. On these terms, the formal difficulties in defining the category described above and throughout this book prove to be humanity's most revolutionary asset. It is the weakness of the loose definition—its productive irresolution—that creates its political strength: its abstract singularity leverages claims to inclusivity because of, not despite, its nonspecificity. The imprecise and non-referential elements that allow the abstraction "humanity" to float also make it capacious.

Indeed, many recent discussions of human rights have drawn attention to—and sometimes embraced as theoretically necessary—this lack of a stringent definition of humanity. "There is no man of the Rights of Man," Jacques Rancière declares, "but there is no need for such a man."[69] Costas Douzinas notes that "humanity" within contemporary human rights discourse is a "'floating signifier,'" albeit one that "carries an enormous symbolic capital,"[70] while Claude Lefort contends that the openness of the concept of humanity—"the idea of man without determination"—helps the rights of man to elude "all power which would claim to take hold of it—whether religious or mythical, monarchical or popular."[71] Étienne Balibar likewise argues that the "negative universality" of human rights depends not on our certitude about which humans possess rights, but on (in Alastair Hunt's gloss on Balibar) "a loss of unconsciousness about the lack of certainty in knowing who bears rights."[72] Designed to forestall the imposition of a normative humanity on those identified as (potential) rights holders, such open definitions preserve the possibility of new claimants, circumventing the impasse created by the restriction of rights to the politically recognized person and the relegation—to return to Arendt—of the merely human to irrelevance. Only by leaving the category of humanity open can those not already empowered claim a place at the table.

It is for this reason that genealogies that derive the rights of man from subjective, property-based claims (rather than from a natural law tradition, for example) often lead to a dead end. When we attribute rights to individuals and then enlarge the sphere of rights-bearing subjects one by one, we are not

really working with a universal; instead, Balibar points out, we are reinscrib-
ing the initial division within an ever-larger class. That is, if human rights
start with two individuals made equal and then expand outward, we must
always grapple with the inequality between the initial two and the rest. We
cannot start with the individual and shift to humanity, as if the latter is the
former writ large. (Indeed, arguments made on behalf of the individual may
be antithetical to those made on behalf of the species.) It is, Balibar claims,
necessary to think humanity immediately in the universal form—a task, as
we saw above, fraught with philosophical difficulties and indeed perhaps cognitively impossible. Balibar registers these difficulties by describing "the universality of individuals" that human rights must "immediately concern" as
"the universality of X's [*l'universalité des X*]."[73] In leaving open the question of
what that X marks, Balibar points to an undefined and perhaps unknowable
humanity as a placeholder for something that remains to be summoned into
being. He thus refuses to instate a template that would compel claimants to
adhere to the likeness of the inaugural rights-bearers. The suspension of decisive knowledge—the refusal to designate the nature of the X—leaves rights
open to all.

Jacques Rancière likewise questions models of human rights that treat
the question of humanity as settled, taking particular issue with Arendt's
confinement of politics to the already-established class of "persons." Instead
of seeing rights as something possessed by given subjects, Rancière argues,
we must understand them as a contested reservoir of potential for a humanity that comes into being precisely by claiming and exercising these rights.
In much the same way that the works of art and literature in this book
make humanity a performative enactment, constituted processually, so too
are rights, in Rancière's account, not "predicates belonging to definite
subjects"—nominal possessions that some humans "have" and others do
not—but generative principles that entitle their claimants to a "sphere of
implementation of these predicates."[74] Rights understood as political predicates "open up a dispute about what they exactly entail and whom they
concern in which cases," as the evident incongruity between the class nominally acknowledged as fully human (by a given regime) and the larger circle
of potential claimants creates the impetus for renegotiating the political order
(303). As the "predicates of a nonexistent being," the rights of man work as
an "inscription, a form of visibility of equality" that creates the humanity
that wields them (303). On these terms, humanity "is not the void term

opposed to the actual rights of the citizen. . . . It is the opening of an interval for political subjectivization," in which subjects *use* rights that they do not (yet) possess (304). Neither an established identity nor an empty term, humanity exists through its enactment. It is not a name but a dynamic form of being instated in performance.

Even as Balibar's "universality of Xs" conjures a humanity to be determined and Rancière's "predicate of a nonexisting being" calls up a human subject able to bear rights, so too does Peter de Bolla, in his intricate reconstruction of the uneven eighteenth-century emergence of the concept of the "rights of man," use what he describes as the " 'ungrammatical' declension of concepts" to generate subjects that can be reconciled with rights-bearing predicates. Inasmuch as individual subjective rights cannot be conjugated with the universal subject of humanity, de Bolla contends, we must create a kind of subject-verb agreement between *universal* rights and "the defining aspiration of being human."[75] Human rights, he notes, "are held by no one in particular, indeed cannot be held *by* the individual, even if all individuals aspire *to* them. Such rights are conjugated in the tense of the future-present" (246). This act of conjugation draws the excluded into the community of potential rights bearers. The claiming of rights transforms humanity from an abstraction into something possessed of performative force through its instantiation in particular beings who come to exercise those rights designated as human. The subject humanity is back-formed through its conjugation with verbs that enable it to come into being. It is for this reason that the performative dimension of the texts analyzed in this book is so important.

The anticipatory structure of the models proposed by Rancière, Balibar, and de Bolla suggests that humanity is always in process, something not fixed or fully materialized. Indeed, in exploiting the incongruity between what humanity is and what it might be, these definitions of the human instate a temporal structure that points to its future realization. That is, the constitutive and performative force of human rights generates a definition of the human from the nature of the rights bestowed, calling up a subject able to realize these ideals. Conceptions of the human subject follow from, rather than serving as the basis for, predicates such as human rights, as writers summon agents and collectives able to realize the aspirations couched in capacious but still empty words. What is important about the category of humanity is not the exhaustive inclusivity of its definition but its constitutive exposure to revision. By withholding a fixed template that would foreclose the category, the fictions without humanity analyzed throughout this book preserve the grounds for a communal order supple enough to embrace those who do not already belong, for the community they call into being is not based on the sympathetic recognition of likeness to a master template, but on the enactment of shared capacities elicited by works of art and literature. On these terms, the processual model of humanity must be understood in relation to the book's argument about forms of realism that are grounded not in mimetic exactitude (the artistic or literary imitation of a stable referential world outside), but in the ability to adopt perspectives that align with (or depart from) a distinctively anthropocentric point of view.

In compelling readers to adopt radically new and alien perspectives, the literary and artistic works analyzed below leverage a fundamental shift in what Rancière calls the "partition of the sensible," that "general law that defines the forms of part-taking by first defining the modes of perception in which they are inscribed."[76] It is for this reason that the argument attends so closely to texts that tamper with modes of perception. Inasmuch as, in Rancière's words, "politics is first and foremost an intervention upon the visible and the sayable," the "partition of the sensible" governs who can take part (who can participate, who is recognized) and who can partake (who is entitled to a share) (¶21). By inviting human writers and readers to adopt the estranging viewpoints of animals and things, the texts addressed in the following chapters unsettle the "partition of the sensible," redistributing visibility, voice, power, admitting the "non-part" into the domain of the political. Although these works often do not represent the humanity they purport to address, they conjure the "predicate[s] of a nonexistent being," to borrow Rancière's phrase, making visible the site on which such a being might emerge. In literally as well as metaphorically rejiggering the "partition of the sensible," the trompe l'oeil, the microscope, the riddle, the fable, and even the novel breach the ossified order of things—that totalized version of the "partition of the sensible" that Rancière calls a "police"—allowing new claimants to appear. They do not settle what humanity is (that would foreclose the category); they reshuffle things so that the question of what counts as human can be posed anew.

The attempt to designate human essence is, Arendt once observed, "like jumping over our own shadows. . . . If we [humans] have a nature or essence, then surely only a god could know and define it, and the first prerequisite would be that he be able to speak about a 'who' as though it were a 'what.'"[77] The works discussed in the chapters of this book ask readers to jump over their own shadows by adopting nonanthropocentric viewpoints—lofting us to the view of a bird, pitching us into the realm of the subvisible, offering the world as experienced by a candlestick, and recasting moral and political life in a zoomorphic guise. This multiplication of extra-human perspectives is one way early writers sought to master an exteriority that would enable the designation of the "who" as a "what."[78] Yet these texts do not offer Arendt's godlike designation of "what" we are; nor do they offer a strict definition of the human. Instead, they embroil their readers in processes that extract the capacities that promise to realize humanity. They do not stipulate what someone is; they enable someone to come to be, by conjugating a not fully defined subject with verbs that transform its nature. Because these experiments with nonhuman perspectives do not produce humanity through mimesis (through a set likeness with which the reader must identify), they offer multiple points of entry to those who do not adhere to the dominant Enlightenment template of "man."

Or so it goes in theory. Abstract universals such as "man" or "the human" excite suspicion for good reason, since they disguise all sorts of ugly exclusions. What appears to be a "*formally* empty" category, Cary Wolfe observes, remains "*materially* full of asymmetries and inequalities in the social sphere."[79] If the broader claim of *Fiction Without Humanity* is that the humanity in human rights is anything but self-evident, the significance of that claim stems from the fact that these rights are not emancipatory for all. As I have argued elsewhere, the lack of a categorical principle that makes the category of humanity so capacious also facilitates the arbitrary exclusion of individuals or groups from its ranks.[80] Elastic definitions simply bend more easily to the will of the strongest. Indeed, the elevation of humanity (and of human rights) as an ideal may conceal, as Saidiya Hartman has argued, "the ways that the recognition of humanity and individuality acted to tether, bind, and oppress." Subjection is to be found not just in the dehumanizing treatment of people as things or animals, but also, Hartman argues, in "the forms of violence and domination enabled by the recognition of humanity, licensed by the invocation of rights, and justified on the grounds of liberty and freedom."[81] Insofar as the language of humanity has not so much been denied to the oppressed as it has been used against them, its ostensibly uplifting appropriation may not be empowering. Under the circumstances, identification with animals and things may not only serve as a refuge from dehumanizing regimes but may also refute the notion that the human as defined by the dominant discourse is the only form of life that possesses worth.[82] In pointing to the ways early Enlightenment definitions of humanity enfold and emerge from encounters with the nonhuman, I seek to recognize the way art and literature offer the disenfranchised the means to elaborate autonomous forms of meaning and value, separate from and even pitted against those sanctioned by the powers that be.

Although the texts I consider below are rooting for a "processual" model of humanity, the category, once ossified, spawns lesser versions of its purportedly universal self. As Sylvia Wynter has argued, the elaboration of European humanism goes hand in hand with the exploitation and immiseration of other populations: the "present ethnoclass (i.e., Western bourgeois) conception of the human, Man, . . . overrepresents itself as if it were the human itself," she writes, securing its monopoly by making "peoples of the militarily expropriated New World territories . . . as well as the enslaved peoples of Black Africa . . . into the physical referent of the idea of the irrational/subrational Human Other . . . and, as such, [into] the negation of the generic 'normal humanness,' ostensibly expressed by and embodied in the peoples of the West."[83] Western modernity's model of the human underwrites its colonial practices. The era that congratulates itself for formulating the Rights of Man, Siep Stuurman reminds us, consolidates gender difference into the (unequal) complementarity of "opposite" sexes and creates racial taxonomies that ground inequality in "an underlying biocultural ontology of the human." Indeed, what distinguishes Enlightenment accounts of humanity in Stuurman's sweeping history of the concept is its imposition of a progressive historical model that places the species on a continuum, affording non-European populations the prospect of eventual ascension to the status of the fully human.[84] Enshrined as the endpoint of a Eurocentric model of transhistorical progress, an idealized humanity ceases to be a historical object, susceptible or open to change, and becomes a gatekeeping construct, a fixed form that furnishes the telos toward which all must purportedly strive.

Once the "processual" models of humanity harden into the fixed template of the Enlightenment's "progressive" model, humanity comes to serve not only as a basis for rights claims but also as an enabling fiction for later eighteenth-century discourses and practices that use race, gender, class, sexuality, and bodily or intellectual capacities to prevent entire populations from being understood as fully human. While the chapters below do not address these specific formations in detail—I hope for that work to be part of a sequel to this book—my argument suggests why the abstraction "humanity" comes to be such a powerful instrument in the consolidation of the very hierarchies it purports to transcend. As the fictions *without* humanity studied below are increasingly edged out by fictions that claim to represent it, the category becomes consolidated around traits that are stipulated in the text rather than elicited by its form. The concept contracts, offering a narrower—exclusionary—sense of what and who counts as human.

My account here may suggest that I believe in some happy mythical time in which humanity was a free, open category, before any one group claimed a monopoly on the right to define it. That is not my contention. Who counts as human was obviously an object of fierce contestation long before the Enlightenment. If there is a determinedly utopian element in my argument, it issues not from some hypothetical prelapsarian moment but from the potential I identify in art and literature—the humanities—to (re)shape our understanding of the human. This book makes a plea for taking painting, fables, riddles, and novels seriously in thinking about the history of concepts (like humanity) that we more frequently associate with philosophy or political theory. It is because works of art and literature treat humanity in and as fiction, carving out a space at one remove from the historical and material forces that in practice govern the workaday world, that the category can be relitigated so that people can work to alter what looks like a fixed status quo.

Without question we must, as Judith Butler urges, recognize humanity as "a differential of power that we must learn to read, to assess culturally and politically, and to oppose in its differential operations," but the concept need not be reduced to yet another Enlightenment ruse.[85] I am not ready to give up on humanity just yet. To be sure, at a moment in which human actions threaten the well-being of the entire planet, species solidarity may seem like an alibi for the more effective exploitation of the environment at the expense of other living things. Nevertheless, we need to preserve the means to imagine collectivities that are able to act and that can be held to account. Sustained programs for political change do not typically arise from being lodged in a permanently selfless state. The recognition that agency is distributed in ways that exceed human command easily leads to hand-wringing paralysis, and critical analysis of the agency of things does not make trees into J. R. R. Tolkien's Ents, able to rouse themselves to defend forests. At a moment in which the ravages of global capitalism, climate change, structural inequality, and systemic injustice offer daily reminders that our deeds—both individual and collective—have consequences that supersede our immediate ken, we perhaps cannot afford to relinquish the strategic essentialism afforded by a category such as humanity as a spur to action and a reminder that collective action is in fact possible.[86] Indeed, in an era of growing disparity and dwindling planetary resources, this book's attempt to provide the formal means to imagine the activity and interests of the nonhuman as a constitutive part of humanity may amount to little more than a plea to recognize the importance of the rights of others (both human and nonhuman) to self-interest. On these terms, the insecure foundation of humanity that I have endeavored to find in early Enlightenment writings may help us reconceive the rights to which we—whoever we are—seek to lay claim. Whether, or in what sense, such rights could or ought to be termed human is one question this book seeks to open.

CHAPTER I

Bird's-Eye View

The introduction offered a rapid survey of the senses assigned to the term *humanity*, showing how the abstraction's tenuous anchorage in concrete particulars created both disquiet about the absence of a clearly delineated model of the human and excitement about its open-ended, revolutionary potential. We now turn to the specific nexus of human, animal, and thing over and against which the abstract category was defined. The "bird's-eye view" of my title is not the lofty and comprehensive top-down viewpoint that we usually associate with the expression: the imagined displacement of spatial orientation that enables the virtual occupation of a stance defined by its identification with a (stationary, single, abstract) avian eye. (I shall return to that below.) Instead, I want to focus on the view from the eyes of a bird: specifically, the view of the birds in the famous classical anecdote of the contest between Zeuxis (who painted grapes so lifelike they were pecked by birds) and Parrhasius (whose painted curtain Zeuxis sought to raise to see the work of art hidden behind it). In the late seventeenth and eighteenth centuries, poets, scientists, art critics, and philosophers use the tale of Zeuxis's grapes as the launching point for debates about realism, verisimilitude, still life, trompe l'oeil, the interpellation of readers or viewers into fictional worlds, and the shifts between narrative and ontological levels—the metalepses—that move people in and out of these worlds. The tale's extraordinary durability—from Pliny to Lacan, with numerous others in between—suggests that this particular fiction about fiction is either very good to think with or else an exceptionally convenient vessel for what has already been thought.

The anecdote (parable, fable) serves as one of the perennial sites on which the representation of things—and the capacity of the work of art to supplant the thing, of the fiction to supplant the real—becomes an object of reflection and contention. Neither fetishism nor idolatry (though at times partaking of both), the error that resides at the heart of this story about mimetic exactitude leads to a set of questions about the materiality of the work of art and the responses it incites. What happens when the eye is confronted by a lifelikeness so vivid that it threatens to erase the boundary between the real and the mimetic, and what difference does the nature of the perceiving eye—human or avian—make? Why are animals, insects, birds so often the canary in the mimetic mine? In the story of Zeuxis and Parrhasius, the lifelikeness of the painted grapes and the curtain leads to errors of perception that not only cast in relief the real and fictive life of the things depicted but also reveal something about the nature of the apprehending subject (the nonhuman birds and the human artist). This chapter addresses the ways late seventeenth- and eighteenth-century writers as well as modern theorists use the tale of Zeuxis's grapes to organize the distinction between humans and animals through the relation each takes to real things, on the one hand, and to works of art, on the other.

The claim that humans and animals are differentiated by the *relation* they are said to take to things such as tools or clothing suggests that the categories of human, animal, and thing are elaborated through these relationships rather than existing as preestablished constructs. When the thing in question is a work of art—as in the example of Zeuxis's grapes—these categories become even more complicated. Although the work of art is, from a certain angle, a thing (considered in its "untouched actuality," as Martin Heidegger puts it, "the picture hangs on the wall like a rifle or a hat"),[1] it is often described in terms of animation in ways that challenge the neat binary of subject and object. Its creation is sometimes characterized as an infusion of artistic spirit, while the work itself is said to "speak to" and "move" its beholders.[2] That birds play such a crucial role in the anecdote of Zeuxis's grapes suggests that animals help distinguish the work of art from a "mere" thing, if only because they cast the human relation to the painting in relief, while the work of art itself provokes responses that demonstrate (or create) distinctions between human and animal.

In the first part of the chapter, I trace some of the permutations of the anecdote of Zeuxis and Parrhasius in seventeenth- and eighteenth-century Europe and England, showing how the story indexes the value assigned to mimetic exactitude in treatises on art as well as in discussions of empiricism and the New Science. I ask how matters of perspective (the "eye-view") as well as of species (the view from the eye of a bird or a human) enter into the capacity to perceive fiction. Is it likeness that produces the error of taking art for life, or some other element of the work that lures the eye—human, avian, animal—into taking the representation for the thing itself? What is it in the object that captivates, substitutes fiction for reality, traduces the eye into error (if error it is)? Drawing on various tales of birds and other creatures tricked by paintings and statues, I examine both mimetic and nonmimetic explanations for the relation animals as opposed to humans take to works of art.

In the second section, I turn to early attempts to imagine what a bird sees in natural histories, physico-theological treatises, and fowling manuals. In endeavoring to grasp the visual experience of other creatures, writers contemplate the possibility that the allure of images for animals resides not in mimetic exactitude governed by human standards of verisimilitude but in something more rudimentary. While natural historical discussions remain conjectural, early optics offered an empirical foundation for these speculations, affording a glimpse of what the eye sees (before its cognitive processing). Experiments by Descartes, among others, deanthropomorphize vision by showing that the eye, whether of an ox or a bird or a human, registers light in the form of an unprocessed retinal image in identical ways. In revealing that what is sensed by the eye—the light that strikes the retina—bears little resemblance to the world as we perceive it, optics challenges models of realism grounded in verisimilitude. If the realist image is not similar to the retinal image, what then deceives the viewing eye, whether human or avian, in art? Drawing on Svetlana Alpers's influential division between Northern European art (with its "retinal" images) and Italian painting (with its use of linear perspective, as codified by the Renaissance architect and author Leon Battista Alberti), I argue that the realistic qualities of Northern still life and trompe l'oeil art issue not only from the lifelike rendering of objects (Zeuxis's grapes as the perfect copy of nature) but also from techniques of perspective designed to capture a specifically human eye.

For it is not only birds that are susceptible to the tricks of pictures. The anecdotes usually cited alongside the tale of Zeuxis's grapes reveal humans to be as much the dupes of art as animals. Zeuxis himself, it is said, "expired of an outrageous *laughing* fit" before his own painting of a grotesque old woman, "hurried" into the grave "by the ludicrous child of his own provoking imagination,"[3] while "*Myro[n]*'s Heifer, so lively shap'd in a Figure of Brass, . . . impos'd not only on the Herd alone, but cozen'd and cheated the Herdsmen too."[4] Praxiteles's statue of the Venus of Cnidos (Knidos) so "mov'd the Blood of the Beholders" that a man hid in the shrine and embraced the statue, leaving "a stain, an indication of his lust," while the seventeenth-century Roman collector Hippolito Vitellesco "was reputed to embrace and kiss the statues in his collection."[5] Binding the response to the refined work of art to the appetites humans share with beasts, these tales of failed sublimation expose—and delight in—the animal drives that course just below the surface of the civilized arts. Works of art do not simply trick the beholder; they also produce a desire that overshoots its designated mark or perhaps mistakes it altogether, as the seduction of a lump of stone, a dab of paint, a piece of wood compels the beholder (human or animal) to try to eat a painting or to have sex with a statue—even after, even though, it is known to be such. While for Zeuxis's birds, the revelation of the trick exhausts the painting—the grapes cease to be of interest once they turn out not to be food—for humans, this proves to be the beginning of the intrigue, and it is here—not in the fact of deception but in the play of fiction—that the distinction between humans and animals resides.

I examine the persistent interest humans have in the fictive object, even once it is revealed to be illusory, through an analysis of three trompe l'oeil paintings of dead birds. Depicting birds drawn to snares by bright berries and mating calls, these scenes offer their human viewer a glimpse of the lethal consequences of being duped by art and in the process enable the beholder to establish a metacritical relation to her own susceptibility to deception. What is at stake in these paintings is less the mistaking of image for real thing (an error common to human and animal alike) than the ability to apprehend a fiction—to grasp that the grapes are not real fruit, for example—and still to remain inexhaustibly invested in the form (without the substance). For humans the ruse is not exhausted by the dissolution of the illusion: the fiction creates an appetite for its own repeated consumption.

For eighteenth-century writers and modern theorists alike, this investment in "mere" form is connected to a capacity to imagine the world from virtual or fictive perspectives, and I conclude by contrasting seventeenth-and eighteenth-century efforts to imagine the view from the eyes of a bird with the late-century interest in the abstract top-down perspective we associate with the metaphorical "bird's-eye view." Long before Lacan and Heidegger, eighteenth-century writers explore the claim that humans alone can project the self into a virtual framework. These seemingly slight quibbles over the meaning of a minor classical anecdote, I contend, raise fundamental questions about the perceptual capacities of humans and animals, about the conceptual and artistic tools humans employ to know the minds of others, about the theoretical fallout from a lifelikeness that promises or threatens to pass for life, and, finally, about the use of the work of art to create and uphold distinctions between human and animal. At the same time, the recalcitrance of the thing before the imaginative facility of the human subject suggests the limits of theories that celebrate virtual perspectives without acknowledging the material constraints that drag them back to earth. Even as the work of art promises prospects—bird's-eye views—that transcend our animal and thingly nature, it recalls and reaffirms humanity's ongoing entanglement in the material and creaturely world from which the fiction of human difference is so painstakingly extracted.

The Canary in the Mimetic Mine

Despite its participation in a kind of transhistorical game of "telephone," the story of Zeuxis's grapes retains in most seventeenth- and eighteenth-century accounts the outline of its form in Pliny, where Parrhasius "entered into a competition with Zeuxis, who produced a picture of grapes so successfully represented that birds flew up to the stage-buildings; whereupon Parrhasius himself produced such a realistic picture of a curtain that Zeuxis, proud of the verdict of the birds, requested that the curtain should now be drawn and the picture displayed; and when he realized his mistake, with a modesty that did him honour he yielded up the prize, saying that whereas he had deceived birds Parrhasius had deceived him, an artist."[6] In Pliny's version of the anecdote, both paintings are fictions (feigned things) so mimetically exact that they provisionally pass for real, the first seducing the birds, the second deceiving the painter, with the superiority of the latter issuing according to seventeenth- and eighteenth-century accounts (although not modern theories) from the greater difficulty of deceiving the human artist. Pliny's anecdote has been something of a straw man, if not quite a scarecrow, in evolutionary accounts of art history, epitomizing the idolatry of an ideal of perfect mimesis: art's aspiration toward what Norman Bryson terms the "Essential Copy." Bryson's influential reading presents Pliny's narrative and its Renaissance humanist successors as offering a progressive model of art history in which one painter succeeds and supersedes another in mimetic aptitude, with the production of the perfect replica as its telos. Since the "world [that] painting is [supposed] to resurrect," Bryson argues, is what "exists *out there*, already, in the plenitude of its Being," all art moves toward an endpoint that is itself the negation of history.[7] Style can only be understood in this account as an impediment to progress, a deviation from the dogged death march toward the perfectly realistic imitation.

Although the comparison—better than Zeuxis, better than *Cats*—is part of the repertory of conventional praise bestowed on artists, the anecdote itself is not invariably invoked to substantiate claims about the superiority of realism. In numerous cases it is employed as a caution *against* the superficial overvaluation of verisimilitude as the criteria for judging works of art. Indeed, a second version of the story, involving Zeuxis's painting of a "Child Carrying Grapes," offers a different ending that seems to demote the Essential Copy to the lesser triumph of honorable mention: "As the grapes were so life-like they attracted the birds," Seneca recounts, "a spectator declared that the birds were making a critique of the painting; for they would never have dared approach had the child been life-like. It is said that Zeuxis erased the grapes and kept what was best in the painting rather than what was most life-like."[8] The perfect imitation here is only partial, incompletely realized, since the boy does not scare the birds away. That Zeuxis rubs out the ostensibly impeccable grapes, retaining the supposedly imperfect boy, suggests that what is valued is not likeness but some other quality left unspecified.

Building on the critique of the "Essential Copy" suggested by the second version of the story, more recent analyses have drawn attention to the fact that the anecdote is *not* a tale of simple mimesis—the exact duplication of actual grapes X here with an image of grapes Y there—but rather involves what Bryson terms "differing ontological levels or degrees, separated by precise thresholds or boundaries, . . . each distinguished by its own particular relation to reality and illusion."[9] The fact that the birds fly up to a "stage-building," Bryson observes, means that they move from nature (the sky) to architecture (the theater, a cultural space that houses representation) to the stage itself (the arena of fictitious representation) and thence into—or rather up against—representation itself (the painted surface, which may be the wall of the theater, since classical paintings are not portable quadrilaterals on stretched canvas separated from the world by a frame).[10] Shifting us beyond a relatively straightforward account of illusionism as lifelikeness measured by its capacity to deceive, the imbricated structure of the tale suggests that fiction is to be grasped in traversing thresholds or in the capacity to follow the passage of another—the birds, Zeuxis—across these thresholds (the trope of metalepsis).[11] The theatrical space in which the contest takes place, that is, shapes the ability to recognize that the curtain is (a) painting.

The anecdote converts the trompe l'oeil (of grape, of curtain) into something that dramatizes and performs as well as represents: this is a fiction about
illusion that operates as narrative or, perhaps, as theater. If the scene in which
the contest occurs frames the image of the curtain, so too does the image
itself frame its own interpretation in producing the expectation—the
anticipation—of a future materialization. The curtain, Stephen Bann observes, creates *"the illusion of a space in which figuration was destined to
appear."*[12] It is Zeuxis's expectation rather than the consummate execution
that shapes the trick here; cleverness, not skill, accounts for Parrhasius's triumph. Praising Zeuxis's grace in yielding victory to Parrhasius, one amateur
critic observes in 1788 that "Parrhasius could not but know, that . . . he was
more indebted to the ingenuity of the device, than the merits of his painted
curtain."[13] We see what we expect or desire to see, what the gaze that structures our field of vision leads us to anticipate. Zeuxis was set up.

The doubly fictive nature of Parrhasius's work resides, however, not only
in the painting itself nor even in its placement in the theater but also in its
insertion in a temporal series in the anecdote. As Bryson points out, "Representation does not *necessarily* produce of itself the idea of competition
between the original and copy, or of the copy's independent power. But
when the copy stands adjacent to or in the place where one would expect the
real thing, something more is involved; the original loses its autonomy, it
becomes the first in a series that also includes fictions."[14] The sequential
presentation of the paintings underlines the differences between them, for
Zeuxis's grapes and Parrhasius's curtains are not identical in their effect (or
at least do not affect birds and men in the same way). Zeuxis's grapes are
usually considered as a realistic representation that in many later accounts is
affiliated with the still life (although it is a trompe l'oeil for the birds), while
Parrhasius's curtain is commonly understood to be a trompe l'oeil, with the
difference between the two kinds of painting being an important part of the
question. Lacan famously argues that only the curtain can be understood as
a trompe l'oeil, since it alone "pretends to be something other than what it
is."[15] The distinction between still life and trompe l'oeil is often left blurry in
seventeenth- and eighteenth-century discussions and, as we shall see below,
continues to present theoretical difficulties to this day.

Although seventeenth- and eighteenth-century readings of the anecdote
do not always share the central preoccupation of many modern interpretations, the story enjoyed something of a vogue during the period, part of a

general interest in optical trickery that accompanied scientific and philosophical empiricism.[16] The importance of still life and trompe l'oeil to Northern European art gave the anecdote a prominent role in Dutch and Flemish treatises, while the masterfully painted trompe l'oeil curtain served as a transparent allusion to the myth of Parrhasius in countless paintings, including Rembrandt's 1646 *Holy Family*, Gerrit Dou's circa 1645–50 *Painter with Pipe and Book*, Nicolaes Maes's 1655 *Eavesdropper*, and Johannes Vermeer's 1657–58 *Woman Reading a Letter at an Open Window*.[17] As its recurrence as a painterly motif indicates, the trompe l'oeil curtain both flaunts the painter's virtuosity and incorporates the painter into a historical tradition and into the rivalries that construct that tradition.[18] Trompe l'oeil was popular throughout Europe, as well as in England, where such painters as Samuel van Hoogstraten, Simon Verelst, and Edward Collier found a thriving market.[19]

The tale of Zeuxis and Parrhasius also crops up with some frequency in the "Quarrel of the Ancient and Moderns" as well as in texts associated with the scientific revolution, such as Abraham Cowley's ode "To the Royal Society," his tribute to Bacon and the New Science, published as the prefatory verses to Thomas Spratt's 1667 *History of the Royal Society*. Stanza four of Cowley's celebration of Bacon's liberation of men from the "scarecrow deity" of Authority is devoted to the figure of Zeuxis's grapes:

> From Words, which are but Pictures of the Thought,
> (Though we our Thoughts from them pervers[e]ly drew)
> To Things, the Mind's right Object, he it brought,
> Like foolish Birds to painted Grapes we flew;
> He sought and gather'd for our use the True;
> And when on heaps the chosen Bunches lay,
> He press'd them wisely the Mechanick way,
> 'Till all their Juice did in one Vessel join,
> Ferment into a Nourishment Divine,
>   The Thirsty Soul's refreshing Wine.[20]

Although the stanza begins by figuring words as visual copies, the second line turns language from the secondary image or "Picture of the Thought" to the origin or source thereof ("we our Thoughts from them pervers[e]ly drew"). In the following lines, words precede but are then supplanted by things, carrying us from a linguistically mediated "Picture" to "Things, the Mind's right

Object," an ostensibly direct encounter with the empirical world. Cowley's use of Zeuxis's painted grapes in the fourth line rhetorically enacts the error he condemns: our gravitation toward the misleading representations of words, those pictures of thought, is repeated in the poet's turn to a simile ("Like foolish Birds to painted Grapes we flew").

The remainder of the passage similarly works against its ostensible meaning. Although Bacon purportedly brings us from words to things, Cowley replaces words not with things but with more words: the "True" grapes that supplant the painted ones become a sustained metaphor for "Things, the Mind's right Object." Rather than returning to things themselves, Cowley puts his metaphorical grapes through a curiously literal and mechanical process that turns them into wine. By converting the fabulous grapes into an object with an extrafictive life—capable of being pressed, metamorphosed, consumed—Cowley replicates the error made by the birds who pecked at Zeuxis's painting, offering the intoxicating fiction that metaphorical grapes can be converted into drinkable wine.[21] The compounding of the metaphor produces a kind of allegory of reading in which the promised empirical ground (of things) can only be revealed through a rhetorical turn. The notion that the mind can be "brought" from the words that are "but Pictures of the Thought" to "Things, the Mind's right Object" suggests that it is possible to circumvent the mediating falsehoods that bar us from the truth, but the "True" grapes ultimately reveal that we cannot get behind the painted curtain of language to encounter the things themselves.

Cowley's repudiation of painted grapes in favor of empirical things is hitched to a kind of aesthetic methodology, delineated in the second half of the stanza:

Who to the Life an exact Piece would make,
Must not from other's Work a Copy take;
      No, not from *Rubens* or *Vandyke*;
Much less content himself to make it like
Th'Ideas and the Images which lye
In his own Fancy, or his Memory.
      No, he before his Sight must Place
      The natural and living Face;
      The real Object must command
Each Judgment of his Eye, and Motion of his Hand.[22]

Here the possibility of making "to the Life an exact Piece" depends on avoiding the copy-of-a-copy distancing from the real. Turning away from both the great masters and the distorting ideas or images of fancy and memory, Cowley's artist converts himself from the subject of the gaze to its object, as the artist who "before his Sight must Place / The natural and living Face" is regarded in his turn. Although the artist avoids slavish imitation, the act of making is characterized by an almost total subordination to the object, as the "natural and living Face" dominates the sight and "the real Object" dictates to both eye and hand. The person must answer to the command of the thing. The scientific and artistic truth of things that Cowley celebrates—the work of the one "who to the Life an exact Piece would make"—is produced through an active confrontation with a gaze that is not quite fully human (or that defines itself as human through the circuit of a virtual perspective that is not human). We shall return to this later.

Whereas Cowley celebrates the primacy of things and is troubled by the deceptive nature of the painted grapes, for many seventeenth- and eighteenth-century critics the problem with the Zeuxis anecdote lies not so much in the trickery of the fiction as in the nature of the objects it imitates, a question bound up in the hierarchy of genres that placed the imitation of commonplace, everyday objects—the matter of still life and trompe l'oeil—at the bottom of the artistic food chain.[23] "To the extent that the Zeuxis's-grapes view of painting was thought to be problematic in the eighteenth century," as Kate Tunstall succinctly puts it, "it tended to be because Zeuxis painted grapes."[24] Notwithstanding Cowley's protracted treatment of the tale, it often merits but a glancing allusion during the period, as an anecdote too well known to require amplification. (In fact, Zeuxis was most celebrated during the period for the "selecting models" myth, his composite portrait of Helen from the best bits of five women.[25])

Over the course of the century, admiration of mimetic exactitude is increasingly dismissed as a crude response to the work of art. Although William Aglionby's 1719 self-help book for wannabe art critics praises Zeuxis's grapes, Apelles's horse (at which other horses neighed), and such moderns as Raphael who make flesh "*so Natural, that it seems to be* Alive,"[26] more canny critics scorn the model of art appreciation it sets forth. Delight in the foolery of masterful replication is the province of the low: "Such deceits are seen every day in works one does not hold in high esteem," Charles Perrault, chief among Louis XIV's moderns, sniffs in his *Parallèle des anciens et des modernes*; the cooks may laugh when they mistakenly try to put a painted partridge on the spit, but the painting stays in the kitchen.[27] Nor is Parrhasius's masterful rendering of a curtain exempt from derision: "Is a painter perfect for having painted a curtain well?" Perrault scoffs.[28]

What is singled out most often by seventeenth- and eighteenth-century readers is, however, not that a painting is mistaken for the thing itself but that such a fuss is made over tricking birds. "Does it require such great artistry to fool a bird[?]"[29] Perrault dismissively asks, and he returns to this question in the *Parallèle des anciens et des modernes*, where the "Chevalier," the helpful sidekick to Perrault's exemplary "modern" abbé, pits Zeuxis against Louis XIV's royal painter, Charles Le Brun:

> I saw an event as flattering to modern painting as the story of Zeuxis' grapes is to that of the Ancients, and vastly more entertaining. The door of Monsieur le Brun was open, and a freshly painted picture had been taken out into the courtyard to dry. In the foreground of this painting was a perfect representation of a large thistle. A woman came past leading an ass, which, when it saw the thistle, plunged into the courtyard; the woman who was hanging on to its bridle was dragged off her feet. If it hadn't been for a couple of sturdy lads who gave it some fifteen or twenty blows each with their sticks to force it back, it would have eaten the thistle—and I say *eaten*, because the paint was fresh and would all have come off on its tongue.[30]

Emphasizing the ludicrous aspect of the Zeuxis anecdote—the notion that the attestation of consummate artistry is to be found in the pecking of birds or (literally) the licking of asses—Perrault's Chevalier points out that the perfect images of the grapes and of the thistle excite the wrong kind of desire (the telos of art is not, ideally, to be eaten). Such moments of mistaken or "improper" use—the reduction of the painting to mere matter through its literal consumption—reinstate the materiality of the work of art: fictions both represent and are incarnated in tangible forms.

Perrault's account, like Cowley's, attempts to grapple with its *own* referential status. His anecdote relies on corroborating narrative incidentals and realist details—the "two sturdy lads," the numbered blows, the paint so fresh that it comes off the canvas—for its truth effect (thus affirming the *story's* own bona fides). It creates the impression in language of a true-to-life verisimilitude that the absurdity of the lifelike painted grapes or thistles potentially undermines. Yet Perrault does *not* offer an ekphrasis of the perfectly realized thistles in much the same way that Pliny omits any description of Zeuxis's or Parrhasius's paintings. We are never given the number of the grapes, the color of the thistles, the pattern on the fabric of which the curtain is made, or any other aspect of the impeccably realized object that so allures the birds, the donkey, the man. In both Pliny and Perrault, the fact of brilliant lifelikeness is stipulated, but no attempt is made to reproduce the purportedly masterful portrayal of the thing itself. The absence of a description embroils the reader in the active production of the fiction, obliging us to represent to ourselves the perfectly realized thing that is not presented to us. That is, the withheld image embroils us in a gratuitous activity of the imagination that satisfies no immediate or biological imperative—an activity whose very gratuity identifies it as distinctively human.

Whereas the human is engaged by the fiction, the bird and the ass are presumed to perceive the work of art only insofar as it is mistaken for what Giorgio Agamben, drawing on the early twentieth-century ethologist Jakob von Uexküll and the philosopher Martin Heidegger, calls a "carrier of significance": one of the limited repertory of objects or elements in the environment that "constitute a close functional . . . unity with the animal's receptive organs that are designed to perceive the mark . . . and to react to it."[31] Uexküll's meticulous reconstruction of the animal's relation to its environment or *Umwelt* identifies unique features that distinguish species' perceptual worlds. The dog encounters olfactory markers that elude the human nose, and the spider spins threads undetectable to the fly's eye, while a tick can be roused from seventeen years of dormancy by the mere proximity of a body of a specific temperature.[32] Seen from this angle, the donkey or the birds perceive the thistle or the grapes *only* because they are mistaken for edible objects, as "carriers of significance" that pertain to their needs. The fact that birds peck at painted grapes or that a donkey licks a canvas suggests a form of captivation that humans purportedly transcend. Only the human being, Heidegger notes, is "open" to the world and thus capable of "apprehending *as* something that to which it relates."[33]

Yet the assertion that what lures the animal to a work of art is its mimetic resemblance to a "carrier of significance" presupposes that we know what would look lifelike to a bird, a horse, an ass, as if realism in representation transcends species. Lacan famously challenges the notion that Zeuxis's grapes are verisimilitudinous, arguing that we cannot understand the fact that the "birds rushed to the surface on which Zeuxis had deposited his dabs of color" to mean that "the grapes were admirably reproduced," since "there would have to be something more reduced, something closer to the sign, in something representing grapes for the birds."[34] Perhaps what captivates in art issues not from resemblance but from some more rudimentary element.

Ernst Gombrich takes this possibility as a point of departure in his 1951 "Meditations on a Hobby Horse," where he argues that it is a mistake to see Pliny's birds pecking at Zeuxis's painted grapes as "a sign of a complete 'objective' illusion."[35] Drawing on Uexküll's fellow ethologists Nikolaas Tinbergen and Konrad Lorenz, who showed that a herring gull chick would peck with the same alacrity at a piece of painted cardboard with a red dot as at the distinctive red spot on its parent's beak, Gombrich argues that an image in a "biological sense is not an imitation of an object's external form, but an imitation of certain privileged or relevant aspects" (48). What allows one object to represent another may lie not in mimetic exactitude but in a functional resemblance that enables the proxy-object to "fulfill certain demands of the organism" (46). The "merest outline of a cow seems sufficient for a tsetse trap, for somehow it sets the apparatus of attraction in motion and 'deceives' the fly," he notes (47). This lowest common denominator of similitude (the minimal qualities such as the herring gull's red dot necessary to elicit the response) points to something other than the lifelike imitation of Zeuxis's grapes or Le Brun's thistle.

For Gombrich, the investment in the functional rather than the mimetic qualities of an object has much to tell us about humanity's relation to art as well. Like the herring gull, humans respond to objects or conscript them into service based on something other than resemblance. The hobby horse from which Gombrich's essay takes its title, for example, possesses a "formal aspect which fulfilled the minimum requirement for the performance of the function" (it can be ridden), but it is not mimetic (it does not look like a horse) (45). What counts for the child who turns a broom into a hobbyhorse is the fact that its properties—its affordances—meet a need (the object, however minimally, however nonmimetically, admits repurposing to the desired end). The fitness of the broom issues not from its resemblance to a real horse but from its serviceability; it is "good enough" for the purpose.

The impetus behind the work of art may thus involve relations and actions rather than resemblances or identities. Creativity embroils us in the world in ways that exceed the static reproduction of fixed forms; mimesis is an inadequate explanation for art. When we make a snowman, Gombrich drily notes, "we do not say 'Shall we represent a man who is smoking?' but 'Shall we give him a pipe?' "[36] We must consider, he argues, that "substitution may precede portrayal, and creation communication."[37] Imitation should be understood not only as the painstaking reproduction of the world according to the conventions of realist representation but also as a dynamic: what it makes the subject do or be (or be in doing). "A child wants to pull something," as Walter Benjamin puts it, "and so he becomes a horse; he wants to play with sand, and so he turns into a baker."[38] What drives us to seize on objects for our own devices and desires may not be an error issuing from mistaken similitude. That is, imitation may involve not the deliberate replication of a discrete object or image by an autonomous freestanding subject but a kind of seizure from without, by something beyond us, that circuits us into a relation that exceeds our conscious grasp. "To imitate," Lacan notes, "is no doubt to produce an image. But at bottom, it is, for the subject, to be inserted in a function whose exercise grasps it." On these terms, we might do well "not to think too quickly of the other who is being imitated."[39]

Gombrich's speculations about what compels in a work of art illuminate the philosopher Pierre Bayle's skeptical description of ancient tales of horses deceived by art in his 1696 *Dictionnaire historique et critique*. Whereas Gombrich asks what might impel a child to mount a broomstick, Bayle asks what might lead a horse to mount an equine statue, investigating in effect the means by which a real horse might transform a sculpture of a horse into one of Gombrich's hobbyhorses. In his curious "Dissertation sur l'hippomanes," a term whose contested meanings include a secretion from mares that acts as a kind of equine aphrodisiac, Bayle initially entertains the possibility that the animal might in fact be capable of appreciating a statue, deliberating over whether

> horses, whose lust is extremely violent, might be fired, when come near to the brazen statue [of a horse], without the aid of any philtre [of hippomanes]. If we suppose them to be endowed with a soul, could they not figure to themselves that a statue is the animal it represents; or, at least, that it is a very fine statue? In the first case, might not the same circumstance happen to them, *mutatis mutandis*, which happened to those birds who pecked at a vine represented in painting? A horse which Apelles painted made some living horses neigh. In the second case, why should they not be subject to the weakness which many men have been guilty of, I mean to lust after a statue?[40]

The horses must not only recognize the verisimilitude of the work of art (like the birds before Zeuxis's grapes); they must also see that the copy is made in their image. That is, in asking whether the horses could "figure to themselves that a statue is the animal it represents," Bayle points to the possibility of equine self-consciousness, of forms of reflexivity sometimes singled out as exclusively human. "Can one not speak of an experience that is already specular as soon as a cat recognizes a cat?" Derrida asks, protesting against Lacan's insistence that animals lack these capacities. "Does not the mirror effect also begin wherever a living creature, whatever it be, identifies another living creature of its own species as its neighbor [*prochain*] or fellow [*semblable*]?"[41]

The fact that the likeness Bayle's horse detects is found not in a living creature but in a statue adds an important twist. For when Bayle contemplates the possibility that the horse's lust is incited not by the statue's resemblance to a horse but by the statue itself, a mere form, he carries the animal beyond the immediate impulses of instinct or nature, attributing to the horse the ability not only to know its own likeness and to recognize that likeness in another but also to find a worthwhile relation between similar forms of different substances (bronze, flesh). In Bayle's (ironic) account, horses, like humans, see through the deception and persist in their delight.[42] The horse may, like a man enamored of a statue, love a work of art—a form—or perhaps, conversely, a human being can come to treat a work of art as something to be used: licked, eaten, mounted.

Bayle's initial speculations on equine art appreciation are succeeded by an intricate reconstruction of the horse's sensorium from within, seeking out the equivalent of the herring gull's red dot. If we grant, Bayle argues, that "in the passion of love, the eye is not the sole guide with which beasts are assisted, as it frequently is with respect to man, and that the smell is the principal vehicle by which that passion is conveyed," then "it follows, that a statue is wanting, or fails, with regard to them, of the chief incentives to love" (10.360; French 4.595). A statue might, he concedes, incite animal desire through the dexterous imitation of "the attitude of a mare fired with the strongest lust. . . . [For] though we should suppose, with the Cartesians, brutes to be mere machines, we nevertheless may suppose that a lively imitation of the postures might have a remarkable effect" (10.360; 4.596). No such compensatory strategy exists for painting, however; since animals are "not excited to copulation solely by the sight, but likewise by motion, by the smell and the voice, none of which three things can be in a picture," he dismisses the tale of Zeuxis's grapes and other remarkable paintings as "mere idle stories."[43] In endeavoring to register the role played by the animal sensorium in the apprehension of the work of art, Bayle conjoins the fabulous stories of the ancients to the discourses of natural history, drawing attention to the complex projections involved in imagining the embodied experience of other creatures. On what terms can the human reconstruct the "something" that represents an object (painted grapes, a statue) for another (birds, horses)? What did they think birds saw? It is to these questions that we now turn.

The World Through Avian Eyes

There is no early modern Uexküll to reconstruct the avian *Umwelt*, and there are few counterparts to the microscopist Robert Hooke's speculations about the temporal experience of flies: "When I hear a Fly moving his Wings to and fro so many times, with such a Swiftness as to make a Sound, I cannot but imagine, that that Fly must be sensible of and distinguish at least 3 Moments in the time that it makes one of those Strokes with his Wings, for that it is able to regulate and guide it self by the Motion of them."[44] Jacques-Henri Bernardin de Saint-Pierre's intricate reconstruction of the experience of a fly landing on a strawberry plant in his *Études de la nature* (1784) is likewise unusual. "Each part of the flower," he writes, "must offer them spectacles of which we have no idea. The flowers' yellow anthers, suspended from white filaments, present them with a pair of golden joists balanced on columns more beautiful than ivory. . . . The other flowering parts [suggest] cups, urns, pavilions, domes, that the human arts of architecture and metalworking haven't yet imitated."[45] Rescaling time and space to the diminutive proportions of a fly, both Hooke and Bernardin reconstruct the world from the point of view of another species. Their imaginings are not the fruits of enhanced sensory powers; indeed, they exceed the limits of empirical observation to create a purely virtual reality. While Bernardin's transformation of the interior of a flower into an architectural space, as Joanna Stalnaker has argued, evokes "surreal perspectives that can only be imagined by the describer," Hooke's use of the sound of a fly's fluttering wings to imagine the fly's temporal experience of the beat between strokes detaches us from an anthropocentric framework altogether.[46]

These fascinating examples are, however, outliers. Speculation about the nature of avian vision in seventeenth- and eighteenth-century natural histories typically begins (and sometimes ends) with an affirmation that birds possess great acuity of sight that enables them to espy prey, detect hazards, and rapidly assimilate visual images in flight. For reasons of length, the discussion here has been condensed, but Oliver Goldsmith's enduringly popular *History of the Earth and Animated Nature* (1774) offers a representative summation. "The sense of seeing in birds," Goldsmith proclaims,

> is infinitely superior to that of other animals. Indeed, this piercing sight seems necessary to the creature's support and safety. Were this organ blunter, from the rapidity of the bird's motion, it would be apt to strike against every object in its way; and it could scarcely find subsistence unless possessed of a power to discern its food from above with astonishing sagacity. An hawk, for instance, perceives a lark at a distance which neither men nor dogs could spy; a kite, from an almost imperceptible height in the clouds, darts down on its prey with the most unerring aim.[47]

Working backward from use to design, Goldsmith deduces capacity from function. Since the kite darts down from high altitudes to strike its prey, it must logically have been able to see it. It is not only the bird's panoptic command of a single point of view but its kinetic processing of information at high speeds that counts for Goldsmith, who favorably compares the avian to the human eye.

While the quantity of anatomical real estate devoted to the bird's eye confirms Goldsmith's conviction about the importance of the faculty, it leads him to unfavorable conclusions about their other capacities: "What great degree of sagacity," Goldsmith asks, "can be expected in animals whose eyes are almost as large as their brain?"[48] Earlier works of anatomy, such as Thomas Willis's *Anatomy of the Brain* (Latin original, 1667; English version, 1681), substantiate Goldsmith's dismissive view of the bird's mental endowments. For Willis, the narrow blood vessels feeding the bird's brain indicate a narrow mind: "The Carotidick Arteries, which carry the blood to the brains of the greater Birds, are so small, that there is no proportion of these to the same in man and four-footed beasts. . . . In truth, the brains of Birds are watered with a very small portion of blood, in respect of other living Creatures; because, where the fancy or imagination is little exercised, there is not much blood required for the refreshing the animal Spirits."[49] As dim as its proverbial counterpart, the ana-tomical bird brain requires little replenishment; avian vision presumably offers few images to be toyed with by the mind. All eye and no brain, the bird sees what it needs to see—and nothing more.[50]

In what is usually considered the first European work of ornithology, *The Ornithology of Francis Willughby* (Latin original, 1676; English version, 1678), John Ray and Francis Willughby rehearse Willis's claims: "The Brains of Birds seem not to be much employed in the functions of Fancy or Memory." While Ray and Willughby offer detailed empirical descriptions of "each Bird from the view and inspection of it lying before us," they neither portray the way birds interact with their environments nor speculate on what birds see.[51] Only in the section on fowling does the *Ornithology* endeavor to reconstruct the perspective of the bird. There readers are advised to smear birdlime on "the brownest Rods, and nearest the colour of the earth" in pursuing wild geese, and to "Colour your Line of a dark green" when snaring heron. Descriptions of the stalking horse—both the real jade trained up to amble along as a walking bird blind and the artificial version contrived out of stuffed canvas, "with his head bending down, as if he grazed, of due shape, stature, and bigness, painted of the colour of a horse"—single out the traits most likely to attract the avian eye (shades of Uexküll's "carrier of significance").[52]

Like the spider spinning a thread just slender enough to evade the fly's eye, Ray's fowler limns the perceptual world of birds in devising methods to snare them. The product of craft and craftiness, his traps are simultaneously a token of humanity's violent claim to dominion over other creatures and an objective expression of the hunter's sympathetic reconstruction of the animals' experience. Yet this understanding is not a one-way street, for birds, Ray acknowledges, have a learning curve. Even the most lifelike mock-up of a stalking horse will not deceive the birds forever.[53] When the fowl "begin to find your deceit, and will not sit, . . . then you may otherwhiles use your Oxe-engine, till the Horse be forgotten, and so by change of your Engines make your sport last."[54] On these terms, traps are not only "lethal parodies of the animal's *Umwelt*," as the anthropologist Alfred Gell has influentially argued, but also the concrete manifestation of "a nexus of intentionalities between hunters and prey animals, via material forms and mechanisms," the site of an intersubjective relation between human and animal.[55] (We shall return to this below.)

Although the passages on fowling and hunting included in the *Ornithology* offer a speculative reconstruction of a bird's-eye view, it is in only in Ray's works of natural theology that he fully steeps himself in other creatures' perspectives. Late seventeenth-century physico-theologians such as Ray, Nehemiah Grew, and William Derham turn from the anatomist's study of isolated specimens and the taxonomist's classificatory schemas to focus on the adaptation of each animal to its place in nature, demonstrating the intelligence of God's design by tracing the close fit of creature to habitat. Their conviction that animals' "forms could not be viewed in isolation from their behaviour and interaction with their respective environments" means that the perfection of God's design of the bird's eye can only be understood by considering the function it was designed to serve *for the bird*.[56] Thus Ray's 1691 *Wisdom of God* contends that the nictating membrane (or transparent eyelid) is given to birds and beasts that lack hands for "the more abundant Defence and Security of the Eye" against branches and grass, while Derham announces in his 1714 *Physico-Theology* that the placement of birds' eyes so "as to take in near a whole Sphere" enables them to "seek their Food, and escape Dangers."[57] (One can hear echoes of physico-theology in twentieth-century ethology: "All animal subjects, from the simplest to the most complex," Uexküll affirms, "are inserted into their environments to the same degree of perfection.")[58]

The physico-theological affirmation that each creature fits seamlessly into its place in nature offers a benign account of a divinely-ordered world, although, seen in relation to the trap, the physico-theological book of nature is the Janus face of the hunting manual. Nevertheless, these reconstructions of other creatures' eye-views challenge anthropocentric assumptions about human dominion. As Joanna Picciotto has argued, physico-theologians serially inhabit the perspectives of other species, elevating each nonhuman actor in turn to the status of "a fellow agent negotiating its way through a larger system beyond its apprehension."[59] The physico-theologians' systematic reconstruction of other animals' experiences seemingly levels creaturely hierarchies, as each being in turn is offered "a shot at full personhood," Picciotto contends. Yet this equality is only provisional, not only because, as we have just seen, humans instrumentalize this knowledge to lethal ends, but also because physico-theological works narrate an inner life that cannot be accessed by the creature itself. The fact that the human feels for the snail "in a way it can't feel for itself" means that man alone can appreciate the ingenuity of providence and the beauties of creation.[60] Humanity possesses a monopoly on the comprehensive knowledge gleaned from this virtual displacement. In conjoining the sympathetic rendering of another creature's consciousness with an exteriorized third-person vantage, physico-theology claims an "epistemological license" that, Picciotto notes, anticipates the later emergence of free indirect discourse (502). We shall return to the way techniques devised for representing the perspective of nonhuman creatures shape the representation of human consciousness in Chapter 5. For the moment, I want to emphasize the extraordinary array of devices (both literal and figurative) that seventeenth-century thinkers contrived to carry the human over the thresholds that separate species, as if the eye can be dissevered from the body.

And of course the eye can be—and was—separated from the body in early optical experiments. While natural historians, physico-theologians, and hunters undertake a primarily speculative reconstruction of the bird's eye-view, optics enabled scientific practitioners to see, quite literally, what another eye sees. Indeed, the exemplary eye used in seventeenth-century optics was often not human. One of Descartes's famous experiments begins with instructions to take "the eye of a newly dead person (or failing that, the eye of an ox or some other large animal)," scrape away the surrounding membranes "so as to expose a large part of the humour without spilling any," and replace them with a white paper onto which the images produced by the light may be projected.[61] The eye here operates as a kind of camera obscura, in which light admitted to a darkened chamber through a pinhole projects the image of the scene outside onto the opposite surface in inverted form. "When you have seen this picture in the eye of a dead animal, and considered its causes," Descartes concludes, "you cannot doubt that a quite similar picture is formed in the eye of a living person, on the internal membrane for which we substituted the white body" (167). The excision of the eye from the body creates a model of vision that, in its automatic functioning, is independent of species and hence not necessarily human. Optics thus severs the possessive that ties vision to a particular subject or kind.[62] The eye thereby becomes, Ofer Gal and Raz Chen-Morris argue, "a natural, material optical instrument[,] . . . merely a screen, on which rests a blurry array of light stains, the effect of a purely causal process."[63]

Our ability to apprehend the means by which the optical image is produced in the eye depends upon processes of splitting and doubling that circuit the apprehension of our own sight through a device. As the illustration from Descartes's *Optics* (Figure 1) shows, the eye becomes a component in an experimental apparatus that offers the optical image in an exteriorized objective form. The plate displays a bearded man looking up at a massive eyeball that diagrams the inversion of the image on the retina. The man sees both the retinal "painting" as it takes shape at the back of the disembodied eye and the eye that is producing the figure. As Victor Stoichita observes, we, like the bearded figure, can "*picture the eye in general*"; we can "*see sight*" as a mechanism and . . .

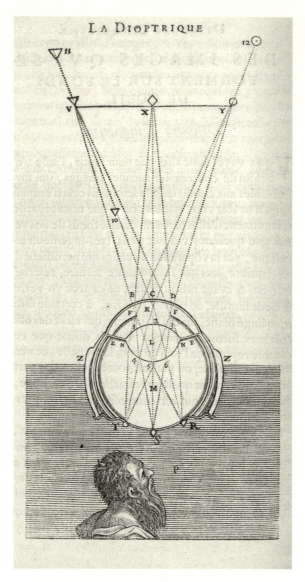

FIGURE 1. *La dioptrique,* in René Descartes, *Discours de la méthode* (Leiden: De l'Imprim. de I. Maire, 1637), p. 36. RB 336029, The Huntington Library, San Marino, California.

imagine it accurately"; we can even see the eye's functioning in *"another* eye," but we cannot "see sight."[64] The eye cannot see itself. (Even when we look in the mirror, we see our face but not our gaze.) Vision issues, as it were, from this blind spot—a blind spot that we encounter in the trompe l'oeil paintings to which we turn below.[65]

If, for optics, the impersonal operation of the eye is identical irrespective of species, what then explains the difference between human and avian vision—between the birds that peck at the image of grapes and the man deceived by the painted curtain? For Descartes, the retinal image is *all* that animals can see. "My view," he explains in a 1637 letter, "is that animals do not see as we do when we are aware that we see, but only as we do when our mind is elsewhere. In such a case the images of external objects are depicted on our retinas, and perhaps the impressions they make in the optic nerves cause our limbs to make various movements, although we are quite unaware of them. In such a case we too move like automatons."[66] The Cartesian animal lacks the capacity to convert sense impressions into conscious perceptions; birds see the retinal or optical image cast on the back of the dead eye—and nothing more. It is only in moments of abstraction—when "our mind is elsewhere"—that the unprocessed retinal image akin to what animals see is before us. At such moments, we become the puppets of our sensory stimuli, as the "impressions [that images] make in the optic nerves" produce automatic responses that leave us little better than the machines Descartes believes animals to be. When we are "aware that we see," our minds refashion the light striking the retina into the coherent images we normally apprehend. Images formed in the back of the eye thus are not "intentional species" (images as copies of things in the world) but light rays that strike the retina in accordance with mechanical laws, producing an image independent of the perceptual processing of the mind.[67] For Descartes, that is, "there need be no resemblance between the ideas which the soul conceives and the movements which cause these ideas."[68] Uncorrected by the faculties, the world as seen through the not-quite-human lens of the disembodied eye bears scant likeness to what the human mind perceives. Put more simply, the image cast on the eye is not a realist image.

What distinguishes humans from animals in this account is not only the refashioning of the retinal image by perception but also the ability to apprehend and reflect on what the eye sees, anterior to its cognitive processing. Humans isolate and play with the distinction between what we see and what we perceive, above all in works of art. We can see this in the interest many Northern European painters evinced in optics, demonstrated by their experiments with the camera obscura in paintings that invite the viewer to experience—to enact—the (re)fashioning of the optical image into what the mind perceives.[69] Thus a Vermeer discloses what the eye sees—light and color blazed on the retina anterior to its formation into a recognizable object—showing how, as Svetlana Alpers puts it, a "hand is assembled out of tone and light without declaring its identity as a hand."[70] Inasmuch as the white, black, red, blue smear of paint on the canvas out of which the hand emerges is closer to the retinal image than a seemingly exact mimetic rendering, it enables us to toggle between vision as it is and the world as we perceive it, between a retinal and a realist image. Northern European art thus invites the beholder to enact a perceptual process that produces or reproduces the distinction of the human from the animal eye.

While this account of the eye's organic functioning helps us understand how the work of art may be used to distinguish human from animal perception, it does not furnish an answer to the question with which we began: what makes an image deceive a human or an avian eye? If it is not mimetic exactitude (as in the tale of Zeuxis's grapes) nor even the replication of the retinal image—what the eye "really" sees—then what enables a work of art to pass for real? In the next section, I want to turn from seventeenth-century speculation about *what* the eye sees to the ways the artifice of perspective shapes *how* the eye sees. For if optics treats all eyes—human, avian, bovine—as interchangeable, perspective as a technique accommodates or creates different eye-views. Perspective operates, as Celeste Brusati has argued, "in much [the] same way as a lens or other optical device to manipulate scale and enhance surface visibility," serving as a kind of "prosthetic" to construct the eye-views to which beholders might accede—eye-views that may or may not be human.[71] In what follows, I want to address the way perspective's impersonal construction of the beholder's eye-view affords the means to see through a point of view not already naturalized as human, on the one hand, while making the experience of seeing into an object of reflexive critique, on the other. What makes the not-quite-human device of perspective "humanizing" in this context is not necessarily that it aligns us with an anthropocentric framework but that it enables us to see through a virtual eye-view not already our own. Our awareness of the artifice of perspective allows us to reflect on the way we see (or do not see), which is one important way art sorts human from avian eye.

The Artifice of Perspective and the Snare of Art

If optics offers us a glimpse of what the eye itself sees, it does so by freezing the living eye's ceaseless movement, aligning binocular and peripheral vision into a single point, and thus circumventing questions of perception, wavering attention, retinal afterimages, and other disturbances (the various defects of the eye that will so vex Hooke in the next chapter).[72] Despite the fact that vision as constituted through the laws of optics does not perfectly line up with the "natural 'judgement of the eye' and . . . the flexibility of the visual process," Martin Kemp argues, early theories of perspective often borrow from geometric optics, bracketing questions of "how we 'see,' how we unscramble sensory impressions, how we understand, how the senses relate to each other," in order to present a "realist" view of the world.[73] Like the optical eye, the eye of geometrical perspective possesses a stability and unity that the embodied organ cannot possess. It rationalizes the visual field, ruthlessly, impersonally, subjecting the eye to a logic that possesses the rigor of a grammar. Yet perspective's alignment with an anthropocentric viewpoint is not intrinsic but constructed: the product of a formal structure that holds both the beholder and the elements of the image in place.

That perspective imposes artificial order on the visual field encountered by the eye is hardly a revelation.[74] In Erwin Panofsky's seminal account of the Albertian models so central to the Italian tradition in painting, the impersonal artifice of perspective "subjects the artistic phenomenon to stable and even mathematically exact rules," offering a framed window on the world organized around a central vanishing point, determined by the placement of an observer at a fixed distance exterior to the picture plane. For Panofsky, perspective is anthropocentric both because it subordinates the represented world to a human-devised system and because "these rules refer to the psychological and physical conditions of the visual impression . . . determined by the freely chosen position of a subjective 'point of view.'"[75] In its orientation around an individual, presumptively human, beholder, Albertian perspective marks the historical moment, as Panofsky puts it, "when modern 'anthropocracy' first reared itself" (72).

Yet perspective in art need not customize the depicted world to Panofsky's subjective, individuated human eye-view. Whereas the Albertian window on the world begins "with a viewer who is actively looking out at objects" and furnishes the appearance of a coherently structured "second or

substitute world" on a "framed surface or pane," Northern European painting, as Svetlana Alpers influentially argued in *The Art of Describing*, offers the
eye's encounter with an "unframed image of the world compressed onto a bit
of paper with no prior viewer to establish a position or a human scale."[76]
In Dutch painting, the eye "inserts itself right into the world" (85). In the
process, Northern art tampers with the tools that tailor the world to the
singular, ostensibly human point of view with which Albertian perspective is
associated.

Northern painting does not dispense with perspective altogether; rather
it deploys different models, as such art historians as Alpers, Brusati, and
Hanneke Grootenboer have shown. Rather than placing the viewer in a fixed
position exterior to the picture plane, the Northern theories of perspective
described in the 1505 *De artificiala perspectiva* by Jean Pélerin (called Viator)
and the 1604–5 *Perspective* of Vredeman de Vries locate the beholder "at the
interface of two visibilities," simultaneously subject and object within the
permeable membrane between the painting and the world.[77] Northern perspective is thus "not only a means of representing three dimensions on two,"
in Brusati's words, "but also a tool for simulating and reflecting upon visual
experience itself." The temporal, aggregative process of viewing elicited by
Northern European perspective opens up other relations to the object-world,
loosening the possessive that anchors perspective to a human eye-view. Thus,
according to Brusati, Dutch interiors "fragment and multiply pictorial
spaces," offering "embedded through-views, open doors, windows and
thresholds" that invite the eye "to wander and to linger,"[78] while studio
scenes, which depict (a) work in progress, represent the temporal-historical
processes of creation as well as the fully realized artifact, a reminder of "the
status of painting as a *human* production, rather than a divine emanation or
imprint."[79] In still-life painting, mirrors, windows, glasses, and polished
metal surfaces reflect each other, in multiple partial views that fracture the
oneness of the thing beheld and of the beholder: we "share the quality of
visibility with the things around us," as Grootenboer puts it, exercising "our
vision while simultaneously being subjected to the vision of surrounding
objects. The things around us occupy possible points from where we can be
viewed, even as we are looking at them."[80] No one eye-view (human or otherwise) presides.

In still-life paintings, such as Willem Claesz. Heda's 1635 *Still Life with
a Gilt Cup* (Plate 1), objects are not organized around the single point of
Albertian perspective. Instead, the eye is invited to rove over the exquisitely

rendered leftovers of a partially consumed meal. The table, seemingly abandoned in disarray, is topped with crumpled white linens, plates, glasses, a
pitcher, a gilt cup, oyster shells, broken bread, and the ubiquitous peeled
lemon, set before a neutral color field that offers no horizon, making it
appear, Grootenboer notes, "as if *we are looking from an empty point of view*."
Both in form and content, the painting offers the "world deprived of a
human gaze."[81]

Although my attention below will be on the trompe l'oeil, I want to
pause briefly to consider the realism of the still life with which the illusionism
of the trompe l'oeil is so often contrasted. In seventeenth-century inventories,
the two kinds of painting are not always clearly distinguished. Indeed, the
Dutch word for deceptively illusionistic paintings (*oogenbedrieger*) was only
coined in the early eighteenth century, and the term *trompe l'oeil* itself in
1808.[82] Like trompe l'oeil, still life makes things present to the beholder, both
through its mimetic exactitude and through its manipulation of perspective.
Both offer the lifelike depiction of what Bryson famously termed the "overlooked": the inanimate objects that usually belong to the margins of artworks,
the *parerga*, or "bywork," that formed the background in narrative pictures
or history paintings.[83] Both represent images of dazzling painterly virtuosity
that make the object seem present, and the often-debased nature of the
objects represented—half-eaten breakfasts, animal corpses, skulls, the detritus
of everyday living—raises perennial questions about the pleasure incited by
the verisimilitudinous representation of objects that would excite disgust in
real life. "Who would hang a Piece of ordinary, unripe, or rotten Fruit in his
best Room, and among a Cabinet-collection," the Dutch art theorist Gerard
de Lairesse grumbled in 1707, "seeing the Life itself is so disagreeable?"[84]
Finally, both still life and trompe l'oeil are characterized by a relative lack of
depth of field (the shallow picture plane means the realistic or illusionistic
effect does not depend on where the viewer stands) and by the seeming
absence of narrative. No story loops the things back into a human world; no
human puts them to use.

Yet still life and trompe l'oeil are quite different in their manipulation of
perspective and in their effect on the beholder. Still life, unlike trompe l'oeil,
enfolds the viewer into the world of the painting. In Heda's still life, for
example, the plates and knife that project over the rim of the table breach
the picture plane, reinforcing the impression of three-dimensional space,
while the absence of a vanishing point lures us into the image. The objects
solicit not only the eye but the touch, for the angle of representation allows

the light to accentuate the textures of the masterfully rendered surfaces: the chasing on the toppled silver tazza, the embossed patterns on the salt cellar, the knurling on the handle of the knife. The still life brings objects close to us while upholding an irremediable distance (since the things are paint). We are "there" and not there at one and the same time.

The impression of nearness in part issues from the way still life approximates the phenomenological experience of things. Even as we can never fully see the objects that surround us in real life, because they always overlap with others based on our vantage, so too are objects only partially visible in Heda's still life. We are located within or at least at the interface of the scene. Nor are the shapes and lines purely geometric. The pristine ellipse of the small plate is broken by an oyster shell; the straight edge of the table is intercepted by the cascading folds of the linens.[85] We catch glimpses of the occluded aspects of things in their reflections on *other* objects: the pale gleam of the underside of a shell or a crust of bread on a plate, the inner surface of the pitcher's handle reflected in its polished side, and the illuminated windowpanes—the unseen but presumptive source of light—mirrored in the green-tinted wine glass and the pewter ewer. While we see things, they "see" each other. The multiplication of vantages means that we do not simply accede to a point of view from which we have command.

Indeed, it is often difficult to know where we stand (literally and metaphorically) with still-life painting. The angle at which we are positioned vis-à-vis Heda's tabletop refuses to offer us a stable vantage: "We are neither sitting at the table nor standing in front of it, but rather 'approaching' it," Grootenboer notes. "Neither a bird's- nor a frog's-eye view—neither occupying a diner's position nor being offered the viewpoint of a fixed viewer—our looking is suspended at an angle relative to the tabletop that we normally would never experience." No designated eye-view secures our place before the scene; no vanishing point anchors our gaze in its depths. The neutral backdrop does not refer to a space outside the frame. Indeed, the beige background does not even seem to be a wall, just a blank color field whose flatness, Grootenboer argues, exposes "perspective's own empty geometrical structure."[86]

This interplay of plenitude and void is a feature of the objects themselves: the filled glass has a toppled counterpart; the oysters are next to empty shells. With the exception of the gilt goblet, the vessels are all open. The pitcher's lid is up; the contents of the salt cellar brim over the top; small grains of pepper have spilled from the cone wrapper—so many containers failing to

PLATE I. Willem Claesz. Heda, *Still Life with a Gilt
Cup*, 1635. Rijksmuseum, Amsterdam.

PLATE 2. Melchior d'Hondecoeter, *Trompe l'Oeil with Dead Birds on a Pinewood Wall*, 1660–70. Suermondt-Ludwig-Museum, Aachen. Photo: Anne Gold, Aachen.

Plate 3. Jacobus Biltius, *Dead Wildfowl and a Huntsman's Net*, trompe l'oeil, 1679. National Gallery of Denmark, Copenhagen. © SMK Photo.

PLATE 4. Cornelis Gijsbrechts, *Trompe L'oeil. Board Partition with a Still Life of Two Dead Birds Hanging on a Wall*, 1670. National Gallery of Denmark, Copenhagen. © SMK Photo.

contain. The only sealed object is the gilt cup that forms the pinnacle of the triangular composition, its gold-plated body standing out against Heda's trademark monochromatic palate. The diagonal from the lower left to the upper right marches the eye upward to the tip of the spear held by the tiny soldier crowning the gilt goblet's ornate cover. With the exception of the skull as memento mori, still-life painting typically does not represent human figures, and the presence of this figurine, presiding over the vestiges of a feast, might be seen either as glorifying or lamenting the "embarrassment of riches" that accompanied the seventeenth-century global ascendency of the Netherlands. Although, as Roland Barthes influentially argued, the abundance of glistening objects depicted in still life indicates a race of beings "at the pinnacle of history, knowing no other fate than a gradual appropriation of matter,"[87] the gilt soldier suggests less human dominion than a strange leveling. Here humanity's avatar is not living flesh but an anthropomorphic figure reduced to an ornamental detail, a metallic gilt-coated body (not pure gold), a glistening surface that reflects the surrounding objects in a scene from which humans have absented themselves. Like our figural proxy, the rigid little soldier, we too cease to hold a position apart from the painting and become one body among others, both subjects *and* objects in the world.

Whereas Heda's still life envelops us in a world of luminescent surfaces that invite the eye to linger and take pleasure in the sumptuously rendered objects, in trompe l'oeil the baleful glare of things supplants the human gaze rather than inviting us to look back. The reciprocal, processual seeing afforded by still life takes on an adversarial valence in trompe l'oeil painting. While both the realism of still life and the illusionism of trompe l'oeil dislodge humanity from its position as the cynosure of the world, trompe l'oeil holds out no compensatory return. Indeed, the illusionism of trompe l'oeil renders us as hapless as Zeuxis's birds, unable to tell real from simulacra. While still life (as we have seen) typically places its objects before a closed, neutral background, trompe l'oeil often pawns itself off as a continuation of real space—a niche, a door, a cabinet, a painting. Whereas still-life objects are typically placed on a horizontal table or surface that gives them, according to Jean Baudrillard, "the weight of real things,"[88] the bodies in trompe l'oeil are usually vertically displayed, often hanging from a hook or a nail hammered into an illusionistically painted surface. The things in trompe l'oeil thus float before us with a hallucinatory vividness that robs us of a sense of "familiar reality," leaving us with what Baudrillard calls the "acute and negative pleasure found in the abolition of the real" (54). Both still life and trompe l'oeil excise the possessive that attaches the eye-view to the human, but whereas still life makes us an object in the world, trompe l'oeil erases our place in it, offering a glimpse of the world not just in our absence but without us altogether.

Still life makes the picture plane dissolve to reveal depth, a third dimension. In trompe l'oeil, the image assaults the eye with the presence of what is not really there. The surface of the painting, as Baudrillard puts it, becomes "an opaque mirror held before the eye, *and there is nothing behind it.* Nothing to see: it is things that see you, they do not fly from you, they bear themselves before you like your own hallucinated interiority" (58). Rendered the object of the relentless gaze of things, the beholder can neither escape into the depths of the image—since the painting has no vanishing point—nor into the depths of the self—since the things "bear themselves before you like your own hallucinated interiority." Confronting us with an image so exact as to pass for the thing itself, the trompe l'oeil short-circuits any turn to a world external to the painting. It proclaims its own autonomous world inasmuch as its objects do not refer mimetically to the world outside: we do not see *through* them to reality or understand them to be copies, but provisionally take them to be the things themselves. In trompe l'oeil, Grootenboer writes, "the gaze of the viewer is no longer able to look 'into' the painting but instead ricochets off the surface of the picture, bouncing back to the viewing eye, the place from which it originated. The blind spot of linear perspective, that is, the vanishing point to which the viewer's eye is directed, can never be reached—or, for that matter, seen—and collapses with the point [of] view from which seeing is made possible."[89] Although this lack in our visual field holds for *all* versions of perspective, only in trompe l'oeil does it become apparent.[90] Whereas linear perspective is constructed *around* the viewer, trompe l'oeil undermines this position of mastery by revealing the ways our field of vision is not aligned with what the mind apprehends. The operation of perspective (which we normally look *through*) becomes dramatically visible precisely in its loss; it exposes a world not assimilated to the humanizing protocols of realism.

The trompe l'oeil offers a view of things that is (by definition) not available to the subjective eye cast directly on the world—a view that can only be attained via the virtual view of an otherwise inaccessible reality made present by the work of art. The "something more" that the trompe l'oeil image delivers—what we see when we look at the trompe l'oeil but do not see when we look at real things—stems from the nonalignment with the gaze that structures our field of vision.[91] "Just at the point where the eye thinks it knows the form and can afford to skip," as Bryson puts it, "the image proves that in fact the eye had not understood at all what it was about to discard."[92] This reflexive recoil, the reassertion of an interval between beholder and surprised self, intimates awareness of the fact, so to speak, of fiction. The startling encounter with the failure of our own perceptual powers creates a heightened self-consciousness about the limits of our intellectual command over the world, for the illusion persists even after the beholder cottons on to the fact that it is an image, not the real thing. The mind cannot master the trick; the message conveyed by the senses outlasts the cognitive knowledge of their deception, inducing what Susan Feagin calls an "ontological wobble" in which what "*one knows to be true*" cannot "*be made to penetrate the phenomenology of one's visual experience.*"[93] We believe our eyes despite the mind's conviction.

Indeed, the persistence of the illusion is precisely the point, for the painting creates a kind of compulsion to repeat that drives the viewer to the surface of the canvas again and again.[94] As we shall see below, this capacity to apprehend the fiction—to grasp that the grapes are not real grapes, that the horse is a statue, that the curtain conceals nothing—and *still* to become inexhaustibly invested in the image, helps define human distinction in early modern discussions of the Zeuxis anecdote in ways that anticipate current theoretical stances on these questions. Like Lacan's human baby who, in contrast with the chimpanzee, finds its own reflection in the mirror to be an object of bottomless interest, the initially deceived viewer keeps coming back to the surface of the painting (even as readers keep returning to the anecdote of Zeuxis's grapes, as if the story itself were a kind of trompe l'oeil holding an unaccountable allure). "This dimension of loving a form is what differentiates, for Lacan, humans from other species," as Barbara Johnson puts it in her discussion of Lacan's mirror stage. "While all other animals measure information by its empirical usefulness, man alone does not have to connect a 'substance' with a 'form.' . . . It is the capacity *not* to tell the truth, to separate forms without substance from the tyranny of the referential, that characterizes the human."[95] On these terms, the difference between the deception that fools birds and the play of fiction that alternately delights and baffles people resides in the willingness to enter into a durable relationship with insubstantial forms (with fictions).

The compelling nature of the trompe l'oeil lies less in the perfection of its replication of reality than in the ongoing and repeatable pleasure of disenchantment it produces. In trompe l'oeil, as Jacqueline Lichtenstein argues, we seek out the "disquieting pleasure born of the sensation of altered reality in which the apparatus and the landmarks of identity waver and fade," because "we are upheld as subjects only by perceiving the tiny difference that lets us distinguish between reality and its image; through the play of resemblances we usually seek not perception of the same but awareness of the non-identical, so as to find in it the assurance of our own ever-uncertain identity."[96] If the dissolution of the barrier between reality and representation disorients the subject in Lichtenstein's account, its restoration reaffirms identity, because the sudden capture or captivation by an image leads to a surprise revelation that produces a doubled consciousness "which comes back to see what has just deceived it" (170). We are compelled not by the perdurability of the material object, its reassuring solidity, but by the reverse: the persistence of the illusion of presence.

Even as the trompe l'oeil dislodges the human eye from its position of command, it reaffirms anthropocentric dominion by letting its reader in on the trick, for the allure of trompe l'oeil resides not in the deception of the viewer but in the disclosure of that deception. The painting seeks not to efface its artifice but to advertise its virtuosic execution, conjoining the pleasures of being duped with a crash course in the mechanisms of deception. It is perhaps for this reason that the periodic renaissance of trompe l'oeil often coincides with the proliferation of new media and new technologies: the invention of optical instruments in the late seventeenth century, the explosion of print in the early eighteenth, the democratization of the public in the wake of the American and French Revolutions, and the emergence of photography and motion pictures in the nineteenth and twentieth centuries.[97]

While, as I argued above, trompe l'oeil generates the means to distinguish humanity collectively from animals, it also produces hierarchies internal to the species, for the superiority derived from illusionism depends on the ongoing subjection of others to its trickery. The capacity to take a reflexive relation to the technology of deception—to see through it—is reserved for the select few. If trompe l'oeil is a humbling reminder that "it is always possible for painting to turn humans into animals, to make them react to an illusion like slaves (or animals) to a master," as W. J. T. Mitchell notes, it also enables the enlightened spectator to stage his or her own freedom from delusion.[98] If the disenchanted eye that declares its freedom from illusion arrogates for itself the right to stipulate what will count as reality, it does so by repeatedly staging the scene of its own liberation from the error into which others fall. Like Zeuxis's birds and Bayle's horses, the ignorant natives deluded by mimesis featured in Enlightenment travel literature naturalize a trajectory of Western modernity from the naïve deception of the primitive to a progressive emancipation from illusion.

The birds that peck at grapes offer an exteriorized image of human susceptibility to images, enabling us to attain a reflexive relation to our own seduction. Yet the complacent spectator who presumes that she has transcended such illusions is the first to fall. In the next section, I want to turn to three trompe l'oeil images that explore illusionism not by representing birds pecking at grapes but by depicting dead birds in relation to the traps that ensnared them: Melchior d'Hondecoeter's *Trompe l'Oeil with Dead Birds on a Pinewood Wall* (1660–70), Jacobus Biltius's *Dead Wildfowl and a Huntsman's Net* (1679), and Cornelis Gijsbrechts's *Trompe l'Oeil: Board Partition with a Still Life of Two Dead Birds Hanging on a Wall* (ca. 1670). By revealing the representation *of* a trap to be itself a trap, these images of snared birds invite metacritical reflections on the operation of the work of art as itself a snare. Drawn to the same berries that captivate the bird, the human beholder only fully grasps the nature of the error by being trapped himself. As these paintings show, the lesson of the trompe l'oeil cannot be learned vicariously, at a safe remove: the viewer must, as it were, put skin in the game. The perils of the virtual are only to be grasped through an encounter with the real.

Trompe l'Oeil with Dead Bird

What is often considered the first modern trompe l'oeil—Jacopo de' Barbari's 1503 *Still Life with Partridge, Iron Gloves and Crossbow Bolt*—features a dead bird. There is nothing particularly odd about this. Like still-life painting, trompe l'oeil features many kinds of things: letter racks, books, musical instruments, cupboards, paintings, curtains, fruit, flowers, and game. Dead birds and fowling equipment feature prominently in works by Willem Van Aelst, William Gowe Ferguson, Frans de Hamilton, Jan Weenix, Frans Snyders, and Johannes and Anthony Leemans. Both intimate Dutch images and the more flamboyant Flemish game pieces featuring large stacks of dead birds were popular among newly rich burghers in the Low Countries, in part owing to the aristocratic prestige associated with hunting. The degree of symbolic meaning to be attached to these images is an ongoing debate in art history, while the "decorative quality" of animal corpses, Nathaniel Wolloch observes, is difficult to take for granted.[99] In what follows, I will argue that the prevalence of hunting trophies and equipment in seventeenth-century still life and trompe l'oeil is connected to the ways art addresses its own duplicitous practices. Whereas the construction of the trap, as we saw above, involves the sympathetic imagination of the animals' world, the work of art is crafted to snare human prey.

Melchior d'Hondecoeter is best known for his vibrantly animated images of *living* birds, but he also painted trompe l'oeils of dead ones.[100] In his 1660–70 *Trompe l'Oeil with Dead Birds on a Pinewood Wall* (Plate 2), two birds and a wire trap baited with red currants hang from a nail on a light pinewood board; a third bird dangles immediately below. Immediately above, a single feather is caught in a crack in the board. On the lower right, three bird whistles are suspended on a nail. The trompe l'oeil effect of the pinewood wall is reinforced by graffiti in the upper-right quadrant of the painting: the profile of a man's head and a male stick figure with a hat, both sketched in white chalk. Hondecoeter's signature, also in chalk, is halfway down the left side of the board.

The center of the image is a riot of browns, umbers, and blacks, with the bright red beads of the currants luring our eye as (presumably) they did that of the birds. Although the wires, wings, claws, and berries are delineated with precision, it is difficult to separate out individual bodies from the strangely beautiful entanglement of mechanism, bait, and prey. The eye gets drawn into the affray in the effort to extricate one body from another: is that springe or sinew, knot or claw, wire, twig, or elongated leg? The thin thread from which the bird at lower left dangles melds into the skeletal foot to which it is fastened, its downward chute underscoring the intense verticality of the composition, and counterbalancing the bird whistles hanging from a nail in the lower-right corner. The three central groupings—the trap with the birds, the third bird, and the bird whistles—form a trinity, crowned with a lofty spirit in the form of the solitary feather caught in the crack at the top of the canvas. Emblematically associated with the soul, birds are here reduced to earthly embodied masses. They hang suspended but no longer in flight. If they symbolically shadow us and foreshadow our death, they also have a shadow of their own; without any regard for our presence or absence, light falls on them as on us.

Although the trompe l'oeil freezes movement and time in a fixed image, the painting *does* imply a narrative: the imitated birdcall has lured the prey to the baited trap. Hondecoeter's trompe l'oeil represents birds and the apparatus used to catch and kill them, depicting both cause—the bait, the lure, and the snare—and lethal effect—the dead birds. The painting simultaneously depicts a trap and exposes the way the work of art—in its play of simulation and dissimulation—itself operates as a trap. For the painting offers multiple forms of imitation: the three decoy whistles (counterpart to the three bird bodies) allow humans to copycat birdcalls to draw their prey in a deception that replicates the lure of Zeuxis's grapes in a sonic register; the imitation birdcall that passes for the original brings death in its train.[101] Whereas the whistle imitates a mating call, enticing the bird with the promise of an encounter with its own kind, the trompe l'oeil draws its human beholder in with the lure of something nonhuman, something alien.

The painting also suggests that the lethal powers of human artifice may be turned against humanity. As Alfred Gell has argued, the trap and the work of art have a great deal in common. Each acts, in Gell's words, as a "dramatic nexus that binds these two protagonists [hunter and prey, artist and beholder] together, and which aligns them in time and space."[102] Like the trap, the trompe l'oeil disguises its nature as art, designating what is seen and what can only be seen too late (or not at all). Conspicuously absent from the trap (and from the trompe l'oeil) are the human hands that designed it, which is not to say that humanity is not present. The trap is, as Gell puts it, "not just a model of the person, like any doll, but a 'working' model of a person" that extends its maker's capacities, acting "as a prosthesis" in his or her stead (27). Although the trap is not fashioned in the likeness of its human fabricator (it does not look like a person), it, like the work of art, condenses human intention and wiliness in an objective form visible in "the congealed malevolence of the arrangement of sticks and cords" (26). The trap once made acts independently of its maker, its lethal autonomous operation doubling down on the trompe l'oeil's pretense to represent the world without us. Yet the trap also implicates the birds in their own fall. Drawn first by the deceptive whistle and then by the berries, the birds spring the trap through their own actions. The trap, Gell contends, thus has a tragic structure. (We shall return to this complex delegation of intention and agency in the next chapter's discussion of instruments as extensions of human capacities.)

The trompe l'oeil shifts from Gell's tragedy to lethal tragicomic joke, if not quite to farce, in its diabolical recapitulation of the trap's structure. The painting both reproduces the image of a trap and imitates its action. However unthreatening Hondecoeter's bird carcasses, stilled and hanging limp from a nail, may seem, they lie in wait for the unsuspecting eye. First prey, the birds are now bait of a different order. The lesson of the painting thus resides not in its content (identification with the bird or contemplation of its iconographic significance) but in its formal operation: the way it closes on us like a trap. In luring us into its toils, the painting redefines the relation we can take to its content: once we have been trapped by the image, we can no longer uphold the same relation to the bird.

The fact that we are trapped, however fleetingly, by the image makes the dead birds harbingers of our own mortality, and indeed, seventeenth- and eighteenth-century descriptions of the encounter with the trompe l'oeil often end in bloodshed. Although the anecdote of Zeuxis's grapes ends benignly—the birds fly off—other descriptions leave us with birds stunned or slain by their encounter with a wall painted like the sky.[103] To be sure, writers assure us that humans are not deceived by the painter Pierre Rousseau's perspectives in the garden of the château at Rueil, so perfect that birds "smash their heads in seeking to pass through the painted arcades." Nor are strollers fooled by Pierre Mignard's cat, so impeccably realized that dogs hurl themselves against the wall to catch it, leaving "traces of their blood." But the fact that trompe l'oeil perspectives *kill*, as Louis Marin argues, is crucial.[104] The bloodstained wall and the carcasses of birds heaped at its base attest to the mortal power of painting to supplant rather than reproduce the world, to change from lure into trap. Such moments reinstate the body in a play of perspective that is, as we saw above, too facilely understood as a play of lines and transparencies encountered by an aloof eye.

To seek to enter the illusory space of a painting—to fly through a painted window—is to annihilate the distance between original and copy on which representation depends. Because trompe l'oeil simulates rather than imitates reality, it converts representation from a making-present of an absent other, which masters loss or lack, into a lethal supplanting of the real by an empty image.[105] Death comes to the beholder through the error into which we are lured and through the completeness with which the image subsumes the original. The difference between the lifelike and the deceptive, the realist and the illusionistic image, resides in this location of meaning: there is no window or way out in the trompe l'oeil, no promised horizon outside the picture where that compensatory presence or significance might be found. In their very lifelikeness, the objects in the trompe l'oeil become privative signs (what is like-life cannot *be* life since likeness is a sign of nonidentity). "In trompe-l'oeil," as Baudrillard puts it, "objects are too much like the things they are:

this close resemblance is like a second state, and their true relief, through this allegorical resemblance, through the diagonal light, is that of death."[106] All you have is what is *here*, and it is only an empty image. "While in other pictorial genres meaning may hide in the layered depth of the pictorial field, as it is symbolized by perspective, for the trompe l'oeil *there is no behind.*"[107] Nothing lies behind the meticulously painted boards that represent the surface of Hondecoeter's painting. The trompe l'oeil offers false surfaces, disguised brushstrokes, and the *mise-en-abîme* of ever-refined detail. There is no outside to which one can refer; no anterior world is being duplicated. This is it.

Yet there is a note of levity in Hondecoeter's trompe l'oeil, and it comes, oddly, in a human form, in the crude graffiti that, Olaf Koester notes, "enhance[s] the trompe l'oeil effect by giving the viewer the impression that the deal board is a quite ordinary wall belonging to the real world."[108] Painted to look like chalk, that most ephemeral and erasable of graphic mediums, easily washed away, the lines that offer up humanity in the form of a flattened stick figure and outlined profile make a mockery of depth. These less-than-realistic figures—childlike fumblings toward the mimetic—perversely augment the impression of realism by signaling the flatness of the surface. The slight tracings on the wall reinforce its opacity and provide a foil for the thrusting presence of the things projected in front of it. The lot of the human figure here is not to bring depth or profundity but to prop up the illusion of two-dimensionality. That Hondecoeter likewise has signed his name with chalk suggests a self-reflexive irony that makes the lines scratched out by the human hand as evanescent as the slender avian bodies. All the reality here is for the birds.

Whereas Hondecoeter's wall features the scrawled signs of human endeavor, the monochrome backdrop to which birds and net are affixed in Jacobus Biltius's 1679 trompe l'oeil of *Dead Wildfowl and a Huntsman's Net* (Plate 3) confronts us with unmitigated opacity. The painting depicts two dead quail, a fowler's net, and a decoy whistle. Here, as with Hondecoeter's trompe l'oeil, the objects figured recapitulate the painting's operation as a trap. Yet Biltius does Hondecoeter one better, adding an illusionistic frame of marbled ebony that converts the image into a trompe l'oeil picture of a trompe l'oeil picture. The monochrome wall turns out to be the painted background of a painting; the frame that at first glance appears to be outside the image is instead integral to it: all the surfaces declare themselves as paint.

Rather than seeking to hide its two-dimensionality by suggesting a third dimension behind the picture plane (as does the still life), the trompe l'oeil flaunts it, and in the process accedes to a higher level of illusionism that radicalizes the premises of realism by presenting itself as the painting that it actually is. The trompe l'oeil painting reveals itself here not as the illusory image that supplants the thing but *as* screen, as an image, in Lacan's words, that "pretends to be something other than what it is." It appears "as something other than it seemed, or rather it now seems to be that something else."[109] It thus makes the deceptive power of painting *more* visible. Yet the trompe l'oeil operates as a trap, even—especially—when it promises to disclose the secret of its own dissimulation, for the promised revelation hides a trick of its own: the metacritical addition of the painted frame, which holds out the possibility of a reflexive knowledge that will allow the canny beholder to escape, instead draws us into an infinite regressive spiral that produces no referential touchdown.

In Biltius's trompe l'oeil, the strong verticality of the image refuses to offer up a ground or horizontal plane on which things can alight. Everything is suspended, literally and figuratively floating in space, tacked to a wall that proclaims its lack of solidity by revealing itself to be nothing more than canvas on which paint has been laid. In the absence of a horizon or vanishing point, the painted surface possesses no beyond that would guarantee the existence of a world behind the picture plane. Biltius's things do not recede or retreat. Instead, the perspective that marshals the representation of the world under a human banner turns against the eye's presumed mastery. And if there is nothing behind or before the thing, there is also nothing behind or before the person who beholds the thing.

Whereas Hondecoeter's whimsical human figures give the intimation of lives lived beyond the borders of the image, the objects in Biltius's trompe l'oeil appear completely dissevered from scenes of human life. They are no longer "bywork"—inanimate things meant to fill out the foreground or background of a painting—but alien bodies plucked away from the syntax that would give them meaning. No hierarchy imposes order on the objects, conjoining them to a specific world or human point of view. We are no longer there. Indeed, we were *never* there. As Bryson puts it, "It is as if we were seeing the appearance the world might have without a subject there to perceive it, the world minus human consciousness, the look of the world before our entry into it or after our departure from it."[110] Biltius's painting is a closed circuit, the coldness of the things' self-containment mitigated only by a stray feather that has worked its way free and is arrested in midair, floating down on the lower-left side of the canvas. Whereas all else in the image is frozen, deathly, the wafting feather promises motion, air, even a form of life. The importance of this insignificant—gratuitous—detail resides in its affirmation of a human capacity to attend to what escapes the captivated animal eye (which sees only the berries). That Biltius has—impossibly, in an era before photography—captured the feather's faint, ephemeral shadow in the background enables us to see the overlooked, indeed, the unseeable. Even as Zeuxis's interest resides not in the curtain but in what lies *behind* it, here the interest resides both in the feather and in the shadow it casts: the object both in itself and in its relation to the world.

While Hondecoeter's and Biltius's images invite the beholder to recognize the analogy between work of art and trap, Cornelis Gijsbrechts's circa 1670 *Trompe l'Oeil: Board Partition with a Still Life of Two Dead Birds Hanging on a Wall* omits the device that ensnared the birds (Plate 4). Gijsbrechts's trompe l'oeil depicts an unmounted still-life image of two dead birds, tacked directly to an illusionistically-painted wooden wall. The upper left-hand nail attaching the still life to the boards has dropped out (leaving a tiny hole in the fabric) and the edge of the still-life painting droops downward, revealing the (ostensible) reverse side of the canvas. The frayed threads around its sagging edge—a reminder that the length of canvas is hacked away from a larger woven bolt—are clearly visible against the dark background of the still life. The canvas has not quite been painted to the edge; both the reddish brown underpainting and a margin of unpainted canvas are visible, giving prominence to the unevenly delineated threshold where representation ebbs back into the materials onto which it is imposed. A band of shadow beneath the right edge of the still life produces a gap between the canvas and the painted board to which it is "attached." Although the painting overtly declares the birds to be painted images on canvas, they are realistically depicted in the manner of still life (as opposed to the illusionism of trompe l'oeil).

Like other trompe l'oeil paintings, Gijsbrechts's image shatters our understanding of surface and, with it, of depth, but it compounds this by multiplying false surfaces. The still-life canvas is tacked to what appears to be a wall, until one comes to recognize that this too is painting, canvas miraculously transformed into the likeness of wood. The imperfections of the background "wall"—the nicks and discolorations in the planks, the cracks radiating from the knots—are consummately rendered to capture its unfinished appearance. And even as the trompe l'oeil wood is revealed to be painting, the still life of the birds is reduced first to its material form (paint on canvas) and then to the simulacra of that material (as a painting). The revelation that the trompe l'oeil is "nothing but 'matter' (canvas, stretcher, colors, and so on)," as Victor Stoichita notes, "is in reality a lie, for the revelation is 'represented' by a painting."[111] On these terms, the surface pulled back simply reveals the same two-dimensional surface. We were *already* there.

Trompe l'oeil pictures often tempt the beholder to verify the fictive nature of the image by touch. Presented with a Simon Verelst flower painting in 1669, Samuel Pepys notes that he "was forced again and again to put my finger to it to feel whether my eyes were deceived or no."[112] Like the birds that peck at grapes, he tests the reality of the object before him. Yet Gijsbrechts's painting is closer to Parrhasius's trompe l'oeil than to Zeuxis's still life of grapes. Whereas the birds are interested in the truth of what is depicted and lose interest once the grapes are revealed as paint, the human cares about what is *not* there, what is concealed. Even as Zeuxis attempts to pull aside the curtain to reveal what is behind it, Gijsbrechts's painting entices us to tug at the drooping corner of the canvas where it has worked free of the (painted) wall to peel the layer away. The impulse to tear the illusionistically painted canvas away from the surface to which it is ostensibly affixed strikes me as somewhat different from the simple act of touching (or pecking) to verify the reality of the image, not least in its empirical impossibility. (Since both surfaces are painted, the image *cannot* be pulled away from its ground.) The desire to tamper with the layers of the image, to shift between, as it were, the different frames or diegetic levels of the canvas, makes it hard to decide on exactly which plane one stands vis-à-vis the painting. Indeed, part of the pleasure of our encounter with the image—and part of the way it elicits a distinctively human response—resides in this undecideability. We may recall that the difference between the human and animal relation to the trompe l'oeil stems from the fact that the human, having recognized the absence or blind spot that structures the field of vision, then "isolates the function of the screen and plays with it."[113] Gijsbrechts's trompe l'oeil invites us to toy with the apparatus that organizes our vision, even as it is dismantled before our very eyes.

The possibility that one layer of the painting might be stripped away creates a myth of detachability, of the easy separation of strata, as if reality can be neatly contained within separate planes. Yet if one layer can be peeled away, what binds them together? What enables us to traffic across different levels of reality and of realism? At the folded-over corner of the canvas, Gijsbrechts has placed a tiny dot of paint to indicate the little hole from which the nail has dropped: what is missing (the nail) has caused or perhaps simply explains the drooping edge. In grandiose (or glib) terms, one might say that tiny (painted) piercing in the canvas is the lack around which the symbolic order of the canvas is structured, but I want to underline that it also indicates the force necessary to make these worlds adhere. What ostensibly holds these worlds together are the nails driven through the canvas into the board, whose visual prominence serves as a reminder of the violent suturing that binds representation to the world "behind" it. The nail that bores through the ostensible layers of the painting breaches the division between the two kinds of painting and the levels of "reality" they support.

Charles Murtagh Peterson perceptively observes that the nail supporting the upper center portion of the canvas is not identical to the other nails tacking the canvas to the board; it is circular and oriented perpendicular to the picture plane. More crucially, Peterson notes, *this* nail belongs to multiple picture planes within the image, for it both tacks the painted canvas to the wall *and* serves as the hook from which the two birds are hanging in the painted still-life image. (The knot attaching the string to the nail is also represented.) Inasmuch as the nail "belongs," as it were, to the still life, it cannot fasten the canvas to the board in the trompe l'oeil. Pointing out that the absence of this nail would make the canvas fold over, "perhaps obscuring both of the birds entirely," Peterson argues that the contradictions internal to the image make the "layers of 'reality' collapse into one: real paint on real canvas."[114] Yet might one not say instead that the nail pierces the multiple layers of the image, becoming a kind of wormhole between dimensions? If the dead bird and the still-life painting are tied to the same nail, the still life and trompe l'oeil hang from the same thread. What might this nail boring through multiple layers—a manifold—suggest about the connection between still life and trompe l'oeil?

Although the painted image of the two birds has some of the characteristic traits of a trompe l'oeil (the void space of the background, the floating bodies, the vertical orientation), both in the style of its execution and in its title, it is a still life *enclosed* in a trompe l'oeil. Critics have disagreed about the degree to which the image is illusionistically painted. Koester claims that the birds are painted in a summary fashion, "without any attempt at a trompe l'oeil effect,"[115] while Peterson points out that the brushwork that creates the *effect* of broad brushstrokes is in fact quite precise. There is an "illusory difference in paint handling," he argues, but "no stylistic break between these two inner degrees of 'reality.' "[116] Despite appearances to the contrary, the picture-within-a-picture is executed with the same refined hand. Although the more "lifelike" rendering of the canvas and the wood board suggests that these things received greater attention than the seemingly casually executed birds, the common style suggests a continuity between the still life and trompe l'oeil that recapitulates the questions raised in the previous section about coexisting modes of representation—of realism and illusionism, mimesis and deception—and the oscillation between ways of seeing—eye-views—that it invites.

For Gisjbrechts's decision to nest a still life in a trompe l'oeil does not simply grant the latter dominion over the former. That is, the trompe l'oeil does not fully master the still life or evacuate the values still life seeks to represent. In Gijsbrechts's image, the still life fights a valiant rearguard action against trompe l'oeil's attempt to annihilate the difference between model and copy. For notwithstanding the irreality of the image proclaimed by the trompe l'oeil, the radiance of the still life persists. The exposed underbelly of the birds, the splayed legs, the awkwardly dangling wings are painted with an unexpected tenderness that lends an element of pathos to the image. No gore mars these images, not even a telltale gob of red paint meant to index blood. Their legs twined together like brittle sticks, the birds plummet downward into the black floating space of the still life, the symmetry of the two figures suggesting an odd solidarity in death, a twinned Icarus rocketing into a void. In Gijsbrechts's trompe l'oeil, that is, the still life does not entirely lose out, for his dead birds are a representation of the *nature* of birds, of death in avian form, that cannot be captured or exhausted by a merely illusionistic rendering. The preservation of this element of still life *within* the trompe l'oeil—the ongoing and persistent demand that we differentiate *between* these two tiers of representation—is more important than the consummate deception that bedazzles the eye. For it allows (or compels) us to toggle between the world assimilated to a human perspective and the world from the standpoint of things. On these terms, the trompe l'oeil does not invite us to occupy the perspective or eye-view of things (our command is never so absolute); rather the trompe l'oeil holds out a perspective that cannot be attached with any certitude to a particular eye-view. And perhaps one expression of humanity's difference from animals resides in this capacity to apprehend the world not only from a viewpoint that is not our own but from viewpoints that we cannot quite identify as belonging to anyone. It is to this virtual bird's-eye view, the hypothetical abstracted perspective with which I began, that I want to turn in closing.

Virtual Prospects and the Speculative Bird's-Eye View

How is Zeuxis's bird, haplessly pecking at painted grapes, or the viewer of a trompe l'oeil, enchanted and disenchanted before painting's mimetic virtuosity, connected to the virtual bird's-eye view, high above the earth? The comprehensive top-down perspective of the bird's-eye view involves a displacement of spatial orientation that enables the virtual occupation of a stance defined by its identification with a (stationary, single, abstract) eye; it is typically traced to the *pianta prospectiva*, the elevated view of cities that became popular at the turn of the sixteenth century—those "ideological expression[s] of urban dominion as an accurate rendering of the urban scene . . . high above the city, distant, commanding, uninvolved."[117] Reconciling the representational protocols of the "lifelike" or "the true" and the perspectival imperatives of a proportioned whole, the city view integrates the flat plan and the perspective view, enfolding in "one glance all the glances that the eye can take from different points of view, searching through the most hidden folds, enjoying the architectural features, perceiving the global shape and the balance between the built-up and the empty spaces."[118] A direct descendant of the models of perspective first introduced in Alberti's *Della pittura*, the bird's-eye view is featured in seventeenth- and eighteenth-century discussions of the mathematical and geometrical models for perspective in treatises on painting and cartography; the term also crops up in discussions of landscape and of art, a complement to the prospect view featured in descriptive poetry.[119]

The hypothetical bird's-eye view is not located in any particular eye. As Alpers points out, "What is normally (and somewhat misleadingly) referred to as a bird's-eye view . . . describes not a real viewer's or artist's position but rather the manner in which the surface of the earth has been transformed onto a flat, two-dimensional surface. It does not suppose a located viewer," but instead operates as a "projection . . . viewed from nowhere" that is not "to be looked through."[120] Consolidated to a single eye that circumvents binocular vision, the bird's-eye view isolates sight from the other senses. It borrows avian command of a visual field by annexing the human eye to that of another species, dislodging it from the body. The panoptic powers seemingly offered by this aerial position are tempered by its frozen stance, high above the world, aloof from contact, interaction, use.

As the product of a purely speculative construction, the bird's-eye view subtracts out messy human perceptual processing, using geometric perspective to project a stable eye, and creating rules that enable the transmission of a particular vision of the world from one person to another. Linear perspective on these terms participates in the rationalization of sight that Bruno Latour, drawing on William Mills Ivins, identifies with the scientific revolution, in which perspective's "'logical recognition of internal invariances through all the transformations produced by changes in spatial locations'" makes it possible to alter one's position (distance and angle) and "obtain the same object at a different size as seen from another position."[121] If optical theory renders the origin of the eye (human, bovine, bird) a matter of indifference, here too the viewing mind is made interchangeable: one individual may assume the eye-view of another and still receive the same information. Irrespective of the beholder's position, the object retains its shape.

What is significant for Latour, however, is not just the way the homogeneous language of geometry and perspective underwrites the "optical consistency" of these "immutable mobiles." Rather, Latour's point is that the very rationalization of sight that makes such regularity possible *also* sutures the real and the unreal: "Perspective is not interesting because it provides realistic pictures; . . . it is interesting because it creates complete hybrids: nature seen as fiction, and fiction seen as nature, with all the elements made so homogeneous in space that it is now possible to reshuffle them like a pack of cards" (9). The optical consistency offered by geometric perspective creates a common ground in which "fiction—even the wildest or the most sacred" may meet "things of nature—even the lowliest" (8). The uniformity made possible by perspective, that is, allows for the fictive and the real to commingle.

The degree of speculative projection necessary to assume a bird's-eye view becomes clear when we recall that before the first balloon flights in 1783, no one had soared untethered above the earth's surface. Until that time, the bird's-eye view was just a purely theoretical displacement of the self from its embodied, local position on the terrestrial globe. The lofty vantage point of the bird affords a vision of the world humans can scarcely grasp, Georges-Louis Leclerc, comte de Buffon, writes in his influential mid-century natural history. "Sailing over the different countries," the bird can "form a picture which exceeds the powers of our imagination. Our bird's-eye views [*plans à vue d'oiseau*], of which the accurate execution is so tedious and so difficult, give very imperfect notions of the relative inequality of the surfaces which they represent. But birds can chuse the proper stations, can successively traverse the field in all directions, and see more, in one glance, than we can guess or judge through all our reasonings, even propped up by all the contrivances of our art" (translation modified).[122] We *use* the bird to project ourselves beyond our bodily bounds. The *"plans à vue d'oiseau"* so laboriously constructed with the tools of reason, geometry, and perspective indicate a human aspiration to rise above the gravitational plane to which we are confined, to imagine the world as seen from another species' point of view. Whereas the earthbound quadruped "knows only the spot where it feeds," Buffon observes, we featherless bipeds indulge in fantasies about the world as experienced by other creatures and yearn to know the place where we are not.[123] The bird's wheeling flight offers it a picture of the world that surpasses both the imagination and the ingenuity of humankind. Even with maps, devices, reason, the human mock-up of the bird's-eye view is at best a pallid approximation—a labored, flattening projection of what the bird sees in the blink of an eye.

The execution of a bird's-eye view requires immense technical virtuosity in perspective, the architectural draftsman and author Thomas Malton (the elder) points out, "for, by no other means is it possible to represent Objects, with any degree of accuracy, which are not immediately before the Eye; which, without being seen, may, by its Rules, be justly drawn, and as they really would appear from such imaginary Station, could the Eye be really placed there."[124] Malton emphasizes the extreme difficulty of the geometric and theoretical projections involved, but what I want to underline is the movement beyond the mimetic to the virtual. The capacity to imagine the world from the impossible perspective (although not, significantly, the sensory or perceptual experience) of a bird involves a speculative projection in a future conditional: what one would see, were one to attain a birdlike prospect not available to the human eye (similar, perhaps, to representations of the planet before the advent of space travel).

Such a virtual prospect both suggests a commanding vantage over all things and, in its lofty detachment from earthly constraint, revolutionary possibilities. It is perhaps for that reason that the bird's-eye view surfaces in discussions of the Enlightenment philosophical project, where it serves as a figure for an aloof stance, freed from the entanglements of the workaday world. "If you enter into the twists and turns and tortuous bends of the

streets of an immense City, it will appear to you an inescapable labyrinth. You
will encounter only hindrances and darkness: everything will thwart you," *Les
lacunes de la philosophie* proclaims in 1783, but "climb a high tower, and look
at the City from a bird's-eye view. The ways out will multiply themselves, all
uncertainties cease."[125] The ability to occupy—whether sympathetically or
dispassionately—a bird's-eye view simultaneously affirms and mocks the
Enlightenment quest for anthropocentric dominion. Seen from above, the
modes of egress from the labyrinth reveal themselves; the bird's-eye view
shows paths through the thicket of empirical details imperceptible from the
ground. Yet the elevated prospect does not offer an exact mimetic reproduction of the world in all its concrete immediacy, like Zeuxis's perfect
grapes. Instead, it requires humanity to abjure its earthbound body and loft
itself into an abstract imaginary point of view. What the bird's-eye view
offers is less a comprehensive or authoritative vantage than a process of self-
displacement that, by dint of the impossible viewpoint it affords, exposes
one's own blind spots and makes possible new ways of seeing.

If the displacement of the eye from one position to another (from one
species to another) transcends the necessary limits of individual human
knowledge and perspective, however, it consolidates human (species) distinction in other ways. The capacity to imagine and reconstruct the world from
the impossible perspective of a bird involves an extrapolation beyond one's
own position, a projection of the self into a virtual framework that, as Anne-
Lise François points out, has been understood from Descartes to Heidegger
to Lacan as a distinctively human trait: "The animal can only be what it is
(the vegetable even more so), while the human can be where he is not." If
the limited ability only to "be what it is" binds the animal at best to the
strictly mimetic, the human capacity to "be where he is not" also produces
the possibility of recognizing the real where no thing is present—in a painting
or a statue, a fiction or an imagined perspective on the world. And if this
ability to move beyond the mimetic to the virtual—the capacity to imagine
a bird's-eye view or the view from the eye of a bird—serves as the basis for
the claim of human difference, then perhaps, as François argues, virtuality
should be understood not only in terms of "the dematerialization of psychic
and sensory experience effected by . . . [various] media" but also in terms of
"its political and philosophical inseparability from the human-animal-
machine dialectic."[126] The tale of Zeuxis's grapes, I have tried to argue, contributes a chapter to the history of that dialectic, for it is the capacity to
imagine the world from a fictive stance utterly not our own—that of a bird,

a thing, a painting, or even no one at all—that helps create the fiction of our own humanity.

Might we argue, however, that this virtual perspective that supposedly distinguishes human from animal *produces* the perception of human difference rather than originating in it—that it is the cause, not the effect, of the human? On these terms, the *human* is the trompe l'oeil produced by the encounter with the trompe l'oeil: an entity that can only be seen from a virtual perspective—from an eye-view that, like Malton's, is the work of a kind of instrumental geometry, a stance that can be occupied by a human being but that has relinquished the claim to belong to a particular human eye.[127] It is worth recalling that the anecdote of Zeuxis's grapes is structured as a repetition: first the birds err, then the man. There is nothing inherently different in the view from the eyes of birds and the eyes of men at the beginning of the story: they both make a parallel mistake. And if only Zeuxis (and not the birds) discovers the trick, the reader of the narrative is always in the know. The anecdote thus operates as a machine for producing the difference between human and animal that it ostensibly reveals. On these terms, the tale of Zeuxis's grapes is not just a story; it is a *fiction* in the etymological sense of a making. And what the fiction of Zeuxis's grapes makes (produces, realizes) is the *real* experience of encountering a fictional image that passes for a real thing—except that the fictional image that passes for a real thing is *not* the grape or the curtain but the human itself. The anecdote, that is, translates one kind of fiction (about the image of grapes that passes for real) into another kind of fiction (about the invented category of the human that passes for real). In the process, it enables us to recognize that the human is an effect, not an entity: not an essence to be discovered but a fiction constituted by looking from an eye-view that proffers the image of that essence in the form of a trompe l'oeil that makes it appear as if it were a thing.

CHAPTER 2

Lousy Bodies

The *forming* of the five senses is a labour of the entire history of the
world down to the present.
　　　　—Marx, "Economic and Philosophic Manuscripts of 1844"

Robert Hooke, the seventeenth-century natural philosopher, astronomer,
microscopist, horologist, mechanist, anatomist, geologist, and architect, had a
lousy body, and not just because, according to his first biographer, he had from
the age of sixteen grown "awry, by frequent practicing, turning with a Turn-
Lath, and the like incurvating Exercises, being but of a thin weak habit of
Body, which increas'd as he grew older."[1] In Hooke's eyes, *all* humanity was
cursed with a frail, lacking body. Whereas most animals are born in a state of
sufficiency—or are rapidly equipped with the essentials necessary for survival—
humans alone require the superadditions provided by reason and technology,
the supplement of education, and the assistance of the material goods of the
world.[2] Whether in the form of a constitutive lack—at birth, as Pliny famously
put it, man is cast "naked on the naked ground"[3]—or in a postlapsarian state,
fallen from Adamic plenitude into insufficiency and need, humanity is defined
by its exposure to the elements and to the depredations of others: what it *wants*.
Despite (or because of) their much-vaunted position at the top of the food
chain, humans prove to exist in a state of piracy, parasitism, and indebtedness,
dependent on provision either willingly volunteered as gift or reluctantly
yielded through acts of theft or of war: this lacking entity *needs* something
outside it to make it functional—indeed, to make itself human.

In this chapter I explore the ways Robert Hooke sought to compensate for this lacking body through the incorporation of devices—prosthetic

extensions of bodily capacities—into his model of man. For Hooke, the insufficiency of the senses creates the impetus for supplementary improvement through *"helps of Art"* such as the microscope, which both extend humanity's powers and compensate for its defects.[4] Humanity's self-formation and its distinction from a bare animal nature are circuited through technological improvements assisted by and incarnated in the instruments Hooke fabricated and operated as curator of experiments for the Royal Society. In amplifying the capacities of the body beyond its previous limits, these prosthetic devices both open up the empirical world to the human senses and estrange humanity from the material world as it is already known to be, as Hooke shows in his dazzling compendium of observations of the subvisible world, the 1665 *Micrographia*. If in Chapter 1 the capacity to dissever oneself from the body and achieve a lofty virtual perspective on the world marks a distinctively human ability, here the quest for prosthetically acquired superpowers extends the body beyond its organic bounds. In redefining humanity's relation both to the object world and to the animal creation, Hooke's devices become the engine of a progressive refashioning of human nature.

Hooke's own career incarnates in small this process of human self-making through *"the helps of Art, and Experience"* (*Micrographia*, sig. a). Son of a curate, scholarship student, and sometime assistant to the virtuoso Robert Boyle and the anatomist Thomas Willis at Oxford during the Interregnum, later the salaried curator of experiments to the Royal Society, professor at Gresham College, and holder of the Cutlerian Lectureship (both founded for the propagation of practical knowledge), Hooke possessed exceptional skills as scientific practitioner, as master instrument-maker, and as operator of such temperamental devices as Boyle's famous air pump.[5] Neither servant nor peer, Hooke was something of a misfit in the context of the Royal Society, both an expert maker of instruments and himself an instrument in the employ of the society's fellows, "the willing and wilful medium through which Fellows' ideas were materialized."[6] Although Hooke's social status deprived him of the gentlemanly autonomy that, as Steven Shapin and Simon Schaffer have influentially argued, guaranteed the Royal Society's consensual establishment of matters of fact, his technical expertise made him indispensable to the society's knowledge production, simultaneously "a free agent in experimental matters" and "the directed instrument of others' free action."[7]

Hooke's amphibious status between mechanic and philosopher exposes the fault lines created by the broader epistemological shifts associated with empiricism and the scientific revolution. His proclaimed ambition in the

Micrographia to "*serve to the great Philosophers of this Age, as the makers and the grinders of my Glasses did to me; that I may prepare and furnish them with some* Materials" affirms his technical mastery and general know-how, at the same time as it rhetorically displays the sobriety and modesty of what Shapin calls the "under-builder," whose quiet industry and disdain of self-interested vainglory attest to his scientific trustworthiness.[8] Simultaneously elevating himself above the "*grinders of [his] Glasses*" and deferring to the "*great Philosophers of this Age*," Hooke at first glance reproduces the traditional Aristotelian hierarchies that elevated abstract theory over practical execution, intellectual over manual labor. Yet Hooke's own methodology, as we shall see, dissolves the neat separation of mind and hand.

Despite his position as a practitioner, Hooke does hypothesize about philosophical matters, going so far beyond his experimental remit in the *Micrographia* that the Royal Society insisted that he add a prefatorial disclaimer taking sole responsibility for his speculative claims.[9] Not only are his writings strewn with metaphysical conjectures and allusions to forces inherent in nature (congruity and incongruity, active matter and sympathies), but his very practice is a form of thinking. For Hooke, theoretical knowledge does not precede the experiment but is created and incarnated in its enactment. Indeed, practice determines the scope of what is known: "According to the choice of the Experiments," he drily comments, "such most usually is the Information."[10] Hooke thus challenges the long-standing division, inherited from Aristotle, between the theoretical knowledge associated with *epistêmê* or *scientia* and the practice or craft associated with *techne*. For Hooke, as J. A. Bennett has argued, "to demonstrate, to control, to manipulate and to measure were a large part of what it meant to understand."[11]

The centrality of experiments to the New Science elevated practical command over the natural world above the syllogisms and geometric proofs of Scholasticism, giving pride of place to what Antonio Pérez-Ramos in his study of Baconian science calls "maker's knowledge," which "postulates an intimate relationship between objects of cognition and objects of construction, and regards knowing as a kind of making or as a capacity to make (*verum factum*)."[12] Dismantling the neat opposition of subject and object, agent and instrument, abstract thought and embodied practice, "maker's knowledge" suggests that doing *is* knowing: not only does manual skill demand mental dexterity but philosophical knowledge also requires mechanical know-how. The experiment does not simply test a hypothesis but itself operates as a form of cognition, while the "demonstration or instrument" is not the secondary illustration of a theory, but "a conceptualization of a problem or the explanation of a phenomenon."[13] To understand *what* something is to grasp *how* it works.

This model of maker's knowledge reconfigures the relation between *Homo faber* and *Homo sapiens*, scrambling the classical division between manual labor (the lot of slaves and animals) and abstract thought (the task of the philosopher)—and, by extension, between humans and other animals.[14] For if the capacity to impose "new forms on matter was a defining human endowment, even a privileged instance of rationally guided action," Joanna Picciotto points out, the Royal Fellow who lacked the technical skills necessary to conduct fact-producing experiments also "lacked the very traits that were conventionally invoked to distinguish humans from beasts."[15] If man is a tool-making animal, are those who cannot make tools men?[16] Inasmuch as knowledge is incarnated in doing, what exactly does the gentlemanly witness understand?

Hooke himself argues for the necessary conjunction of philosophy and art, of abstract thought and maker's knowledge, in the preface to the *Micrographia*. Echoing Bacon's second aphorism from the *Novum organum* (1620), he insists that philosophy make a circuit "*to* begin *with the Hands and Eyes, and to* proceed *on through the Memory, to be* continued *by the Reason; nor is it to stop there, but to* come about *to the Hands and Eyes again.*"[17] While the reciprocal relation between intellectual and manual labor here suggests their indisseverability, Hooke's incorporation of the "*Hands and Eyes*" into a circuit with memory and reason erases the devices that mediate between the senses and the world. His silent assimilation of instrument into hand or eye blends the collective labor and thought contained in the tool into the body of the individual practitioner. Yet the question of where our tools end and we begin was a pressing one for Hooke. The various ways he and other early Enlightenment thinkers attempt to draw this line is a central concern of this chapter.

Understood as imitations or extensions of the senses, instruments blur the boundaries of the body and the external world in ways that undermine the distinction between them. Indeed, they invite us to see sensory organs as themselves instruments, like the ox and human eyes that Descartes interchangeably uses in his experiments, as we saw in Chapter 1.[18] (Hooke himself tests the consistency of his astronomical findings by switching from right eye to left in much the same way that he swaps out lenses.)[19] We *use* our eyes and open our ears, serving as both the subject and object of our own sensory powers, making our organs means to other ends, and thus "blur[ring] the precarious distinction between human and mechanical instrumentality."[20] Hooke's experimental practice on these terms should be considered not as the magisterial inquiry of an autonomous subject into a stable objective world but as what Sean Silver describes as a form of extended cognition involving "the codevelopment of an instrument to answer a question or set of questions, and the corresponding adaptation of the mind to the instruments that it puts to use."[21]

It is not always clear whether instrument or user has, as it were, the upper hand. While tools allow their users to appropriate the powers they incarnate—the lever allows a slender hand to dislodge a boulder, making the ingenuity contained within the device available to new constituencies—they also actively redistribute power. "Not only do machines materially transform the mediatory capacity of our sensual faculties," as Jessica Wolfe has argued, "but they also participate in refashioning relationships between human beings and their instruments, from readers and their texts to rulers and servants." In the milieu of the Royal Society as in the Renaissance contexts Wolfe discusses, the mediating role of both human operators and their tools draws attention to "the moral and epistemological ramifications of instrumentality—the use of human, mechanical, or intellectual instruments to achieve a particular end."[22] Like the word *agent*, which betokens both the autonomous actor and the substitute or deputy, a creature in the derogatory sense, the word *instrument* in Samuel Johnson's 1755 *Dictionary* signifies not only "the agent or mean [sic.] of anything" but also someone "who acts only to serve the purposes of another."[23] The compliant proxy may change its vote in favor of a hostile takeover; delegation may slip into usurpation. It is perhaps for this reason that the language of Daedalean *metis* or cunning—machination, manipulation, device, instrument, and tool—is so often bound up with trickery.[24]

Instruments are not docile subordinates that reflect preexisting hierarchies; they redistribute agency and authority not only between classes of people and kinds of knowledge but also between humans and things—a particularly volatile matter during the Restoration, which sought to secure order "through the correct attribution of powers to bodies," not least the royal body in the wake of the regicide.[25] Hooke's circuit of the senses through artificial devices and his creation of instruments able to surpass the body's physical limits challenge the notion that the human body is a stable circumscribed entity to which elements may be added and detached without alteration of its original nature. As we shall see below, the prosthetically augmented body claims a kind of life of its own.

The opening section of this chapter explores the way Hooke enfolded the instrumentally augmented body into a broader account of the progressive history of humankind. Technology reconfigures what might be called Hooke's anthropology: his understanding of humanity as a historical object. Even as Hooke's devices expose the fallibility and inadequacy of the senses, they supplement human lack, fostering collective advancement. Yet the intimate connection of tool to body, instrument to eye, poses questions about the model of humanity to which Hooke aspires and appeals in turn. Does the prosthetic involve the imitation of a prior template of human nature—the reinstatement of the sensory capacities of Adam's prelapsarian body—or its supersession? Are instruments the means of recapturing an Edenic wholeness or the engine of human progress organized around technology? Inasmuch as the nature of man is expressed in the embrace of artificial helps, humanity is incarnated in the prosthetic devices that estrange it from itself.

If Hooke's instruments expand the capacities and even the bodily bounds of the subject, they also explode the seeming unity and integrity—the morphological discreteness, solidity, defined edges—of the object, whether natural body or crafted artifact. The second section of the chapter turns to his 1665 *Micrographia* to analyze the strategies Hooke devises to represent the hitherto unseen world that the instrumentally enhanced senses brought into view. Hooke's text repeatedly slams up against the limits of the human body in comparison with the powers of its tools, for the objects revealed by Hooke's optical devices bear scant resemblance to those encountered by the naked eye. Whereas in Chapter 1, trompe l'oeil tricks the beholder (human, avian, mammalian) into taking the painting for the real thing, the microscope offers not the hyperreality of a perfect replication of the world, but the revelation that the world is nothing like it seems. At first glance this simply suggests that the microscope offers a defamiliarizing glimpse of everyday objects. Hooke after all enjoins the would-be scientist to consider himself a stranger in a strange land (GS, 62). Yet the microscope does not simply magnify or distort an already known thing—a formula that can be run in reverse, as in anamorphosis—it suggests that the object that we thought we knew might be something else entirely. Although Hooke insists that the *Micrographia*'s images accurately depict what he saw, the very nature of the microscopic world means that empiricism cannot be neatly aligned with realism. There is no way to verify what the microscopic world "really" looks like.

Moreover, some of what interests Hooke lies beyond the compass of even the prosthetically augmented senses. Physical minima, such as atoms and corpuscles, elude even the instrumentally enhanced eye. Notwithstanding all his confident assertions about the utility of artificial helps, Hooke devotes much of his energy to the place where things drop completely below the horizon of human perception, straining to tell whether there is actually something to be seen at the place where sight falters. The *Micrographia* veers between two poles, spitting out arrestingly detailed visions of the microscopic world that exceed the shapes and concepts available to receive them, while also repeatedly pointing to a beyond—to a referent, a cause, hovering just outside of view. Indeed, at times all Hooke can do is point to a produced effect that is the sign of an otherwise inscrutable cause. I argue that Hooke's mode of reference may best be understood as indexical rather than strictly mimetic.

Cast adrift without a template for the microscopic objects that swim into his ken, Hooke derives form from function, offering blueprints of the shared mechanisms and structures of the microscopic world that explain how the articulated parts of bodies act upon each other as "fit Agents to Patients" (GS, 3). Rather than creating exact portraits of things, Hooke seeks to discover how they can be made causes of sought-after effects, stressing what bodies *do* over what they *are*. Designed to circumvent any appeal to occult causes or natural magic and to accommodate the invisible atoms and corpuscles of mechanistic and materialist philosophy, Hooke's realism is grounded not in mimesis but in operability, not in how something looks but in how—whether—something works. He seeks not to observe or describe nature but to change it. In striving to harness the "*small* Machines *of Nature*" to his own anthropocentric ends, Hooke enfolds bodies into circuits that embrace human and nonhuman, living body and inorganic instrument (*Micrographia*, sig. g).

What may at first glance seem like Hooke's resolutely anthropocentric framework buckles under the weight of his close encounter with the alien entities harbored within and upon the human form. If the fusion of organ and instrument in Hooke's experimental practice implies that humanity may be a hybrid thing, the magnified and often unidentifiable creatures detected by Hooke's ocular "helps" destabilize the body's organic wholeness. The final section of the chapter turns to Hooke's famous depiction of the louse to analyze the way the microscope reconfigures the relation of humans to other creatures in the world. Even as Hooke's dependency on his prosthetic devices suggests that humanity's self-definition depends on its parasitical relation to objects outside the self, the body swarming with a life not its own suggests a more profound dispossession that Hooke only half-acknowledges. If the teeming world unveiled by the microscope dismantles the object, it also shatters the integrity of the subject—and with it, the definitions of humanity that that subjectivity sustains. It's not that the world is not ready for its close-up; it's that *we* aren't.

Robert Hooke's Prosthetic God

> With every tool man is perfecting his own organs, whether motor or
> sensory, or is removing the limits to their functioning. . . . By means
> of spectacles he corrects defects in the lens of his own eye; by means
> of the telescope he sees into the far distance; and by means of the
> microscope he overcomes the limits of visibility set by the structure
> of his retina. . . . Man has, as it were, become a kind of prosthetic
> God. When he puts on all his auxiliary organs he is truly
> magnificent; but these organs have not grown on to him and they
> still give him much trouble at times.
> —Sigmund Freud, *Civilization and Its Discontents*[26]

For all its reverence toward the miraculous activity of the Creator, Robert Hooke's 1665 *Micrographia* documents the coronation of a prosthetic God. The book revels in the possibility of a technologically enhanced humanity, equipped with *"Mechanical helps for the Senses"* that will offer a glimpse of the intricate machinery of nature hovering just beyond the threshold of the visible (*Micrographia*, sig. d2r). In this section of the chapter, I explore Hooke's incorporation of devices—prosthetic extensions of the senses—into his model of man. Even as Hooke's instruments serve as the defining mark of human difference from animals, they fuse person and thing, body and implement, into a working unit able to transform the physical world, in the process renegotiating humanity's place within a divinely ordered creation. Whereas some contemporary thinkers depict these devices as the means to recapture humanity's prelapsarian state, Hooke increasingly sees them as the engine of future progress organized around techne and incarnated in scientific works. If the exquisite images gleaned from the microscope offer an estranging and disorienting glimpse of an unknown world—a reminder that these artificial organs have not, as Freud puts it, grown on to us and still give us much trouble at times—they also point to a distinctively human aspiration to claim dominion over entities that exceed our grasp.

From its opening line, the *Micrographia* strives to distinguish humans from other animals: "*It is the great prerogative of Mankind above other Creatures, that we are not only able to* behold *the works of Nature, or barely to* sustein *our lives by them, but we have also the power of* considering, comparing, altering, assisting, and improving *them to various uses*" (sig. a). Hooke converts man from a lacking creature who lives off of the lendings of nature to an empowered agent able to transform both nature's works and itself. Like animals, humans "behold *the works of nature*" and "sustein *our lives by them*"; what exalts humanity above other species is the capacity to exercise various powers that transform the immediately given world. Whereas the first two capacities (considering and comparing) elevate mere "beholding" into more active contemplation and even preference, the latter three (altering, assisting, and improving) treat nature not as something to be followed or obeyed, but as "*works*" that may be converted "*to various uses*." It is both the variety and plurality of these "*uses*" that merit consideration here, for the proliferation of purposes suggests the plasticity of humanity's relation to the material world, on the one hand, and its open-ended nature, on the other. If Baconian "maker's knowledge" involves a kind of past tense of the object—to know what something is is to know how it was made—Hooke's model of improvement casts forward beyond the already realized, conjugating the present object in a future tense. His method requires him to dwell in a polymorphously perverse world in which things are not bound to their origins or slated ends.

To convert nature "*to various uses*" is to suspend knowledge of its foreordained purpose—the predestination of the object, the identity indicated by its signature—in order to recognize the alternate ends to which its form may be put: both to see what it is and to see what it could be. Invention courts misuse, abuse, a vagrancy of purpose, producing the choice, freedom, play, that can only issue from an unfinished nature. It thus pitches us into a historical narrative, in which humanity is also a work in progress, striving but not yet fully fashioned. And since, as the cliché goes, one cannot improve on perfection, Hooke's progressive model of human nature simultaneously depends on a kind of incompleteness, a mis-fit between human need and material world.

Indeed, inventiveness exists because of (not despite) the deficiencies of mankind: the apprehension of a lack serves as the impetus for technological innovation in Hooke's account, as "watchfulness over the failings" of the senses leads to the desire for an "inlargment of the[ir] dominion" (sig. a2r). Defined by a capacity that is missing and by the promise of a future power, Hooke's humanity aspires to become what it is not. For Hooke, this is an open-ended model of anthropological progress. The human ability to "improve" the works of nature does not imply that something *specific* is missing (as if the addition of one last piece of the puzzle could make us whole). Nor does it insinuate that God's creation is imperfect; it simply announces something could be there and is not there (yet), gesturing toward an unconstricted domain defined only by the imperative to overcome the inventory of human infirmities with which the *Micrographia* begins. It is by recollecting these deficiencies, Hooke affirms, that "*we may the better understand how to supply them, and by what assistances we may* inlarge *their power, and* secure *them in performing their particular duties*" (sig. a). From privation, the impetus for its technical overcoming; from Epimethean forgetting, Promethean foresight; from necessity, invention.

Our flaws, however, are less easily known than one might think. Even our senses, "the most knowable of our faculties," elude understanding, according to the West Country divine Joseph Glanvill: "Our eyes, that see other things, see not themselves."[27] How then can humanity come to recognize the nature of its own defects? Hooke takes the measure of human potential via a circuit through the nonhuman, judging our sensory powers against the capacities of animals, the divinely wrought prelapsarian Adamic body, and the impersonal perfection of the instrument or machine. Human striving after perfectibility requires humanity to find itself wanting vis-à-vis fictions and artifices of its own devising.

Indeed, one of the ironies of Hooke's text is that the human quest for technological superiority comes from the recognition of our inferiority to beasts. Finding our organs in "*many particulars much outdone by those of other Creatures*," we create devices to refine human senses "*to as great a degree of perfection as it is in any Animal*" (*Micrographia*, sig. av, sig. c2r). Technology simultaneously marks the difference between human and animal and bridges the distance between them. If humanity is distinguished from other creatures by the capacity to improve itself, it perversely uses these helps to reinstate sensory capacities that animals possess and we lack. The realization of human nature thus entails a turn toward the artificial, the manufactured, even the unnatural, for rather than simply "sustein[ing] *our lives by* [*the works of nature*]," we transform them, in effect removing them—and ourselves—from nature. Given that "human nature" for Hooke is defined through its propensity for altering both itself and the natural world, man's nature is to be denatured, or rather, to denature itself.[28] We are *made* to make ourselves into something other than what we are, in the double sense that we are both fashioned by God to alter ourselves and compelled to do so.

This exceptional capacity for self-transformation that separates humanity from other creatures—the distinction of species—also creates the individuation that divides one man from another. If the capacity to improve, Hooke notes, "*is the peculiar priviledge of humane Nature in general, so is it capable of being so far advanced by the helps of Art, and Experience, as to make some Men excel others in their Observations, and Deductions, almost as much as they do Beasts*" (sig. a). Even as man's nature is to separate himself from nature, here the shared trait of "*humane Nature in general*" becomes the impetus for the individual's attempt to divide himself from his kind—to make himself singular: a first-person "I," distinct from and elevated above others. The passive voice, in which the advancement of collective human nature "*make[s] some Men*" surpass others "*by the helps of Art, and Experience,*" initially deflects agency from the man to the instrument, but it subsequently converts the man himself into an instrument for the advancement of collective humanity, as capacities lodged in these artificial "helps" are transferred to the human beings who wield them.

Nor does Hooke recognize any check on this future advancement. By following experimental method, Hooke proclaims, "*there is nothing that lyes within the power of human wit (or which is far more effectual) of human Industry, which we might not compass*" (*Micrographia,* sig. b2r). Privileging "industry" over "wit," practical works over theoretical knowledge, Hooke traces the progressive refinement of humanity through technological endeavor, through what is made rather than what is given. The *Micrographia,* like Hooke's other texts, is riddled with references to what *will* be possible and *will* be known once technology has achieved a sufficiently advanced state. Hooke's devices improve, but do not achieve perfection. "After a certain degree of magnifying," Hooke confesses, his contrivances "leave us again in the lurch," a failure that must spur future labors by others: "It were very desirable, that some way were thought of," Hooke repeatedly notes.[29] The incompleteness of Hooke's project means that it must be pursued by others, by humanity communally conceived.

Hooke's model of progress thus involves a dialectical movement not only between individual and collective but also between instrument and instrumentally assisted humanity. The pride of place Hooke gives to devices suggests a historical anthropology grounded in techne, in which human and instrument become subjects and objects of each other's formation. The fact that we are made to make ourselves through "*the helps of Art, and Experience*," that is, underwrites the "invention of the human"—an expression whose double genitive implies, the philosopher Bernard Stiegler notes, both "the technical inventing the human" and "the human inventing the technical." This reciprocity means that the questions " 'Who' or 'what' does the inventing? 'Who' or 'what' is invented?" are hopelessly entangled.[30]

Stiegler's discussion of the role of technology in creating evolutionary distinctions between *Homo sapiens* and its antecedent species forms draws on the work of the paleoanthropologist André Leroi-Gourhan. For Leroi-Gourhan, the glacial-paced, collectively enacted coevolution of knapped flint and human body cannot be assigned to a single subject (a Eureka moment) or to a sudden evolutionary leap. Instead, shifts in technology precede and precipitate the evolution of the species and vice versa. Thus the "achievement of bipedalism" that liberated the hand not only contributed to the elaboration of the tool, but also gradually remade the cortex. The subject makes and uses the object, but the object also anticipates the subject, for the brain is "not the cause of developments in locomotory adaptation" for Leroi-Gourhan, "but their beneficiary."[31] In lodging the impetus behind human evolution in things exterior to the body and the mind, Leroi-Gourhan affords an intriguingly nonanthropocentric account of the emergence of the species. Rather than considering the instrument a copy or extension of an existing human organ or capacity, we must understand it to anticipate these powers and to place them *exterior* to the body into which they will subsequently be incorporated.

Stiegler helpfully spells out the implications of Leroi-Gourhan's analysis. While the "human invents himself in the technical by inventing the tool—by becoming exteriorized techno-logically," he argues, it is paradoxically "an exteriorization without a preceding interior." Although we typically assign agency to humanity, it is "rather the evolution of the *what* that has a return effect of the *who* and governs to a certain extent its own differentiation."[32] (Stiegler refers to these exteriorized technologies as *prostheses*, a term to which we shall return below.) In this version of things, humanity is not differentiated from other creatures by the possession of some trait, essence, or organ (the size of the brain, the opposable thumb) but comes into being through a relation to tools. Whereas animals are born into the world equipped with the means necessary to thrive—modifications are internal to the species—

humanity realizes its being in an exteriorized form. "The whole of our evolution," Leroi-Gourhan writes, "has been oriented toward placing outside ourselves what in the rest of the animal world is achieved *inside* by species adaptation."[33] Humanity's self-formation, that is, is circuited through processes of technical improvement in which instruments embody human know-how and in which an instrumentally improved human, whose bodily capacities are extended by technology, is able to delve ever deeper into the operation of the natural world. It is not, in other words, just the initial making of the flint or of the microscope that counts but also the fact that these tools become repositories of technology bequeathed to successive generations. We outsource cognitive labor and store it in objects as well as books so that we do not have to reinvent the wheel every time.

For Hooke as well, human difference from other living creatures originates in our distinctive power to improve ourselves—advances that are exteriorized and perpetuated in material artifacts and tools (*"the helps of Art"*), which in turn transform the human user. Humanity makes itself in and through works, which by virtue of their exteriority, can be shared: they perpetuate knowledge beyond the labors of an individual or single generation, and they forge communities and institutions that redistribute that knowledge. Hooke is acutely aware of the importance of this intertwining of technics and time. He celebrates the power of writing to amend the defects of memory by creating an external repository, a kind of prosthetic organ more powerful than that belonging to a single individual: *"What ought to be thought of that man, that has not only a perfect register of his own experience, but is grown old with the experience of many hundreds of years, and many thousands of men"* (*Micrographia*, sig. d). Intelligence for Hooke is likewise stored in devices, both mechanical and linguistic, that convey knowledge (or knowledge of how to produce knowledge) in the form of "know-how." The microscope itself, like other tools and instruments, is a vessel for the knowledge and craft that went into its making.

On these terms, Hooke's "helps" constitute what Francis Bacon terms *opera* and what Hannah Arendt in *The Human Condition* calls *works*—the "'artificial' world of things, distinctly different from all natural surroundings," that condition human nature, making a world that houses each individual life but "meant to outlast and transcend them all."[34] Humanity's "ability to leave non-perishable traces behind" distinguishes it from animals by creating a perdurable culture that allows for knowledge to be bequeathed in the form of "things—works and deeds and words."[35] To be sure, Hooke's endless squabbles over credit for inventions—most famously with Isaac Newton—and his increasingly secretive and miserly ways toward the end of his life ("to a Crime close and reserv'd," in one posthumous biographical note)[36] make it difficult to incorporate him into a communal project for the advancement of humankind, or even into the model of collectively authored scientific consensus central to many accounts of the Royal Society. Yet his texts abound with directions for replicating his work: diagrams, explanations of how to make and use various instruments, step-by-step breakdowns of experimental processes, and meticulous reconstructions of the trial-and-error means by which he jury-rigged solutions to problems encountered along the way. Hooke may have wanted credit for his works, but he also sought to transmit knowledge to posterity and to provide the impetus for humanity's future labors. Indeed, the devices he bequeathed to humanity at large are the material incarnation of his thinking.

This future orientation is, however, defined by a relation to the past; the devices that serve as the engine of future progress are the fruit of an anterior deficiency, an emendation for the Fall. "*By the addition of such* artificial Instruments *and* Methods," Hooke writes, "*there may be, in some manner, a reparation made for the mischiefs, and imperfection, mankind has drawn upon it self, by negligence, and intemperance, and a wilful and superstitious deserting the Prescripts and Rules of Nature, whereby every man, both from a deriv'd corruption, innate and born with him, and from his breeding and converse with men, is very subject to slip into all sorts of errors.*"[37] The compounding of imperfectly subordinated clauses makes it difficult to isolate a single original cause: the "mischiefs and imperfection" are caused by inaction ("*negligence*"), excess ("*intemperance*"), and deviance ("*deserting the Prescripts of nature*"), which are themselves the product of "*deriv'd corruption*"—itself simultaneously inherent ("*the innate corruption of fallen humanity*") and produced (the "*breeding and converse with men*" that produces the Baconian idols of the mind). The crux here for Hooke concerns the compensatory possibilities offered by artificial organs and the possibility that they reinstate an Edenic perfection. Hooke presents, as Nick Wilding argues, "a rereading of the Fall to offer the possibility of a technologically supplemented cyborg postlapsarian body that would be functionally equivalent to the prelapsarian Adam."[38] On these terms, we grasp the capacities of Adam's body through the prosthetic technology's revelation of our own defects.

In the seventeenth century, Adam was conventionally invoked as the natural philosopher's Biblical precedent, his naming of the animals deemed

a sign of his wisdom and dominion over the creation (although Hooke himself is skeptical about how much knowledge the mere bestowal of a name
indicates).[39] The perfections of the Adamic body purportedly made possible
the immediacy of Edenic knowledge of nature. "*Adam* needed no Spectacles,"
Glanvill affirms in his 1661 attack on scholasticism; his unassisted eye could
see the effluvia that creates magnetism, the pulsing of the blood, and the
movement of the earth.[40] Adam's prelapsarian body, on these terms, possessed all the powers painfully clawed back through prosthetic devices such
as the microscope; it serves as a defamiliarizing device that makes the deficiencies of fallen perception visible, allowing writers such as Glanvill to sub-
tract out Edenic powers in order to reinstate them, evacuating a space in
order to fill it up again.

Not all thinkers, to be sure, concurred in according Adam such perfections. The physician and Royal Society fellow Henry Power—himself the
recorder of microscopic observations in his 1664 *Experimental Philosophy*—
considered "*the Constitution of* Adam's *Organs . . . not divers from ours, nor
different from those of his Fallen Self.*" Adam, Powers argued, would have been
unable to see the entities that "*we do by the Artificial advantages of the* Tele-
scope *and* Microscope."[41] Hooke likewise shows a certain dry skepticism:
"Whatever men's eyes were in the younger age of the World, ours in this old
age of it need spectacles."[42] If humans never possessed such perfection, then
our relative shortsightedness is not a derogation from a happier state but a
constitutive lack, and such artificial aids as the microscope are not the restitu-
tion of a lost whole but the invention of a new body.

These divergent understandings of the Adamic body govern the status of
the instrument as compensatory or as superaddition. Indeed, they define both
the limits and the proper ambit of scientific ambitions within the broader
scientific milieu to which Hooke belonged. As Peter Harrison has argued,
seventeenth-century beliefs about what could be known and by what means
depended on which physical or cognitive attributes Adam and Eve were
understood to have lost at the Fall and which could be reinstated.[43] What
science and technology could (or should) do, that is, was shaped by a kind of
theological anthropology. These arguments determined whether instrumental
alterations could be naturalized as proper to the human.

Whereas Harrison addresses how varying religious beliefs about the
impact of the Fall on human nature govern scientific practice, Joanna Picciotto identifies a seventeenth-century shift from a collective investment in
the sacrificial figure of Christ to Adam the innocent laborer as a figure that

"distributed intellectual authority rather than concentrating it: first, by privileging the perspective of humanity prior to its fall into social difference, and second, by offering people a perspective to which their own persons provided no access."[44] In Picciotto's argument, identification with the innocent figure of Adam underwrites corporate identities—a consolidation of the public not through the exchange of ideas but through the shared labor of a collective making of fact (5). The approximation of Adam's powerful senses made possible by such artificial organs as the microscope, Picciotto argues, offered "their users prosthetic access to a body capable of seeing through the 'false Images' of fallen perception" (191). By restoring "the first person to the first person"— consolidating a "we" through the primacy of Adam's "I"—Picciotto's intellectual laborers use Adam's unprepossessed eye as a shared impersonal medium through which to access the subvisible world (62). Adam's body on these terms naturalizes the instrumental alterations Hooke advocates.

When Hooke pits the backward-looking reinstatement of a long-lost Eden against the future-oriented discovery of hitherto unknown worlds, he also proposes two different models of human perfectibility.[45] On the one hand, the prosthetic understood as the emulation of an already existing (Adamic) form reinstates a prior wholeness; on the other, the Promethean improvement that issues from Epimethean lack suggests the constitution of an entity that supersedes its ostensible origins and shatters the notion of a stable master template. If the "*helps of Art*" recapture a prelapsarian state, permitting us to "recover some degree of these former perfections" by "rectifying faults," then the supplementary device belongs in a "natural" theological order, and the Adamic body can indeed offer the kind of symbolic unity that Picciotto argues it incarnates for the New Science. If, however, the "*addition of such* artificial Instruments *and* Methods" is the emendation of an essential lack (something that was never there), then it does not reinstate something lost but extends humanity's capacities beyond the original bounds of the senses, enabling us to "inlarge *their power*" (sig. a). (Although Hooke at intervals pauses to remind his reader that the miraculous order, detail, and ingenuity displayed in the works of nature are a sign of divine wisdom, it is hard to argue that the man who bragged of having devised "thirty several ways of Flying"[46] was solely interested in reinstating an organic prelapsarian unity.)

Hooke's technological model of progressive history, with which we began, keeps punching holes in the organic or god-given body meant to naturalize it. Whether Hooke's artificial helps compensate for an inherent lack or replace a prior plenitude governs the question of whether the instrument mimics a lost but essentially human function or extends beyond originally bestowed organic capacities in a self-vaunting attempt to amend or exceed the divine template—an imitation not of what humanity already is but the creation of something else altogether. The questions raised by Hooke's instruments on these terms anticipate modern theoretical discussions of the prosthetic. Alternately understood as imitating the activity of the body or as supplementing its powers, a prosthetic either replaces something that fails to work (serving as a placeholder for a lost limb or capacity) or improves what it supplants (bringing forth capacities that may never have been possessed by the body). As David Wills has argued, the distinction between the wooden leg's direct attempt to emulate the missing human limb and the modern prosthesis's endeavor to supersede and perfect its operation offers us "two competing conceptions of the human."[47] While the wooden leg replicates the body's normative shape, the technologically improved prosthesis "takes a big step towards the reproduction of a functioning more strictly analogous to that of the human leg, but that is also a step towards the more strictly mechanical functions of the human, hence toward the nonhuman" (26–27). In focusing on the "reproduction of a *functioning*" rather than the imitation of a part, Wills raises the question of whether the prosthetic is designed to imitate a leg or to imitate what a leg *does*. Is the aim, that is, to reproduce the illusion of a whole—an artificial reinstatement of a lost original—or to further the capacity or end for which the part was designed (or perhaps used)?

Whereas the understanding of the prosthetic as reinstating a prior unity makes the prosthetic compensatory—adding what is missing to re-create the likeness of an original—the notion that the prosthesis is designed to perform a function converts it into a means, potentially able to outdo the original, and able to do so in multifarious ways. The original template no longer governs. Inasmuch as what we are able to do redefines what we are thought to be, the add-on tampers with the essence. To the extent that the prosthesis imitates not what a leg or an eye looks like but what it does, it discards the mimetic in favor of the practical, defining the human body not in terms of appearance but in terms of functioning. (We shall return to the ways this shapes Hooke's scientific realism later.)

If the superadded part (ostensibly) reinstates what is missing, it is only because there is a concept of an organic whole or of a functioning ensemble in the first place. What is lost in losing a limb is not only the part and the actions it enabled one to perform but also the integrity of the body: the sense of being one, of being whole. But what if, Wills asks, "the whole never was anywhere" (15)? The perturbing possibility that the "organic form might always have been a fantasy," in Barbara Johnson's gloss on Wills's question, implies that "the difficulty of getting used to its artificial substitute is the difficulty of living without that fantasy."[48] A "whole" body on these terms need not be a fully "able" or maximally *enabled* body; it may simply be a body that has embraced its own limitations as the final word on the matter. Indeed, the belief that we know in what our wholeness consists—that somewhere there is a tidy organically given form, a neat shape that we can fully and comfortably occupy—is challenged not only by the relations of dependency and lack into which we are born but also by the microscope's revelation of the swarming worlds beneath the visible surface of things. As we shall see in the discussion of Hooke's louse at the end of the chapter, the one is *always* the many.

Hooke's prosthetic improvements do not just tamper with the fantasy of a whole body; in their quest for infinite perfectibility they cancel it out altogether. That the prosthesis exceeds its supplementary function suggests that the body's boundaries furnish no calculable limit as to what humanity might be or do, a possibility that is both promise and threat. Although Hooke's preferred term, "helps," affirms human primacy ("helps" exist to serve us), the "prosthetization of the animate or the human" makes it hard to "distinguish the human from its inanimate other," leaving us, as Wills puts it, "forever removed from ourselves."[49] This alienating circuit outside the self moves us even further away from the notion that the prosthetic reinstates a lost whole. Hooke's artificial helps turn away from the pursuit of humanity's prelapsarian semblance to a spectral vision of what humanity might become. We have here the creation of a kind of bionic man.

Yet Hooke's utopian model of cyborg empowerment is visited upon and experienced unequally by bodies of different genders, ranks, races, occupations, ages, and endowments: the defining lack that spurs humanity into compensatory excess does not produce a world accessible to all. The instrumentally enhanced body that is Hooke's engine of future human progress simultaneously generates a class of lesser bodies. While the prosthetic compensates for a frail or aging body and supplements a typical one, it also designates those bodies that lack its superadded powers as defective. As Sarah Jain puts it, "A prosthesis can fill a gap, but it can also diminish the body and create a need for itself," validating a normative or enhanced body while

designating others as not "fully whole."[50] The promise of universal, technologically engineered equality is further belied by the unequal distribution of
its benefits. While the books that Hooke represents as a kind of prosthetic
memory (which Hooke considered an organ)[51] serve as shared repositories of
knowledge, for example, they also consolidate a cognitive elite, contributing
not just to the evolution of humanity over time but to its differentiation.
Moreover, although it is grotesque to apply the term *prosthetic* to another
human being, the incorporative logic naturalized by Hooke's instruments
facilitates the silent assimilation of the labor of other humans into the self.

And even those most empowered by Hooke's instruments may be sur-
passed and even supplanted by them. Data registered by devices, Hooke
notes, reveals "how many faults and inequalities the naked eye and unma-
chined hand do commit."[52] The undeviating accuracy of the mechanical
attains an impersonal authority, as the circuit through the nonhuman instrument tempers the subjective conceits that deform perception. "*Many things,*"
Hooke warns, "*which come within their* [the sense's] *reach, are not received in
a right manner*" (sig. av). Long before objectivity emerges as a value for the
culture more generally, we find Hooke praising the superior exactitude of
instruments over the fallibility of the human senses.[53] Yet what begins as an
extension of human powers takes on a life of its own, as humanity devises
the tools for its own supersession.

Hooke even designed instruments—a self-recording surveying instrument, a subaquatic way-wiser, and a clock-driven paper-feeder added to a
weather clock—able to record indices in the absence of a living percipient.
Operating independently of the subject, these mechanisms circumvent
human bodies altogether, creating a literally objective observer of events.
They make available information about what one would see if one were
present—indeed, what one would not see were one present, since the phenomena they record often pass below the human perceptual threshold. In
measuring "*the least variation of heat or cold, which the most Acute sense is not
able to distinguish,*" these devices carry us beyond the proverbial tree falling
in the forest (*Micrographia,* sig. c2v). By opening up what Ann Banfield
describes as "vast and terrifying epistemological perspectives that 'no one had
ever seen'," Hooke's instruments cease to mediate between the human senses
and a divinely wrought nature and themselves reign as prosthetic gods.[54]

Yet the messages of the gods are rarely immediately intelligible to their
mortal recipients. How is one to identify, let alone describe, what "no one
had ever seen"? The price exacted for the augmentation of human powers is

the world as we know it to be. At the same time as Hooke enthrones an instrumentally augmented humanity as the engine of his model of human progress, his devices expose the subject to disorienting shifts in scale and strange new worlds whose veracity is impossible to substantiate. By revealing that the magnified object does not fit its visible shape, the microscope creates a space in which bodies shuck off their identities, squirm out of the grasp of language, and turn an unrecognizable face to the lens or the eye.

Even as the *Micrographia* dazzles with images of the exotic, exquisite micro-world literally at our fingertips, it punctures the hubris of our prosthetic superpowers by underscoring how little we definitively know or master. Many of the *Micrographia*'s plates elicit not recognition but bafflement; without the supplement of language, it is often difficult to know what the image depicts. Once magnified, mold becomes a lush, rank forest; the tip of a needle, a torpedo cruising across the top of a plate; the insignificant flea, a fearsome scaled marauder. Objects under the microscope are often discrete particulars unmoored from any context, stripped of their nominal identities and reduced to a lump, a churning mass of light and shadow, a smudge or a smear on a screen. The fact that the microscopic world revealed to Hooke's instrumentally enhanced senses bears scant (or no) resemblance to the world known to the naked eye means that verisimilitude is no measure of the truth of his observations, raising epistemological, ontological, and methodological problems for the *Micrographia*.

Because the microscopic world, while contiguous, does not necessarily resemble this one, it is difficult to represent mimetically, while the corpuscles, atoms, and other physical minima central to late seventeenth-century strains of materialist, vitalist, and alchemical philosophy *cannot* be represented mimetically, for they fail to materialize at all. As "a science without object, or without an empirical object," philosophical materialism challenged empiricism's commitment to the reality of what is perceived through the senses and, by extension, to the realist protocols devised by the Royal Society to secure its truths.[55] Although some claimed to have seen "'not only mites . . . but the atoms of Epicurus, the subtle matter of Descartes, the vapours of the earth'"[56] through their instruments—claims scornfully dismissed by the Dutch microscopist Antonie van Leeuwenhoek—physical minima hover tantalizingly outside of microscopic view, as elusive as the active matter and occult causes that they were designed to supplant. Hooke, like the corpuscular chymists analyzed by Helen Thompson, must "elaborate modes of figural, formal, and experimental access to imperceptible things, crossing the epistemological pretenses of empirical knowledge with the awareness that such knowledge is *produced*."[57]

We saw above that the prosthetic alteration of the senses grounds Hooke's definition of humanity not in a master template that delimits what humanity *is*, but in a historical anthropology that involves the progressive transformation of the capacities of the species—what humanity *can do*. In the next section, I want to turn from the effect of the instrument on the humanity of its user to the difficulty in establishing object relations with the alien world unveiled through its mediation. Given the difference in scale and the lack of resemblance between micro and macro worlds, Hooke grounds his realism not just in mimesis or the testimony of the senses but in practice or operability: how—and whether—things work. What can guarantee that the world encountered by the prosthetically altered eye is indeed the world as it actually is? For Hooke's experimental practice, the proof lies less in the eye than in the hand: not in what something looks like, but in what it does.

Bricoleur Realism

While Hooke's preface celebrates the way technology extends human powers beyond their organic limits, the *Micrographia* itself explores the simultaneous rapture and menace of a world made strange through the mediation of these "*Mechanical helps*" (sig. d2r). Hooke's compendium offers magnified images of a splendid hodgepodge of things: mold, moss, snowflakes, sparks from flint, shards of mica, frozen urine, fish scales, fly's eyes, fleas, all strangely beautiful and wonderfully strange. The text begins with defamiliarizing representations of homely human artifacts—a needle's point, a razor's edge, a scrap of silk—wrested from their domesticating contexts and divorced from use. Seen through the microscope's merciless lens, the most perfect fruits of human art are not the polished finished objects that they appear to the naked eye but botched irregular forms, a humiliating contrast to the flawless works of nature with their ever-receding delicacy of infinitely refined detail. The most elegantly crafted human objects prove to be crude fumbling replications of God's masterful handiwork, while great technical achievements such as the microscope only reveal how mortifyingly short our most accomplished efforts fall.

When viewed through the microscope, even the text we are reading is not what it seems. Hooke's masterstroke in beginning the *Micrographia* with the full stop—a point he punningly expands to embrace mathematical, logical, and discursive points—exploits the parallel between physical things, geometrical constructs, linguistic signs, and their idiomatic counterparts, dispatching in a single rhetorical thrust both our image of the world and the methodologies devised to understand and represent it.[58] The mathematical point, with its promise of indivisible unity, is "the most natural way of beginning" in geometry, Hooke notes, but its integrity crumbles the moment we shift from a pristine Euclidean world to its physical counterpart (*Micrographia*, 1). When viewed under a microscope, a point proves to be a swirling centrifugal excrescence, a molten ball, an inchoate blotch, "like *smutty daubings* on a matt or uneven floor with a blunt extinguisht brand or stick's end," Hooke snarls, or "a great splatch of *London* dirt" (3). When magnified, the words on the page cease to be text and become scratches, gouges, stains on a crude surface, binding the most exalted of human arts—mathematics, writing, the printing press, and reading matter—to an inescapable sordid materiality. "No more rapid subversion of a program conceived *a priori* is imaginable," Catherine Wilson notes.[59]

How, moreover, is one to interact with this alien world, given the vast difference in scale? Hooke illustrates the abyss between the micro and the macro worlds by contrasting the magnified point with an actual-size full stop, framed by a circle and annotated with the letter *A* (Figure 2). While the other elements in the image have been heavily mediated by the microscope, by Hooke's eye and drawing hand, by the labors of the engravers and their tools, the actual-size point alone has the appearance of being transcribed "as is." The juxtaposition of "actual" and magnified points invites the reader to toggle between the two, echoing the movement between the deceived and the disenchanted eye before the trompe l'oeil discussed in Chapter 1. *This* cannot be *that* (contiguity is incompatible with identity, and these two points are next to one another), and yet this, Hooke tells us, *is* that (or would be were we to look at it under a microscope). Whereas elsewhere Hooke rescales the world at will, making the moon into a dot and converting a speck into a sun, here we encounter a kind of referential touchdown, in which the "actual size" image reinstates the body of the beholder, checking the imaginative play by which we loft ourselves into other dimensions. As the art historian David Summers observes, "We can only touch things at the size they are."[60] Gulliver cannot have an anatomically impossible affair with a Lilliputian court lady any more than we can shake hands with a louse. The contrast between the magnified and "actual size" points both exposes the perspectival systems that

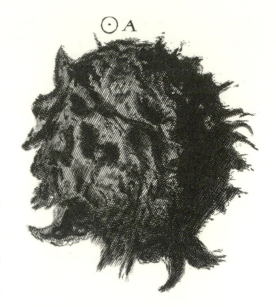

FIGURE 2. Detail of Schema II
[The Needle and the Full Stop],
in Robert Hooke, *Micrographia*
(London: Jo. Martyn and Ja.
Allestry, printers to the Royal
Society, 1665), opposite p. 2. RB
487000:0930, The Huntington
Library, San Marino, California.

organize the world as artifice and reminds us of the pragmatic limits on what
we can *do* with the microscopic world.

What the juxtaposition between the two points underscores is that the
magnified object is not "the same thing" except smaller—nature's "mini-
me"—but an alien form that resists assimilation to known templates. The
microscope shatters the "optical consistency" guaranteed by linear perspective
that creates Bruno Latour's "immutable mobiles" (discussed in the previous
chapter). In peering through a microscope, we do not "obtain the same object
at a different size as seen from another position" but are instead confronted
with an object that cannot quite be squared with or restored to its original
likeness.[61] The world viewed through the microscope cannot be reconciled
with the one seen by the naked eye simply by altering one's point of view,
and the inability to reconcile these worlds undermines the stability of subject
and object alike. For if, as Hooke avers, a magnified "O" (simultaneously
letter, circle, and zero) would not live up to its billing, the "I" (letter, line,
and pronoun) fares no better (*Micrographia*, 5). To the extent that the point
as the irreducible (but invisible) minima of the physical world finds in
the first person an irreducible subjective counterpart, the disaggregation of the
former menaces the unity of the latter. The microscope's dissolution of the
neatly delineated point into a misshapen swirling morass transforms the point

that orients the eye and anchors the viewing subject into the point where the subject as well as the object vanishes. Like Wallace Stevens's blackbird winging out of view, the moment when something flies out of Hooke's sight marks the edge of one of many circles. As the point disintegrates before our eyes, it threatens to take us down with it.

Notwithstanding Hooke's insistence in the preface to the *Micrographia* that he is committed to the "*plainness and soundness of* Observations *on* material *and* obvious *things*" (sig. b), there is little plain or obvious in this tricky world in which unidentified bodies commingle with shadows, bathed in an uncertain light that gutters, flares, and winks out. As Barbara Stafford observes, seventeenth- and eighteenth-century microscopes offered "a mine field of incomprehensible chiaroscuro . . . glaring and distorting refractions . . . [and reflections that] made certain portions of the object so bright that they annihilated the whole."[62] Under the lens, enigmatic forms strike an array of poses, without ever declaring their proper name. Inanimate objects skitter across the slides, while Hooke's squirming ants and mites refuse to stay still unless stunned, frozen, inebriated, or killed. Since any increase in power (by compounding lenses) decreased the light, magnification was accompanied by a loss of resolution, and even where their users had command of optical theory, the imperfections of the lenses made a mockery of their hypotheses. Looking more closely did not bring clarity. Many first-time users of the microscope looked through the eyepiece and saw nothing.

Hooke himself does not know at first glance what he is seeing. He coaxes coherent bodies out of churning aggregates of matter, offering multiple comparisons to known objects in an effort to conjure an intelligible form. Conventional tropes, however, do not quite hold up in the microscopic world. Metonymy falters before the difference in scale, while metaphor often points to an absence of resemblance rather than a commonality able to bind two worlds. Thus, the eyes of a fly "*in one kind of light appear almost like a Lattice, drilled through with abundance of small holes. . . . In the Sunshine they look like a Surface cover'd with golden Nails; in another posture, like a Surface cover'd with Pyramids; in another with Cones; and in other postures of quite other shapes*" (sig. f2v). While such analogies ward off the mental anarchy produced by the inchoate, the cascade of metaphors prevents one likeness from rising to the surface; no master template stabilizes the kaleidoscopic images flickering across the lens. In Hooke's world, a thing never looks the same way twice, which is to say that we cannot be sure what it looks like at all. Instead of producing confirmation through the orderly reproduction of experimental results (probability produced by iterability), repeated observation yields a provisional image without an authoritative original to which one can appeal—an image that, once fixed, gradually comes to be taken for the thing itself.[63] It is in part because of the immense difficulty of seeing *anything* through the microscope that Hooke's images so rapidly achieve iconic status, reproduced endlessly by authors who return to the master for a template to tell them what it was they saw, after all.

The early microscope's deficiencies and the difficulty of using one have been catalogued by many, starting with Hooke himself: "*It is*," he observes, "*exceeding difficult in some Objects, to distinguish between a* prominency *and a* depression*, between a* shadow *and a* black stain*, or a* reflection *and a* whiteness in the colour" (*Micrographia*, sig. f2v). Protuberances prove to be hollows; a ridge is a trough; what seems to be a colored patch turns out to be a trick of the light. Then as now, it is hard to determine whether what is observed is actually a property of the specimen or an artifact of the apparatus: the chance result of the angle of vision, misshapen lenses, bubbles in the glass, inadequate illumination, the decay or mutilation of the object, the fallibility of a tired eye, or Samuel Butler's trapped mouse. As Hooke's "faithful *Mercury*," the microscope serves as a courier between nature and human understanding, delivering intelligence not apparent to the naked eye; as a fallible or duplicitous instrument, it misdirects rather than relays (*Micrographia*, 211). Whether our devices are compliant emissaries of the gods or the rogue purveyors of false reports is at times difficult to tell.

Even the subtitle of the *Micrographia*—"Some Physiological Descriptions of Minute Bodies Made by Magnifying Glasses"—allows us to hesitate over whether it is the description or the minute body itself that is "made" by the magnifying glass. Seen as an agent that *produces* the apprehended object, Hooke's microscope operates less as an instrument that allows a separate, preexisting world to be observed than as a participant in an experimental process that loops subject and object into mutually constitutive relations. For Hooke's endless complaints about recalcitrant specimens, flawed lenses, an uncooperative sun register the multitude of other agencies at work in the experimental processes. Indeed, Hooke's method perhaps somewhat surprisingly anticipates elements of what the physicist and philosopher Karen Barad calls "agential realism," in which bodies emerge through "a dynamic process of intra-activity . . . through which part of the world makes itself differentially intelligible to another part of the world and through which causal structures are stabilized and destabilized."[64] Drawing on the work of the physicist Niels

Bohr, Barad argues that there is no stable, inherent, or unambiguous "cut" that sunders the individuated Cartesian or Newtonian observing subject from outward preexisting entities. Bodies are "not objects with inherent boundaries and properties," existing independently of the systems that produce them; nor are they self-contained individuals with fixed borders or essential traits (153). Rather, phenomena emerge in specific configurations, within apparatuses "constituted through particular practices that are perpetually open to rearrangements, rearticulations, and other reworkings" (170).

Barad's model questions the anthropocentric assumptions underwriting experimental practice. In her account, the agencies that shape the world and make it knowable cannot be "aligned with human intentionality or subjectivity"; rather, bodies are summoned into being through the apparatus in which they participate (177). (We might think here of the way the instrument or prosthetic device enfolds the body into a working configuration.) Inasmuch as reality involves "not a fixed essence," but *the ongoing dynamics of intra-activity*," Barad's realism entails not a crystalline portrait of an observation-independent referent but an account of the agencies that enable phenomena to become intelligible to one another (206, 170). Indeed, the observing subject is herself an element in this dynamic process, "part of the configuration or ongoing reconfiguring of the world—that is, they/we too are phenomena" (206). While Barad's model dislodges humanity from its monopoly over the experimental process, her insistence that realism pertains only to that "reality of which we are a part" and not to some "imagined and idealized human-independent reality" leaves us with a realism only imaginable in relation to ourselves (207). There is no world without us.

Hooke, to be sure, does not understand himself to be a mere "phenomenon" conjured by his own experimental practices; he characterizes himself as a scientific Columbus discovering a new world through the microscope (GS, 20–21; *Micrographia*, sig. d2v). Nevertheless, his objects are not camera-ready, waiting to be seen, but must be brought "to such a Constitution, as to bring them within the Power of the Sense" (GS, 38). While Hooke's "sincere Hand" and "faithful Eye" purportedly record "*things themselves as they appear*," in practice, things have to be cajoled or dragged into view through precisely the kinds of intra-actions that Barad describes (*Micrographia*, sig. a2v). Because the qualities of objects are "obscur'd or buried in the matter, so as not at all to affect the Sense," they must be "excited and made active and vigorous by Art" (GS, 40). Specimens must be sliced, bruised, stained, rubbed, struck, dissolved, and calcined; light must be passed through prisms or filtered through screens; liquids must be heated, diluted, distilled, and their precipitates extracted. Hooke must make "the sensible Qualities of the Object more powerful than naturally they are of themselves for affecting the Sense, or more proportionate to the Power and Faculties of them," enticing phenomena into becoming available for apprehension (GS, 40). What this suggests is that Hooke's realism does not depend upon the mimetic description of an ontologically stable world, neatly dissevered from the observing subject, but involves the conscription of eye, instrument, and specimen into circuits of making and doing that confer provisional form upon subject and object alike.

Hooke's account of the genesis of the *Micrographia*'s plates draws attention to the multiple mediating layers between what he "saw" in his serial viewings of the object and the synthetic composite he turns over to the hands of the draftsman. "*I never began to make any draught before by many examinations in several lights, and in several positions to those lights, I had discover'd the true form*" (*Micrographia*, sig. f2v). Whether seen as a composite forged by combining elements from different viewings or as a kind of lowest common denominator realized by subtracting out anomalies, Hooke's "true form" scarcely merits the definite article. Indeed, as Matthew Hunter has argued, "The true forms the draftsman aimed to represent were not really *seen* forms at all" but "a concretion of data collected from discrete, observational acts conducted in time, then integrated, projected, abstracted."[65] Since objects too large or bulky for the microscope had to be sliced up and could only be observed in parts, Hooke reverts to the macro-scale (known through the naked eye) to correlate the fragments into a recognizable morphology, adjudicating form through "inferences from sensory data to project the nature of targets that could never actually be seen in full."[66] Hooke's "empiricism" thus involves a marked degree of conceptual abstraction, a reminder that hand and mind cannot be easily dissevered. Since it is impossible to count the number of cells in a piece of cork from a minute sliver, for example, he must use mathematical reasoning to extrapolate what cannot be observed. Hooke projects wholes that, like Wills's integral body, might not be anywhere.

The elusive nature of subvisible bodies, I argue, leads Hooke to ground his realism not in outward likeness but in function—in what the bodies glimpsed through the microscope (and their invisible counterparts) *do*. The authority of Hooke's descriptions, both verbal and visual, resides less in the detailed rendering of a likeness (hard to gauge, since we cannot see what he saw) than in the formal relations between working parts. Hooke's realism appeals to what Margaret Cohen in her study of maritime fiction calls a "performability effect," which "solicits a pragmatic use of the imagination . . . for expedients that do not violate the laws of nature, that could be performed, and that could plausibly work."[67] Drawing on J. L. Austin's performative utterance, which assesses language based on "effectiveness rather than referentiality," Cohen's performability effect is measured by "plausibility of performance" rather than "plausibility of mimesis"—felicity or efficacy, not likeness or truth.[68] Hooke substantiates his claims about the invisible world through its practical manipulation, elaborating a formalism grounded not in mimesis but in operability. *Process*—the viable relation of cause to effect—serves as the gauge of the real.

Hooke's apprehension of microscopic objects is governed by this interest in efficacy. His bricoleur's eye appraises bodies based on their affordances, stripping them down in order to piece them together into Arcimboldo-like composites, so many components in nature's erector set. The sharp points of nettles are like "Syringe-pipes, or Glyster-pipes"; spiders' legs are "long Leavers"; and the cells of cork are "small Boxes or Bladders of Air" (*Micrographia*, 143, 199, 114). Hooke's descriptions partake of what Abigail Zitin calls a "practitioner's formalism," a disciplined attention to the formal attributes or "linear scaffold of an object" that enables artist or artisan to reconstruct the empirical processes by which things are made.[69] To be sure, Hooke describes the outward appearance of objects, but the meat of his descriptions lies in the disposition and interaction of parts. Thus, cork sucks nourishment from the tree it encases in a fashion "something *analogous* to the Mushrome, or Moss on other Trees, or to the hairs on Animals," while the venomous point of the nettle works like the stinger of a bee and also like the poisoned arrow devised by humankind (*Micrographia*, 115, 144). These are not the visible signatures of Renaissance similitude famously described in Foucault's *Order of Things*, but homologous working parts, impartially shared by mechanical and organic forms.[70] Even as the prosthetic leg may imitate the operation of the limb rather than the likeness of the body, so too does Hooke emphasize the function of a part instead of its outward appearance.

Rather than offering a static mirror of a fully realized world (no new inventions there), Hooke's process-oriented descriptions explain how the affordances of bodies allow them to be turned to novel uses. Hooke appropriates parts in much the same way that animals conscript empty shells or rotting carcasses as proxy wombs for their eggs (actions that "seem to savour so much of reason," but that are, Hooke insists, a result of "the excellent contrivance of their machine" [*Micrographia*, 190]). His mix-and-match mode echoes nature's own infinite capacity to repurpose objects, "the Mechanism of Nature," Hooke notes, being "usually so excellent, that one and the same substance is adapted to serve for many ends" (165). Because Hooke sees bodies as aggregates of working parts rather than integral wholes, they can be recombined, creating hybrids that traffic across the boundaries that separate living and nonliving entities: animal, vegetable, mineral. Hooke's flying machine reportedly involved "contrivances for fastening succedaneous Wings, not unlike those of Bats, to the Arms and Legs of a Man," while the ghastly vivisection experiments he performed in the mid-1660s created a kind of early modern respirator, replacing the hollow circularity of the dog's windpipe with a tube connected to a bellows in what Hunter aptly calls a "violent literalization" of the Cartesian beast-machine.[71]

Hooke is no Lévi-Straussian engineer, with a comprehensive sense of all that is available to him within a circumscribed system. Instead, he has a bricoleur's appreciation of the limitless variety of uses to which an object may be turned. When there is no "piece of oyly Paper" at hand, "a small piece of Looking-glass plate" coarsened with sand may do; a pipe or joint designed for one device can be transferred to another (*Micrographia*, sig. d2v, sig. e). Hooke's ear trumpet begins its life as a wind detector.[72] There are no single-use items in Hooke's world; he can always find another way to skin a cat. Hooke underlines the "scores of ways, for perfecting Instruments" that he has devised, "each of these very differing from one another. . . . I have various ways of fixing those instruments, and appropriating them for this, that, or the other particular use. I have various mechanical ways for making and working the several parts of them with great expedition and certainty, which is a knowledge not less useful th[a]n the knowledge of the theory and use of them when made, there being so very few to be found in the World that can or will perform it."[73] Hooke's variety in contrivance adheres to no one theoretical model; he offers multiple expedients to produce a single effect. Hooke thus preserves a promiscuous recombinatory openness, a technical indeterminacy, that allows entities to be plied to various ends. He does not pretend to engineer a second nature but to craft new possibilities from the heterogeneous oddments extracted from this one. This defiance of the object's predestination creates a polymorphous world whose reality may be governed by God the engineer but whose realism belongs to the partial, provisional, ongoing, and open-ended makings and doings of the bricoleur.

Hooke puts nature to work, finding new and various uses—*abuses*—for bodies that fracture their given identities by delivering them into relations that were no part of their originally designated end. Hooke's realism, that is, is grounded not in the description of what something is or what it looks like but in *how* (and sometimes just *whether*) it works. Thus Hooke dismisses the "needless insisting upon the outward Shape and Figure, or Beauty" of things as "not of such a Knowledge of Bodies as might tend to practice" (GS, 4). The reader absorbed by the beauty of Hooke's stunning images misses the point, for form is of no interest for its own sake: "it seems . . . contrary to that great Wisdom of Nature," he remarks of the exquisite petrified shells called serpentine stones, "that these prettily shap'd bodies should have all those curious Figures and contrivances . . . for no higher end th[a]n onely to exhibit such a form" (*Micrographia*, 112). Form and detail must have a purpose, for Hooke has no patience with insignificant notations. What matters is what something does.

This instrumental relation to form is an extension of the utilitarian relation Hooke takes to knowledge: "Knowledge," Hooke insists, "is not barely acquir'd for it self, but in order to the inabling a Man to understand how by the joyning of fit Agents to Patients according to the Orders, Laws, Times and Methods of Nature, he may be able to produce and bring to pass such Effects, as may very much conduce to his well being in this World, both for *satisfying his Desires*, and the relieving of his *Necessities*" (GS, 3). Here, as we saw in the opening section of the chapter, the intense labor required for the "*satisfying*" of man's "*Desires*, and the relieving of his *Necessities*" is a constant reminder of humanity's inadequacy and its need for Hooke's artificial helps. Natural knowledge is no end in itself but enables humanity to enter into new configurations through the "joyning of fit Agents to Patients."

Hooke offers elaborate descriptions of how these "Agents" and "Patients" may be conjoined in the form of step-by-step instructions about how to replicate his experiments. Yet for all his insistence that what matters is how or whether things work, he does not *know* exactly what he is doing. His methodical directions are littered with approximating references to the best or proper distance ("*four or five inches*"), rough timing (when "*you see the colour . . . to be greenish, but no sooner*"), and ball-park amounts ("*about as much as will lye upon a half Crown piece . . . others will require more, or less*") (*Micrographia*, 23, 22, 23). The Goldilocks adjudication of the measure of the "just right" belongs neither to the theoretical knowledge of the savant nor to the droning rote repetition of the mere mechanical; it is neither fully of the mind nor fully of the hand. Technical skill cannot be excised from the experienced body. Hooke can tell us there is a screw to adjust the lens, but he cannot tell us how far to turn it, a reminder that prose cannot impart the embodied know-how that determines the precise degree of pressure necessary to tighten a knob or the exact proportion of light required "that it may not singe or burn the Paper" (*Micrographia*, sig. d2v–e). The maker's knowledge that enables Hooke to shape the real escapes cognitive grasp. His bricoleur realism invites a performative reenactment that can neither be fully represented nor exactly reproduced.

The corporeal nature of maker's knowledge—the deftness of the hand that eludes language and cognition—also hints at a mechanical element at the heart of acts of human making. The technician who has internalized the skills of his art works "with the automatism attributed to natural processes" or at least cannot claim to be fully aware of all elements of his own actions.[74] It is not just that we outsource capacities to instruments and machines in experimental practice; even our own bodies are vessels for knowledge that escapes our conscious apprehension. If the fact that knowledge inheres in the flesh belies Cartesian dualism, attaching the singularity of Hooke's "first person" to body as well as mind, it also points to the automatism that haunts all acts of making. There is always a blind spot in the accounts Hooke offers of the processes through which things have been made, and thus there is also a blind spot within the practitioner's knowledge that supposedly substantiates Hooke's account of the real.

Like the bricoleur, Hooke "makes do" in the face of obscurity or incomplete information. Indeed, as long as he can produce results, Hooke is often strangely content with partial knowledge; he offers an account of working parts while suspending the question of the causal agent altogether. What lurks behind the curtain pierced by the microscopic eye is no Oz-like natural magician but an assemblage of Munchkin-sized machines operated by unidentified hands. We have, Hooke notes,

> some reason to suspect, that those effects of Bodies, which have been commonly attributed to Qualities, and those confess'd to be occult, are perform'd by the small Machines of Nature, which are not to be discern'd without these helps, seeming the meer products of Motion, Figure, and Magnitude; and that the Natural Textures, which some call the Plastick faculty, may be made in Looms, which a greater perfection of Opticks may make discernable by these Glasses; so as now they are no

more puzzled about them, then the vulgar are to conceive, how Tapestry
or flowred Stuffs *are woven.* (*Micrographia*, sig. g)

Hooke's strategic recourse to the passive voice ("*are perform'd by the small*
Machines," "*may be made in* Looms") points to the machinery without identifying what makes it run; absent from this Queen Mab fantasy are the tiny
textile workers laboring upon these looms. What distinguishes the Lilliputian
engines that drive the natural world from the "plastic faculty" or "occult
qualities" that Hooke dismisses would seem to be Hooke's ability to manage
them—to tamper with the workings of nature.

Hooke has little patience with purely speculative beings; he wants to be
doing. Once we have discovered that "the fiery Sparks struck from a Flint or
Steel" are microscopically identical to the particles left after casting steel or
iron filings into a flame, we may conclude, Hooke notes, that "Iron does
contain a very *combustible sulphureous Body*" (*Micrographia*, 44, 46) and thus

> need not trouble our selves to find out what kind of Pores they are,
> both in the Flint and Steel, that contain the *Atoms of fire*, nor how
> those *Atoms* come to be hindred from running all out, when a dore
> or passage in their Pores is made by the concussion: nor need we
> trouble our selves to examine by what *Prometheus* the Element of
> Fire comes to be fetcht down from above the Regions of the Air, in
> what Cells or Boxes it is kept, and what *Epimetheus* let it go; Nor to
> consider what it is that causes so great a conflux of the atomical
> Particles of Fire, which are said to fly to a flaming Body, like Vul-
> tures or Eagles to a putrifying Carcass, and there to make a very
> great pudder. (46)

The pores and doors, the self-propelling "atomical Particles of fire" hurling
themselves pell-mell toward the flames of which they are the purported cause,
are as absurd as accounts that feature the mythical Prometheus. Hooke here
recapitulates the logic of operability (if a surface is breached, atoms must
pour out) in order to mock the very homologies he elsewhere deploys. Yet
Hooke himself does not explain *how* the "large Iron-Bullet, . . . should set
fire to those [coals] that are next to it," leaving it unclear why his "*combustible
sulphureous* Body" possesses greater explanatory power than the "atomical
Particles of Fire" he dismisses (46, 45, 46). Here as elsewhere the capacity to
produce outward effects trumps speculative knowledge about inward causes.

For even as Hooke jeers at the absurdities of occult qualities—"what . . . should I trouble my self to enquire into that which is never to be understood, and is beyond the reach of my Faculties to comprehend?"[75]—he believes that he can *do things* with these intangible and invisible bodies. The trouble with a mystical agent such as Henry More's hyclarchick spirit—that puzzling chimera made up of "I know not what, and to be found I know not when or where, and [that] acts all things I know not how"—is not that it is invisible (or even that it is a tautological personification that explains nothing), but that Hooke cannot *do* anything with it. "If it were a Spirit that Regulated the motion of the water in its running faster or slower," he mockingly asks, how "should I signifie to it that I had occasion for a current of water that should run eight Gallons in a minute through a hole of an Inch bore?"[76] It is the capacity to create measurable effects that substantiates (invisible) causes: what matters for Hooke is not the identification of the specific agent but the ability to manipulate outcomes.

Science is filled with theoretical agents of uncertain ontology, from More's hyclarchick spirit to the Higgs boson. Such speculative entities, Ian Hacking has argued, become real to experimentalists through use: "Experimenting on an entity does not commit you to believing that it exists. Only *manipulating* an entity, in order to experiment on something else, need do that." Experimental science, Hacking contends, leads us to "count as real what we can use to intervene in the world to affect something else, or what the world can use to affect us."[77] It is not that we discover real things and then learn to use them; rather, in using things we know them to be real. We do business with entities that we only imagine, and we use those transactions to sanctify our belief in their existence. The practitioner finds conviction not in the mind but in the hand.

Hooke's emphasis on operability rather than mimesis as the gauge of the real commits him to the immediate relation of object and sign that the nineteenth-century philosopher Charles Sanders Peirce termed the index. Peirce's semiotic taxonomy distinguishes the resemblance of the icon and the conventionality or arbitrariness of the symbol from the index, which is defined by an existential or physical (spatiotemporal) relation between sign and referent. Embracing diverse examples—the footprint, the sundial, the bullet hole, and the photograph as well as pointing fingers, letters annotating diagrams, deictics such as "that" and "there," and shifters such as "I" and "you"—the index refers "to the Object that it denotes by virtue of being really affected by that Object."[78] The sun strikes the dial; the foot sinks into the sand; the light leaves a print on the photosensitive surface; a "low barometer with a moist air," Peirce notes, "is an index of rain."[79] Offering an imprint rather than a mimetic reproduction, the index attests to the material contact of sign and referent. It is, in Marianne Doane's words, the "only sign for which . . . [the physical world] can be seen as *cause*."[80]

Because the index indicates a relation in which one body has been affected by another, it corroborates the existence of the object that caused the sign, verifying that something is (here) or was (there), without reproducing its likeness. To be sure, the index as impression may partake of the iconic—a footprint, such as the one Robinson Crusoe encounters, mirrors the foot that produced it—but the connection it makes to its object issues from a proximate or causal relation, not from resemblance. "While realism claims to build a mimetic copy, an illusion of an inhabitable world," as Doane argues, "the index only purports to point, to connect, to touch, to make language and representation adhere to the world as tangent—to reference a real without realism."[81]

While the index attests to the existence of its referent, it tells us little more, for it involves the absence or displacement of its object: the foot that made the print, the object toward which the pointing finger gestures. Inasmuch as the index creates a sign that confirms the existence of an object without representing the cause that produced it, it holds questions about the nature of the agent or action at bay. As Peirce puts it, "The index asserts nothing; it only says 'There!' "[82] Hooke traces "*the footsteps of Nature*," pursuing these indices through all nature's "doublings *and* turnings" (*Micrographia*, sig. a2r). He both reads the marks left by the actions of nature on the "Superficies and out-sides" of things and seeks to produce indexical signs that attest to a relationship between the visible world and the inner workings of nature (GS, 8). Hooke's hygroscope, for example, is designed to detect "*watery steams volatile in the Air . . . which the Nose it self is not able to find*" (*Micrographia*, sig. c2r). The turning of the hygroscope's dial attests to Hooke's ability, through the medium of a plant, to make the otherwise undetectable action of nature into a separable, recognizable phenomenon—"differentially intelligible" to return to Barad's terms—to the observing subject. From slight objects, vast portents: "From the turning of a Straw," Hooke marvels, we can "foresee a Change in the great Ocean of the Air" (GS, 63). The hygroscope thus references what Doane calls "a real without realism."

Hooke's description of the hygroscope is nested in his observations about the (anthropomorphically named) beard of oat (Figure 3), which "turn[s] and

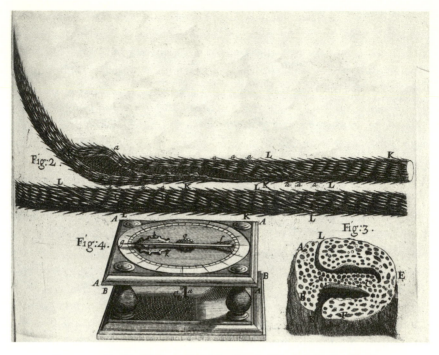

FIGURE 3. Detail of Schema XV [The Beard of Oat], in Robert Hooke, *Micrographia* (London: Jo. Martyn and Ja. Allestry, printers to the Royal Society, 1665), opposite p. 143. RB 487000:0930, The Huntington Library, San Marino, California.

move[s] round, as if it were sensible" when exposed to moisture, and gradually "unwreath[s] it self, and by degrees, [appears] to streighten its knee" (*Micrographia*, 147). While charlatans pawn this "oddly constituted Vegetable substance" off as "the Legg of an *Arabian Spider*, or the Legg of an inchanted *Egyptian fly*" (149), Hooke, here as elsewhere, seeks an explanation for this curiously animated behavior in "the make and shape of the parts" (151). Yet Hooke's analysis of the plant's inward structure is truncated. His initial hypothesis—that the beard bends owing to a "Spongie substance" at the "knee"—collapses when he discovers that the pores run the entire length of the plant (149). Notwithstanding his grandiose claim that the plant offers "the very first footstep of *Sensation*, and Animate motion, the most plain, simple, and obvious contrivance that Nature has made use of to produce a motion," Hooke never fully spells out what drives "the influx and evaporation of some kind of liquor or juice" that accounts for the movement of the plant and even "the *Mechanism* of the Muscles" in living creatures (151, 152, 152). More-over, the reader who tries to follow Hooke's explanation of the internal work-ings of the plant may find herself frustrated, as the lettered sections noted in the text are not fully correlated with the diagram (space running short, Hooke omitted part of the plant altogether [148]). The confirmation of his account of the beard of oat resides less in the "practical realism" of his description of the plant itself than in the uses to which he puts it. The best evidence Hooke offers for his account is the fact that the hygroscope works.

Fully half of the entry is devoted to directions about how to harness the beard of oat to the device, so that "the pointing of the Hand or Index, which is moved by the conjoin'd Beard" will show "all the *Minute* variations of the Air" (*Micrographia*, 150). The hygroscope does not materialize a body; it places plant, air, dial, hand into relations that point to causes or bodies that lie beyond Hooke's representational and even sensory purview, indicating a fact about the world—the invisible presence of moisture in the air—without representing that fact mimetically. Indeed, because these alterations in the atmosphere escape the senses, the fact to which the hygroscope attests rests solely on the device. Without the instrument, there is no there there.

While Hooke, as we saw above, dismisses entities such as the hyclarchick spirit, Prometheus, and the "atoms of fire," he accepts the existence of other-wise imperceptible moisture in the air because the swiveling hand of the hygroscope indexes its action. The importance of the index to Hooke stems from the fact that it registers the existence of agents not fully materialized by his experimental practice, serving as an interface through which these agen-cies may become legible to one another. And since the index may be pro-duced by human and nonhuman actors, it affords a more expansive understanding of the agents at work in the world than other signs. It is for this reason that such anthropologists as Terrence Deacon, Webb Keane, and Eduardo Kohn have found in Peirce's index an important resource for addressing the sign-making and sign-interpreting capacities of nonhuman beings, from the chemical-emitting roots that signal peril to adjacent trees to the rustling leaves that indicate the presence of a predator to a monkey.[83] As Keane points out, the classification of different signs carries with it beliefs about "what kinds of possible agent (humans only? animals? spirits?) exist to which acts of signification might be imputed," thus making visible assump-tions "about what kinds of agentive subjects and acted-upon objects might be found in the world."[84] Whereas the symbol and the icon depend on lin-guistic and perceptual capacities typically reserved for humans, the index admits nonhuman bodies as sign-producing and sign-reading agents, enabling Hooke to acknowledge the multitude of "agentive subjects" and "acted-upon objects" that populate his world.

Humans for Hooke do not have a monopoly on agency. To be sure, his insistence that knowledge be harnessed to human ends is overtly anthropocentric, but his *method* often dislodges humanity from its place at the center of the universe. "We ought," Hooke writes, "to conceive of things as they are part of, and Actors or Patients in the Universe, and not only as they have this or that peculiar Relation or Influence on our own Senses or selves" (GS, 9). Considered inasmuch as they act upon or react to one another apart from "our own Senses or selves," his actors and patients, like the actants of Latour's actor network theory or the differentially intelligible phenomena of Barad's agential realism, suspend an anthropocentric framework in which things are apprehended only insofar as they relate to us. Indeed, Hooke's human—that prosthetically refashioned entity—may be just another interlocking part in dynamic configurations.

I noted previously that the instrumentally enhanced senses reveal alien worlds that undermine the normative protocols of realism, and I argued that Hooke substantiates his claims about the subvisible world less through verisimilitudinous description than through operability: the fact that parts interlock in a way that works. While Hooke seeks to put these bodies to work, however, the microscope reveals that some of these bodies seem to be using *us*. In the closing section of this chapter, I want to address the oscillation in Hooke's oeuvre between empowered (human) agent and acted-upon patient, between parasite and host, by focusing on the most famous image from the *Micrographia*, Hooke's magnificent portrait of a louse. The fact that, as the microscope revealed, the human body teems with life that is not solely its own proclaims the lie of that basic unit of modernity: the autonomous, self-possessed individual. "Every part of Matter," Joseph Addison would note some fifty years later in the *Spectator* 519, "is peopled."[85] If tiny leaves turn out to harbor innumerable infinitesimal insects that are themselves the hosts of other creatures, then what are *we*?

Even as the microscope, as Barbara Stafford puts it, "drastically transformed how people perceived coherent organisms" by pulverizing "a well-behaved anthropomorphic unity . . . into tiny and teeming minima,"[86] it also menaced the integrity of the subject. The louse-infested body is not a unity but a reminder that, as Cary Wolfe puts it, the human institutes itself only by repressing, mastering, or denigrating its "unruly, asynchronous, material heterogeneity."[87] Under these circumstances, it may become difficult to

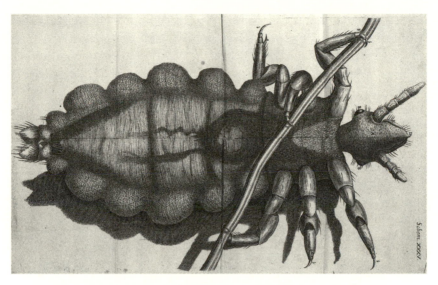

FIGURE 4. Schema XXXV [The Louse], in Robert Hooke, *Micrographia*
(London: Jo. Martyn and Ja. Allestry, printers to the Royal Society, 1665),
between pp. 212 and 213. RB 487000:0930, The Huntington Library,
San Marino, California.

determine who exists in service to whom. No respecter of persons, the louse's
voracious appetite produces relations of dependency and lack that return us
to the figure of human insufficiency with which this chapter opened. As we
shall see, the frail but insatiably devouring parasite offers the Janus face of
the lacking and prosthetically enhanced human with which we began.

Of Lice and Men

The immense fold-out engraving of the louse in the *Micrographia*—the
largest in the collection, showing a louse some twenty inches long—dwarfs
even the folio pages of the book (Figure 4). Depicted in isolation, without
any caption or indication of scale, the creature floats on the space of the page,
unmoored from a context that would help identify this alarmingly alien,
militaristic creature. Like other bodies glimpsed through Hooke's microscope, the louse belongs to a world neither peaceful nor orderly. While
Hooke's human-made artifacts seem pocked, stunted, scarred, his natural

objects appear as hostile forces amassed at the borders of our world: swollen with poisoned sacs, encased in scales, bristling with spikes and barbs. Only the written description clarifies that what might be construed as a weapon clutched in its claws—"the long transparent Cylinder FFFF"—is in fact "a Man's hair," an identification (as with the full stop) that helps rescale the louse to its actual size (*Micrographia*, 212). Indeed, so bizarre are the images produced by the microscope that "if a louse or flea, or such like insect, should look through a microscope," Margaret Cavendish observed, "it would be . . . much affrighted with its own exterior figure."[88] The louse gets a glimpse of its magnified form and screams in horror.

The louse was a common figure of perverse sociability in satires, doggerel verse, riddles and mock-epic poetry from the period, and would have been a familiar creature to Hooke's readers from the perpetual war waged against all manner of vermin. While principally the scourge of the poor, the louse infested all ranks, from the crowns of princes in St. James to the "sturdy Beggar's Smock" in St. Giles, as one Grub Street hack put it, binding high and low together through a common revulsion.[89] "The antipathies of mankind"—like their tastes—"are various," Oliver Goldsmith would observe a century later, but "all seem to unite in their dislike to the Louse, and regard it as their natural and most nauseous enemy."[90] The host of a perpetual house party populated by gate-crashing guests, the louse-ridden body suggests that the individual is never not embroiled in relations with an other, exposing the difficulty of defining the literal threshold of individual beings, where one body—one life—ends and another begins.

Although, as Addison argues, the microscope shows that "every living Creature is inhabited," Hooke's famous image presents the louse in solitary splendor, connected to the human world by a single hair.[91] Its isolated figure is thus cut off from what was generally understood to be the most distinctive aspect of insect life: its teeming multiplicity.[92] There is, in real life, never one louse or one mouse. The anthropomorphic allegory with which Hooke opens his observation acknowledges the louse's ubiquity, while casting the louse as a singleton, a thrusting social climber:

> This is a Creature so officious, that 'twill be known to every one at
> one time or other, so busie, and so impudent, that it will be intrud-
> ing it self in every one[']s company, and so proud and aspiring withall,
> that it fears not to trample on the best, and affects nothing so much
> as a Crown; feeds and lives very high, and that makes it so saucy, as

to pull any one by the ears that comes in its way, and will never be quiet till it has drawn blood: it is troubled at nothing so much as at a man that scratches his head, as knowing that man is plotting and contriving some mischief against it, and that makes it oftentime sculk into some meaner and lower place, and run behind a man[']s back, though it go very much against the hair; which ill conditions of it having made it better known then trusted, would exempt me from making any further description of it, did not my faithful *Mercury*, my *Microscope*, bring me other information of it. (*Micrographia*, 211)

After pages of description of the articulated joints of a flea's leg or the mechanisms that allow an insect snout to bore into flesh, the shift to narrative, as Cynthia Wall points out, renders "an unseen world visible and *alive* with motion, plot, characters, space," restoring vivacity to a text that is perhaps getting too mechanical.[93] Oscillating between agent and object, the louse pinned beneath the microscope is nevertheless rhetorically active in its own self-presentation, pushing itself forward without a proper introduction. Common ("known to every one") and yet elite (it lives and eats "high"), the louse at once moves beyond its proper place and is always in its proper place, for it makes its home anywhere. A great leveler, the louse, like its social analogue, refuses to acknowledge or respect individual borders or social distinctions. Simultaneously democratic in its favors (it infests all heads impartially) and aristocratic in its aims (it aspires to the crown), the louse possesses the attributes of human character (it is officious, impudent, proud, and saucy).

Hooke's brisk, cheerful description masters the horror-movie potential of the monstrous creature in the plate through the deflationary humor of an anthropomorphic allegory that is as much of its historical moment as the compromised apologetic masculinity of *Honey, I Shrunk the Kids* is of an era of suburban domesticity. Extreme magnification impels a kind of affective downsizing, an economic adjustment that rechannels the surge of horror and disgust at the magnified object into a comic register. Hooke offers a sequence of puns that brings together bodies personal and politic, playing on the literal and metaphorical senses of crown, drawing blood, pulling others by the ears, going behind another's back. Such rhetorical acrobatics run counter to the "plain style" of the New Science celebrated in Sprat's *History of the Royal Society*, which strives to "separate the knowledge of *Nature*, from the colours of *Rhetorick,* the devices of *Fancy*, or the delightful deceit of *Fables*."[94]

Hooke's puns suggest an irresistible human impulse to play with words—Hooke the bricoleur tinkering with his prose. Yet the pun that reduces the word to sound, like the ink splotch that converts writing to shapeless mass, also brings us into abrupt contact with the intractable material core of language, suggesting the way words, those most human of artifacts, escape our complete mastery. (We shall return to the pun in the next chapter's discussion of the riddle.)

Hooke's wordplay suggests a state seething with plotters—surely not what Hooke intended in a book printed under the auspices of the Royal Society and dedicated to the king. Indeed, the allegory itself manifests unexpected sympathy for the traitor louse, as Hooke reverses perspective (and sides) mid-passage. If initially it is the seditious louse that undermines the peace "till it has drawn blood," it is subsequently the human that is perceived by the louse as "plotting and contriving some mischief against it" (211). To the human its unwelcome visitor is a noxious irritant; to the louse the scratching hand is an interruption of its meal, as the reach of the hand of the Crown sends the louse into hiding, in a "meaner and lower place," itself part of the body that shelters the seditious vermin. Yet Hooke's playful allegory and his toying with perspective do not on their own tell us anything new about the louse. Indeed, the ubiquity of the louse, Hooke remarks, would "exempt me from making any further description of it, did not my faithful *Mercury*, my *Microscope*, bring me other information of it" (211). You think you know the louse, Hooke implies, but what you know is the *anthropomorphized* version, refashioned after a human image. The magnified louse, as the plate indicates, is something else altogether.

Hooke shares with writers of the period a sense of the nigh unbridgeable alterity of insects: they are, as one writer put it, "formed of parts so different from ours, that we can probably conceive no more idea of the use of some of their organs, than a man born blind or deaf can of the senses of vision or hearing. They may have senses different from ours."[95] He does not, however, use the louse as a prompt for an occasional meditation on God's presence in the natural world, after the fashion of his patron Robert Boyle, and his praise for the ingenuity of God's workmanship never reaches the exalted heights of the Dutch naturalist Jan Swammerdam: "Herewith I offer you the Omnipotent Finger of god in the anatomy of a louse."[96] Nevertheless, he finds the intricate assemblage of interlocking parts that make up the insect's mechanism to be a miracle of design, taking pleasure in the seamless connection of function and form celebrated by physico-theologists, such as William Ray and William Derham.[97] Thus, although the placement of the eyes on the side of the head robs the louse of "foresight," it enables the forelegs to cleanse its lidless eyes; the want of eyelids, Hooke surmises, must be a product of its customary haunts in the dark recesses of the hair: "The open and clear light, especially that of the Sun, must needs very much offend them" (*Micrographia*, 211). The louse's claw—furnished with "joints, almost like the joints of a man's fingers, so as thereby it is able to encompass or grasp a hair as firmly as a man can a stick or rope" (171)—does not quite rise to the level of an opposable thumb, but it is ideally suited for its purpose (locomotion) and its environment (scalp as landscape). Nature, Hooke notes, appropriates "instruments, so as they are the most fit and convenient to perform their offices, and the most simple and plain that possibly can be" (171). The louse's foot is shaped like this because this is what it does.

Nevertheless, Hooke is not always sure what he is seeing. Poor illumination, he complains, makes it difficult to discern the nature or purpose of various parts of the louse: "If it be plac'd on its back, with its belly upwards . . . it seems in several Positions to have a resemblance of chaps, or jaws, as is represented in the Figure by EE, yet in other postures those dark strokes disappear" (*Micrographia*, 212). Worse, the disposition of organs is not a reliable sign of function: the louse's eyes, Hooke notes, are "where other Creatures['] ears stand"; its long horns are "in the place where one would have thought the eyes should be" (211, 212; for other examples, see 177, 183). Only careful observation of the body in motion reveals the nature of the parts, as the mysteries of anatomy are dispelled through mechanism: "About A there seem'd a contrivance, somewhat resembling a Pump, pair of Bellows, or Heart, for by a very swift *systole* and *diastole* the blood seem'd drawn from the nose, and forced into the body" (212). It is not likeness but use that ultimately enables Hooke to determine whether what looks like a mouth is in fact one: Hooke finds, "upon letting one creep on my hand" to feed, that it "did neither seem to thrust its nose very deep into the skin, nor to open any kind of mouth" (212). From the visible passage of blood from his body to the louse's belly, Hooke infers that the snout must "have a small hole, and to be the passage through which he sucks the blood" (212), but he cannot see it. He perceives the effect, but not the means, and back-forms a cause from the observed outcome. (Hooke elsewhere finds it necessary to amputate crustacean appendages to determine the purpose of various organs based on the creatures' subsequent behavior [178].)

Yet Hooke's observations are marked by a haptic and visual intimacy with the louse that exceeds the strictly mechanical. After starving the louse for several days, he places it on his skin and watches his own blood surge into its body, documenting the lankness and tautness of the belly when empty and engorged, the altered textures of its shell or skin as it feeds. Simultaneously subject and (partial) object of his own observations, Hooke watches his blood course through the louse's organs, becoming a hydraulic element in the mechanical processes of digestion. "I could plainly see the blood, suck'd from my hand, to be variously distributed, and mov'd to and fro" (212). The objective distance of the impartial observer is belied by the fusion of bodies, though Hooke underlines that he feels nothing, not "the least discernible pain, and yet the blood seem'd to run through its head very quick and free" (212). The incorporation of his hand into a living circuit with the louse prompts observations on the human body as well: since the louse's minuscule snout can so easily siphon off its dram, human blood, Hooke concludes, must be dispersed through the skin very close to the surface.

The Protestant Hooke's use of his own body as food for his experimental subject possesses no Christ-like sacramental valence, although the blood's alteration in color suggests a kind of transubstantiation: "The digestion of this Creature must needs be very quick, for though I perceiv'd the blood thicker and blacker when suck'd, yet, when in the guts, it was of a very lovely ruby colour, and that part of it, which was digested into the veins, seemed white" (213). Hooke is particularly struck by the louse's insatiability and by the rapidity with which the blood is expelled as excrement—the conversion of Hooke's own body fluids, before his eyes, first to food and then to feces. If the transfusion creates a material link between man and insect, between vital matter (blood) and waste, it also suggests the limits of autonomy and bodily self-possession in creatures bound together in a food chain. At what point does the substance of Hooke's body come to be part of the louse? Is it, as Sterne's Tristram asks of Locke's paradigmatic apple, "when he digested?—or when he——?"[98]

Like Hooke's gleeful characterization of social-climbing vermin, the blood transfusion suggests a kinship between louse and man that belies the abyssal difference of kind. On these terms, Hooke's anthropomorphic allegory does not simply domesticate the alien form of the louse by casting it into a human guise; it recalibrates our understanding of the *anthropos* by suggesting that the louse may already be integral to what we are. The louse suggests that we are always already bound up in exchanges—sometimes reciprocal, sometimes not—with other bodies and things. Living beings do not start out in serene autonomy and gradually open up channels to the outside; instead, we are constituted through these relations. The anthropomorphic allegory that depicts the louse in human guise conversely suggests that the human might be understood as a parasite. "We have made the louse in our image," as Michel Serres puts it, "let us see ourselves in his."⁹⁹ Hooke's anthropomorphism of the louse on these terms seems less an effort to bring a deeply alien species closer than a recognition that human and parasite are already kin. For if the allegorical louse undercuts the fiction of human autonomy, it is a fiction that Hooke, as we saw in the opening section of this chapter, never fully endorsed. Hooke's confidence that human lack can be supplemented through devices that expand the body's powers beyond its immediate bounds results in an artificially enhanced creature that is parasitically dependent on its instruments. Put more simply, the louse recapitulates the prosthesis in another register.

The spiraling turn from Hooke's prosthetically enhanced Promethean figure, to louse, to louse-eaten body suggests the exclusions and inequalities instituted by human "advancement," but it would be up to other writers—above all, a witheringly skeptical Margaret Cavendish, Duchess of Newcastle—to recognize the shortcomings of Hooke's prosthetic gods. A full half-century before Swift's excoriating portrait of the New Science in Book Three of *Gulliver's Travels* (1726), Cavendish's *Observations upon Experimental Philosophy* (1666) and her utopian *Description of a New World, Called the Blazing World* (1666)—that "work of fancy" she joined to her "serious philosophical contemplations"—mocked the delusions of experimental philosophy.¹⁰⁰ Empowered by her rank but marginalized by her sex, Cavendish famously dismissed Hooke and his confederacy of gentlemen scientists as so many boys with their toys, who "play with watery bubbles or fling dust into each other's eyes."¹⁰¹ The aspiring scientist does not perch on the shoulders of giants but lurches on stilts seeking to elevate his or her views. "Magnifying glasses," in Cavendish's trenchant appraisal, "are like a high heel to a short leg, which if it be made too high, it is apt to make the wearer fall." The prosthesis meant to correct or amend instead causes the body to totter, as those who become absorbed in these "deluding arts" stumble from the path of right reason.¹⁰²

Thus when the Empress of Cavendish's Blazing World is shown a magnified louse by her proud experimental philosophers, the hybrid "Bear-Men," she is prompted not to wonder at its glories but rather to pity "those that are molested with them, especially poor beggars, which although they have nothing to live on themselves, are yet necessitated to maintain and feed of their own flesh and blood, a company of such terrible creatures called lice, who instead of thanks, do reward them with pains, and torment them for giving them nourishment and food."[103] The human resurfaces here not as autonomous observer, political subject, or possessive individual but as suffering body. The privation of the beggars who "have nothing to live on themselves" does not exempt them from becoming food for vermin; cast from the pinnacle of the food chain, the human body becomes a literal and figurative host, so vulnerable that it cannot even claim thanks rather than pains for its provender. The vermin-infested body that constitutes the first property of the Lockean individual cannot be counted as fully his (or her) own. The sovereign subject has become occupied territory.

If this chapter began with a fusion of body and prosthesis that fostered Hooke's fantasies of cyborg empowerment, it ends with the devouring of a starveling's flesh by vermin. The prosthetic devices on which Hooke erects his "empire of the senses"[104] prove to be pilings driven into marshy ground. For even Hooke's devices did not protect him from the gnawing depredations of animal nature. Hooke apparently became something of a miser in his old age, clutching at his worldly goods and increasingly disinclined to impart his ideas in a bitter affirmation of his sole propriety over his inventions. But he did not die alone. It was reported by one Thomas Kirke that Hooke "was soe lowsy when He dyed that there was no comeing near him & his own Cloathes or rather raggs wrapt him like Searcloth [i.e., cerecloth, a winding-sheet], this is the exit of Dr Hooke."[105] Hooke's louse-ridden corpse is an admonitory reminder of the body's base materiality: irrespective of our Promethean aspirations and accomplishments, we are all food for worms. Michel Serres's incisive if cryptic insistence that "one has to speak of Prometheus from the bird's-eye view—that of the eagle"[106]—knocks us from the lofty perch of the soaring raptor at the pinnacle of the food chain to the debased position of a parasite picking at the liver of a fallen demigod. Neither the eagle, from its lofty heights, nor Prometheus, the master thief cursed by the gods for stealing fire to relieve a lacking humanity, can escape from the circle of devouring or being devoured. And even as the bringer of fire to humankind is reduced in the end to bird food, so too does Hooke become fodder for the very vermin he studied beneath his microscope. On these terms, humanity's Promethean aspirations to exceed our organic limits give us the instruments with which to scrutinize the depredations to which our animal bodies are inescapably bound. Hooke's prosthetic gods chisel away the ground on which he aspires to stand.

CHAPTER 3

Anthropomorphic Things

Mouth of a jar, eye of a needle, head of a nail, face of a mountain. Our daily vocabulary teems with anthropomorphisms—so much so that the humdrum everyday world might seem a mere inch away from the fanciful animated kettles and dancing brooms of a Disney film. Such borrowing from the human body to describe things, the Neapolitan philosopher Giambattista Vico argued in his 1725 *New Science*, resides at the origin of human language:

> It is noteworthy that in all languages the greater part of the expressions relating to inanimate things are formed by metaphor from the human body and its parts and from the human senses and passions. Thus, head for top or beginning; the brow and shoulders of a hill; the eyes of needles and of potatoes; mouth for any opening; the lip of a cup or pitcher; the teeth of a rake, a saw, a comb; the beard of wheat; the tongue of a shoe; the gorge of a river; a neck of land; an arm of the sea; the hands of a clock; heart for center (the Latins used *umbilicus*, navel, in this sense); the belly of a sail; foot for end or bottom; the flesh of fruits; a vein of rock or mineral; the blood of grapes for wine; the bowels of the earth.[1]

Like the invasive species of the trope world, anthropomorphism crowds out all other forms, replicating human likenesses everywhere. Vico's extraordinary catalogue of anthropomorphisms—the beard of wheat, the tongue of a shoe, a vein of rock—restores the living flesh in the dead metaphor, awakening the monstrosities slumbering within language made unremarkable by long use.

Why, Vico asks, do humans have this tendency to recast things in their own image? Our propensity for anthropomorphism, he argues, is

> a consequence of our axiom that man in his ignorance makes himself the rule of the universe, for in the examples cited he has made of himself an entire world. So that, as rational metaphysics teaches that man becomes all things by understanding them (*homo intelligendo fit omnia*), this imaginative metaphysics shows that man becomes all things by *not* understanding them; and perhaps the latter proposition is truer than the former, for when man understands he extends his mind and takes in the things, but when he does not understand he makes the things out of himself and becomes them by transforming himself into them (*homo non intelligendo fit omnia*). (129–30)

Anthropomorphism is elicited by the opacity of the world to our minds. Rather than envisioning an empowered bestower of names, such as Adam in Eden magisterially labeling a world created for his rule, Vico offers us a confused projection of the self onto a dimly understood world, the imposition of human likeness a sign not of mastery but of incomprehension. Borrowing from the substance of the human body to paper over a gap in knowledge, the human wields anthropomorphic language so as to substitute the self for a void. Like a tyrant who erects a statue of himself on every corner, Vico's man thinks he is seeing an endorsement of his power, but what might at first glance seem to be a sign of anthropocentric dominion proves instead to be a mark of humanity's tenuous command over the external world.

Indeed, the wanton projection of self onto thing ricochets back onto the human. If, as Vico's "rational metaphysics" would have it, understanding allows man to "take in" all things through an extension of the mind that preserves the integrity or essential difference of external objects, the anthropomorphism of his "imaginative metaphysics" compels man, in his incomprehension of the nature of things, to make "the things out of himself." And this refashioning of things after a human image not only falsifies their nature, it also entails a form of self-loss. In seeing himself in things (in making "things out of himself"), Vico's man makes himself into a thing ("becomes them by transforming himself into them"). Humanity comes into being in a reified form forged out of its own ignorance. The anthropomorphic thing is thus both a symptom of humanity's overweening drive to refashion the world in its own likeness and a sign of its blind dispossession before things and forces that exceed its comprehension: a testament both to enduring bafflement before the enigmatic face of the world and to the unending endeavor to recast it into intelligible form.

In this chapter, I want to explore the work of anthropomorphism in a minor literary form, what was, in the eighteenth century, not much more than a parlor game: the riddle. In the riddle, as in Hooke's *Micrographia*, the nature of things is not revealed through mimesis—the rendering of an object with detailed exactitude in order to achieve a realistic effect—but through the deliberate estrangement of a normal human (anthropocentric) perspective. Both the microscope and the riddle are devices that wrest familiar objects from the preordained constructs that make them immediately recognizable by dislodging the eye from its accustomed point of view. Whereas Hooke's *Micrographia* affords a glimpse of the disaggregated sensory data of raw experience, the riddle offers the *disjecta membra* of a body without giving us the identity—the name—that would unite them. Both riddle and microscope shatter the integrity of the individual object, offering a defamiliarizing glimpse of the world without its organizing categories and, in the process, challenging the primacy of humanity as exclusive agent and organizing center of the world.[2] In making visible what Michel Serres calls "the brackets and parentheses, syntheses, whereby we shove multiplicities under unities,"[3] the riddle does not simply magnify or distort an already known thing (a formula that can, like anamorphosis, be run in reverse); it suggests that the entity that we thought we knew might be something else entirely. By prying objects from ready intelligibility, from their unremarked assimilation into habitual practice, the riddle interrogates our presumption that we know what a thing is in the first place. The inexhaustibility of certain riddles, I shall argue, lies not just in the infinitely transformative power of language but also in the opacity it offers up for contemplation.

In what follows, I focus on the tropes and figures that guide us through the collapse—deliberate or undesigned—and reassembly of the scaffolding of the world. The riddle tampers with the machinery that aligns the order of things with language, dismantling the world as we know it to be and even undermining the notion that a human subjective standpoint is the one from which that world is to be known. Riddles play with anthropomorphisms, not only punning on the hands of clocks, the heads of pins, the faces of coins, but also attributing humanlike actions and motives to creatures lacking the proper organs or capacities: "No tears I shed, and yet I always weep," the pen

affirms; "man I ne'er was known to kill,/But ladies blood I often spill," the
needle proclaims.[4] If, as Vico argues, we turn to anthropomorphism when
we are ignorant, when language bottoms out, it is because there is no term
for what one seeks to name. Anthropomorphism, that is, often involves catachresis.[5] Whereas other tropes entail a substitution of figural for literal meaning, of one word for another (part for whole, like for like), catachresis balks
such exchanges (there is no proper term for which to substitute). The slit at
the top of a needle is its eye; there is no other word in English. If anthropomorphism allows us, as Vico puts it, to make "an entire world" from ourselves, it also, like catachresis, spawns monstrosities—cups with speaking lips,
mountains with glowering faces—that convert the likeness discovered in
nature into a grotesque composite. Breaching categories, spawning mutant
hybrids, anthropomorphism undermines the serene human empowerment it
otherwise seems to proclaim.

Vico's use of the term *anthropomorphism*, it should be noted, is an early
outlier. The preferred term employed by writers and critics to describe the
attribution of life, agency, or intention to inanimate things was *personification*
or, less frequently, *prosopopoeia*.[6] The few occurrences of the word *anthropomorphism* to be found in seventeenth- and eighteenth-century texts usually
involve the representation of God with human features. (Anthropomorphism
was, as Lorraine Daston points out, "a theological sin long before it became
a scientific one.")[7] The *OED* lists the first use of *anthropomorphism* in 1650,
while the word only arrives in the 1798 fifth edition of the *Dictionnaire de
l'Académie française*. Although I draw on modern theories to distinguish
between anthropomorphism and personification, my claim is that eighteenth-
century texts are in practice alive to a distinction not made in their language.
Even as anthropomorphism recasts the world in a reassuringly familiar
human form (albeit as a sign of our ignorance), it also hints at forces not
susceptible to refashioning in a human guise—forces that, I shall argue, surface in the form of personification.

Anthropomorphism is not, on these terms, as irredeemably anthropocentric as it appears at first glance. Indeed, inasmuch as it expands the category
of entities deemed capable of acting and responding, by redistributing power
to other forms of life or matter and reanimating elements of the environment,
it may—or so Jane Bennett has recently argued—help "counter the narcissism of humans in charge of the world" by registering what she calls "the
agentic contributions of nonhuman forces (operating in nature, in the human
body, and in human artifacts)."[8] Riddles use anthropomorphism not only to

compel readers to acknowledge a more expansive sense of the agencies at work in the world, however, but also to confront the reader with the limits of human knowledge about the familiar objects that surround us.

For not every riddle yields a neat solution. Although the riddle is overtly dialogic, at its heart lies something resistant to thought, to representation, to communication. The riddle unmasks the fact that, as Walter Benjamin claims, the mimetic must have "something alien as its basis."[9] There is always something leftover, something not incorporated. The question this chapter addresses is why the trope used to give expression to these elusive aspects of the world is so often anthropomorphism. In converting the anthropomorphizing tendency that Vico associates with human incomprehension into an instrument to access the enigmatic properties of things and other creatures, I argue, the riddle reinstates precisely the bafflement that Vico suggests anthropomorphism is designed to dispel.

By withholding the identity of its speaker, the riddle obliges the reader to imagine the world through another's eyes in order to determine the "proper" identity of the riddle-creature.[10] Its first-person form invites an experimental extension of the self beyond the purview of our own species in a deliberate courtship of self-loss. Rather than mirroring the reader as she already is or offering a figure with whom to identify, the riddle steeps us in the lived experience of a radically different form of being. For while the riddle's use of anthropomorphism attests to Vico's human propensity to project our own likeness onto the incomprehensible, it also exposes a human yearning to yield to and become other, to be something different from what we already are. This desire for a first-person experience of other forms of being reminds us that, as Benjamin argues, "mimetic modes . . . of behavior . . . [are] by no means limited to what one person can imitate in another. The child plays at being not only a shopkeeper or teacher but also a windmill and a train."[11] To affirm that our identifications and imitations are restricted to human roles is drastically to curtail the sweeping range of our desires and imaginings.

If the anthropomorphized riddle-creature is partly human, the human is thereby revealed to be partly nonhuman—sometimes animal, sometimes thinglike. On these terms, the shifting use of anthropomorphism in riddles affords a glimpse not only of what Daston calls the ever-altering "sine qua non of the human," but also of "the shape of . . . the nonhuman—the 'morphos' of anthropomorphism."[12] If, as I contended above, the riddle tries to reinstate some of the bafflement that Vico claims anthropomorphism eradicates, it also puts the definition of the human back into play by monkeying around with the shapes assumed by the nonhuman—Daston's "'morphos' of anthropomorphism." It undercuts the assurance that one already knows what the human is. In tracing the shifting line between these broader categories, this chapter explores the ways the riddle uses language—that capacity that supposedly separates human from nonhuman—to explode the division between them.

The riddle makes visible the entangled relations of an ostensibly sovereign humanity with things and other creatures, suggesting that there is no bright line between the human and the nonhuman. Yet the process of solving the riddle is designed to make that bright line appear. Riddles, like the fables to which we will turn in the next chapter, ask us to see ourselves in and differentiate ourselves from animals or inanimate things. But they also do something more, for they demand our highest cognitive skills as humans, requiring that we use language to see what is *not* explicitly there, abstracting an object (or ourselves) from embodied being. Thus, although the imaginative dabbling in a radically other perspective may slide into an ontologically perilous immersion in an alien point of view—the nonsocial, nonhuman, antagonistic vantage of a thing or an animal—the riddle's structure of address ultimately bars full absorption into the perspective of another. In soliciting the reader to exercise the reason that allows for the logical determination of identity through language, the riddle insistently reinstalls its human interlocutor at the heart of its enterprise. Even as it invites us to imagine what it is like to be another creature, it repeatedly marks the distance between its first-person speaker and who (or what) we humans are.

Categorical Questions

Inasmuch as riddles demand to be solved, the claim that riddles reinstate the enigmatic properties of things may seem counterintuitive. To the extent that it has only one answer, the riddle operates as a kind of rhetorical question: a ruse ostensibly open to multiple possibilities that really only accepts one outcome. Such riddles are diversions for an idle hour. Like the microscope, which (as Hooke himself lamented) had rapidly devolved into a trifling "Diversion and Pastime,"[13] the eighteenth-century riddle may be seen as an easily exhausted novelty, a minor suitor pleading for a share of the newfound leisure hours of a growing middling class. Featured in almanacs, jestbooks, puzzle collections, gentlemen's periodicals, and ladies'

magazines, eighteenth-century enigmas are at best dim echoes of the enduringly cryptic Exeter Book riddles, the inscrutable pronouncements of Del-
phic oracles, and Oedipus's life-or-death dealings with the Sphinx. Often
derivative (copycats crop up, uncredited, across the century), they vary
widely in quality, from the mainstream versions that circulated as what we
might now call memes to the more sophisticated enigmas composed by
Jonathan Swift in the 1720s (on which I will largely draw below). Literary
periodicals used riddles, rebuses, and charades to create a community of
readers, publishing the puzzles in one number of a journal or almanac and
the answers in the next (often as verse epistles from readers), a strategy that
not only furnished ready-made copy for the editor but also built a solid
subscriber base.[14] Yet even the mediocre examples offer some of the most
sustained and detailed endeavors in eighteenth-century literature to imagine what it is like to be something else.

Although the fundamental structure of the riddle, as folklorists have
explored, is strikingly perdurable across cultures and epochs, eighteenth-
century riddles tend to be more expansive than the single-line versions of my
childhood ("what is black and white and re(a)d all over?"), usually consisting
of multiple stanzas of rhyming couplets in which an entity (animal, thing,
abstraction, body part, letter, passion) offers a defamiliarizing description of
itself, often in the first person.[15] I single out the riddle in the context of this
argument not because it is unique to the eighteenth century but because both
its form, which attributes a (human) first person to a nonhuman entity, and
its content, which offers a nonhuman perspective on the world, have a great
deal to tell us not only about the conflation of human, animal, and thing
during the period but also about the shifting terms of their separation.

Like it-narratives, those tales told by things and animals that have
recently attracted considerable critical interest, riddles borrow a nonhuman
point of view that underscores the role of objects in the constitution of subjects.[16] Their popularity may be traced to some of the same causes that
account for the proliferation of it-narratives: a burgeoning economic system
that commoditized persons and things alike, the growth of literacy, the swelling
market for entertainment. Whereas the it-narrative typically presents a sweeping portrait of commercial society by offering the backstory of the human
characters encountered by the object (or animal) narrator, the eighteenth-
century riddle is usually a short poem that speculatively confers an "I" on an
unidentified nonhuman other, offering an estranging description of its origins, physical properties, activities, typical history, and ultimate end. In the

riddle as in the it-narrative, the nonhuman speaker traces human social relations through the circulation of commodities, while offering an account of
the origins and uses of these newly available but increasingly familiar objects.
Riddles, however, have a far more expansive catalogue of narrators than it-
narratives, as they assign a speaking voice not only to animals and things but
also to abstract qualities, letters of the alphabet, body parts, and celestial
bodies.

Both the it-narrative and the riddle belong to the discontinuous, epi-
sodic, and often satiric strain of eighteenth-century literature that critics have
recently proposed as a counternarrative to the canonical "rise of the novel,"
offering first-person accounts without much in the way of psychological
depth or continuous action. Because riddles (again like it-narratives) use an
ostensibly human first-person form to point to something inhuman, abstract,
and impersonal lodged within human forms of life, they are able to explore
the mechanisms and structures—economic and political but also linguistic—
that are made by people but that also supersede them. Both take the literally
objective stance of a nonhuman thing seriously in ways that anticipate the
abstract impersonal voice associated with free indirect discourse. Recounted
by a first person without a self, a grammatical subject without a subjectivity,
the unliving historian of a life, the riddle offers an anthropomorphizing narrative without a human to anchor it. By withholding the identity of the
speaker, riddles expose the difficulty of knowing when and whether one is
dealing with a human being to begin with—a pressing question at a moment
in which industrialization, urbanization, global expansion, and above all, the
slave trade thrust person and thing into violent new relations.

My aim is not to insist on the literary greatness of the eighteenth-century
riddle as an undiscovered subgenre (a fruitless endeavor). Many of the riddles
I discuss below are literary one-offs, easily guessed or of no great interest
once the answer is known. As Joseph Priestley observed, "Books of jests,
apophthegms, or any species of mere *wit*, are seldom read a second time.
They will only bear to be repeated in *company*, and in fresh company."[17] The
renewable pleasure of the casual riddle lies less in its content than in its
dialogic performance and the sociable encounters it initiates. The riddle
about the blushing zebra does not furnish any startling revelations about
the occult qualities of a certain striped African equid; instead, the gratifying
repetition of the already known marks childhood initiation into a shared
vernacular. The seeming arbitrariness of the answer—the blushing zebra may
also be a sunburned skunk or a newspaper—suggests that riddles operate as

a shibboleth, consolidating community through an insignificant difference like the pronunciation of a sound, a "ciphered singularity: irreducible to any concept, to any knowledge."[18] They secure the continuity of culture (and of subcultures) not through official nomenclature but through perdurable rites inhering in language: the formulaic repetition of a common idiom in boundary-policing rituals. The riddle combines, as Daniel Tiffany puts it, "obscurity and transmissibility in ways that have distinct implications for social being," serving as a "medium . . . of negative sociability" that creates underground solidarity by marking the password-protected borders of groups.[19]

The question-and-answer form of the riddle establishes a renewable intersubjective dynamic marked by a demand that the interlocutor supply the missing answer: the unidentified first person solicits the second person "you." Possessing, as John Frow puts it, "the agonistic dynamics of question and answer, and the social force of the secret,"[20] the riddle divides power between the riddler (who asks the question and also knows the answer) and the interlocutor (who guesses but without whom the riddle is left suspended, incomplete). If riddles are the language of the disempowered or disadvantaged, they are also a gambit in a power game in which the holder of the answer possesses the power to denominate the nature of a riddled reality: to state *what things are.* Simultaneously overt contest and passive-aggressive negotiation, riddles enact forms of mastery in the guise of play. When told in group settings, riddling, like other guessing games, involves a triangulated display of knowledge and ignorance, although the ability to answer the riddle correctly may or may not be what is truly at stake in a given social situation.[21]

Eighteenth-century riddle collections offer a procession of questing object-supplicants in pursuit of an identity, so many words in search of an author to name them. Riddles recall, Andrew Welsh argues, an Edenic scene in which "an unsurpassed Master of Riddles" brought the beasts to Adam to see what he would call them as a "part of Adam's education, a teaching based on the theory that to find the name of something it is necessary to know it, and to know something it is necessary to see it with clarity."[22] Adam's naming of the animals, as we saw in the previous chapter, was also central to the New Science's understanding of an immediate Edenic insight into the natural world that bound word to knowledge. As befits a fallen world, the riddle runs this process in reverse order, inducing its reader to work backward from the enigmatic description of the object to its name, as it were, christening the object anew. (We return to these questions in Chapter 5.)

Riddles understood in this way obey rules that usually (but not always) facilitate the reinstatement of a "rightful" order of things. Even as the distortion of anamorphosis is corrected when one stands in the proper spot, so too is the riddle's controlled distortion of reality dissolved when one utters the answer. The riddle seen from this point of view becomes an inversion of predicative definitions: whereas definition "leads from a name to its multiple, consistent predicates," as Daniel Heller-Roazen puts it, riddling, by contrast, wends its way "from a set of seemingly incompatible attributes to the common term that can be substituted for them all."[23] The revelation of the name reconciles these incompatibilities and restores the world to intelligibility. The solution distills the elaborate periphrases that make up the poem into a single word that reasserts the proper measured distance between subject and object, promising (or threatening) to contain the mysteries of a thing in the fixity and singularity of the noun. Indeed, one might see the final answer as committing a kind of violence in yoking together the heterogeneous elements of the riddled description, forcing the riddle-creature to cleave to the parameters of its nominal identity.[24]

The riddle understood in this way yields a disenchanted take on the world. Even as it unleashes the power of language to reconfigure reality, it offers the means to break its spell, operating, Northrop Frye argues, as "a charm in reverse: it represents the revolt of the intelligence against the hypnotic power of commanding words. In the riddle a verbal trap is set, but if one can 'guess,' that is, point to an outside object to which the verbal construct can be related, the something outside destroys it as a charm, and we have sprung the trap without being caught in it."[25] Like the magic herbs bestowed by the gods on Greek heroes to protect them from ensorcellment, the solution in Frye's account allows us to pass unscathed through the illusory world woven by the riddle's lexical hex. We witness the power of language without being snared in its toils.

At its most basic, a riddle is a (confusing) comparison. Aristotle classed it as a species of metaphor, which describes one thing in terms of another. ("Clever enigmas," he observed in the *Rhetoric*, "furnish good metaphors; for metaphor is a kind of enigma, so that it is clear that the transference is clever.")[26] Yet the riddle also tampers with the smooth operation of metaphor, producing conceptual gridlock by trafficking between the literal and the figurative. In the folklorist Archer Taylor's account, the riddle contains, on the one hand, a positive description that actually "impl[ies] the answer" but confuses the interlocutor because it is "understood figuratively rather than literally," and, on the other hand, a negative description or "block" that "also contains the answer, but, taken literally, baffles the hearer."[27] Thus the potato, riddled as "has eyes and cannot see," pits the figurative (the potato's eye) against its literal (unseeing) nature, while the louse, described as "a Bosom-friend" who "generally turns a Back-biter,"[28] produces a seeming paradox that can only be resolved by entering into a whirligig between anthropomorphizing idiom and nonhuman referent. The assumption is that the answer will resolve the conflict between literal and metaphorical levels, assimilating all the contradictory elements under the unity of a proper name. Although they are designed, as Taylor argues, to confound what something is and what something is not, riddles typically adhere to a surprisingly rigorous logical structure, as each line of the riddle refines the description to eliminate rival answers. Because the riddle-creature leaps rather than crawls, we know the solution is a flea, not a louse; "head, no eyes" is a pin, while "eyes, no head" is a needle.[29] If riddles tease the imagination with visions of strange hybrid creatures, they also summon reason to tell things apart.

To understand the riddle as a simple bait and switch of answer for question is, however, to miss the point of the exercise, which involves the nonequivalence between the two. If the riddle at first glance possesses the symmetry of a chiasmus, in which the estranging description can swap places with the solution, it also presents the costs exacted by or losses incurred through such an exchange—what is omitted or occluded by the answer. "In the process of finding the name, of reading the unknown in terms of the known," as Andrew Welsh puts it, "paradoxes arise because the unknown never completely fits into the known. The riddle is more than simply substituting one name for another."[30] Riddles make audible the excluded elements necessary to constitute a unity: what must be eliminated as noise or static to produce intelligible speech.[31] Although the notion that a riddle can be solved seems to indicate that the complexity of a body, an idea, a thing can be decanted into the vessel of a single word, riddles also present those aspects of an entity that fall outside the linguistic structures that lasso the world into nominal forms. "Objects," Theodor Adorno observes, "do not go into their concepts without leaving a remainder."[32] The riddle offers a glimpse of that remainder, making it apparent that the word is never entirely equal to the thing: the thing exceeds the word, and the word is a vehicle for more than its ostensible referent.

The point I want to underline here is not that the riddle reveals the poverty of the word vis-à-vis the thing but rather that the riddle unveils the complexity of the linguistic tools that allow the world to become a play-thing of the mind. As Aristotle affirms in *De Poetica*, "The very nature . . . of a riddle is this, to describe a fact in an impossible combination of words (which cannot be done with the real names for things, but can be with their metaphorical substitutes)."[33] By unmooring language from its fixed referential anchorage, metaphors in riddles allow aberrations impermissible in reality and thus reveal the truth of things beneath the logical ordering of the world. The pleasure of the riddle resides less in the solution (which reasserts the normative world) than in the way it allows words and things to swim before our eyes—and admits movement between them. The imagi-nation elects to dawdle in the sensory and intellectual mishmash that pre-cedes or exceeds the assimilation of experience to idea, delighting in the capacity of words to mask and reveal at one and the same time. "The real answer to the question implied in a riddle is not a 'thing' outside it," Frye argues, "but that which is both word and thing, and is both inside and outside the poem."[34]

To give a name to a riddle-creature on these terms is not to exhaust the description or settle the question; it is to reinstate what Benjamin calls the "core that is the symbol of noncommunicability"[35] harbored within language. Riddles allow us to contemplate the prospect that the fog will not be dis-persed, that looking closer does not bring clarity (as we saw with the *Micro-graphia*), that obscurity itself may possess meaning or power. At the margin of every riddle is the possibility that there may be no solution—that there are things in heaven and earth beyond philosophy and language, for which there is no name, no metaphor, no idiom: what has not been assimilated to or mastered by an idea. It is when we encounter this opacity that we summon anthropomorphism, in Vico's account, but riddles, I contend, also point to where anthropomorphism falters. They reinstate the impenetrability of things and other creatures and even ourselves—what refuses the anthropomorphic taming of an alien nature.

Because it withholds the name bestowed on the thing—the missing ele-ment that organizes the poem is the name of its speaker—the riddle provi-sionally balks the work language does to tailor the world to a human perspective, requiring the reader to dabble in an alien perspective in order to work the object into its "proper" identity or category. In the process, the riddle makes the "thingness" of the thing visible. As Tiffany puts it, the riddle "withholds the name of a thing, so that the thing may appear as what it is not, in order to be revealed for what it is."[36] It lures the interlocutor into a series of category errors that present an animal in a human guise, an inanimate thing as an animate creature, revealing the singular object to be a kind of hybrid compounded from incommensurables. Thus the speaker in Jonathan Swift's pen riddle mutates from a part of a living animal as feather, a made thing as quill, an instrument plied by human hands as pen, and the issue of the human mind as writing:

> In Youth exalted high in Air,
> Or bathing in the Waters fair;
> Nature to form me took Delight,
> And clad my Body all in White:
> My Person tall, and slender Waste,
> On either Side with Fringes grac'd;
> Till me that Tyrant Man espy'd,
> And drag'd me from my Mother's Side.[37]

Swift's riddle-creature proffers a series of possible identifications (as human, as mythological creature, as animal) and snatches them away. We encounter what might be seen as a bird or an aerial spirit ("exalted high in Air"), a nymph ("bathing in the Waters fair"), or a human being (possessed of a "Person tall" and "slender Waste").

If the pen is initially described as a work of nature—"Nature to form me took Delight,/And clad my Body all in White"—it is subsequently refashioned by human hands, savagely plucked from its "Mother's Side," seized by "Tyrant Man," and tortured. Although the riddle turns away from the directly mimetic reproduction of what is seen by the naked eye, it requires the imaginative reconstruction of the origins, activities, and properties of its speaker—what Northrop Frye describes as the riddle's distinctive "fusion of sensation and reflection, the use of an object of sense experience to stimulate a mental activity in connection with it."[38] In reinstating the material and labor that produce the finished object, and recalling the uses to which it is put, the riddle reminds us of the obscure origins and ends of objects that we treat as known entities. Like Hooke's efforts to imagine the fly's experience of time from the rapid beat of its wings, the riddle involves a virtual reconstruction of the empirical world from another point of view.

The process by which the feather is converted into a pen is described in unrelentingly brutal terms. The anthropomorphism reconfigures the trimming of the down and barbs from the feather's shaft as a kind of rape and torture of the quill:

The Tyrant strip't me to the Skin:
My Skin he flay'd, my Hair he cropt;
At Head and Foot my Body lopt:
And then, with Heart more hard than Stone,
He pick'd my Marrow from the Bone. (ll. 10–14)

The passage confers the properties of an entire living body—skin, hair, head, foot, marrow, bone—on the unidentified speaker (an entity that miraculously outlives its evisceration to tell its own tale). That we do not know the class of being to which the violated body belongs lends ethical force to the riddle, as we judge the actions described through a kind of Rawlsian veil of ignorance, assessing their savagery without reference to the nature of the victim. Without knowing who or what is being injured, we have no scale to appraise the damage: is a child being beaten, or a carpet? The nature of the action is determined retroactively by knowledge of the object.[39] In this sense, the riddle's withholding of identities exposes the sliding ethical scale by which we appraise our deeds. Although the solution to the riddle mitigates the horror of the stripped and flayed body by identifying it as a feather, the bait and switch of one body for another brings home the immense violence harbored in the artifacts of high culture (such as writing).

   Although the opening lines tempt us to think we are in the presence of a being like ourselves, the riddle rapidly disabuses us of any sense of fellowship. The speaker despises humanity:

To me he chiefly gives in Trust
To please his Malice, or his Lust,
From me no Secret he can hide;
I see his Vanity and Pride. (ll. 21–24)

Privy to its owners' hidden desires, vanities, and malevolence, the pen—like the it-narrator—is witness to and instrument of human self-exposure. The pen admits no complicity in the deeds it enables, although it relishes the unacknowledged dependency of humans on its support: "Without my Aid, the best Divine / In Learning wou'd not know a Line" (ll. 29–30). The pen prevents the lawyer from "forget[ing] his Pleading" and allows the scholar to "shew his Reading" (a phrase that reduces learning to mere display) (l. 31, 32). Writing ceases to be an aid or prosthetic and replaces the mind altogether, even as the pen as metonymy for the writing hand comes to supplant it. Human capacities are outsourced to or overtaken by our tools, converting us into pawns in a larger game that the riddle enables us to recognize. If anthropomorphism (as Vico argues) gives expression to what we do not understand, then perversely, paradoxically, it presents in humanlike form those very aspects of our own humanity that escape our control and our understanding.

The agency of the pen in Swift's riddle goes well beyond the movement of quill over paper. Although the pen may seem a tractable servant, it wields immense power over the very lives from which its anthropomorphic form has been siphoned: "Nay; Man, my Master, is my Slave: / I give Command to kill or save" (ll. 33–34). The pen does more than we know; usurping the first person of the writer, it makes and breaks people. If the pen's arrogation of the "I" enables it to personify executive powers that exceed even the individual, it simultaneously negates (or consummates?) its own anthropomorphism by revealing its inhumanity toward man. The bleak truths recorded by Swift's pen involve not the way humans use things but the way we use one another.

Like other pen riddles, Swift's is a song of lost innocence, as the oritinal white of the feather is literally soiled by ink and metaphorically defiled by the sordid transactions in which it is embroiled. It is telling in this regard that the closing lines of riddles deictically reference the present and ongoing activity of the riddling object—which should (but does not necessarily) tip us off to the identity. Thus, Swift's pen:

> while I thus my Life relate,
> I only hasten on my Fate.
> My Tongue is black, my Mouth is furr'd,
> I hardly now can force a Word. (ll. 37–40)

Choking on its own words, the speaker self-referentially annihilates itself in producing the text we are presently reading, converting "its autobiography into its own obituary," as Luke Powers notes.[40] The anthropomorphism here simultaneously makes the pen human (with its black tongue and furred mouth) and reminds us of the thinglike elements of humanity. The ease with which we take nonhuman for human, inanimate for animate, in our daily practices suggests that we are (and treat one another) more like things than we thought.

Riddles deliberately call the nature of humanity into question. Although the attribution of first-person speech anthropomorphizes the riddle-creature, the speaker repudiates the identification. The riddle-creature takes on the human capacity for language and then, as Tiffany wonderfully puts it, "by speaking, sheds its human qualities yet goes on speaking. The thing becomes human and then performs a verbal striptease in the dark, before our eyes, divesting itself of its human attributes."[41] The riddle, that is, presents the creature or thing in an anthropomorphic guise and then systematically unveils the differences between human and nonhuman forms. In the process, riddles also call into question the presumption that we already know what humanity is—an assumption that seems to lie at the heart of anthropomorphism.

Yet perhaps anthropomorphism, rather than simply applying a received prior definition of humanity, as Vico presumes, helps produce it. In his analysis of Nietzsche's famous definition of truth as a "mobile army of metaphors, metonymies, anthropomorphisms," Paul de Man argues that anthropomorphism is a distinctive trope precisely because it posits what the human is. Whereas metaphor and metonymy involve "proposition[s]" about the likeness and proximity of entities *to one another*, anthropomorphism "is not just a trope but an identification on the level of substance"; it does not point to a relation but imposes a form on the entity so figured, turning anthropomorphism from a trope into an absolutely singular designation. "Anthropomorphism freezes the infinite chain of tropological transformations and propositions into one single assertion or essence which, as such, excludes all others," de Man argues; it "takes one entity for another and thus implies the constitution of specific entities prior to their confusion, the *taking* of something for something else that can then be assumed to be *given*."[42] That is, anthropomorphism, by claiming to figure an entity *as* human, stipulates what humanity is. The traits that the pen ostensibly borrows from humanity produce the concept of what humanity is then said to be. Like the residue left in an alchemist's crucible, humanity is a kind of precipitate of anthropomorphism.

On these terms, de Man argues, anthropomorphism operates not as a trope but as "a proper name, as when the metamorphosis in Ovid's stories culminates and halts in the singleness of a proper name, Narcissus or Daphne or whatever" (241). De Man designates anthropomorphism as a proper name rather than a trope, Barbara Johnson explains, because what it figures is arbitrarily designated but irremediably fixed. Yet the examples of proper names he singles out are peculiar, for they are drawn from myths of metamorphosis: Narcissus and Daphne. Johnson focuses on the symptomatic fact that gender surfaces at this particular juncture in de Man's theory, which otherwise has little to say about sexual difference.[43] That a definition of anthropomorphism brackets gender exposes the fact that the *anthropos* is a normative figure that excludes some humans from its template; I return to this below. For now, I want to point out that Narcissus and Daphne attain fixed forms that are not or are no longer human (a flower and a laurel tree). The proper name that for de Man illustrates the fixed form of anthropomorphism, that is, belongs to a *former* human being. What is "human" in the proper name de Man represents as a figure for anthropomorphism is at best a weird remainder or residue that outlives all these transformations or metamorphoses in order to give its name to *something other* than what it was (a flower rather than a beautiful lad).

The temporal structure of the trope is crucial here. De Man suggests that anthropomorphism institutes the idea of the human in the process of exchange or rather in its wake; it is when something else is taken for the human that the human "can *then* be assumed to be *given*" (first italics added). The *then* in the final clause is important; it is *after* we anthropomorphize an entity that we think we have established what the human is. We point to something and claim it is made in our image to know what we are. On these terms, metamorphosis (ceasing to be human) is essential to the establishment of a definition of humanity on the far side. The riddle, which obliges us to pass through the anthropomorphic figure, produces a definition of the riddle-creature but also of the human from which that creature is finally distinguished. In the process, it rattles the epistemological grid that holds the order of things in place, precipitating a collision between the organizing categories that sort the world into kinds—animal, vegetable, mineral—and revealing the falsification involved in treating things as if they happily roost in neatly demarcated pigeonholes. It is to the challenge that riddles pose to the order of things as articulated in language that I now want to turn.

Talking Tropes in Riddles

Riddles expose the tension between the unique properties of individual bodies and the fact that words spill across the partitions that separate bodies into kinds. As one folklorist observes, "Riddles play with boundaries, but ultimately to affirm them (like a child playing with mud to find and define the boundaries of his body). Shared characteristics between categories are a threat to the distinctiveness of the categories; riddles examine those things that are shared and pinpoint those that divide."[44] In this section I focus on the tropes (anthropomorphisms, puns, catachreses) that incessantly traffic across the thresholds that ostensibly separate human and nonhuman. If bodies prove to be extraordinary hybrids, words too pertain to more than one kind; indeed, they possess a versatility that bodies cannot attain. "We have no way of defining, of policing, the boundaries that separate the name of one entity from the name of another," as de Man puts it. "Tropes are not just travellers, they tend to be smugglers and probably smugglers of stolen goods at that."[45]

Tropes in de Man's terms are telltale signs that our cultural baggage needs to be searched: commonplace things prove to be compounded of those elements from which they are ostensibly the most distanced. Even a familiar object such as a glove marks the spot where animal, human, and thing converge and are divided. Made from the skin of calves, sheep, goats, and other animals, the leather glove is a thing that sheaths the hand, the body part often understood to be a signal distinction between human and animal. Glove riddles foreground this category confusion, proffering a series of possible identifications (as human, as animal, and as thing) and then snatching them away.

> Tho' my parents were poor, and had nothing to leave,
> But their coats on their backs, when they went to their grave;
> I soon got them dy'd; and as spruce as an heir,
> Who mourns for the loss of his father, appear.[46]

The glove-child literally inherits the coat on its parents' backs; it *is* the skins flayed from their bodies. Indeed, its parents' death is the condition of the glove's existence. Recasting the dyeing of the gloves into the bereaved son's flaunting of his newly inherited fortune, the riddle satirizes the brutally unsentimental relation taken by humans to loss, converting the material fabrication of the thing into a chapter in a human life history (and perhaps the other way around, insofar as human rites of passage are marked in a commercial society by cosmetic makeovers).

Like the it-narrative, the riddle often offers a kind of autobiography of its speaker. Thus the glove traces its life history from birth and the softening education that removes its (literal and figurative) "roughness" to its social circulation in the world and ultimate demise:

> And though to Brutes my Birth I owe,
> And so my Pedigree's but low,

By Education's friendly Aid,
See! what Improvement may be made.[47]

What is described as an animal ("to Brutes my Birth I owe") possesses the grammatical powers of a human speaker that behaves like a person but proves to be a thing. Both metonymic and synecdochal figures for their possessors, the gloves describe themselves as enjoying a social life contiguous with but separate from the hands that wear them ("At plays, at balls, we your diversions share, / With your devotion mingle when at pray'r") but they also take on human guise ("I dress like the ladies.—A girdle my waste [sic] / Surrounds, that my shape mayn't be farther increas'd").[48] Yet the anthropomorphizing of the thing does not give it equal standing with the human, or rather it exposes the inequalities that mar human relations with one another. Like the sylphs in *The Rape of the Lock*, the gloves are unremarked laborers: "All night we sport it with the fair, / Play with her fan, or . . . adjust her hair." They acquire a voice in order to proclaim their joyous servitude and perpetual readiness to hand: "Your entrance on the stage of life we wait, / Attend your youth, your nuptials celebrate."[49]

In mimicking the capacities (and making up for the fragility) of the hand, the glove incarnates both the human ability to instrumentalize nature and the inadequacy of the body without the supplement of things. It thus indicates the capacity of humanity to make itself an object in its quest for perfectability (discussed in Chapter 2). Even as the glove is the product of labor and technology, so too is the hand an artifact "highly perfected by hundreds of thousands of years of labour," as Frederick Engels puts it.[50] The refinement of the object or artifact involves a refashioning of its maker, and in this sense, the retroactive structure we discovered in de Man's analysis of anthropomorphism is also central to the fabrication of objects, which likewise come to remake the template on which they were modeled. If humans have fashioned an object that copies a hand, the glove in turn imitates and even supplants it. "I have never seen as yet," one of the gloves brags, "A HAND I could not counterfeit."[51] Punning on the hand as body part and as penmanship, the glove boasts of its skill at forgery, but the reciprocal shaping of glove and hand, of subject and object, reminds us that imitation is a two-way street. The copy may refashion the original.

The melding of hand and glove suggests that the riddle's anthropomorphism is less the confused or terrified projection of human likeness onto

inanimate others that Vico describes than a way of acknowledging the mirroring relations between persons and things, humans and animals. Each contributes to the elaboration of the other. The recognition of similarities in the
riddle form points to the mimetic faculty that Benjamin describes as a vestige
of a primal human propensity to become other: "Nature creates similarities.
One need only think of mimicry. The highest capacity for producing similarities, however, is man's. His gift of seeing resemblances is nothing other than
a rudiment of the powerful compulsion in former times to become and
behave like something else."[52] Nature makes similarities, but humans are
prompted by resemblance to remake themselves. What for Benjamin lies
behind the recognition of likeness in others is this distinctively human
impulse toward self-transformation. We seek to become like things, not, as
in Vico, to make things like us.[53] We recognize likeness in things beyond
ourselves because we ourselves possess a capacity to become something other
than what we already are, because we yearn "to become and behave like
something else."

Not someone. Something. It is not the imitation or mirroring of another
person that is at stake here but the impulse to become the thing, the something, one is not. The compulsion that leads us to find similitude in other
entities issues in Benjamin's account from a form of mimesis that involves
not the fabrication of objects but the making and remaking of the self: "Our
gift for seeing similarity is nothing but a weak rudiment of the once powerful
compulsion to become similar and also to behave mimetically."[54] Anterior to
our fearful or magisterial refashioning of others after our own image is a
prior imitation—the vestige of that "powerful compulsion in former times to
become and behave like something else." Anthropomorphism as the recognition or production of similarities in other beings is less the empowered refashioning of other creatures in our likeness (or the terrified projection of our
semblance upon them) than the recollection that we make ourselves after
theirs: it is not that we make things and other creatures to be like us but that
we recognize what it is in them that we have copied. The riddle repeatedly
directs our attention to the complexity of this two-way street—not least by
foregrounding the work done by language in capturing these similarities.

In Swift's candle riddle, for example, anthropomorphism reveals how the
properties of things have furnished figures for the most fundamental human
experiences and elements, including the soul. The poem opens with a self-
description that emphasizes the speaker's hybridity: "Of all inhabitants on

earth, / To Man alone I owe my birth," Swift's candle begins. "And yet the
Cow, the Sheep, the Bee, / Are all my parents more than he."[55] Molded by
human hands but made of tallow or wax, the candle describes itself as the
impossible offspring of human and animal (ruminant, ungulate, and insect).
In describing both the provision of raw material (tallow or wax) and the labor
of fabrication as forms of parentage, the riddle presents its speaker as both an
organic and a manufactured body—and an explicitly female one at that. The
candle is

> Big like *Bess*, and small like *Sue*;
> Now brown and burnish'd like a nut,
> At other times a very slut;
> Often fair, and soft, and tender,
> Taper, tall, and smooth, and slender. (ll. 28–32)

Alternately squat pillar and slender stick, the candle suggests various women's
body types.

Anthropomorphism surfaces in the candle's physical resemblance to the
human body, but it is the candle's properties, baked into idiom, that shape
human descriptions of ourselves (to carry a flame, the light of one's life).
Objects are conscripted into figurative service that yanks them away from
their ostensibly proper function. What drives the riddle are the figurative
associations of the candle derived from its physical form—the nursed flame
of unrequited love, burning desire, the ephemerality of life—that operate
independently from the object. The riddle puts these idioms back into contact with the material bodies from which they are derived, at times to bawdy
effect. The guttering flame that indicates the wick requires trimming is recast
as a "languid . . . love-sick maid" to whom "steel . . . affords present aid" in
a lewd double entendre (l. 41, 42). The extended pun on "die" with which
the poem concludes likewise fuses erotic consummation with the snuffing
out of life and the extinction of physical desire (the snapping of the "fatal
thread" to which the wick is compared [l. 45]). The candle is said to

> Die like lovers as they gaze,
> Die for those I live to please;
> Pine unpitied to my urn,
> Nor warm the fair for whom I burn. (ll. 49–52)

Casting more light than heat, the riddle-creature's demise is central to its figurative life. The riddle's polysemy moves us between different linguistic planes and invites us to recognize that words enjoy a life of their own.

This polysemy is marked by the fact that riddles are riddled with puns. Along with anthropomorphism, the most common trope in the riddle is paronomasia (or pun), whose etymology from *para* (beside or beyond) and *onomázein* (to name) suggests the secret lives led by the word, independent of the object. If, as we saw above, the name that solves the riddle cannot exhaust the mystery of the thing, the opposite is also true: the thing cannot exhaust the word. The pun requires us to recognize that the same names can be annexed to radically different entities and, indeed, can mean completely different things. "The eye" is not exclusive to humanity but shared by animals and even by needles; the horn-speaker in Swift's riddle describes itself as "The Joy of Man, the Pride of Brutes, / Domestick Subject for Disputes," simultaneously musical instrument, animal antler, and metaphorical sign of human cuckoldry.[56] Riddles play on the multiple valences attached to single words, taking off as full-fledged puns when the riddle-creature acts: when, for example, the eye and the needle "see well" or when "Spirits" raised "from below" by Swift's riddling corkscrew "rise, walk round, yet never fright."[57]

The pun—"two meanings competing for the same phonemic space or . . . one sound bringing forth semantic twins,"[58] in Geoffrey Hartman's neat definition—traffics across contexts and organizing systems, offering an estranging glimpse of what a word might point toward when inserted in another signifying chain—what happens, say, when an object bolts between dimensions or when the ostensible referent proves to be something else entirely. As Hartman's phrasing suggests, the pun entails simultaneously the contestation of multiple meanings in a single word and the irrepressible fecundity of language associated with Bakhtinian heteroglossia. It suggests both the proprietary struggles over sense that occur in language and its overflowing abundance.

Mikhail Bakhtin's famous dictum that "the word in language is half someone else's"[59] is fully realized in the pun, which hijacks meaning from the mouth of its speaker. Whether deliberate or inadvertent, clever or cheesy, the pun snatches the word from the syntagmatic operation of the sentence, making it impossible to maintain a stable perspective on the sentence as a whole (as if one word, magnified out of all proportion, becomes the fulcrum that turns the rest of the sentence into a teeter-totter). The pun's disorderly conduct violates Augustan decorum, exciting the disdain of Joseph Addison and

Richard Steele in the *Spectator* and the *Tatler*. Punsters, Steele complains, "need not be concerned with you for the whole Sentence, but if they can say a quaint thing, or bring in a Word which sounds like any one Word you have spoken to them, they can turn the Discourse, or distract you so that you cannot go on, and by Consequence if they cannot be as witty as you are, they can hinder your being any wittier than they are."[60] Steele's punster takes pleasure in the *wrong* kind of relation—one grounded in an arbitrary homonymy rather than a reasoned connection between ideas. In reducing intelligible speech to syllables, fragments, mere sound matter, the pun strips language of its expressive legitimacy and communicative functions. As the epigram to the issue of the *Spectator* devoted to false wit puts it, "*Operose Nihil agunt*," or "They laboriously do nothing."[61] Like the riddle's circumlocutions, the pun's divergences are a kind of Rube Goldberg linguistic machine that diverts the proper channel of the discourse, introducing contortions that add no value or that bring rational conversation to a standstill. Derided by Addison as "a Sound, and nothing but a Sound," the pun becomes a kind of *res*, a sonic filibuster or linguistic roadblock to useful communication or true wit.[62]

Steele is concerned not just about the abduction of meaning but also about the violation of sociable conventions: the disruption of the hierarchies that govern conversational norms. Even as punning mixes senses through a similitude of sound, so too does it puncture Steele's careful divisions among kinds of wit and classes of men. The condemnation of the pun by arbiters of taste suggests an effort to hold upstarts at bay, above all, in the coffeehouses, taverns, and clubs where the mixture of ranks challenged the intellectual elite's monopoly on wit. On these terms, Alexander Pope's assertion that punning is "a contagion that first crept in amongst the first quality, descended to their footmen, and infused itself into their ladies" recasts potentially subversive wordplay as a derivative practice in a defensive assertion of social control.[63] For inasmuch as the pun undercuts the unitary nature of the word, it is often antiauthoritarian, "an agent of disorder, a disturbing influence."[64] In precipitating a collision "between accident or meaningless convergence and substance or meaningful relation,"[65] it levels hierarchies of language through the arbitrary affiliation of words. The pun's subversion (playful or earnest) of the rules of proper diction helps align the riddle with the off-kilter perspective of the underdog.

Puns expose the fact that language is never univocal, and like the riddle, they remind us that language's sole function is not "the clean transmission of a pre-existing, self-sufficient, unequivocal meaning."[66] In the riddle as in the pun, the shortest distance between two points is not necessarily a straight line. We must swerve to arrive at the solution. Thus, when Swift's circle describes itself as "up, and down, and round about, / Yet all the World can't find me out," it offers a telltale self-description (it is "round about" in appearance) that also points to its immediate presence (it is somewhere "round about" us) in lines that enact (in a "roundabout" description) our failure to see what is before our very eyes, while playing on the larger mathematical failure to "find [its] measure."[67]

The riddle exploits the pun to spin literal and figurative meanings together in an engineered breakdown of official meaning. It takes what Addison and Steele consider to be the leaden weight of the word as mere sound and uses it to release language from its anchorage in a single object. Puns in riddles allow the reader to cast off into a new dimension: the contingent sonic connection provides a switchpoint for one-track minds, opening up the multiple meanings borne by an individual word or thing. The pun parasitically siphons meaning from a word's primary sense, or rather, it asks us to consider how we decide which sense is primary. Indeed, language itself might be said to originate in a similar splintering of unitary sense. Samuel Beckett's parodic aphorism in *Murphy*—"in the beginning was the pun"[68]—strips the world of its founding logos, offering as origin a language divided and playing against itself. It can be difficult to sequester the pun from other forms of language, to know which words *are not* puns.[69] Is there any word that might not be turned from its purported proper use? (Indeed, etymology at times seems like a pun tricked out in respectable guise.)

Even Addison's abhorrence of the pun does not lead him to characterize it as an unnatural aberration: "The Seeds of Punning," he acknowledges, "are in the Minds of all Men" and "will be very apt to shoot up in the greatest Genius, that is not broken and cultivated by the Rules of Art." The detection of similitudes (as we saw with Vico's anthropomorphism and Benjamin's mimetic faculty) is essentially human: "Imitation is natural to us, and when it does not raise the Mind to . . . noble Arts, it often breaks out in Punns and Quibbles."[70] Understood as a kind of unchecked overflow, punning may thus simply be our shape-finding, similitude-seeking minds exercising their powers—Benjamin's mimetic faculty doing its thing. But it may also be the nonhuman agency or *instance* of language asserting itself, as if, in Culler's words, "language has ideas of its own."[71] Inasmuch as unintended wordplay makes us the plaything of the language we ostensibly control, punning defies neoclassical aspirations to see wit as "an act performed by a free human agent and a practice regulated by norms of sociality," as Neil Saccamano has argued. The pun suggests that the speaker or writer is governed by "the perverse contingency of linguistic materiality."[72] Humans become the material used by language rather than the other way around. As Saccamano puts it, "The moment that nonsignifying, chance relations of language direct poetic production, the human face of sense seems to become only a figure drawn by language to express its own proper agency."[73] We retroactively represent the effects of language as if they were caused by our conscious designs in a desperate effort to keep language *human*. The riddle, I want to argue, marks humanity's effort to turn this contingency to its own ends—and yet the moment the speaker in the riddle is revealed to be nonhuman, the anthropomorphized first-person "I" comes to appear uncannily like Saccamano's "human face of sense" drawn by "language to express its own proper agency."

Indeed, in some riddles, language itself acquires a voice to "express its own proper agency." In riddles by letters, vowels, and parts of speech, language talks back to those who wield it. Swift's vowels—"little airy Creatures / All of diff'rent Voice and Features"—describe themselves variously as "in Glass . . . set" or found "in Jet," obliging the reader to switch from semantics to orthography, from imagining the object (glass, jet) to seeing the word in which the letter is embedded.[74] If the pun reduces the word to its sonic form, here the vowel riddle-creatures transform themselves into alphabetic ciphers on the page, obliging the reader to fracture the word into its component parts. In interposing the letter between word and meaning, Swift makes the medium into the message. To solve Swift's riddle, one must toggle between text and page in the kind of now-you-see-it-now-you-don't movement we encountered with the trompe l'oeil.

In emphasizing the material form taken by language, Swift draws attention to the kinship between the riddle and the rebuses or "hieroglyphic epistles" that enjoyed a vogue during the period. If the vowel-riddle-creatures materialize as alphabetic figures on the page and the pun transforms the word into its sound image, the rebus compels the reader to move between literal and figurative, between writing and speech, between the syntagmatic and paradigmatic orders of language. Often presented as epistles, rebuses such as the "Hampton Court Letter Being a Reply to the Epsom Lady's Answer" (Figure 5) convert language into a series of graphic puns, requiring the reader to derive the message from the sound of the word associated with the object that the image denotes. If the presence of text in a painting, as Michel Butor has argued, reminds us "that writing is a visible thing[,] . . . drawing,"[75] here pictorial and written language meet in a visual tabula that can only be made meaningful by recourse to another sensory dimension (sound). The rebus creates a kind of sensory metalepsis.

To decipher the rebus, the reader must convert the image of an object first into its name and then into a sound and thence into a word to be threaded into a sentence. Thus the picture of a "witch" becomes the homonym "which"; images of a yew and a ewe stand in for "you." At times, objects (the stars, for example, or the joined hands) stand for themselves, while at others they require the reader to shift between literal and metaphorical registers: an eye placed under a mine becomes "I undermine." Alternately the object may allude to the spelling of the word ("s" before an image of a "hall" is "shall"). Since the individual objects may represent an entire word or simply a syllable, the gaps do not indicate discrete syntactic units. Producing meaning involves a slow movement from one fractured sign to the next, a practice less like reading than like translation or the painstaking sounding-out of letters in learning to read.[76] The reader accepts and rejects possible meanings for each image, based on their compatibility with the overall sense of the sentence. Only retroactively does the coherent phrase or sentence become apparent.

Although the sentences obey the laws of English grammar, the rebus itself is a veritable smorgasbord. Nothing unites these objects on the same tabula. Indeed, they defy categorization: a coin is juxtaposed with a comb, a hart with a hat, their position in the syntax of the image governed by the sound image associated with the name of the represented thing. Moreover, there are typically no logical links between the object depicted and the meaning of the word. The rebus converts language from a sequence of univocal signs that permit the exchange of preestablished messages into an instrument whose plasticity and capacity to reconfigure the world is itself the object of representation. Words cease to be the fixed tokens of a meaning that resides elsewhere and become themselves objects of play. The reduction of word to sound, rather than serving as a deadening reminder of the materiality that encumbers lofty ideation, offers an occasion for the mind to exercise its powers, as the rebus disaggregates language to allow for its pleasurable reconstitution.

Although Swift disdained the rebus as "a *Paraphrase* made on a *Punn*,"[77] his riddles similarly explore the processes by which mere sound becomes meaningful language—and vice versa. His echo riddle, for example, converts

Figure 5. "Hampton Court Letter Being a Reply to the Epsom Lady's Answer." (London: Andrew Johnston, 1710). 1868.0808.3433, British Museum, London. © The Trustees of the British Museum.

the hollow repetition of others' voices into dialogue. As the speaker of the riddle, the echo ceases to be a void that simply bounces words back and itself becomes the originating speaker. Yet in making its mimicry of others' words into an object of play, the echo sports with the way language escapes intentions as it is produced and reproduced. Indeed, it threatens to transform the most personal of laments into the mechanical repetition of empty cries reflected back from an abyss.

> Let the Love-sick Bard complain,
> And I mourn the cruel Pain;
> Let the happy Swain rejoice,
> And I join my helping Voice.[78]

Usurping the first person of the plaintive poet or the joyous shepherd, the echo poses a problem of possession: Whose words are they? And how is one to know the difference?

While the echo replicates the original utterance, the echo *riddle* offers a distorted semblance and demands that its reader work to detect a similitude. Even as Swift's echo exults in its ability to imitate all, it dissolves the singularity of its first-person voice into other creatures:

> Now I am a Dog, or Cow,
> I can bark, or I can low,
> I can bleat, or I can sing,
> Like the Warblers of the Spring. (ll. 9–12)

The first person here fractures into multiple voices as it describes, in human language, its mimicry of animal sounds. The riddle (like the echo) both splinters (or doubles) the first person and usurps the singularity of each successive "I." Worse, the echo's repetitions level human language and animal sounds, suggesting that the lovesick bard's complaints are no different from a calf's bawling or an alley cat's yowling.

The simultaneous plenitude and vacuity of the echo means that the "I" is always a hair's breadth away from disappearing altogether—"I hate a silent Breath, / And a Whisper is my Death" (ll. 29–30). Like the echo, the riddle offers a first person without an actual speaking subject or reflexive consciousness, a pronoun without a real-world antecedent, an "I" without a face. On these terms, what ultimately unifies the fragmented elements of the riddle-creature's self-description is little more than the persistence of the first-person "I"—a continuity secured not through psychological depth or a referential body but through a grammatical subject: the person in a purely linguistic sense. In its first-person impersonation of (third-person) nonhuman entities, the riddle reveals the impersonal elements that eighteenth-century grammarians and riddlers locate at the heart of the "I," exposing in the process the nonhuman linguistic elements that shape anthropomorphism.

First-Person Impersonal

One of the more surprising genealogies in literary history derives the subjective immediacy of the lyric from the impersonal voice of the nonhuman riddle-creature, threading the emotional outpourings of the first-person subject through the figure of the nonhuman other. In the form of the Anglo-Saxon riddle, Daniel Tiffany argues, "lyric poetry first emerged in English as the enigmatic voice of certain highly wrought objects."[79] To see the riddle as the nonhuman antecedent of the lyric, that most humanly expressive of poetic forms, is to acknowledge the impersonal elements that potentially reside at the heart of first-person speech. If, as Northrop Frye argues, "in the history of literature the riddle, the oracle, the spell, and the kenning are more primitive than a presentation of subjective feelings," the beginnings of lyric are to be found not in an understanding of poetry as "a *cri de coeur* . . . the direct statement of a nervous organism confronted with something that seems to demand an emotional response" but in modes that turn away "from obvious (i.e., descriptive) meaning."[80] Milton's *L'Allegro* is not an exposition of "'I feel happy,'" Frye acidly notes. Lyric, like riddle, insists that opacity is part of the speaker's essence. It tells its truths slant, through "a subtle and elusive verbal pattern that avoids, and does not lead to, such bald statements" (81). Rather than seeing subjectivity or self-expression as the alpha and omega of lyric, we must reenfold the unassimilable into our account.

Indeed, it is perhaps the mysteries of the outside world that summon the inner world into being. In steeping us in the impossible first-person viewpoint of a nonhuman entity, the riddle, like lyric, sounds the mysterious depths of the self, offering an oblique image of the subject that it calls into being. It reminds us that lyric, like narrative fiction, offers unattainable knowledge of other human beings: "what writers and readers know least in life: how another mind thinks, another body feels."[81] The impossible imagining of the somatic experience of an object is a dry run for imagining that of another human being. We accede to the first person by taking a circuit through the impersonal.

Not all riddles, to be sure, use the first person. Perhaps the most famous riddle in the Western literary tradition, that of the Sphinx, does not. Many eighteenth-century riddles do, however, and in extending the first person to non- or extra-human entities, the riddle brings to the surface the complex modes of reference implied by the pronoun "I." Like the riddle, which gives voice to an unknown entity, "I" always harbors within it a certain mystery. The pronoun conveys, as one eighteenth-century grammarian puts it, "no precise idea of itself."[82] Not unlike the *cogito*, it affirms a speaker's existence, without stipulating content. The fact that "I," the most personal of personal pronouns, is shared by all speakers means that it is simultaneously singular and general—an infinitely replicable structure of absolutely specific indexical self-reference that is not bound to anyone in particular. As the twentieth-century linguist Émile Benveniste succinctly puts it in his *Problems in General Linguistics*, "The instances of the use of *I* do not constitute a class of reference since there is no 'object' definable as *I* to which these instances can refer in identical fashion. Each *I* has its own reference and corresponds each time to a unique being who is set up as such." *I* and *you* are thus not mere proxies (substitutes for an antecedent), but self-constituting in their immediate reference to the speaker. That is, the reality to which *I* or *you* refers is discursive, not referential; it does not refer to "'objective' positions in space or time but to the utterance, unique each time, that contains them."[83] The pronoun relocates the site of enunciation deictically, recalibrating the entire linguistic GPS in relation to a new point of view. On these terms, the extension of the first person to nonhuman entities not only breaks the human monopoly on language but also organizes the world around a nonanthropocentric center.

Eighteenth-century grammarians were alive to the oddity of the pronoun—the complexity of its modes of reference; its status as a placeholder for a (sometimes uncertain) antecedent; the problems of (deictic) reference to the here and now that it raises. (They even contemplate versions of what is now called the "answering machine paradox": the simultaneous truth and untruth of "Hi, it's me; I'm not here right now.") Inasmuch as it implies capacities such as language and self-referentiality, grammarians consider the first-person "I" to be exclusive to human beings. "*I* and *we*," William Ward argues in his 1765 *Essay on Grammar*, "are equally the names of *any one or*

more objects who speak and name themselves," whereas the third person refers
to an entity lacking those capacities: "All objects which are neither considered
as speaking and mentioning themselves in what they say, nor as distinguished
by being mentioned in words particularly addressed to them, are of the third
personal species."[84] To bear the first- or second-person pronoun is to be able
to wield or be interpellated by language; the third person, on these terms,
belongs to an entirely different class of being. "Nouns," the grammarian
James Elphinston asserts in his 1765 *Principles of the English Language
Digested,* "can neither speak nor be spoken to; and so are all of the third
person."[85]

Benveniste elaborates on the implications of the sharp distinctions
between the *I-you* dyad and the third person made by these eighteenth-
century grammarians. Inasmuch as the first-person "I" is the one who speaks
and the second-person "you" is the one who is addressed, the "I-you"
together form a relation through which each person is specified, defined
uniquely each time. The third person is excluded from this dyadic relationship as the object spoken of; indeed, Benveniste insists, the third person is
"not a 'person'" at all.[86] (Anyone who has been referred to in the third person
while standing in front of the speaker can attest to the occasionally alienating
effect of this form of speech, although the convention may also be a polite
deflection of direct address—*and for the gentleman?*) Inasmuch as the difference between the third person and the *I-you* dyad is the difference between
being a person and a "non-person" (Benveniste's word),[87] the riddle's conversion of the third person of a thing or animal to the first person potentially
carries high stakes, for the dialogic structure of the riddle both animates the
riddle-creature and gives it the power to solicit *us.* By conferring a grammatical person on a nonhuman entity, the riddle, like the apostrophe, "enables
the poet to transform an 'I-it' relationship into an 'I-thou' relationship, thus
making a relation between persons out of what was in fact a relation between
a person and non-persons."[88] In assigning an "I" to an entity, and in addressing another as "you," the riddle instantiates a person—which is not to say
that the person is human or even, necessarily, anthropomorphic. (We shall
return to this later.)

We saw above that the solution to the riddle (the name) does not necessarily equal the sum of its described parts. The pronoun "I" likewise exists in
excess of the proper name. The pronoun, the eighteenth-century rhetorician
César Chesneau Dumarsais insists, is *not* a simple substitute for an antecd-
ent; it marks out a point of view. Neither *I* nor *you* is "*a simple deputy, whose*

duty is confined to figuring in the place of another."[89] Whereas some personify the pronoun as a dogged understudy diligently reproducing the figure of the other for which it stands, Dumarsais argues that the pronoun is not just designed to revivify an idea while avoiding the repetition of the noun. (Indeed, he notes that discourses often *begin* with the pronoun and thus have no antecedent. In such cases, the pronoun *posits* its subject rather than pointing back to an anterior subjectivity.) Instead of serving as a surrogate for the person who holds a point of view, Dumarsais argues, *I* and *you* "are like so many proper names for these points of view" (3.332). We see this when we replace the pronoun with a noun or proper name. The latter cannot, he contends, "express all the idea, the entire point of view of the mind [*de l'esprit*], the full sentiment of the one who speaks" (3.333). The "I" is thus *not* entirely interchangeable with the name that serves as the solution to the riddle.

The asymmetry between the first person and the denominated speaker is apparent in Swift's riddle of the five senses. Speaking in a collective "we," the senses disaggregate the unity of the subject into a *plural* first person, describing themselves as emissaries who carry reports of their empirical experience to a council room over which a common or internal sense presides. Although they are a close-knit band of brothers—"All of us in one you'll find, / Brethren of a wond'rous Kind"—each is absolutely sundered from the rest: "Yet among us all no Brother / Knows one Tittle of the other."[90] The personified senses lead curiously autonomous lives both vis-à-vis one another and vis-à-vis the body of which they are part. No one sense can be taken synecdochally for the whole; each offers separate intelligence about the world, and none shares the experience of the other, which means that the poem's speakers do not know and cannot disclose their own identity. Although the "we" speaks as one voice, the riddle multiplies the speaker into five separate entities that do not add up to the unity of an individuated self. Swift creates a sensory division of labor so absolute as to balk any communication between them:

> Pierce us all with wounding Steel,
> One for all of us will feel.
> Tho' ten thousand Can[n]ons roar,
> Add to them ten thousand more,
> Yet but one of us is found
> Who regards the dreadful Sound. (ll. 21–26)

Whereas in the previous chapter the prosthetic augmentation of the senses with Hooke's "artificial helps" exposes the unprotected body to overwhelming assault, in Swift's riddle, no augmentation of the stimulus (ten thousand cannons firing) can overcome the partition of the sensible. The ear cannot see and the eye cannot smell.

Rather than representing the objects we see, hear, smell, taste, touch, the riddle embodies the processes of the mind, inviting us to reflect on *how* we sense and how we are able to reflect on how we sense. Yet it is hard to know how entities that know nothing of one another can come to speak with a collective "we," particularly given that the synthetic consciousness to which they report also escapes their knowledge:

> We in frequent Councils are,
> And our Marks of Things declare,
> Where, to us unknown, a Clerk,
> Sits, and takes them in the Dark.
> He's the Register of All
> In our Ken, both great and small. (ll. 5–10)

If the senses are part of the unity of the body ("All of us in one you'll find"), Swift's clerk "to us unknown" suggests the mysterious impenetrability of the consciousness to the senses, or of ourselves to ourselves. The riddle-creatures themselves encounter a kind of riddle-creature. What Swift personifies as the "Register of All" seems to be a version of Locke's "thinking thing,"[91] the consciousness that allows for reflexivity and continuity of identity. Yet that consciousness is precisely what the poem's unnamed first-person speakers describe as unknown. That is, what we would normally consider the first person, the governing consciousness or "I," is presented here as a shadowy third person, a clerk industriously recording "our Marks of Things . . . in the Dark" (ll. 6, 8). The complete dissevering of the senses from the unifying consciousness make it difficult to locate the "thinking thing" that integrates their reports. How can the riddle-creatures inform us of what they do not know? Where, so to speak, are "we"?

By giving a separate anthropomorphic life to the senses, Swift's riddle destabilizes any tranquil vision of centralized human command. The speakers simultaneously acknowledge the dominion of a unifying common sense— "He's our master, we his Tools"—and insist on their blind power to convert their master to a puppet: "We can, with greatest Ease, / Turn and wind him where we please" (l. 12, ll. 13–14). The reader is called upon to exercise the very faculty that has been described as unknown to the senses in order to recognize a disarticulated version of herself or himself. Swift's riddle allegorizes the opacity of the self to the self. I argued earlier that the riddle is designed to expose the non-fit of word to thing (the fact that there is always some surplus not assimilated to language). Inasmuch as the grammatical subject ("we") possesses powers the referential subject (the five senses) lacks, the first person itself implies a kind of excess vis-à-vis the noun as well.

Presenting a first-person account of a third-person entity, the riddle offers a symmetrical inversion of free indirect discourse, with its third-person rendering of a first-person consciousness. Whereas free indirect discourse often uses the authority of the narrator to offer both the character's thought processes and commentary thereon, the riddle withholds a normative vision of the world until we arrive at its solution. The first-person self-description of the riddle-creature proposes an equivalence between subject and predicate that may or may not be realized—that may or may not add up to the (fixed) identity proposed by a proper name. The unanswered riddle allows the unidentified first person to "float," but it also exposes the possibility that there is no there there: that subjective effects may emerge without a subjectivity to produce or anchor them. And even after the speaker is identified, the first person points to a remainder that cannot be captured or exhausted by the name—an asymmetry that leaves a mystery at the heart of the riddle, even after it has been "solved."

Indeed, the first-person voice in riddle is strangely impersonal, grounded in the continuity of the grammatical subject (the person in its reduced sense). The particularity the riddle unveils is not psychological but categorical; it involves not the identification of *who* but the designation of *what* one is. The answer to the Sphinx's riddle is "man," not "Bob." The riddle-creature's name refers not to a human individual but to the irreducible particularity of a general class, usually introduced by an indefinite article: *a louse, a cat, a vowel.* Indeed, the rare riddles that describe specific humans gravitate toward personalities or types: such famous politicians as William Pitt and Charles James Fox or such biblical figures as Adam and Eve.[92] These riddles usually read like a game of twenty questions or offer their answer as a kind of antonomasia—a proper name (Nero) invited to stand for an entire category (tyrants).

Riddles often conclude with a plea: *now tell me my name.* They thereby make visible the classificatory systems that govern the basic units of cultural

distinction and similitude, indicating both the minimal differences that separate proximate categories and the levels of taxonomical specificity at which a
given culture operates. Systems of classification, as Claude Lévi-Strauss argues
in *The Savage Mind*, determine the point at which we arrive at the proper
name, the term "assigned to a level beyond which no classification is requisite,
. . . represent[ing] the *quanta of signification* below which one no longer does
anything but point."[93] A name designates the level of particularity that makes
one thing *not* interchangeable with another, that renders it categorically *itself.*
Yet proper names, Lévi-Strauss observes, are not the sole province of individual human beings; we name pets, for example, and exceptionally valuable
objects such as the *Mona Lisa*. What allows an entity (including a human
being) to acquire sufficient particularity to merit a proper name?

Lévi-Strauss argues that the operations by which individual personalities
are differentiated are similar to those by which we distinguish the quiddity
of classes of animals or things. The extreme particularity we associate with
the individuals on whom we bestow proper names, he argues, is not a manifestation of reason or self-consciousness but the result of a social development
in which biological individuals are urged to develop a "personality" that renders each human being a class of its own (which perhaps also helps to explain
the evolution of lyric from the riddle, as individuals acquire the particularity
previously associated with classes of things). That the differentiation of an
individual human personality parallels the differentiation of a class or species
is perhaps most evident in the perturbing eighteenth-century use of proper
names to mark an entire class: an "abigail," generically, for a maid; "Mungo"
for an African man.

Eighteenth-century uses of the term *personality* bear out Lévi-Strauss's
claim that the particularizing of a class parallels the particularizing of an
individual. In period usage, *personality* primarily signifies the "quality, character, or fact of being a person, as distinct from an animal, thing, or abstraction" or "the quality, condition, or fact ascribed to God of consisting of three
distinct persons."[94] In its political and legal senses, it refers to the status of a
civil or juridical subject. The modern sense of *personality* as that "quality or
collection of qualities which makes a distinctive individual" first emerges,
according to the *OED*, in 1711, in an entry describing the duplicity of a man
who "seems to be two Persons for he hath two Personalities in him." (The
1795 example likewise merits quoting for its coupling of individual personality as a quantifiable something one "has" with a type-casting antonomasia:
"Marmontel observes that even a French girl of sixteen, if she has but a little

personality, is a Machiavel.") Although personality in the psychological sense would seem to be a far cry from the earlier categorical uses of the term, these impersonal classificatory valences shape the modern usage. Even as personality comes to be "decisively internalized," Raymond Williams observes, it is "internalized as a possession, and therefore as something which can be either displayed or interpreted."[95] Personality on these terms *reifies* the distinctive traits that particularize a person. Indeed, as personality ceases to be something one 'has' and becomes something one 'is,' it becomes the object of a cultic fixation: "The empirical person, just as he happens to be, is posited and transformed into a fetish."[96]

If personality assumes a fixed form that enables us to classify individuals as types, it is because, as Frances Ferguson points out, personality for Lévi-Strauss operates according to the logic of totemism, the cultural practice that arrests the "incessant process of analogizing that searches out meaningfulness and represents its own motives indexically—by pointing to something whose sacredness to a particular group is demonstrable (and particularly demonstrable because of the unlikelihood that anyone outside that group would recognize its power)."[97] Whereas the totem organizes and particularizes groups, "personality" creates human singularity. "Among ourselves," Lévi-Strauss argues, "this 'totemism' has merely been humanized. Everything takes place as if in our civilization every individual's own personality were his totem."[98] Ferguson describes Lévi-Strauss's totemic personality as a form of personification, which animates a set of traits to create a postulated individual essence to which we simply point, declaring those qualities to be inherent. Rather than personifying trees or lightning, "we personify persons now . . . creating 'sainted mothers,' 'honored fathers,' and 'cherished offspring,' among others."[99] Although it is tempting to affirm that human individuals cannot be personified—you can make me the personification of kindness or cattiness, but you cannot personify *me*—Ferguson's argument suggests the particularity of individuals issues from the impersonal operations of personification rather than from emotional or psychological attributes.

The consolidation of the disaggregated self around personality makes the individual—the "first person" that bears a proper name—distinct within the broader class of humankind. Riddles reveal this process of particularization in much the same way that the estranging self-description of the riddle-creature makes visible the traits that define the category to which it belongs. In the final section of this chapter, I argue that this particularizing of persons through personification is connected to the particularizing of humanity through anthropomorphism. Whereas for Lévi-Strauss and Ferguson, personifications produce individual personality through the totemic elevation of specific traits as the sign of individuality, anthropomorphism produces species difference through the totemic elevation of specific traits as the sign of humanity: by abstracting and condensing particular traits, anthropomorphism creates the illusion that the category of humanity exists in a knowable form. That is, anthropomorphism depends on a kind of personification of humanity—a stipulated definition—that we take as given. It is to the interplay of personification and anthropomorphism in the riddle's first-person animation of nonhuman entities that we now turn.

Riddle Me This

Shifting between proper (human) names and species identifications, Swift's riddle "Louisa to Strephon" is a parody of amatory and pastoral poetry. A kind of literary parasite on these antecedent forms, the riddle also savages a long tradition of works from Ovid to John Donne that present the flea as erotic *entremetteur*. The poem is almost completely conventional except for its speaker, whose identity, once revealed, transforms our understanding of the whole. As the title indicates, "Louisa to Strephon," unlike many other riddles, is not immediately addressed to the reader: the "you" is Strephon, not us. Bemoaning the unreciprocated affections of an unfeeling beloved shepherd—"Ah, *Strephon*, how can you despise / Her, who, without thy Pity, dies?"[100]—Louisa unlooses a barrage of clichéd questions and complaints. The answers to these questions become self-evident the second one has solved the riddle, for the reply to each of them is the same: the unriddled identity of the louse. How can I despise you? Why do I take it amiss that you wake me with a kiss? *Because you are a louse!* The meaning of the poem is determined by an extratextual reference to the nature of the speaker that converts the ostensibly rhetorical questions into literal ones. (Louisa's rival likewise appears to be a Medean psychopath until one grasps that "the tender Pledges of our Joy" that Chloe will "with relentless Hands destroy" are lice [ll. 22, 21].)

Lice may turn lovers into scourges, but how is one to know the difference between paramour and parasite? The difference between "Louse" and "Louisa," after all, comes down to the letter *i* and the final vowel. That Louisa is a louse turns romantic platitudes—"When thee I leave, I leave my Life"—from formulaic protestations into biological facts; the metaphorical yearning for the beloved proves to be physiological dependency on the other's flesh (l. 8). The separation of host and parasite ("thee I leave") in the first half of the line, by cutting the louse off from its sustenance, enacts the second half ("leave my Life"). While the chiastic structure of the line suggests a reciprocity that no parasitical relation permits, it also indicates the difficulty in separating speaker and addressee—or even telling them apart. Indeed, one of the central questions raised by the riddle (and by the parasite) involves the ability to distinguish between bodies and lives. What initially looks to be an easily parsed (and thus manageable) difference *between* individuals (Strephon, Louisa, and Chloe; parasite and host) turns out to be a difference *within* in the form of a devouring desire that cannot be eradicated or extricated from the flesh.[101] Nor, it turns out, can language manage these divisions.

In Swift's riddle, as in other louse riddles, the bonds of blood are physical; Louisa's claim to be "of as noble Blood as you" stems from her feeding on Strephon's body. Whereas most louse riddles toy with the debased creature's exalted lineage, Swift uses Louisa's amorous avowals to expose the multigenerational incest that logically follows from her devotion. Parasitism undermines exogamy. Louisa the lover is also child and mother, the "Fair Issue of thy genial Bed," who has produced "tender Pledges of our Joy," all "born from thy Embrace" (ll. 5–6, 22, 24). Louisa's exuberant description of her incestuous transgressions exposes the fragility of the artifices that cleave us into beings distinguished by species, family, generation, individual self-possession, and (easily pregnable) bodily bounds; the louse's declaration that she "Embrac'd thee closer than a Wife" (l. 7) suggests that proximity to our vermin produces an intimacy greater than that experienced with our kin or our own kind.

The ironic displacements in the poem prevent us from siding with Louisa, but it is worth remarking that from the louse's viewpoint, its claims of virtuous affection might be construed as genuine. Like Nietzsche's bird of prey, with its love of the lamb, the louse is sincere in its attachment. Because enjoyment of the riddle depends on an oscillation in perspective that moves the reader from the pleasurable provisional half-misrecognition to an understanding that puts one "in" on the joke, it implicitly lures the reader over to the side of the disenchanted. Although our sympathies may go astray (and we may miss the joke) until we recognize that Louisa is a louse, the solution only yields a deeper riddle, one involving the very nature of human desire and the impulses that drive us to feed on one another in violation of sociability, respect, or care.

Whereas the riddle is nominally meant to reveal something about the nature of the object riddled (the louse), it reveals something about the nature of the object harbored in the *form* of the poem (amatory love). "Passion," Carol Houlihan Flynn observes of the riddle, "becomes the urge to scratch where it itches, desire a physical need to feed on one's host in a condition of perpetual consumption that can only lead to the most radical of solutions."[102] Flynn's "radical solution" entails wholesale destruction, as devouring by another becomes in the final stanza indistinguishable from self-devouring:

> Consider, *Strephon*, what you do;
> For, should I dye for Love of you,
> I'll haunt thy Dreams, a bloodless Ghost;
> And all my Kin, a num'rous Host . . .
> Shall on thee take a Vengeance dire;
> Thou, like *Alcides*, shalt expire,
> When his envenom'd Shirt he wore,
> And Skin and Flesh in Pieces tore;
> Nor less that Shirt, my Rival's Gift,
> Cut from the Piece that made her Shift,
> Shall in thy dearest Blood be dy'd,
> And make thee tear thy tainted Hyde. (ll. 25–28, 37–44)

Louisa compares the shirt bestowed upon Strephon by Chloe to the blood-soaked, poisoned cloak of the centaur Nessus, given by Nessus to Alcides's (Hercules's) wife, Deianeira, with instructions to bestow it upon her adulterous husband in the hope of guaranteeing his constancy. The object meant to arrest the desire of the beloved upon the self proves instead to be the instrument of his destruction; Hercules dies in agony. Should "I dye for Love of you," Louisa declares, her progeny will avenge her death, converting Chloe's charm against infidelity into an instrument of torture, to "make thee tear thy tainted Hyde." Even as the lice are and are not quite part of Strephon, so too does the detachable clothing fuse into the flesh. What once was outside as louse is now located within.

Put another way, the riddle makes Louisa both an anthropomorphized louse *and* a personification of consuming desire. The reader who thinks that (anthropomorphized) "louse" is the solution to Swift's riddle has stopped too soon; Swift requires another turn of the screw. The unriddling of the poem is not simply the revelation that Louisa is a louse but also that the anthropo-morphism is a personification of the not-quite-human drives within. Here it is necessary to underscore the key distinctions between anthropomorphism and personification. Whereas anthropomorphism (as we have seen) stipulates a human form, personification, as Heather Keenleyside has argued, transfers capacities—movement, life, consciousness, sensibility—that are not the exclusive province of humanity but are shared with animals.[103] Personifica-tion does not anthropomorphize an entity (and may even reveal the persis-tence of nonhuman agency within an anthropomorphized body), while anthropomorphism may not bestow the active capacities associated with per-sonification (but may simply attribute a human likeness to an object).

As an *anthropomorphized* louse, Louisa gives a psychological gloss to desire, rendering it subjective and intelligible, communicable in language, directed toward a defined object (Strephon). For as long as Louisa remains a louse, the riddle remains human (so to speak), projecting an anthropomor-phic face on desire (albeit in zoomorphic form). As the *personification* of desire, however, Louisa becomes the figure for inexpressible, even inhuman drives. Personifications resolve inchoate or enigmatic forces into the sem-blance of subjectivity in what Barbara Johnson describes as so many "subjec-tivizations performed . . . upon the unintelligible."[104] If desires were *like* vermin, they would remain two separate entities; if desires *were* devouring vermin, they could be exteriorized and killed; if, however, the devouring desires come from within, they can only be annihilated through the acts of self-destruction with which the poem concludes. Our desires gnaw at our vitals, but unlike lice, they cannot be exterminated. Swift's riddle thus sug-gests that there is a nonhuman element within even the most anthropomor-phic personifications. Louisa understood as personification is *not* a louse, and the sexual impulses the riddle encodes are not animal; they are extra-human drives that propel Strephon to self-destruction. The nonhumanity of Louisa does not lie in the fact that she is a louse, but in the fact that she is a personification, asked to incarnate something that exceeds or is exterior to the human individual. The riddle itself is an anthropomorphism of a personi-fication that reveals the way we recast the extrahuman impulses that drive us in a human form.

Unlike many riddles, "Louisa to Strephon" does not end with a plea to "tell me my name." We were given the proper names up front in the title; they just did not lead to any clear identification of the nature of the charac-ters. Swift's riddle involves a more complex form of reading that goes beyond an easy deciphering. The question raised by the poem's speaker is not only "what am I?" but also "what are you?" When a person, an "I," addresses us and turns out to be something other than what we thought—when what we thought was a human lover turns out to be an anthropomorphic louse and then turns out to be a personification of our own desire—we (as the second-person addressee) are changed in turn. The unraveling of Louisa's identity—that she is a louse—reconfigures Daston's *anthropos*, for the question posed by the riddle revolves around the identity not of the louse but of the human. And the truth of that identity, once the amatory gloss is removed, is brutal in its simplicity: *you are food*. We are left with mere devouring.

What makes Swift's poem simultaneously funny and menacing is not that we may mistake our lovers for lice (or vice versa), nor even that we only recognize the impulses that drive us in the estranged form of a personification. The alarming element of Swift's poem involves the fact that personification does *not* make desire any more comprehensible to us. To say that desire is a devouring louse is to give figurative form to the forces that drive us, but the skin-tearing destruction with which the poem ends is itself a kind of unresolved riddle within the riddle: an insoluble element that makes humanity fundamentally unknowable to itself (and in this sense, the riddle undercuts the notion of humanity as a "given," as "knowable," on which de Man's account of anthropomorphism depends). Louisa as personification at best tells us something about the forms we impose on the obscure impulses of desire to make its operation legible, while Louisa as anthropomorphism would seem to be yet another version of Vico's wanton projection of a human form onto the unknown—a projection that allows us to treat as intelligible what we do not in fact understand. The triumphant moment in which we think we have unmasked Louisa and "solved" the riddle of her identity turns out to be the moment in which our claim to know ourselves is unmasked as a lie. To "know" Louisa is to know that you are not what you thought you were.

This being Swift, the message may be even bleaker still: for it is not just that these tropes allow us to pretend that what we do not understand looks like us; it is that we use these tropes to avoid recognizing that there *is* something that we do not understand, and that what we do not understand may do violence to ourselves and to others. By offering grounds for the assumption that "the human *has been* or *can be* defined," Johnson argues, anthropomorphisms sanction presuppositions that underwrite the laws that govern the world: the indispensable self-evident "truths" that designate the boundaries of human community.[105] The work of anthropomorphism, with its stipulated version of humanity, is stealthy and hard to detect, and it is here, for Johnson, that personification does its most important work. Because personification reveals the humanity created by anthropomorphism to be the effect of a trope, it allows the great begged question of "what humanity is" to rise to the surface. By revealing the rhetorical sleights of hand that instate persons where none exist, Johnson argues, personification reveals the suppositions that we make about the "givenness" of the human in anthropomorphism, yielding (negative) knowledge of what these tropes hide.

For personifications and anthropomorphisms really explain nothing, which is what riddles help us see. Riddles reinstate the opacity of bodies and things—what refuses our anthropomorphic taming of their alien nature—and in the process they remind us of the performative force of obscurity: what is not cognitively mastered may nevertheless act. The significance of the riddle on these terms lies not in the fact that it reveals the "true" identity of the riddle-creature through a defamiliarizing description; it lies in the fact that it reinstates what Johnson calls (in another context) those "gaps in cognition," which, "far from being mere absences," possess "the performative power of true acts. The *force* of what is not known is all the more effective for not being perceived as such."[106] Johnson's point is that this ignorance, and the devices like anthropomorphism that cover over this ignorance, have a great deal of power. "We may perish by cracks in things that we don't know," as Henry James put it in *The Golden Bowl*.[107] What you don't know *can* hurt you.

At the beginning of the chapter, we saw that Vico's anthropomorphism projects a human face onto things to cover over what we do not know. We pretend that what we do not understand looks like us. Riddles revel in exposing the way false resemblances cover over these gaps in comprehension or cognition. Claiming the casual intimacy of the first-person "I," the riddling object addresses us with a familiarity that indicates long acquaintance, only to slap us with our own ignorance. "Do you know what I am?" the riddle-creature asks. "Do you even know my name?" This is an accusation as much as a question, and the inability to answer is not the awkward faux pas of forgetting the name of a one-night stand in the throes of blear-eyed hangover; it is instead the failure to recognize a spouse of twenty years over the breakfast table—or worse, an admission that you have never really known the person with whom you thought you were sharing a life. Riddles show that we do not know or see what is smack-dab in front of our face. The insistence with which the riddle-creature "I" addresses its interlocutor "you" necessitates a recalibration of the ways we measure ourselves, in much the same way that Daston argues the "sine qua non of the human" (the *anthropos*) is transformed when we alter the shape of the nonhuman (its *morphe*) within anthropomorphism.[108] Riddles force us to acknowledge our failure to recognize both another and ourselves at the very moment in which we think we have divined the answer and crow "I get it; I know."

As we toggle between anthropomorphized thing and reified human, the likeness between human and thing seems to involve less the projection of human traits onto things than the revelation of a thinglike aspect only intermittently recognized within the human. If, as Vico puts it, man "makes . . . things out of himself and becomes them by transforming himself into them," then the relations we take to things may not be all that different from the relations we take to people. The riddle tricks us into taking one thing for another in order to expose the delusive assumption that we already know what something (or someone) is. It puts literal and metaphorical, human and anthropomorphism, on the same footing, and in the process it makes "the lack of certainty about what humanness is come to consciousness,"[109] prying the human loose from the exclusivity of a singular form or a proper name. It is when we anthropomorphize a thing that we start thinking we know what a human is; it is when anthropomorphism falters that we glimpse not the narcissistic reflection of our own likeness but the rictus of our own ignorance. In staging the impossibility of an equivalence between the enigmatic description and the name of the thing, the riddle suggests that one can never really take one entity for another—or assume that what has been taken is now a given.

CHAPTER 4

Flea, Fly, Fable

"It was," Francis Bacon writes in his essay "Of Vain-Glory," "prettily devised of Aesop; 'the fly sat upon the axle-tree of the chariot wheel, and said, "What a dust do I raise!" ' "[1] Planted at the axle about which the whole world wheels—the provisional still-point at the center of a turning universe—the fly attributes to itself effects of which it is in no way the cause. A hitchhiker on a vehicle infinitely greater than itself, the fly is unable to grasp its incidental place, its irrelevance, its triviality. Less easily apprehended than one might guess, one's insignificance is best to be glimpsed by starting from something other than oneself: by identifying, through the form of the fable, with a position that is not one's own in order to procure a fleeting glimpse of where one might be perched, in the estranged image of one's self as fly. Yet the reader who kicks up a dust in priding himself or herself on this insight falls into a further trap within the fable: as the fly hitchhikes on the chariot, the reader is likewise carried by the vehicle of the fable, a kind of stowaway. Bacon, in crediting the pretty device of the fable to Aesop, carefully keeps himself low on the vainglory food chain, although the receding origin—Bacon quoting Aesop quoting a gnat—creates a suspiciously long chain of citations in a fable explicitly concerned with the mistaken association of cause and effect. And there is an additional irony to be found in the fact that the source of the fly's pride is, literally as well as metaphorically, dust.

Yet even the apprehension of the fly's insignificance is misplaced, since the form of the fable paradoxically *does* make the fly the engine and solar center of its universe, trailing moral dust in its wake. The narcissism against which the fable warns (the assumption that the world revolves around the self) is, in fact, the necessary precondition for reading it. You're so vain; you probably think this fable is about you—as indeed you must, to get the point.

The anthropomorphic fable about the evils of anthropocentrism requires that the human recognize itself in—indeed, substitute itself for—the fly, thus enacting the lesson (that one is not the center of the universe) before explicitly grasping the moral. Whereas the natural history, as we saw in Chapters 1 and 2, offers a glimpse of a bird's- or louse-eye view, and the riddle, as we saw in Chapter 3, offers an estranged view of the insect's nature through a first-person account that withholds the identity of the speaker, the fable grants speech to a broad cast of animals in order to scrutinize the terms on which humans may separate themselves from their constitutive animality.

This chapter raises two main questions: what definitions of the human do the fable's anthropomorphized animals offer, and how does the fable as a form seek to produce humanity in its readers? If the purpose of the fable is "to make Men lesser Beasts," as the verse in John Ogilby's frontispiece to the 1651 *Fables of Aesop* (Figure 6) would have it, why pursue this end by depicting them as animals?[2] What version of humanity issues from the diminished but ineradicable animality of men made "lesser Beasts"? Ogilby's epigraph raises a set of questions—theological, philosophical, and political—about the connection between humans and animals and the terms on which they may be dissevered; it suggests that the conjunction "and" that serves as the fulcrum in the titles of so many fables involves what Giorgio Agamben calls both the "metaphysical mystery of conjunction" between human and animal and "the practical and political mystery of [their] separation."[3]

In what follows I want to make a dust about the most trivial characters featured in the fable: the flea and the fly. In focusing on noxious minute pests rather than on the charismatic megafauna—the wolf, the lion, the fox, and the lamb—and busy insects—the bee, the ant, the grasshopper—that generally have pride of place in discussions of the fable, I want to think about the value the fable assigns to or extracts from the seemingly worthless lives of vermin.[4] The flea and the fly serve as the baseline, the not quite vanishing point, for relativizing comparisons designed to puncture human vainglory.[5] Their insignificance is proverbial and their lives are disposable. As they cut man down to size, the flea and the fly disrupt rather than reaffirm the anthropocentric cast of the fable. Even as the fable imagines a nonhuman world animated for the edification of its human reader, it questions humanity's absolute primacy over nature and its own animal life. This chapter examines how the thematic concerns and pedagogical aims of the fable, which seek to establish the humanity of its reader, are connected to its form: the figures of personification and anthropomorphism it employs and the reading practices

FIGURE 6. Frontispiece, in John Ogilby, *The Fables of Aesop Paraphras'd in Verse, and Adorn'd with Sculpture* (London: Thomas Warren for Andrew Crook, 1651). RB 106524, The Huntington Library, San Marino, California.

it institutes. What definition of the human emerges from zoomorphic fictions that offer the reader a likeness in a nonhuman image?

The Pedagogy of Beasts

More than most literary genres, the fable treats the threshold between human and animal as moveable and permeable. Even the fable's purported progenitor, Aesop, is characterized as only marginally human in the accounts of his life that accompanied most fable collections during the period. Aesop's precarious right to personhood is evident in his physical proximity to the animal, his status as a slave, and his tenuous claim, even upon manumission, to justice; his ascendancy to the role of seer and counselor to kings ends with his false accusation and summary execution by the people of Delphi ("*by so extrajudicial a violence*," as Francis Barlow puts it in his polyglot 1666 edition).[6] The original author of the fables has a tenuous claim to fully human status.

Invariably described as "slow, inarticulate and very obscure" of speech, such that "people could very hardly understand what he said,"[7] Aesop is depicted both in verbal descriptions and images (Figure 7) as a monstrous figure, disfigured in body, with "a sharp head, flat Nos'd, his Back roll'd up in a Bunch or Excrescence" and a "Complexion black, from which dark Tincture he contracted his Name (*Aesopus* being the same with *Aethiops*)."[8] That Aesop's name fixes his racial or national origins in language stages the movement between particular (proper name) and general (common noun), between individual and class, between character and allegory, enacted in the fable. While the implied alignment of racialized skin color and physiognomy with disfigurement points to an aesthetic that elevates white over black, it is the purpose of the *Life* to expose the error behind such a reading: the figure of Aesop himself operates as a kind of meta-fable in which the correlation of outer sign and inward being is foregrounded as an interpretive conundrum. "We learn the Spirit of Fable from what these Authors have written of him," the French critic and fabulist Antoine Houdar de la Motte writes in his 1719 *Discours sur la fable*, "and perhaps they have given him such a monstrous Body, only to make him, with the Beauty of his Wit, and the Uprightness of his Heart, the greatest *Contraste* in the World."[9] If the fable depends upon the conjunction of sign and meaning (the equation, say, of a lamb with innocence), it also addresses the lack of symmetry between external form and

See here how Natures Book vnclasped lies,   Who th[e] wise Apologues from Beasts, deriued.
Whose Pages Æsop reads with pearcing eyes. Tells man they for his conduct were contriu'd

FIGURE 7. Frontispiece, in Francis Barlow, *Aesop's Fables with His Life* (London: H. Hills Jun. for Francis Barlow, 1687). RB 110968, The Huntington Library, San Marino, California.

internal capacity: the stunted body houses an exalted spirit, as if "Nature by a more even Retribution had endow'd him with a most accomplish'd Mind, capable of the most sublime and elevated Speculations."[10] Yet his unprepossessing appearance and "monstrous" body mean that the already human Aesop must acquire the traits that enable him to be acknowledged as such. Although he will ultimately be granted articulate speech as a gift in return for an act of hospitality toward visiting priests of Diana, Aesop lacks the outward identifying traits of a human. How is he to be known to be a man?

The problem turns out to lie not so much with Aesop himself as with the form and content of definitions of the human. Aesop's stunted body and lack of articulate speech present the same problem as the imperfectly human "Changeling" (simple-minded child) in John Locke's 1690 *Essay Concerning Human Understanding*. "I would gladly know what are those precise Lineaments, which . . . are, or are not, capable of a rational Soul to be joined to them," Locke writes. "What sort of outside is the certain sign that there is, or is not, such an Inhabitant within?"[11] Noting the propensity to resolve the "whole Essence of the Species of Man . . . into the outward Shape," Locke subjects his Changeling to a gradual experimental makeover, asking the reader to descry at exactly what point the figure morphs into a subhuman. Although one may be persuaded of the changeling's humanity, Locke notes, "Make the Ears a little longer, and more pointed, and the Nose a little flatter than ordinary, and then you begin to boggle: Make the Face yet narrower, flatter, and longer, and then you are at a stand: Add still more and more of the likeness of a Brute to it, and let the Head be perfectly that of some other Animal, then presently 'tis a *Monster*; and 'tis demonstration with you, that it hath no rational Soul, and must be destroy'd. Where now (I ask) shall be the just measure; which the utmost Bounds of that Shape, that carries with it a rational Soul?" (IV.iv.§16, 572). Minuscule deviation—the length of a nose, the shape of a face—gradually mutates into monstrosity, as anomaly beyond measured degree leads to a lethal slippery slope that ends in the conclusion that the figure possesses no rational soul, no humanity, and hence may—indeed "must"—be put to death. Locke's "figure [of man]," Paul de Man affirms, "is not only ornamental and aesthetic but powerfully coercive since it generates, for example, the ethical pressure of such questions as 'to kill or not to kill.'"[12]

Carrying his speculations beyond the changeling to fantastic creatures, part human, part beast, Locke asks his reader to isolate the specific element that would decisively thrust an individual from the party of humanity:

Had the upper part, to the middle, been of humane shape, and all
below Swine; Had it been Murther to destroy it? . . . So uncertain
are the Boundaries of *Species* of Animals to us, who have no other
Measures, than the complex *Ideas* of our own collecting: . . . The
precise number of simple *Ideas*, which make the nominal Essence,
[is] so far from being setled, and perfectly known, that very material
Doubts may still arise about it: And I imagine, none of the Definitions of the word *Man*, which we yet have, nor Descriptions of that
sort of Animal, are so perfect and exact, as to satisfie a considerate
inquisitive Person; much less to obtain a general Consent, and to be
that which Men would every where stick by, in the Decision of
Cases, and determining of Life and Death.[13]

Because for Locke we only know the nominal and not the true essence of
things, we have no way of knowing whether we are operating with the proper
definition or description. Complex ideas are here assembled piecemeal from
contingent, arbitrarily selected traits, culled from a potentially infinite fund.
How is one to sort incidental detail from essential trait? Which feature, once
lost, banishes someone from the species? The categories produced by these
enumerative definitions yield templates that are neither capacious enough to
accommodate all who should fall within the category nor restrictive enough
to exclude those who should be omitted. Without a decisive catalogue of
fixed traits to rely on, who can say where the species begins or ends?

As we saw in the introduction, definitions of humanity are often little
better than tautologies—humanity as "the Nature of Man, or that which
denominates him *human*."[14] Habituated to the circular logic that creates such
concepts, people cease to recognize their vacuity, even as these concepts come
to wield immense power in the world. Locke's version of the dead-end
reached by such tautologies (as "a soul is a soul") is especially evocative: "It
is but like a Monkey shifting his Oyster from one hand to the other; and had
he had but Words, might, no doubt, have said, Oyster in right hand is *Subject*, and Oyster in left hand is *Predicate*: and so might have made a self-
evident Proposition of Oyster, *i.e. Oyster is Oyster*; and yet, with all this, not
have been one whit the wiser . . . and that way of handling the matter,
would much at one [sic.] have satisfied the Monkey's Hunger, or a Man's
Understanding."[15] Locke's recourse to animal metaphor breaches the tautological equivalence, offering a monkey in place of a man, and an animal (the
oyster) in lieu of a word—in much the same way and for much the same

reason, I want to argue, the fable endeavors to circumvent the tautology (a human is a human) by passing through the figure of the animal. It thereby constitutes humanity not as a defined property possessed by its readers (an equivalence to be sought and found in the fable), but as a quality to be realized or acquired through a *process* of reading.

Definitions that try to reduce humanity to a nutshell definition invariably arrive at an impasse. It is perhaps because of the fallibility of such enumerative definitions that the Swedish natural historian Carolus Linnaeus, in placing man in the class of Anthropomorpha alongside monkeys and sloths in his influential 1735 *Systema naturae*, offered a definition in the form not of a catalogue of traits but of an imperative: *nosce te ipsum* (know thyself). In using a command (what Swift's Houyhnhnms would term an exhortation) as a defining trait, Linnaeus offers a strangely empty model of humanity that can only be realized in its performance: man, as Agamben observes of this passage, "has no specific identity other than the *ability* to recognize himself," which means that humanity is "neither a clearly defined species nor a substance; it is, rather, a machine or device for producing the recognition of the human." If man "is the being which recognizes itself as such, . . . *the animal that must recognize itself as human to be human,*"[16] this recognition is enacted by presenting humanity to itself in something other than its own image: the reader of fable produces her humanity by recognizing herself in the figure of the animal.

Although the taxonomical name, *Homo sapiens*, seemingly embraces all who are capable of self-reflexivity, Linnaeus fractures the category's inclusiveness in the enumerative lists of defining traits assigned to the four human varieties—European, American, Asian, and African—and in the addition in the 1758 tenth edition of the category of "feral man" (*Homo sapiens ferus*), sandwiched between human and ape in the renamed order of "primates."[17] Even internal to the broader category of man, questions of recognition move beyond specular self-knowledge to embrace the possibility of otherness *within* as well as *between* species. Nor does the fable represent humanity as a generic or homogeneous class; it too splinters the species into kinds. The process of identifying with or distinguishing oneself from an essential animality produces and confirms other hierarchies of nation, race, gender, class. If the fable underscores a common creaturely nature, it simultaneously shows that some are more equal than others.

Inasmuch as the reader must determine what is added to (or subtracted from) the human to make an anthropomorphic animal, the fable demands a

degree of critical reflexivity about the intrinsic bestiality from which humanity ceaselessly seeks to separate itself. Fables might on these terms be better
understood, as Annabel Patterson has suggested, not as a literary genre but as
a *"function"*[18]: a device that, like perspective in art, the microscope, and the
riddle, rescales and repartitions objects, redistributes power, and makes new
aspects of familiar objects visible. But fables do something more than recast
the relation of subject and object, for the fable's language is meant to be not
only descriptive but performative: it must instruct, persuade, and thus *transform* its reader. The fable offers lessons in reading that are focused not only
on the reproduction (or critique) of moral and political principles but also
on the production of a reflexive human subject that defines itself by its distance from its own creaturely needs and nature. It is in the reading protocols
that the fable institutes—in the movement across that "unarticulated space
between the fable's 'animalized' narrative and its 'humanized' *moralitas*"—
that the reader distinguishes himself or herself from the beast.[19] The fable
does not so much blur the line between human and animal as it thickens that
line into a field where the two commingle.[20] Producing a definition of
humanity out of the reader's self-recognition in an array of animal figures,
the fable operates as a kind of anthropological machine through a process of
zoomorphic reading.[21]

   That the fable attains such popularity at a moment in which humanity's
emergence from its own bestial existence in the state of nature becomes an
object of speculation reflects the importance of questions of animality to the
period's political thought. Ogilby's *Fables of Aesop* was, after all, published in
the same year as another great animal fable, Hobbes's *Leviathan*. Born in
translation, the fable serves as a channel both for homespun wisdom and for
the pan-European circulation and dissemination of potentially inflammatory
philosophical thought. Thus the fables of Johan and Pieter de la Court, composed in Holland in the 1660s and translated into English in 1703 as *Fables
Moral and Political*, bind Cartesian animal spirits and the elements that make
up the Hobbesian body politic to individuated passions incarnated in beasts,
while Bernard de Mandeville's 1703 translation of La Fontaine and his
expanded 1704 edition, *Aesop Dress'd*, paves the way for his 1705 *The Grumbling Hive*, the 433-line hudibrastic foundation of his 1714 *Fable of the Bees*.[22]
William Law and Bishop Berkeley (among others) would vilify Mandeville's
infamous description of a market society driven by passions and vices for its
treatment of "Man, *merely* as an *Animal*, having like other Animals, nothing
to do but follow his Appetites."[23]

Although the fable finds tributaries in many earlier literary forms—the medieval *Physiologus*, Chaucer's tales, Spenserian allegory, biblical parable, Oriental and Arabian tales, popular folklore, emblem books, and proverbs as well as philosophy and natural history—its revival in the course of the English civil war and its enduring popularity through the Restoration and the Glorious Revolution and well into the eighteenth century stem from the fable's ability to serve as a self-protective medium of political expression for the underdog—what Patterson describes as the fable's "flexible and constantly renewable system of metaphorical substitutions for actual events, persons, or political concepts that can, but need not, be recognized as such."[24] The fable likewise enjoyed great popularity in France in the wake of the Fronde as a medium of expression under the absolutist Louis XIV. Its mythical origins in the utterances of the enslaved Aesop made it a mode for communicating truth under tyranny; under the veil of allegory, the fable conveys advice to superiors without giving offense and offers criticism in a guise that avoids persecution or punishment. (The tyrant who sees himself in the rapacious lion is self-incriminating.) The indirection of the fable—the often indeterminate relation between story and moral, the obscurity of the allegorical or topical references, the obfuscatory cast of animal characters—renders it a propitious genre at a moment in which the shifting political and religious landscape made the overt assertion of loyalties and principles risky.

Although the focus here will be on the British tradition, with some attention to the French, the fable flourished on a pan-European scale, with translations and adaptations in Dutch, German, Italian, Russian, and Spanish.[25] Because many fable collections were published anonymously (typically with at least a partial attribution to Aesop, Phaedrus, and Pilpay/Bidpai), they provided an excellent cover for political opposition and radical philosophical thought.[26] Aesop, along with Ovid, Epicurus, and Lucretius, becomes a repertory player in debates about the mechanistic, corpuscular, and neoatomist philosophies of Gassendi, Hobbes, Descartes, Spinoza, and Lamy, among others. Radical readers found in fables a form able to accommodate and propagate materialist speculation about the connections of human, animal, and thing, as in the covert but sustained engagement with Spinoza that critics have uncovered in La Fontaine's poems.[27]

Simultaneously a translation exercise for schoolboys (*quia ego nominor leo*, Barthes remarked, means "*I am a grammatical example*"),[28] a mirror for princes, a weapon in the trench warfare between political factions, and a commodity in a burgeoning print market, the fable is turned to multiple

ends throughout the period. References to fables creep into novels, periodicals, conduct books, political theory, philosophy, and natural history; they
find a readership among individuals of every rank, age, religion, gender, and
political stripe, in formats ranging from the ephemeral pamphlet to the lavish
folio. Ogilby's stunningly successful 1651 collection, which went through five
editions before 1670 with a second volume in 1668, was followed by the
exquisitely illustrated editions of illustrator and Stuart sympathizer Francis
Barlow (1666, 1687, the latter with verses by Aphra Behn) and the enduringly
popular pithy prose versions published in two voluminous tomes in 1692 and
1699 by Roger L'Estrange, Stuart propagandist, Catholic sympathizer, and
royal censor.[29] Fables were composed both by literary eminences such as John
Dryden and by swarms of lowly Grub Street hacks who churned out broad-
sides and pamphlets satirizing nonconformists under Queen Anne.[30]
Although the fable was often the genre of choice for political outsiders—
Royalists, Jacobites, Catholics, and Tories, such as Ogilby, L'Estrange,
Dryden, Behn, and Anne Finch, thrust from power or stripped of their traditional status by the shifting political order of the age—writers from every
part of the spectrum sought to harness the fable's popularity to their own
ends. The Hanoverian Samuel Croxall would attempt to supplant Roger
L'Estrange's influential Jacobite version with his 1727 edition, with only partial success.[31]

     In its simplest form, the fable is a tool for the reproduction of homely
virtues, much praised for the clarity of moral instruction it offered. Although
the deist John Toland objects to allegory and metaphor as the instruments of
bamboozling priestcraft designed to dazzle common sense, he praises the
straightforward morality of the animal tale in his 1704 edition of the *Fables
of Aesop,* dedicated to the freethinker Anthony Collins. The brevity of the
fable and its overtly didactic content suits eighteenth-century literary tastes
and neoclassical ideals, while its distinctive blend of instruction and entertainment won the endorsement of such eminences as François Fénelon in his
Traité de l'éducation des filles and Locke in *Some Thoughts Concerning Education.*[32] Capitalizing on the Lockean trope of the mind as blank slate in the
preface to his *Fables,* L'Estrange delights in the power of the fable's pedagogy
to mold the child-subject: "Children *are but* Blank Paper, *ready Indifferently
for any Impression, Good or Bad, for they take All upon Credit; and it is much
in the Power of the first Comer, to write Saint, or Devil upon't.*"[33] L'Estrange's
Hanoverian adversary Croxall is outraged at this use of the fable as an instrument of seditious instruction: "What poor Devils," Croxall demands, "would

Lestrange make of those Children . . . ? Not the Children of *Britain*, I hope; for they are born with free Blood in their Veins."[34] The subject-forming powers of the fable raise the political stakes of its pedagogy.

Accessible to readers of different educational levels and classes, and deemed suitable for ladies and children, the eighteenth-century fable is gradually purged of topical political references and gentrified for the swelling market of middle-class readers. Later in the century, collections such as Thomas Marryott's 1771 *Sentimental Fables* make it a vehicle for fashionable sensibility, even singling out the oyster, that minimally sentient bivalve, as an object of pity in such poems as "The Oyster, the Eel, and the Lobster." From the midcentury forward, editions aimed at juvenile readers dominate the market. Anna Letitia Barbauld, Sarah Trimmer, Dorothy Kilner, and Mary Wollstonecraft—the cluster of rationalist educators that Charles Lamb famously lambasted as "the cursed Barbauld Crew, those Blights and Blasts of all that is Human in man & child"[35]—use the fable to inculcate moral and humanitarian principles in children. The fable plays a key role in the pedagogical processes that help convert children from persons in potentia—human but not legal persons, capable but not yet possessed of speech and reason—into political subjects within the Lockean "full state of Equality" to which they are born.[36] The fable's educational value, as Heather Keenleyside has argued, is thus closely connected to the political aim "of making persons—in the sense of speakers—out of animals."[37]

The speaking animals of fable also mystify the hierarchies implicit in these pedagogical structures. Numerous eighteenth-century critics note that the fable's indirection is necessary not because it delivers unpalatable truths but because the recognition of the teacher's implied dominion incites revolt. Readers, La Motte observes, "would not be corrected at all, if they thought that to suffer Correction implyed Obedience."[38] The fable's naïve narrator and its cast of animal characters mitigate the humiliation of requiring instruction, disguising the wizard of Oz–like fabulist orchestrating the pedagogical scene.[39] "We do not like to receive lessons from our peers," Batteux observes in his 1764 *Principes de la littérature*. Animals are ideal preceptors "because they are not men. As they judge us without passion, one receives their verdict without revolt. That is how we are tamed. The trick [artifice] is not subtle; nevertheless men allow themselves to be taken in."[40] The dispassionate gaze of the animal becomes the estranging medium through which we can gain an exteriorized glimpse of our own fallible nature. The form of the fable flatters human *amour propre* by presenting our faults in a bestial guise. In

Batteux's account, animals tame us rather than the other way around, as we are knowingly snared in a trap of our devising (shades here of the trompe l'oeil in Chapter 1). Our vanity, our dislike of being told what to do, necessitates the trickery that blinds us to our own blindness, disguising our inferiority and creating the *illusion* of equality.

Notwithstanding the many laudatory comments about their pedagogical utility, fables are prone, as L'Estrange observes in his 1692 *Fables*, "*to a Thousand Abuses and Mistakes, by a Distorted Mis-application of them to* Political, *or* Personal *Meanings*."[41] Sometimes, as Rousseau acerbically noted in *L'Émile*, the examples are bad or are misread—the child reader cheers for the victorious wolf not the innocent lamb—or the message is heard by the wrong addressee; sometimes the moral has no obvious relation to the story, or the friction between them creates suave ironies that undermine the ostensible lesson; at times the allegory is confused or the topical references are difficult to decipher.[42] Worse, young people swallow the moral pill without having digested the point, "*as we Teach* Pyes *and* Parrots, *that Pronounce the Words without so much as Guessing at the Meaning of them*," L'Estrange scoffs. "*The Boys Break their Teeth upon the Shells, without ever coming near the Kernel*."[43]

The fable's utility as a vehicle of moral education could also render it a kind of literary bread and circuses, its sugarcoated lessons operating as a form of insidious dominion where brute force fails. The famous use of "The Belly and the Members" to pacify the Roman crowd shows the power of the fable to quell discontent not through raw military power, traditional authority, or reasoned argument but through literary seduction: "What neither the authority of the law, nor the dignity of the Roman magistrates, was able to do, was accomplished by the charms of the apologue," as Dumarsais puts it.[44] The fable's simplicity and clarity render it the ideal vehicle for the dogmatic instruction of the masses. "If a rude multitude cannot readily comprehend a moral or political doctrine, which they need to be instructed in," the essayist James Beattie suggests later in the century, "it may be as allowable, to illustrate that doctrine by a fable, in order to make them attend."[45] While the fable at the beginning of the century serves as a subversive instrument in the arsenal of the political opposition, it increasingly comes to be seen as an instrument of class domination.

Beattie's scene of literary reception involves moral lessons dropped like worms into the receptive beaks of a rude multitude. Operating by indirection and as misdirection, the fable's message is, however, apt to go astray. If the essential lineaments of the fable remain the same from one version to the next, its significance is protean. Although eighteenth-century critics repeatedly praise the neoclassical unity, moral rectitude, and stylistic purity of the fable, it proves to be cursed or blessed with an interpretive volatility that turns the most seemingly solid of principles into quicksilver. No one-to-one correspondence secures the alignment of example and precept: what seems to be the same maxim may be attached to multiple tales, while multiple (sometimes conflicting) morals may be gleaned from the same story. Indeed, dissension about the meaning of words and their connection to deeds often resides at the heart of the fable's lesson. "It is," as Jayne Lewis puts it, "fables' demonstration of their own contingency—of the way meaning is made—that, in Augustan eyes, invested them with something akin to natural authority."[46] The point of the fable resides less in any portable bromide it might yield than in the ways it dismantles its own authority by revealing the machinations by which meaning is produced.

It is for this reason that the debate over whether, as the critic John Dennis would insist in a 1700 debate with Richard Blackmore, "the very first thing that he who makes a Fable does, is to fix upon his Moral,"[47] or the other way around, is so significant. What seems at first glance to be a trivial chicken-or-egg question lies at the heart of a broader debate about the unity of the form and its moral closure. Fabulists endlessly debate whether maxims should be dogmatically trotted out up front, divulged at the end, or left unstated. While frontloading the moral guarantees that the reader will get the point, La Motte argues, it also "ravish[es] from your Readers the Pleasure of the Allegory."[48] The reader knows the lesson from the get-go and simply subordinates the story to the pre-fab rule. Placing the moral at the end, by contrast, implicates the reader in the interpretive labor of extracting a rule from contingency, while ensuring that obtuse readers will get the correct "takeaway" from the poem. The bookseller and author Robert Dodsley admits in his 1761 "Essay on Fable" that "every story is not capable of telling its own Moral," so that sometimes a supplement may be necessary, but he claims that a well-constructed fable should "render needless any *detach'd* or *explicit* moral."[49] Indeed, it is not always clear whether it is possible to excise the moral from the story in which it is intertwined; once the sententious proposition is woven into "the cloth of discourse," Geoffrey Bennington points out, "its extraction can no longer be simple."[50]

Fables at their best do not transmit ossified truths—gilding the self-contained pill of a neatly delineated moral—but persuade by embroiling readers in interpretive activity. Defined in the *Encyclopédie* as a "discourse that contains something more than it seems at first,"[51] the fable partakes of the structure of a riddle, both because its origins in the culture of slavery require that the truth be told in disguised form and because it involves a reading process in which one looks for what is missing or withheld from the story proper, "leav[ing] the *reader* to collect the moral," as Dodsley puts it, by "discovering more than is shewn him."[52] But the reader who understands the moral to be the "solution" to the fable (in the same way that the simple riddle has an "answer") usually misses the point—not least because the lesson of the fable is not necessarily its moral. The fissure between the practical lesson of the fable and the precept it purports to promote resides at the heart of the fable's subject-producing capacities. It is the *process* of reading the fable—the substantial interpretive labor that ideally alters the very nature of the reader—that teaches the lesson, not the nugget of truth to be mined from it.

In Jean-François Marmontel's account of fable in the *Encyclopédie*, the moral is *not* an ossified lesson to be swallowed by a compliant reader; rather "the illusion must end in the development of some useful truth; we say *the development* and not *the proof*, for it must be observed that the fable proves nothing." The extraction of this "useful truth" is essential to the enactment (not simply the articulation) of the morality. Because for Marmontel the fable is designed to "direct the attention, and not to coerce the consent; to arouse the imagination to what is evident to the reason," it embroils the reader in a process; the fable sets the mind in motion in an ongoing elaboration of a principle, rather than offering the finality of a fixed maxim.[53] It thus involves, as Louis Marin puts it, not only the conflict "between fact and value, between an objectively established given and an ethical and ideal teleology," but also the creation of a "moral subject, acting within the sphere of practical reason."[54] The fable acts not just as a machine for the production and reproduction of knowledge but also as an engine for the interpellation of subjects into its human-making toils.

To illustrate this claim, let me turn to John Gay's 1727 "The Man and the Flea."[55] Although Gay's reputation today largely rests on his 1728 "Newgate pastoral," *The Beggar's Opera*, he was best known for his two volumes of *Fables* (1727, 1738), which went through more than 350 editions before the end of the nineteenth century.[56] "The Man and the Flea," like Bacon's tale of a vainglorious fly, concerns the overweaning pride of "man." Whereas Bacon's fly misapprehends itself as the origin of all things, however, Gay's flea is their end: the one for whom the world is made. The poem begins with a trait common to animal and human alike: "Whether on earth, in air, or main, / Sure ev'ry thing alive is vain!"[57]—an assertion that converts the titular yoking of man and flea from the incidental metonymy of narrative encounter ("a man and a flea walk into a bar . . .") into the metaphorical equivalence that will be the fable's moral. In the opening stanza, the crab and the snail each in turn survey the world and celebrate their privileged relation to it: the crab

> crawles beside the coral grove,
> And hears the ocean roll above;
> Nature is too profuse, says he,
> who gave all these to pleasure me.

Meanwhile, the snail,

> When bord'ring pinks and roses bloom,
> And ev'ry garden breaths perfume,
> . . . looks round on flow'r and tree,
> And cries, all these were made for me! (ll. 9–12, 13–14, 19–20)

Simultaneously a proprietary claim (the arrogation of the common earth for one individual's or one species' pleasure) and the revelation of the impossibility of such propriety (since not everyone can own the same thing), these sequential declarations of delight—the crab on the strand, the snail in the garden—mockingly compare the way each creature considers itself incomparable.

Introduced as just one in a series of equivalences that undermine his exclusive title to a place at the center of the world, "Man, the most conceited creature," who "from a cliff . . . cast his eye, / And view'd the sea and arched sky," proves to be exceptional only in conceit (ll. 22, 23–24). Whereas the apostrophes of the other creatures meet with no reply, however, man's soliloquy is punctured by a riposte that reorients the world, shifting from the man's lofty perspective high upon a hill (Figure 8) to that of the flea perched on the nose that one cannot see on one's own face. Gay moves the reader from comparisons grounded in similitude (we are like the crab, the snail) to identification with a position of alterity that reverses the order of things, converting man from the recipient of nature's gifts into food for fleas. " 'Tis vanity," the flea informs him,

FIGURE 8. A. Motte, "The Man and the Flea," in John Gay, *Fables*, 3rd ed.
(London: J. Tonson and J. Watts, 1729), p. 186. RB 145209 v.1, The Huntington
Library, San Marino, California.

that swells thy mind.
What, heav'n and earth for *thee* design'd!
For thee! made only for our need,
That more important Fleas might feed. (ll. 43–46)

In acknowledging the possibility of a system organized around the needs, desires, imperatives of another creature, Gay invites the reader to adopt a flea's-eye view so as to more fully recognize the limitations of human perspective. The flea's place at the bottom of the animal hierarchy belies its place at the top of the food chain: it feasts on man. To the flea, one is but food.

If the flea topples man from the summit, teaching humility through humiliation, Gay suggests we learn from the vertigo as well as the fall. To know thyself—to "learn thyself to scan," as Gay's flea, riffing on Pope, puts it (l. 41)—is to relinquish the secure position from which one already knows oneself. The reflexivity that the flea lacks—the capacity to recognize its own lack of reflexivity—is what the human reader must strive to attain, and this capacity to objectify and critique the self (by seeing oneself in and as a flea) is both what the fable elevates as a distinctive capacity of the human and what it compels its reader to perform. That the tutelary genius that moralizes against vanity is blind to its own vanity would seem to give man the last laugh, but the reader who snickers and stops reading with a sense of superiority (triumphing over a flea!) has missed Gay's point.

For we see through the flea a bit too easily, and the finger-wagging moral "don't be vain; you are food for fleas" is true but trite. Moreover, the assertion that we are objects as well as subjects in the world, that other creatures make use of us even as we use them, implies a simple reversibility of position—an equivalence of man and flea—that is not entirely borne out in the poem. What, after all, does it mean to consider the other as made *for you*? The animals turn out to have two different interpretations of how the world is made *for* them: one aesthetic and the other instrumental. On the one hand, the crab, the snail, and the man delight in the beauty and bounty of nature. As Mark Loveridge observes, the rhapsodic tone of the poem and the "poetic delight" the animals as well as man take in their surroundings offer a "robust vision of a world where animal and human energies are in reassuring emotional unity."[58] On the other hand, the flea exalts its place in a world made for it *to eat*. On these terms, the ostensible admonishment (don't be vain) yields a slightly different moral that issues from and extends the first: do not, in your vanity, presume that it is righteous to eat or harm others. (Indeed, one might argue that the second position makes the first one impossible: those who eat their fellows cannot enjoy their beauty.) The problem is not vainglory per se (however unattractive a character trait it may be) but the actions that vainglory sanctions. Gay's "Man" on these terms seems to be on the good (or less bad) side of the equation: conceited and flea-bitten but not predatory.

To read the fable in this way is, however, to take a partial view of the relation of flea and man, recognizing man only as fodder for fleas, while disregarding *his* acts of predation or parasitism. As Michel Serres points out in his analysis of La Fontaine's fables, man's assumption that "everything is born for him . . . hides the fact that man is the universal parasite, that everything and everyone around him is a hospitable space. Plants and animals are always his hosts; man is always necessarily their guest. Always taking, never giving."⁵⁹ Human relations with other beings always bend the logic of exchange in our favor. The assertion that the world is made for us mystifies real, existing relations of dependency and vulnerability, on the one hand, and of force and exploitation, on the other.

Something like this interpretation is intimated in the opening stanza of the fable, where two parallel questions posed to the addressee of the poem compare man not to the crab and the snail, these happily self-absorbed but basically harmless creatures, but to the hawk:

> Does not the hawk all fowls survey,
> As destin'd only for his prey?
> And do not tyrants, prouder things,
> Think men were born for slaves to kings?⁶⁰

Splintering the unity of "man" into slave and tyrant, the fable turns the enmity between species into predation on one's own kind. It is not only fleas that feed on men, after all: humans (like birds) feed on one another. Although Gay's dedication of the fable collection to the six-year-old Prince William gives these lines a faint political edge, the insinuation of possible future royal tyranny is muted by the form of the rhetorical question. Rhetorical questions look like questions but require no response, or rather they ask for only one response, unthinking assent. Isn't that right? They thus avoid the actual questioning that might challenge or alter the status quo—a lesson that Gay, a self-aware sycophant striving through the fables to win preferment at court, slyly insinuates into his form. Gay ventures the possibility of an abuse of power, but he does so in a mode of rhetorical indirection that manifests his deference to the potential tyrant. (Even where "grammar allows us to ask the question," Paul de Man observes of the rhetorical question, "the sentence by means of which we ask it may deny the very possibility of asking.")⁶¹

Gay's decision to frame one of the poem's morals as a self-defeating question may indicate his sense of the ultimate inefficacy of the fable form—a prescience borne out by the fact that William would grow up to be known as the Butcher of Culloden for his role in crushing the Jacobite Rebellion in 1745 (and would be depicted in caricatures as an ox with a calf's head wielding a butcher's bloody cleaver and axe [Figure 9]).⁶² His use of the rhetorical question might also amount to a covert claiming of the upper hand (since the one who asks a rhetorical question can only be sure the answer is truly

FIGURE 9. "The Butcher, taken from ye sign of a butcher in ye Butcher Row."
(London: George Bickham the Younger, 1746). 1868.0808.3806,
British Museum, London. ©The Trustees of the British Museum.

settled if she or he has complete mastery over the discourse and its context), or it might even be a lure to the reader to convert the rhetorical question into a serious one. If the lesson of this particular fable lies in the form of an endless questioning of one's proper place in the world (rather than in an answer that would settle the matter), then the decision to couch one of the moral takeaways in the form of an unanswerable rhetorical question presents a method of reading whose value stems from its unresolvability. If, as Samuel Johnson lamented, it is "difficult to extract any moral principle"[63] from Gay's fables, it is because their spiraling ironies make it difficult to get the text to stay still long enough to excise a portable sentiment. And it is this interpretive process—notwithstanding Johnson's complaint—that makes the fable an engine for the production of the humanity of its reader.

For although many eighteenth-century discussions of the fable emphasize its doctrinaire aspects (the fable as moral Pez dispenser), they also acknowledge the ways it exercises the mind. The fable, Addison argues in the *Spectator*, produces delight in the mind's own self-creating powers: "If we look into Human Nature, we shall find, that the Mind is never so much pleased, as when she exerts herself in any action that gives her an Idea of her own Perfections and Abilities. This natural Pride and Ambition of the Soul is very much gratified in the reading of a Fable: for in Writings of this Kind, the Reader comes in for half of the Performance; Every thing appears to him like a Discovery of his own; he is busied all the while in applying Characters and Circumstances, and is in this respect both a Reader and a Composer." Simultaneously "Reader and Composer," monitor and admonished, the subject and object of interpretation, producer and consumer of meaning, the reader is the author of his or her own experience: "We are made to believe we advise ourselves."[64] The mind's fierce pleasure in its own exertion creates reflexivity and self-awareness as part of an ongoing process of self-constitution that makes the reader responsible for his or her decisions.

It is here, as Thomas Keenan has argued, that we find the ethical challenge of the fable, its call to a form of personal responsibility that only exists with "the withdrawal of the rules or the knowledge on which we might rely to make our decisions for us." The interest or payoff of the fable resides not in the rule offered in the maxim but in what does not quite add up: the excess or remainder that cannot be assimilated to a pat moral. The fable's power to create a responsible subject depends on its ability to interrupt the very structures of authority on which pedagogy ostensibly depends. How, after all, can one *compel* someone to be free or to think for herself? In

Keenan's account, the fable instates "subjectivity as the sine qua non of responsible action and the claim to rights" precisely by withholding the rule that would enable one to go through the motions automatically. When "we fall back on the conceptual priority of the subject, agency, or identity as the grounds of our action," he contends, ethics and politics fall by the wayside.[65]

It is in this context that we might connect the fable's use of animals to Derrida's contention that ethical responsibility in the fullest sense of the word emerges from an encounter with an unrecognizable other. "So long as there is recognizability and fellow," Derrida writes, "ethics remains dogmatic, narcissistic, and not yet thinking. Not even thinking the human that it talks so much about." Where moral or legal obligations are only recognized in relation to one's kind, Derrida argues, "not only can one cause hurt without doing evil," one has in effect exempted oneself from ethical responsibility toward those humans not recognized as fellows and also "toward any living being foreign to the human race."[66] It is when we smack up against the unrecognizable—something not in our likeness, not already established as our neighbor, someone not a priori embraced by a categorical imperative— that these kinds of ethical questions surface. By offering us moral lessons in the guise of animals rather than humans, fables repeatedly stage this decision about the boundaries of the ethical community. Although, as Gotthold Lessing argues, fables use animals as readily intelligible shorthand "to avoid the necessity of explanatory detail"[67]—the docile personifications of human qualities that make the fox "cunning" and the peacock "vain"—in many fables, we do not entirely know who or what we are dealing with. Seen in this light, the animal visage in the fable is not a mere fanciful mask; it is the essence of the question.

Prêt-à-Manger

For all the Law is fulfilled in one word, *even* in this; Thou shalt love thy neighbour as thyself. But if ye bite and devour one another, take heed that ye be not consumed one of another.

—Galatians 5:14–15

The fable asks who should fall under the embrace of its moral or its law. It is a question of some importance in the fable, since the answer often decides who will eat and who will be eaten—whether it is okay to have a neighbor for dinner. This is often (but not always) a matter of life or death for the parties on both sides of the equation: the one who is eaten and the one who must eat to survive. Self-preservation concerns the wolf as well as the lamb, and these driving imperatives of the animal body bind humans to beasts in the fable. The animals' actions, as Hegel points out in the *Aesthetics*, "spring from the same vital needs which move men as living beings."[68]

The addition of speech that anthropomorphizes the animals does not liberate them from the body. Although some fable creatures display considerable rhetorical skill, the fable generally revolves around forms of necessity that cannot be paraphrased or made metaphorical. Words cannot substitute for food: one must eat to live. The metaphor that casts humans *as* animals thus always involves the inescapable fact that humans *are* animals. As Annabel Patterson puts it, "When, as in the fable, the role of metaphor is to mediate between human consciousness and human survival, the mind recognizes rock bottom, the irreducibly material, by rejoining the animals, one of whom is the human body."[69] In translating self-preservation (treated in more abstract terms by political theory) into the incontrovertible need to eat, the fable addresses the way animal life, as biological imperative, underwrites the supposedly human life of the "political animal."

In fables, characters talk to—and play with—their food: they discourse with the next course of their meal, the creature they are planning to swallow. The regular debates between predator and prey in fables allow the terms on which this need will be satisfied to become a matter of critical reflection (if not negotiation). Fables, M. Richer observes in 1729, "suppose that a Wolf can suspend its appetite after carrying off a Lamb, gobbling it up only after holding a disputation with it."[70] By producing a hiatus between the desire to eat and the act of consuming (for animals in fables do not talk with their mouths full), the speech of the fable's animals introduces a measure of choice, deliberation, freedom: the possibility of evaluating imperatives rather than simply executing them. Discourse, as Louis Marin puts it, establishes "a new boundary between the need that drives the animal and the act of devouring."[71] Language provisionally suspends and occasionally reverses the brute relations of force that allow the strong unchecked dominion over the weak.

Whether the flea should live or die for feeding is the central question in yet another fable titled "The Man and the Flea." The story follows more or less the same lines in its various iterations, although its moral varies dramatically from one version to the next: a man bitten by a flea threatens to kill it; the flea advances multiple arguments against its immediate execution—its prior suffering at the hands of man, necessity, the slightness of the offense, the right to self-preservation—but the man rejects the plea and crushes the flea beneath his nail. Although the fable follows the basic structure of, say, "The Wolf and the Lamb," the flea is not a sympathetic victim like the lamb but a parasite, and the man, unlike the wolf, is not cast as a predator but as a host (the one who is eaten). While the outcome of the story is predictable— the flea, like the lamb, dies—the man struggles to justify *la loi du plus fort* ultimately affirmed by the wolf. Notwithstanding the seeming symmetry of fable titles ("the X and the Y"), who comes first always counts when we are talking about the food chain.

The nature of the animal *does* matter in the fable: the cultural baggage of the fox is not interchangeable with that of the lion. The smallness of the flea, its alien form, and its noxious means of subsistence shape the reader's sentiments about the man's decision to crush it; swap in a baby seal, and the story looks very different. The fable capitalizes on a kind of residue in which the specific qualities of the animal are not fully absorbed or superseded by the allegorical work it is asked to perform. Whereas fables such as "The Belly and the Members," in which the respective parts dispute their relative importance, emphasize the interdependency of the body (human and politic), the flea lives in a relation of dependent nonreciprocity (it eats people, but people do not eat fleas). Like other parasites, the flea cannot live without its host, and although it eats without offering any return, it does not kill. The flea thus bites the man, but it does not—pace Galatians—consume him.

John Ogilby's version, "Of the Rustick and the Flea," opens with the yeoman's address to the flea whose bite has awakened him: "Blood-sucker! thou that thus hast broken in, / Committing Burglary upon my Skin."[72] Aligning the reader with the perspective of the man (or, perhaps, placing us in the position of the flea as addressee), the rustic's speech casts the flea's bite as an act of trespass and theft, a violation of the prior title of the host to his own body. Neither equitable exchange nor mutual contract is present in this fable: the parasite operates in a state of nature in which, as Hobbes contended, "every Man has a Right to every thing, even to one another[']s body."[73] If the flea in Ogilby's fable prevails over the more powerful man, usurping the man's property in his own body, its dominion is temporary, secured neither by might nor right, and once caught, the flea admits his trespass, acknowledging his "Crime," his weakness, and the man's right over his "Life thus forfeited" (Ogilby, 96). Exalting the rustic into "Great King of Creatures" (95), the flea attempts first to exchange flattery for food—to use

one kind of orality (speech) to make up for the ravages of another (eating)—
and then to excite pity, with a pathetic account of its exploitation at the
hands of men in a flea circus:

> Me when my Master had with no small pains
> Truss'd like a Murderer, up to hang in Chains,
> He tuter'd to such Activeness and Strength,
> That Laden I leap'd ninety times my length. (96)

In effect a fugitive slave, the flea has sought asylum amid the rustic's "shel-
t'ring Flocks," only creeping out to feed when necessity left it no choice:
"Rather than die, [I] made bold with your Relief" (96). Claiming the prerogative of self-preservation, the flea pits its paltry need against the yeoman's
abundance. Far from treating the yokel's body as an all-you-can-eat buffet, it
took but

> a little Sop,
> Not much above a quarter of a Drop,
> Which from your Purple Isle, your Crimson Sea,
> Could not be mist, yet sav'd a wandring *Flea.* (96)

An uninvited and unwelcome guest, the flea claims hospitality not as a right
but as a gift in the rustic's dispensation.[74] Amid such plenitude, might not
the starving flea avail itself of a dram? Should pity lead one to turn a blind
eye to minor predations, particularly those necessary for the survival of the
poor? Why are these questions raised by a flea—a universally despised pest,
to be sure, but also a powerless creature, unable to resist? Indeed, the flea's
emphasis on its powerlessness eggs the rustic on, suggesting that "insight into
the physical vulnerability of some set of others" may inflame "the desire to
destroy them."[75]

The flea's plea raises questions about the efficacy or performative power
of a declaration with no force to back it up: "what Rhet'rick can prevail," the
rustic muses, before an interlocutor who is not only victim but also "your
Executioner and Judge"?[76] A word order that places the death sentence before
the verdict indicates a foregone conclusion, and the flea proves to be no
Scheherazade, able to defer execution through fantastic yarns: "Thou Fables
dost devise," the rustic sneers. "Hast hope to save thy Life by telling Lies?"
(97). Drawing on the multiple senses of the word *fable,* which embraces not

only the Aesopian "feigned story intended to enforce some moral precept" but also, in Johnson's 1755 *Dictionary*, "the series or contexture of events" in a "poem epick or dramatick," the playful counterfactual of "fiction in general," and the deliberate fabrication of "a lie," the rustic claims that the flea is offering empty language rather than a profitable moral in exchange for its life.[77] Yet Ogilby's version adds another twist: for the flea's crime is not that it has sucked the man's blood, nor even that it has told the wrong kind of fable, but that its bite interrupted the fable the swain had pleasurably devised for himself, awakening the rustic from a dream paradise of willing women, bounteous bread, and a life without toil: "me of all my Hopes thou didst bereave, / And with one Pinch awakening, undeceive." The flea has robbed the rustic not so much of blood as "of a Heavenly Wife / And hast confest, so forfeited thy Life."[78] The fable, on these terms, tells of the fate inflicted upon those who rob others of their fantasies—who, even inadvertently, disenchant rather than enchant.

The parallels between the flea's servitude in the circus and the rustic's unremitting toil pass unremarked in the fable proper, but Ogilby's moral draws attention to the similitude of the bloodsucking flea to the fabrication of the man's fancy (and perhaps even to Ogilby's own fable): both are "*Night-walking Jades*," that, "*whilst they Embrace, they Rob; / The sweet Dream flying, leaves an empty Fob*" (98). The willing seductress proves to be a thieving prostitute; what looks like a gift turns out to be a cover for a theft, and Ogilby's moral would seem to be more a cautionary tale about self-deluding collusion with sweet-talking trulls than anything else, with the death of the flea a gratuitous incidental outcome. Ogilby's moral on this front is oddly inconclusive, neither vindicating nor condemning the rustic's killing of the flea. Although he seemingly acknowledges the legitimacy of the flea's plea of necessity—"*Most steal for Want; for Pleasure few, or Spite*"—he refuses to endorse it. The rustic's decision may be a matter of contingency, even whim, but it is not necessarily inconsistent with justice: "*some in Frolicks do the Gallows right*" (98).

Later versions of the fable, such as Roger L'Estrange's 1692 colloquial version, dramatically truncate the flea's plea, attributing the impetus behind the flea's bite not to privation but to nature. The flea feeds on the man because human blood is "the Livelyhood . . . that Nature has Allotted" to it.[79] Thus determined by its nature, the flea cannot be held to account—an argument that L'Estrange makes cut both ways: "It is as Natural," he writes in his "Reflection on the Moral," "for a *Man* to kill a *Flea*, as it is for a *Flea* to Bite a *Man*. There's a kind of self-Preservation on Both sides, and without Any Malice on Either Hand" (127). The flea's snacking and the man's smacking are reciprocal, impersonal acts, requiring no reflection or justification.

And why should they need to be vindicated? After all, we are presumably talking about a flea. Although the sparing of the life of a fly will become a sentimental cliché in the second half of the eighteenth century (achieving its apogee in Uncle Toby's "why should I hurt thee?—This world surely is wide enough to hold both thee and me" in Sterne's *Tristram Shandy*), fleas, like lice, pretty much remain fair game throughout the period.[80] "The Man" in L'Estrange's fable is no Prufrock centuries ahead of his time (do I dare to kill a flea?), but a pragmatist who moves quickly to crush a pest: "now I Have ye, I'll secure ye for ever Hurting me again, either Little or Much."[81] What is surprising in all this is not that the flea winds up as a purple stain on the nail of its former host but that the fable expends so much energy to affirm what most would hold to be self-evident (that it is okay to kill fleas when they bite you).

L'Estrange's reflections on his moral are extensive. "Live and Let live," he notes, "*is the Rule of Common Justice, but if People will be Troublesome on the One hand, the Obligation is Discharg'd on the other*" (127). The seeming symmetry of "*on the One hand*" and "*on the other*" masks the potential disproportion between the "troublesome" behavior of the offender and the unchecked license to punish permitted by the discharged "obligation." If the exemplary story of "The Man and the Flea" involves the power of the man (and, by extension, the state) to *make* examples, the moral involves the power to make exceptions, for it offers a rule about the suspension of a rule, explaining the terms on which the seeming compact to "Live and Let live" may be annulled. L'Estrange strains to justify the abrogation of "*the Rule of Common Justice*," in part because the outcome of the story (the death of the flea) converts the casual idiom "live and let live" into a literal matter of life or death, which only seems trivial for as long as we are talking about fleas. When L'Estrange extends the analogy of the flea to those "Impertinent People" who break in on "Men of Government and Bus'ness"—"One Importunity upon the Neck of Another, is the Killing of a Man Alive"—the violent retribution for a proverbial fleabite comes to seem excessive (127, 127, 128). Once the flea becomes a figurative human—once the personification refers to a person— the logic and the moral start to seem dubious.

It is for this reason that both the argument and the moral of "The Man and the Flea" are so often overdetermined; there are invariably more explanations given than seem strictly necessary, an excess that excites suspicion (the pot that I did not borrow already had a hole in it, and it was a badly made pot anyway). Thus, in a 1706 version, the flea's first two arguments—that the bite was a first offense and that "she but little harm could do"—are overturned by her final excuse, that she is impelled by a force beyond will, "by Nature prone thereto." If, the man points out, the flea is by nature "prone to Mischief," the crime is only small because the criminal is small.[82] The three morals from a 1708 version are likewise not strictly compatible: "*Wickedness ought to be discourag'd, even where there is little Power to Hurt. Little Offences repeated are Troublesom, and no Man is obliged to bear a Trouble, which he may prevent by lawful Means. A Man's Quiet is of greater Value than the Life of a Flea.*"[83] Whereas the first moral offers a kind of zero-tolerance policy against all manner of "*Wickedness*" and the second sanctions action against nuisances within the parameters of the law, the third entails a determination about the relative value of the parties that sanctions taking life without reference to the law—perhaps all very well when it comes to a flea, but dubious when one tries to rescale the lesson for humans. How do we know if we are dealing with fleas or humans provisionally represented in the guise of fleas? If the fable, as Jayne Lewis puts it, seeks to "press language back to its literal foundations" and thus to expose "the figural as arbitrary and manmade," it also suggests that the power to draw the line between the literal and the figural may adjudicate who lives and who dies.[84]

The essence of the flea seems to lie in the fact that it may be killed without consideration (a kind of *pulex sacer*). "Nothing must be done *hastily* but killing of fleas," as a contemporary proverb would have it.[85] The flea's very expendability raises questions about the applicability of the fable's moral to different classes of being—or rather, the lesson of the fable involves the question of whether the moral applies to different kinds of creature, whether what holds for a man when talking about fleas is valid when the pest in question is human. To be sure, some versions claim that the fable advocates equity in justice:

Or great or small th'Offence, the power of Law
And Justice, with severity must awe
Offenders, future mischiefs to prevent,
Lest . . . villainous Examples fill the Times.[86]

In its insistence on the imperative to punish major and minor infractions without exception, the moral extols the power of the example to prevent future crime, affirming the necessity of stern but impartial justice. Other versions, however, contend that the law is anything but evenhanded in its selection of examples of villainy.

In John Toland's 1704 version, for example, the fable's justification for crushing a flea is exposed as a vindication for dispatching the defenseless poor to the gallows: "The smaller any Creature is, the less he ought to be pardon'd, being guilty of a higher Crime, and less capable of making any Resistance. Hence 'tis that we every Day see, that the lesser Criminals are made Examples to the rest, to deter them from the same Crime; because in their Deaths there are but few who concern themselves, or sue out for an Arrest of Judgment."[87] The ostensible applicability of the law to all—forbidding, in Anatole France's famous aphorism, rich and poor alike to sleep beneath bridges—does not generate equity in punishment; an unjust penal system makes examples of the weak, not the powerful, crushing the petty criminal, like the flea, in its gears. This fable about the making of examples reveals the less-than-exemplary fashion in which they are made. By steeping us in a world in which we take for granted the valuelessness of the flea's life (in the story), and then transferring that logic back onto human relations (in the moral), the fable exposes and tampers with the norms that designate lives as valuable or worthless. Crushing a tomato is not the same as crushing a flea or a man.

All this may seem to drop a portentous load on the back of a tiny flea, assigning life-or-death stakes to a slight, even lighthearted fable. Yet the fable's ubiquity gives it a constant supporting role in the low-grade reproduction of normative cultural standards. If the Rabelaisian belly laugh at the excesses of the lower body allows for a carnivalesque release of energy, the twinges of disquiet excited by the fable mark the unprocessed uneasiness at naked injustices that have been absorbed into "the way things are done." The comic treatment of the flea's mortality excites a flutter of nervous laughter that registers discomfiting daily facts made unremarkable by dint of their omnipresence.

If anthropomorphizing a flea lends it a value it normally lacks, rendering a man a flea exposes the fact that some lives are held cheap. The zoomorphism of the fable thus jostles the epistemological frame that allows some creatures (human and animal) to be seen as worthless. When the fable sets up the flea as a figure for a man and then puts the man in the place of the flea, it makes visible the greater or lesser value assigned to different orders of being. Those lives that are "not first apprehended as living," as Judith Butler has argued, "are never lived nor lost in the full sense."[88]

Given the proverbial insignificance of the flea's life, its acquisition of figurative life in the fable would seem intuitively progressive. And yet the figurative life bestowed by the fable lasts only as long as the personification or anthropomorphism forestalls recognition of the real powerlessness of the entity it animates. Although eighteenth-century thinkers such as Joseph Priestley see personification as a powerful trope, capable of transforming figures by "a voluntary effort of imagination, into real persons,"[89] the artificial "life" added through personification may be limited in quality and of short duration; the rhetorical attribution of qualities or capacities need not produce a shift in the epistemological status of a being and thus may not give value to a life in the strong sense. Worse, the two-way street that allows figurative entities to act in the world (allowing fleas to dispute their fate) may also transfigure literal agents into metaphorical ones (make men into fleas). As Steven Knapp has influentially argued, eighteenth-century disquiet over the nature of personification involves "not merely its inherent primitiveness and irrationality, but its *reversibility*. Once the boundaries between literal and figurative agency were erased, it seemed that nothing would prevent the imagination from metaphorizing literal agents as easily as it literalized metaphors."[90] If "The Rustick and the Flea" lends the qualities of humans to fleas, what is to prevent it from working in the opposite direction? The characterization of human beings as vermin, as history has shown countless times, is one step in a process of vilification used to justify extermination.[91]

But fables do not just make figurative and literal reversible; they make it hard to know precisely when the fable shifts from a literal to a figurative register (when the flea as such becomes the flea as a figure for man). Indeed, part of the interpretive labor exacted from the reader concerns precisely this determination. Priestley recognizes the complicated workings of the trope of personification: although it starts out as a comparison "derived from the idea of sensible and thinking beings" wherein "the difference between any two objects is preserved," personification may easily slide into metaphor and even metamorphosis, in which things "are confounded, and one of the things is changed as it were, in idea, into the other."[92] The fable's conversion of man as metaphorical flea into a flealike figure to be crushed suggests that the placement of the line between literal and figurative has lethal consequences. The fable, in its uncertain fluctuations between the real and the metaphorical, between the animal and the human, exposes the tenuous nature of our claims to know what the human is. It asks humanity to sort out what it is by deciding where that line is to be drawn. Indeed, the fable suggests that we may only be able to figure out "what the human is" in this estranged form.

In the final flea fable to which I want to turn, in which a man apostrophizes the gods to avenge a flea-bite, anthropomorphism does not humanize the animal but gives shape to divine power. In La Fontaine's "L'homme et la puce," the bite of a flea, which then escapes into the bedsheets, leads the man of the title to call first upon Hercules to "purge the earth of this Hydra" and then upon the Gods to annihilate the entire species: "Que fais-tu, Jupiter, que du haut de la nue / Tu n'en perdes la race afin de me venger?" (What occupies you, Jupiter, that from the pinnacle of heaven, / You don't destroy the entire race to avenge me?)[93] Whereas in the other fables we have examined, the flea is given a speaking role, here it is nothing more than a biting pest. It is neither the man nor the flea but the apostrophized gods, invoked to witness and avenge the injurious fleabite, who are given form by the trope. Their inclusion here reminds us of the twinned origins of Aesopian apologue and myth (both called *fable* by early modern French writers) in humanity's propensity to anthropomorphize the external world. We bestow eyes on our deities that they may behold us and give them weapons that they may smite down our enemies.

La Fontaine's man petitions the gods not for sympathy but for revenge; his language is not simply an expressive outpouring but an active wish. The fable concerns the propriety of such invocations, as manifested in the moral of the fable with which La Fontaine's version opens: "Par des voeux importuns nous fatiguons les dieux: / Souvent pour des sujets même indignes des hommes" (With tiresome wishes we weary the gods / With prayers unworthy even of men).[94] Falling below the threshold of human as well as divine interest, the man's complaint repeats the flea's bite in a different register: to the gods, the man's importunities make him a noxious pest. Flea is to man as man is to god. If the poem opens with a description of how we see the gods seeing us—"Il semble que le Ciel sur tous tant que nous sommes / Soit obligé d'avoir incessamment les yeux" (it seems that the gods are obliged to keep their eyes eternally trained upon our affairs)—the fable proper is designed to reveal how the gods see us seeing them (ll. 3–4). It is the human not the flea that is "le plus petit de la race mortelle" (the smallest of the mortal race), a mere speck from a god's-eye view (l. 5). The indifferent gods, paring their fingernails, do not reply to the man's addresses. The deities may attend to the fall of a sparrow but acts of petty vengeance fall outside their bailiwick.

What makes the man's prayer "indignes des hommes" (unworthy of men) is not only the triviality of his complaint but also the violence of his wishes (l. 2). He asks not just for damages but for retribution in the form of extermination, and not just of the offending flea but also of its entire "race," thus inflating a small injury, not life-threatening (fleas were not yet understood to be plague vectors), into grounds for the annihilation of a species. The fable thus raises questions about the relationship between the literal order of magnitude separating flea and man and the metaphorical scale that weighs the nature of the injury and the proper measure of retaliation. It is, in other words, concerned with questions of proportional response, the attempt to calculate and apportion violence by establishing what Eyal Weizman calls "a 'proper relation' between 'unavoidable means' and 'necessary ends.'" Debates about proportional response, Weizman argues, preempt questions about justice and the "clear lines of prohibition" on certain forms of violence, asking not *why* or *whether* one should act, but *how much* one should do?[95] The fool's apostrophe to the gods circumvents the question of right and justice, simply exposing his will to maximize power without regard to cost or consequences.

It is precisely this conversion of welt into world-shattering war that resides at the heart of Anne Finch's version of the fable. Written in the wake of the Glorious Revolution, in exile from the court where Finch had served as maid of honor to Mary of Modena, "The Man Bitten by Fleas" offers what Charles Hinnant describes as a "witty travesty of the kind of perspective that can lead to demands for drastic political action" in a society "tormented by threats—real and imagined—to its stability," where men nurse slight wounds into calamity and fleas become threats to homeland security.[96] The flea in Finch's fable becomes the force behind what Henry Home, Lord Kames, calls a passionate personification, in which the intensity of the emotion excited by an injury requires the objects of passions to be persons, capable of will, motion, agency. When I stub my toe on a stone, Kames claims, my anger "forces the mind to personify a stock or a stone when it occasions bodily pain, in order to be a proper object of resentment. A conception is formed of it as a voluntary agent," retroactively attributing will to a thing incapable of desiring harm.[97] For Kames, this belief that the stone (or the flea) was "a voluntary agent" must be sincere. "So long as the mind is conscious that it is an imagination merely without any reality," our anger will find no relief (1.192). We thus must commit ourselves to our fictions, pledging allegiance to the personified cause we have contrived to explain the effect of a personal injury. Our belief, however provisional, that the personified entity is *truly* a live, conscious, voluntary agent drags the figurative over the threshold of the real, as the personification takes on the force of the real thing, producing "an actual conviction, momentary indeed, of life and intelligence" (3.62).

To commit ourselves to our fictions in this way is dangerous, even foolhardy, however, for once personified, the injury takes on a curious autonomy with respect to the injured and injuring parties. The personification carries on, as it were, without the (human) person, serving as the life support for emotions that would (and sometimes should) die. "The physical body that is the cause of my desire for revenge," Miguel Tamen notes, "can only become an object of revenge as long as it is *embodied by*, i.e., made into, personification."[98] The life thus created takes on a life of its own. Even Kames acknowledges that the risk of personification is that poets will get carried away and make "this phantom of their own creating behave and act in every respect as if it were really a sensible being."[99] If the efficacy of the trope depends not on its ability to imitate life but to *create* it, we must take responsibility for the Frankenstein's monster we have spawned, for the fiction acquires the power to inflict harm and to justify further action in response. The human becomes the puppet of a personified threat that was once a flea, a stone. Kames's insistence that we pledge allegiance to our fictions is one beginning of a politics of fear.

For while Kames insists that the attribution of malevolence to the stone relieves anger, in Finch's poem, the personification perpetuates and even amplifies the bad feeling. It is for this reason that Finch insists that we must resist the temptation to personify or anthropomorphize the flea. Whereas La Fontaine's flea-bitten man magnifies the injury and feeds his own rage in accusing the flea of malevolent intent, Finch argues that we must refrain from inflating its creaturely action (the flea doing its thing) into intentional encroachment, making it the vehicle for emotions or actions that exceed the original harm.

Finch's insistence that a fleabite is just that and nothing more reveals the way rhetorical inflation invests agents with an intent and a capacity to harm that they may not unto themselves possess.[100] In her fable, the origins of catastrophic violence lie in the overvaluation of our own losses ("The Strife, ye Gods! is worthy You, / Since it our Blood has cost"); the exaggeration of personal injury ("scorching Fevers must ensue, / When cooling Sleep is lost"): prognostications of global disorder based on unlikely eventualities ("Strange

Revolutions wou'd abound, / Did Men ne'er close their Eyes"); and the hyperbolic consequences ("Confusion, Slav'ry, Death and Wreck") attributed to inaction ("whilst you keep your Thunders back, / We're massacr'd by *Fleas*" [225]). The mighty contests that arise from trivial things are driven by the narcissistic outrage of the injured party. We possess no scale to determine the "actual size" of the injury and hence no way to adjudicate the appropriate level of response—a response that may produce effects that exceed our desires and may even damage ourselves in unanticipated ways.

Finch recognizes that our actions may cause effects (unintended consequences, collateral damage) that we cannot foresee. Deeds have repercussions not visible from our present limited perspective:

> *For Club, and Bolts, a* Nation *call'd of late,*
> *Nor wou'd be eas'd by Engines of less Weight:*
> *But whether lighter had not done as well,*
> *Let their Great-Grandsons, or their Grandsons tell.* (226)

Even as the fable's personification condenses inchoate historical forces into discrete actors (the man and the flea), so too are "*Clubs and Bolts*" self-contained tools that allow one to see where the blow falls and where the lightning strikes. Yet Finch's poem suggests that we may still not know what we are doing; indeed, such knowledge may only be available to our "*Great-Grandsons,*" from the position of a future's past. The summoning of forces beyond our narrow compass through the apostrophizing of deities may unleash hell if our prayers are answered, and in this sublunary world, the clamor to act may animate entities that supersede our ability to control them. "Action and reaction among men never move in a closed circle and can never be reliably confined to two partners," as Hannah Arendt puts it—that is the great lie of the fable's titular contraction of its action to a counterpoised pair such as "The Man and the Flea."[101]

The lesson of Finch's fable is to let the flea be. Finch's gods, unlike La Fontaine's, answer the blustering fool, and the reply they give is not a call to arms but an admonishment to return to the homely tasks of the "good Housewives" who "sweep, and wash, and strew [the] Floor," quietly whisking fleas—real fleas, not chimerical threats—from the home.[102] Finch thus advocates an ethics of minimal action, in which it is better to leave well enough alone—the reticence of what Anne-Lise François describes as "a choosing often inflected as no more than the continuation of earlier choices, ready to be dissolved but for revision and renewal."[103] Sometimes a flea is just a flea.

The restraint in speech and deed that Finch advocates in her version of the fable suggests the importance of carefully considering *who* or *what* merits personification before unleashing its powers upon the world. One may elect *not* to personify—to leave the flea abidingly a flea, and the fleabite a mere nip—and thereby check the forces animated by the imagination. Under certain circumstances, this may be the ethical thing to do. In the next section, I focus on eighteenth-century debates among critics over the kinds of figures that may be properly personified and the significance of those elements left untransfigured. For although the fable is populated by talking animals and animated pots and kettles, it also presents characters, such as "the man," in their own proper form. If, as I argued above, the fable is designed to *produce* humanity (rather than treating it as a property already possessed), what is the status of an already realized, fully fledged man within this economy of personified characters? Given that animals personify human traits, enacting them in anthropomorphic guises, what exactly does "man" exemplify?

L'exemple que donc je suis

The animals in fables, it is often remarked, are not "really" animals but proxies for human traits, impulses, needs, desires. Insisting that we cannot draw moral instruction "from beings who act not upon the same principles with us," Kames in his 1762 *Elements of Criticism* contends that Aesop's "lions, bulls, and goats are truly men under disguise; they act and feel in every respect as human beings."[104] For Kames, the animal guise is decorative tinsel, nothing more. His insistence that the creatures of fable are just humans in animal masks—a humorous device with all the wit of a poster of dogs playing poker—dismisses the possibility that zoomorphic figures may unsettle the fable's broader anthropocentric stance. In this final section I want to return to the question of the animal by addressing the untransfigured human characters who disrupt the fable's zoomorphic economy. Are we meant to read "the man" differently from "the flea"? Does categorical commonality—an example in our own likeness—trump other forms of allegorical resemblance? To what degree are the fable's animals to be seen as representative of their species?

Some seventeenth- and eighteenth-century writers, illustrators, and critics took the relationship between real and fabulous animals seriously. As

Diana Donald has argued, fables "constituted a locus where restrictive views of animal intelligence were frequently questioned, and where the very subjectivity that gave rise to sweeping theories about other species was itself subjected to destructive satire."[105] Writers used the fable as a point of entry into broader debates over the Cartesian characterization of animals as mere machines and explored the naturalistic representation of animal behavior in the illustrations.[106] What Frank Palmeri calls the autocritical fable—an apologue depicting the wolf, say, not as a brutal human being but as a representative of its own species—allows animals to exceed their allegorical status or subject it to reflexive critique, as they protest their treatment by unjust or degenerate man.[107]

Over the course of the eighteenth century, writers increasingly insist that fabulous animals comport themselves in keeping with the general character of their species: the lion, we are repeatedly told, should not be cowardly. Thus, Edmé-François Mallet maintains in the *Encyclopédie* that the wolf and the lamb must say only "what those of whom they are the images would say,"[108] while Joseph Warton condemns modern fable writers for "ascribing to the different animals and objects introduced, speeches and actions inconsistent with their several natures. An elephant can have nothing to do in a bookseller's shop."[109] Although the presence of speaking animals immediately marks the fable as fiction, it too is governed by standards of verisimilitude: "Brute animals, and vegetables too, may be allowed to speak and think" in fables, James Beattie concedes, but "nature should not be violated; nor the properties of one animal or vegetable ascribed to a different one."[110]

Beattie's observations present the immediate conundrum of how the personality of a carrot might differ from the disposition of a turnip, but they confirm the kinship, recently analyzed by Bruce Boehrer, between the bestiary or natural taxonomy, on the one hand, and Aristotelian and Theophrastan traditions of classifying character types by their shared attributes, on the other. Critics, Boehrer argues, have too readily assumed that literary characters (which are, after all, linguistic constructs) are by their very nature human. Rather than reproducing a preestablished division of humans and animals, literature in Boehrer's account helps *create* these divisions. Pointing out that the Cartesian cogito and the *bête machine* emerge "hand in hoof," Boehrer contends that "the notion of character develops in English writing as . . . a means of manufacturing and perpetuating the distinction between people and animals." The attribution of psychological depth to humans is part of a shift from marking character through shared attributes (written marks or signs) to a model of "personal identity as singular and doubtful" that leaves inner life the exclusive province of the human.[111]

Neither "the man" nor "the flea" could be mistaken for characters from a Henry James novel, and little distinguishes man from flea (indeed, the possibility that there is no distinction—that men may be crushed as fleas—is part of the question the fable asks). When considered as literary characters in the tradition of novelistic realism, not much besides a name separates "man" from the other personified or anthropomorphic figures within the fable. Indeed, in his influential 1675 *Traité du poème épique*, René Le Bossu draws on Aristotle to argue that the poet only decides the proper names and species of his characters after he has determined the moral and the action. Because the deed requires a doer—"this action is the action of someone"—one must assign it to a personage, but Le Bossu's species-blind casting call is unusually elastic in its parameters: "It matters little for the nature of the Fable [a term that for Le Bossu embraces Aesopian apologue as well as Homeric epic] whether one takes the names of Beasts or the names of Men. . . . [Aesop] called Sheep what the poet [Homer] called Greeks."[112] That human might be interchangeable with ungulate by a mere change of name reflects the degree to which character is solely the instrument of plot—a kind of afterthought. Having no existence prior to or in excess of the action, the hero exists only to get the job done: for Le Bossu, we do not read fables for information about the mating habits of rabbits or the dietary preferences of foxes, let alone the philosophical or psychological reflections of Odysseus or Penelope. "The Hero," Le Bossu argues, "exists only for the Action."[113] The doer here is truly a fiction added to the deed.

That actions might be carried out indifferently by any kind of entity—by Greeks or sheep or stones—suggests that the role of the cat in one version may be played by the rat in the next. "The Fox and the Hedgehog" is "The Frogs Petitioning for a King" with different animals. "Change the names," as Charles Batteux would put it in 1749, "and the Frog that Wished to be as Big as the Ox, becomes the Bourgeois Gentilhomme."[114] Inasmuch as agents in this version of fable exist simply to perform the action, they are to be understood less as characters than as what narrative theorists call "actants." Actants are defined not by the nature of the personage (who they are) but by the functions they carry out (what they do). The actant is of interest "*from the point of view of its significance for the course of the action*," as Vladimir Propp argues in his *Morphology of the Folktale*.[115] The same function might be fulfilled by a bed-knob, a broomstick, an eagle, a thought in a child's mind, or a band of feral cats; the actant thus includes but is not limited to the kind of figure we normally recognize as a character. The significance of the actant issues from its capacity to produce results.

Attending not to the nature of the actor but to the act creates the possibility of moral judgment based on the ethics or efficacy of what was done, independent of who did it. To see "The Man" simply as one actant among others, then, is to question his presumed place at the pinnacle of the social and political hierarchies in the fable, underwriting the jujitsu through which the weaker defeats the stronger. Yet given that the lesson of the fable (as opposed to the moral) is often that the articulated dictum is imposed by the most powerful, it is difficult not to conclude that the strictly formal possibility of such interchangeability in the fable serves to expose its real-world impossibility: the role of the wolf can never be played by the lamb.

Seventeenth- and eighteenth-century discussions of the fable make it clear that the form grants emergency executive powers to its author to generate whatever agents are necessary to conduct the action: the fabulist may personify at will. A poet's power to animate extends beyond the beast to all sorts of entities: "Though Animals may be Actors never so proper and convenient in Fable, they are, however, not the only ones that have Right thereto," La Motte affirms. "The Spring may complain against its Stream; the File laugh at the Serpent."[116] Dodsley's 1761 "Essay on Fables" likewise grants the fabulist the "authority to press into his service, every kind of existence under heaven. . . . Even mountains, fossils, minerals, and the inanimate works of nature, discourse articulately at his command; and act the parts which he assigns them." Less an Adamic bestower of names than a God fashioning a second nature, Dodsley's fabulist should be understood as a "*Creator*," able to "bestow life, speech and action, on whatever he thinks proper," including animals, plants, body parts, inanimate objects, abstract qualities, duties, and an array of human types.[117] Fables on these terms create, if not a level playing field, then one in which agency is distributed among animals as well as humans, inanimate objects as well as abstractions. The fable, La Motte affirms, may "make Persons of every Thing it imagines."[118]

Such indiscriminate personification is affiliated with the primitive imagination in Enlightenment philosophy, which connects the anthropomorphisms of fable (both as Aesopian apologue and in its enlarged seventeenth-century sense of myth) to the first stirrings of natural philosophy and primitive efforts to understand and govern the mysterious operations of nature. The fable is a kind of holdover from these animistic prerationalist paradigms, the vestige of an earlier cosmology. "Man sees only as a human being can," Johann Gottfried Herder writes in his 1787 essay "On Image, Poetry, and Fable"; "he transfers the sensations and passions in his breast to other creatures, and hence also the intentions and actions typical of his manner of thinking and acting; he sees everything in terms of his own person, according to his measure." Given the universality of the impulse, Herder notes, "it was only a matter of time before the Aesopian fable was born."[119] The animism that "must have been common to the human species when languages were invented" still holds for the young, Thomas Reid argues in his 1788 *Essays on the Active Powers of Man*, which explains why the "rational conversation of birds and beasts in Aesop's Fables do not shock the belief of children."[120] Yet eighteenth-century fabulists increasingly pay obeisance to the division of human and nonhuman, animate and inanimate. Late-century fables are crammed with reminders to susceptible children not to be fooled: of course mice do not speak.[121]

Although the presence of "man" in fables such as "The Man and the Flea" might seem to create a certain automatic alignment between the reader and "the man," human characters in fables lead us back not to individual subjectivity or a "self" but to the abstract noun *man* or to some subset thereof. Whereas animals in fables are categorized by their species, humans are either representatives of mankind as a general singularity or classed by roles or types: the miser, the sculptor, the hunter, the gardener. When humans enter into the scene—the *Who Framed Roger Rabbit?* interaction of animated creatures and human actors—they are equally subject to the demands of the allegory, their actions constrained by the moral teleology of the fable. Yet if the fox illustrates, say, human cunning, and the fly, human vainglory, what is the specific property of man illustrated by "man"? If, as I have tried to argue above, the fable is designed to *produce* humanity (rather than treating it as a property already possessed), what is the status of untransfigured man within this economy of personified or anthropomorphic characters?

Addison observes that fables "are raised altogether upon Brutes and Vegetables," with "some of our own Species mixt among them, when the Moral hath so required," but he leaves unstated why the moral would occasionally require the inclusion of man in the fable's system of animal representation.[122] The presence of untransfigured humanity may signal a prelapsarian fantasy of an Adamic man, one among the creatures; it may plant humanity on the treacherous ground of a materialist philosophy that threatens to swallow up the difference between them; it may embroil readers in structures of reading that require them to rearticulate their difference from animals; or it may bring to the surface a fundamental incertitude about the nature of that humanity. Inasmuch as the "mingling of personifications on the same footing as 'real' agents," as Barbara Johnson has argued, "threatens to make the lack of certainty about what humanness is come to consciousness," the encounter of untransfigured "man" with anthropomorphic animal requires the reader to toggle between the two classes and decide the difference between them.[123] In inviting personifications to interact with anthropomorphized beasts, that is, fable reveals the uncertain status of the humanity that both these tropes take for granted.

For most eighteenth-century theorists, the preservation of the categorical distinction between human and animal is essential to the fable's operation. If the animal is totally absorbed into the human, in Herder's succinct formulation, "the Aesopian fable as such is thereby destroyed." The animals of fable must act *"as animals but like men,"* preserving an essential identity ("as animals") while admitting resemblance ("like men").[124] Although both "as" and "like" customarily introduce similes, here they point toward markedly different relations. Whereas the comparative "like" creates analogies while upholding categorical distinctions between species, "as" marks an equivalence: the animal is a subset of the category to which it belongs. To be sure, the insistence that animals act "as animals"—like the enjoinder to "just be yourself"— reasserts precisely the difference it pretends to overcome, postulating a given essence to be realized or repeated in the performance. Nevertheless, the circularity of animals acting "as animals" (like the presence of untransfigured man in fable) verges on a tautology that evacuates the fable of meaning. We are back in the presence of Locke's monkey, passing the oyster from the right hand to the left.

The animal acting "as animal" does not, however, only exemplify itself; it also is asked to exemplify human qualities within the anthropomorphic economy of the fable. It is this likeness to man that breaches what would otherwise be a tautology. "In the Aesopian fable," Herder notes, "every animal speaks precisely only in *its* sphere, in keeping with *its* character; not as a man, but like man."[125] That the animal speaks "not as a man" (as an individual) "but like man" (as a class) underscores the distinction not only between identity and resemblance ("as" versus "like") but also between the particular (*a* man) and the general (man). Inasmuch as Herder's animals speak and act not "as a man but like man," they lead us to no particular, fixed, already-instantiated template; the abstract universality of mankind is not out there in the world to be mimetically reproduced in the fable. What human nature *is* cannot be settled referentially, by pointing to a particular individual. It is here, in its openness about the nature of man, that the fable enacts its human-making labor.

The fabulist offers us not a unified vision of humanity but human nature disaggregated into separate traits and packaged in zoomorphic form. "The human soul is, as it were, dispersed among all the animal characters," as Herder puts it, "and the fable seeks only here and there to fashion this scattered reason into a whole."[126] The beasts represent the *disjecta membra* of an elusive unity in a theoretically endless train of examples that need not add up to anything. For although Herder claims that the fable only seeks "here and there to fashion this scattered reason into a whole," no composite figure pieces together an ideal human from the best bits of the animals, as in the Zeuxis collecting model myth in Chapter 1. Even where untransfigured man is present, as in "The Man and the Flea," he does not blend all the traits represented by the fable's bestiary into an all-in-one figure. Certainly the one-dimensional "man" fails to offer an elevated template to which humanity might aspire. On these terms, fable's exemplarity curiously stems from the partiality of the examples it offers.

Inasmuch as the fable does not treat humanity as a finished product but as a process involving multiple agencies, not all of them human, it challenges a settled vision of human beings as serene, self-sufficient entities, securely planted, like Bacon's fly, at the center of the world. The multitude of things animated in the fable thus splinters the meanings of the *anthropos*—that tautological version of "humanity as what makes us human"—by showing how a creature defined by its ability to "know itself" (to return to Linnaeus) can learn "who it is" by coming to terms with "what it is" or what it thought it might be. The lessons the fable offers about human nature do not issue from mimesis or from the invitation to identify with anthropomorphic figures. Instead, humanity is elaborated through the presentation of examples that are (literally and metaphorically) hard to follow.

The title of this section—"*L'exemple que donc je suis*"—somewhat coyly borrows from the title of Derrida's influential essay "L'animal que donc je suis," itself a play on the Cartesian cogito: "Je pense, donc je suis." Working off of the double sense of "je suis" as "I am" and "I follow," Derrida's title names the animal as what the first-person "I" both "is" and "follows." The fable reader endeavors to know what she is (or to become what she ought to be) not by doggedly copying the examples offered in the story but by following them in the way we "follow" an argument. Inasmuch as education involves the endless endeavor to breach the tautology of being what we already are, the ability to follow an example—to commit to a principle that is not intrinsic to one's being, to cleave to a form or figure that is not one's own—is part of what allows us to be or become human. By following an example, we endeavor to become a different kind of first person, seeking to be more like the thing we are not, be it animal, vegetable, mineral, or human. To encounter an example is, then, to expose ourselves to transfiguration; it is to rupture the tautology of likeness. If, as Michael Taussig puts it, "*to give an example, to instantiate, to be concrete*" is to allow "the replication, the copy, [to] acquire . . . the power of the represented," then to follow an example is to allow ourselves to be "thereby lifted out of ourselves into those images."[127] Even as the illustrating example in fable brings the abstract precept to the level of the concrete, the reading of the example operates as a sort of metalepsis, traversing the border between the fiction and the real world.

Yet the example in the fable does not involve identification with a particular figure but the derivation of principles to govern action. We saw above that a single story may produce multiple conflicting morals. The imperfect alignment between particular practice and universal rule means that the fable does not invariably lead to a stable moral principle. "However well adopted the example may be to the moral [*moralité*]," Marmontel contends in the *Encyclopédie*, "the example is a particular fact, the moral is a general maxim. . . . The example contained in the fable is the indication [of the morality] and not the proof."[128] A map without GPS, the fable offers possible routes to a destination without pinning a particular one down. And while an individual fable may leave us with a clear takeaway, fables are presented in *collections*, often offering wildly contradictory lessons.

For the most part, fables do not issue enjoinders: "do this" or "be that." They ask us what to do, and they insist that what we do will define what—and thus who—we are: wolf or lamb, ant or grasshopper. The practical morality offered in fable suggests that the question "who am I?" (or "who will I be?") is an open question—one to be answered by deciding "what I [will] do." For if the fable is designed to teach, it must leave its student free to learn: a compulsory example ceases to be an example and becomes a rule. The liberty to adopt or to refuse the moral lesson is central to the fable's pedagogy. It is for this reason that fabulists underscore that readers possess and perform a freedom that animals ostensibly lack. "We give the Proprieties of Animals, though necessary and unchangeable, for the Image and Representation of our Inclinations the most free," La Motte tells us.[129] In taking "the actions of animals, [which are] always necessary, for the image of our own, which are free," in Richer's words, we both attest to the imperatives underlying the fable's morality and embrace a distinctively human interpretive license.[130] It is telling that many fables offer *bad* examples—what *not* to do.

Fables oblige readers to engage in multifarious comparisons—of self to fable-creature, of narrative to precept, of example to practice, of one fable to another—without necessarily elevating one choice decisively above the rest. By offering a plurality of figures in which we can trace a human likeness, they rupture any vision we might have of humanity as a fixed form. Fable offers us not a cookie-cutter singularity but a multitude, not a mirror image of the human but rules for action that unfold metonymically. On these terms, "the man" in the fable, that consolidated figure that bestows a discrete coherent shape on our reflected image, is *not* an example of humanity that we are invited to imitate; the man is simply one figure among many. The version of humanity presented in fable is a proposal rather than a model—an example that we can choose to follow (or not).

To follow, Paul de Man observes, "is not at all the same as *match*. . . . We have a metonymic, a successive pattern, in which things follow, rather than a metaphorical unifying pattern in which things become one by resemblance."[131] To follow an example is not to identify with a character or to adopt a precept; it is to enact a choice about what one should become. The morphisms proposed by fable invite the reader to enter into a potentially infinite catalogue of possibilities: we could do—or be—this or this or this. Humanity is not depicted as a static figure (moreover, most of the figures in fable are animals) but a dynamic elicited or even enacted in processes of reading. "My Mind through the whole Fable," as La Motte puts it (in an argument in favor of saving the moral for last), "has all the Exercise and Employment it is capable of."[132] The nature of our humanity has *yet* to be determined, although we only recognize its not-yet-formed nature when anthropomorphisms proliferate and show us all the other things we might be.

Humans, David Hume declares, have a universal propensity "to conceive all beings like themselves, and to transfer to every object, those qualities, with which they are familiarly acquainted, and of which they are intimately conscious. We find human faces in the moon, armies in the clouds."[133] Hume's anthropomorphism discovers and projects human likenesses everywhere, (confirming the assumption that we already know and invariably recognize what humans are). On these terms, Hume's anthropomorphism would seem to be irredeemably anthropocentric. Yet in asking us to find humanity *in others*, anthropomorphism preserves the possibility that humanity may be something other than what we already recognize it as being. Inasmuch as anthropomorphism expands the category of entities deemed capable of acting and responding, allowing the powers possessed by other forms of life and matter to become visible, it may—or so Jane Bennett has recently argued—help "counter the narcissism of humans in charge of the world" by registering what she calls "the agentic contributions of nonhuman forces (operating in nature, in the human body, and in human artifacts)."[134] Inasmuch as the fable's anthropomorphism does not treat humanity as a finished product but as a process involving multiple agencies, not all of them human, it questions humanity's place at the still center of a turning world.

Bruno Latour has argued that "the expression 'anthropomorphic' considerably underestimates our humanity" and has advocated seeing how other forms of "morphism . . . define the *anthropos*,"[135] while Lorraine Daston roots for an anthropomorphism that uses analogies with the human to find the "multitude of *anthropoi*, of kinds of humanity—in this case, of kinds of mind—as well as the multitude of *morphoi*, of shapes of understanding other minds" hidden beneath "the smooth word 'anthropomorphism.'"[136] It is by understanding that the *anthropos* that resides behind anthropomorphism is not fixed that we can use fable as an instrument for self-making. In its seemingly indiscriminate anthropomorphizing of animals, minerals, plants, abstractions, and men, the fable offers a plenitude of entities in and through which a reader might (as Linnaeus enjoined) "know thyself." Rather than simply giving the reader an image after humanity's own likeness—showing it, tautologically, to be what it is—the fable asks the reader, in its playful and sometimes sinister fashion, to find an anthropomorphic image in the nonhuman elements and forms that make—or personify—that humanity. And in inciting us to find that image, fables offer us a glimpse of something other than ourselves as we are already known to be, presenting us with, in every sense, an impossibly hard act to follow.

CHAPTER 5

Crusoe's Island of Misfit Things

[In *Robinson Crusoe*] there are no sunsets and no sunrises; there is no solitude and no soul. There is, on the contrary, staring us full in the face nothing but a large earthenware pot. . . . Defoe, by reiterating that nothing but a plain earthenware pot stands in the foreground, persuades us to see remote islands and the solitudes of the human soul. By believing fixedly in the solidity of the pot and its earthiness, he has subdued every other element to his design; he has roped the whole universe into harmony. And is there any reason, we ask as we shut the book, why the perspective that a plain earthenware pot exacts should not satisfy us as completely, once we grasp it, as man himself in all his sublimity standing against a background of broken mountains and tumbling oceans with stars flaming in the sky?
—Virginia Woolf, *The Second Common Reader*

"A thing is identical with itself."—There is no finer example of a useless proposition, which yet is connected with a certain play of the imagination. It is as if in imagination we put a thing into its own shape and saw that it fitted.

We might also say: "Every thing fits into itself." Or again: "Every thing fits into its own shape." At the same time we look at a thing and imagine that there was a blank left for it, and that now it fits into it exactly.

Does this spot   "*fit*" into its white surrounding?—*But that is just how it would look* if there had at first been a hole in its place and it then fitted into the hole. But when we say "it fits" we are not simply describing this appearance; not simply this *situation*.
—Ludwig Wittgenstein, *Philosophical Investigations*

This book began with a tautology—humanity is what makes humans human—so it is perhaps appropriate to end with Ludwig Wittgenstein's example of a useless proposition—"A thing is identical with itself."[1] The chapters of this book have examined the various ways writers and artists sought to breach such tautologies, by recognizing the ways humanity, far from subsisting in serene autonomy, defines itself in and through relations, sometimes adversarial, sometimes complementary, to the world outside itself: animals, material objects, other human beings. As we have seen, these attempts to elaborate a definition of humanity entail a trial-and-error process that keeps punching holes in the categories available to describe what we are. If there is a moral to my argument (though morals, as we saw in the last chapter, are not to be trusted), it would be that nothing—least of all humanity—is identical to itself. There is no neat outline delimiting the human, like the silhouette of a cartoon figure that has crashed through a wall or the line chalked on asphalt where a corpse once lay. There is instead a restless play of the imagination in the face of Wittgenstein's useless proposition: a willingness to try on all manner of shapes, as it were, just for size. Perhaps the most sustained experiment in this imaginative play occurs in the literary form for which the period is now celebrated: the novel.

It may seem counterintuitive to end a book that has been devoted to nonhuman figures and perspectives with a chapter on Daniel Defoe's *Robinson Crusoe*, a novel often recognized as a locus classicus of modern individualism. It may also be surprising to conclude an argument that has addressed estranging, nonverisimilitudinous representations with a work celebrated as the Ur-text of formal realism. Jonathan Swift's satire *Gulliver's Travels* would in many ways seem like a more logical endpoint, with its funhouse distortions of great and small, its mockery of the New Science, its riddle-like descriptions of familiar objects, and its rational horse-like Houyhnhnms in the political fable of Book 4. In closing instead with *Robinson Crusoe*, I want to think about how the literary and artistic depictions of nonhuman points of view discussed in the first four chapters of this book—the world as seen by literally mindless things and by animals—contribute to the techniques used to render the world according to human characters. What happens when we consider the novel's investment in individual particularity and empirical description in light of these experiments with nonhuman perspective? What might this genealogy reveal about literary character (which, as critics have recently argued, is not necessarily human)?[2] Does the novel's commitment to formal unity perforce imply that the world must be organized around a single narrative vantage point, and must that vantage be human? If so, does the anthropocentric framework underwrite the novel's realism by tailoring its descriptions to a human eye-view?

While the first four chapters explored fictions that largely banish humanity from their purview, *Robinson Crusoe* offers a first-person narrative of a man stranded on an island without other human beings for companionship. Vulnerable and isolated, Crusoe struggles to domesticate the world both literally and metaphorically by harnessing animals and things to his needs, on the one hand, and by mustering the creatures and objects he encounters into intelligible forms, on the other. Even as the descriptive labor that coaxes entities into their "proper" classes as human, animal, or thing secures the epistemological authority of the novel's human narrator, it strives—not always successfully—to align the novel's claim to realism with an anthropocentric framework. Whereas the texts in the preceding chapters dislodge humanity from its position as the still point of a turning world, offering the estranging perspectives of nonhuman creatures identified as classes of being (a bird, a louse, a flea, a glove), here the human individual is planted front and center, offering a first-person account of his own adventures.

Enshrined as the epitome of novelistic individualism, Robinson Crusoe has been depicted variously as homo economicus, as quintessential man of nature, as exemplary spiritual autobiographer, and as imperial prototype.[3] Samuel Taylor Coleridge famously characterizes Crusoe as "a representative of humanity in general," who "makes me forget my *specific* class, character, and circumstances, [and] raises me into the universal man."[4] Yet these celebrations of Crusoe as a type or as an abstract model of humanity are hard to reconcile with the novel's preference (in Ian Watt's words) for "the discrete particular, the directly apprehended sensum, and the autonomous individual" over "the ideal, the universal, and the corporate."[5] How can the novel's commitment to gritty empirical details be brought into line with its elevation of the particular individual into Coleridge's "universal man"?

Heather Keenleyside has addressed this seeming contradiction by arguing that Defoe's novel invites us to read Crusoe as an "allegorical personification" —"the embodiment of an abstraction (Man) rather than an aggregate or average term (a representative of men)."[6] In this account, we read Crusoe straight into the universal, as the incarnation of a representative idea in exemplary form. Yet we not only read Crusoe *as* an "allegorical personification"; we also, I want to argue, read *through* him. Indeed, so steeped are we in Crusoe's perspective that (in Edgar Allan Poe's apt words) we ourselves "become perfect abstractions in the intensity of our interest," so absorbed by his activities that we adopt him as a kind of human eye-view.[7] The novel realizes—makes real—its concept of humanity both through its descriptions, which single out those properties of objects that answer to human needs, and through the focalization of these descriptions through our first-person protagonist. Like the microscope, the riddle, the fable, and the bird's-eye view, *Robinson Crusoe* serves as a device for adjudicating perspective, its realism a function of its alignment (or not) with a human vantage.

It may seem unnecessary to argue that Defoe's novel crafts an anthropocentric point of view. What could be more emblematic of humanity's dominion than the famous frontispiece of Crusoe clad in his goatskin costume? Yet this freestanding exemplar of human individuality is the *product* of Defoe's novel, not fully realized in the text proper. Seen in relation to the estranging viewpoints analyzed in the first four chapters, Crusoe's "human" vantage is as much an artifice as a flea's- or a fly's-eye view. In *Robinson Crusoe*, the descriptive labor required to impose provisional order upon the irremediably heterogeneous elements that make up the world of the novel exposes the force necessary to coax things into line with an anthropocentric (and Eurocentric) framework. Inasmuch as the privileged perspective that emerges from the novel is merely one eye-view among others, the novel's claim to verisimilitude issues less from mimesis than from the fact that it describes the world in accordance with human interests and needs. And if the novel's realism hinges on this description of the world from an anthropocentric perspective, it is because the perspective produced by realism is the one we elect to denominate "human." This too is part of the labor of the novel.

Despite its claims to mimetic fidelity, description does not just mirror a preexisting world; it creates it. Things in Defoe's novel do not possess the obduracy or clarity of outline that Woolf's earthenware pot in the epigraph seems to possess.[8] Even the pots in *Robinson Crusoe*, after all, are not exactly pots: they are initially, Crusoe informs us, "large earthen ugly things, I cannot call them Jarrs," and even after Crusoe discovers the trick of baking his pots, "the Shapes of them," he tells us, continue "very indifferent" (88, 89). To imagine Woolf's pot is to come precariously close to enacting the useless proposition Wittgenstein lambastes in the epigraph: "It is as if in imagination we put a thing into its own shape and saw that it fitted." In treating objects as if we already know their shape and morphology, as if they have a cookie-cutter outline, we engage in a version of Wittgenstein's game of linguistic *fort-da*, which vaporizes and rematerializes an object that cannot quite escape its own identity. Descriptions are meant to evoke something that is not present—to "put a thing into its own shape" when we do not already have a blank imagined—and yet they rarely create a neat hole or a neat whole into which an object can step (that is where a certain vagrancy of the imagination comes in). Even the figure of Crusoe himself needs to be laboriously demarcated in the novel, as if he does not quite know his own edges. Language in Defoe's novel describes the world in the double sense of rendering its objects in words and delimiting entities as one might describe a circle or a line in geometry.

Language describes, but *description* tends to emerge precisely at those moments when nomenclature falters or when the names assigned to objects fail to render them adequately. The world almost never resembles its linguistic mug shot. Descriptions become necessary at those moments in which objects do not align with the words or names available to receive them. They give shape and delineated form to subjects and objects (human, animal, and thing) and work to articulate divisions between them, a process that (as we saw in Chapter 4's discussion of Locke's changeling) pits the particularizing detail, which distinguishes the unique properties of an entity, against the classificatory detail, which categorizes individuals.[9] In the opening section of this chapter, I analyze Crusoe's efforts to muster the things and creatures he encounters into forms readily intelligible to a human eye. While Crusoe often treats objects and animals as analogous to familiar entities, the world also refuses to cleave to the categories provided by language. I examine how Crusoe's descriptions strive to custom-fit things and animals to human needs and interests, constraining what we are able to see about the thing (as property, as commodity, as tool, as fetish) and about the animal (as food, as threat, as fellow creature, as pet). Things and animals appear only in partial view, insofar as their affordances allow them to be incorporated into Crusoe's designs, leaving the human enshrined at the novel's center.

Yet novelistic description *also* exposes the labor involved in making things ply to human will or cleave to a human form. In the second section of the chapter, I show how Crusoe's figurative struggle to fit names to bodies and bodies to categories finds a counterpart in his literal efforts to fit body to skin, self to world. Even as Crusoe's things must be coaxed into their "proper" linguistic forms, so too must skins be first molded into clothing and then fitted to his human form. The goatskins that Crusoe fashions into his wardrobe and the botched shoes or "Pair of somethings" (109) he contrives for his feet redefine the thresholds of his body, making it hard to know where one kind of thing or being ends and another begins, to decide when one has arrived at a whole. It is difficult to determine what Judith Butler calls the *morphe* of things or of bodies: "the shape by which their material discreteness is marked."[10] Crusoe as an autonomous being is *not* a given in Defoe's novel.

If bodies do not neatly fit into their discrete shape or *morphe* in *Robinson Crusoe*, they also do not fit neatly together. There is always a remainder. Even as Crusoe tailors things to the human eye or makes them fit for human use, something—the unpaired shoe that washes up on the shore following the shipwreck, the footprint discovered in the sand—always exceeds the instrumental relations Crusoe wishes to take to the object world. At those moments in which the world fails to match up to its "proper" (material or nominal) form, Crusoe encounters the resistance of things and animals to human mastery—to what we "know" them to be. This is a problem for Crusoe *within* the novel, but it is also, I argue in the final section of the chapter, the problematic *of* the novel, which must rope the world into some kind of unity. Put another way, the difficulty in making things fit first to their "proper" forms and then to Crusoe's body encapsulates in small the difficulty in making the disparate elements of the novelistic world fit together. This chapter explores the role played by description in creating that formal unity.

Description is the red-headed stepchild of literary history. Like the bywork featured in the "lesser" genres of still life and trompe l'oeil—the mere things that make up the background to the human drama of history painting—description is often understood as subordinate to the narrative that delivers the stories of (human) subjects.[11] Dismissed by early writers as an ornamental superfluity that offers the individuating particular rather than the universal essence, or snubbed as what Cynthia Wall terms a "*res non grata*"[12] blocking the forward momentum of the narrative, description (like the riddle) exposes the inadequacy of the word to compass the thing, as it takes on the thankless task of representing the misfit things that cannot be immediately assimilated to the world as we already know it to be. It thus serves, Joanna Stalnaker contends, "as a heuristic device, as a virtual perspective that reveals something about our relationship to objects, or about the relationship between words and objects, that we cannot perceive in our everyday experience of them."[13] Description is a reminder that the fit of words to things, parts to wholes, individuals to categories, is laboriously produced rather than freely given.

These questions of fit are central to Georg Lukács's influential account of the novel. In *The Theory of the Novel*, Lukács argues that the novel is born out of the loss of the concrete rounded totality of the world of epic, in which the "immanence of meaning" coincided with empirical reality. Epic raises no question of fit because everything is always already fitting, while the novel, as "the epic of an age in which the extensive totality of life is no longer directly given," must struggle to reconstitute that lost totality through "the paradoxical fusion of heterogeneous and discrete components into an organic whole which is then abolished over and over again."[14] The loss of the organic wholeness of the world of epic structures the relation of subject to object in the novel, as the hero must endlessly seek to overcome the hiatus between the immanent meaning of life and outer reality. Indeed, it is this hiatus or estrangement between the hero and his world that makes the individual subject possible. Whereas the rounded totality of the world of epic is "too organic for any part of it to become so enclosed within itself," so that no part of it (no individual within it) is able "to find itself as an interiority: that is, to become a personality," the novelistic hero as the "product of estrangement from the outside world" produces his individuality as he undertakes to create a unified world out of "elements essentially alien to one another."[15] One might understand Crusoe's efforts to wrest meaning from his experience and to fit seemingly random events into a providential order as a version of this (subject- and world-producing) activity, and in this sense for Defoe, as for Lukács, the novel is generated out of a ceaseless attempt to engineer a relation of heterogeneous part to unified whole, to overcome the distance between what Lukács calls the "mutually alien worlds of subject and object."[16]

But in what ways and to what extent *are* these two worlds mutually alien in Defoe? The fact that it is difficult to know where the edges of particular entities begin and end, and to delineate where the categories of human, animal, and thing begin and end, suggests that the relations of subject and object do not operate according to the strict binary of the "mutually alien." If humans, animals, and things in Defoe's novel do not fit neatly into their own shape and form, then they cannot be neatly and symmetrically opposed. On these terms, the problem with which the eighteenth-century novel grapples is twofold: on the one hand, how to describe subjects and objects—to confer on them discrete shapes, make them fit into their own forms, and thereby articulate the distinction between them—and, on the other hand, how to make them fit together in the world of the novel. The two questions have to be posed together. In *Robinson Crusoe*, subject and object are not "mutually alien"; they are mutually constituting, both in the material sense that persons and things, humans and animals, make one another and in the formal literary sense that Crusoe, like his readers, must struggle to work the heterogeneous elements of the novelist world into meaningful unity, making things—shoes, skins, or even footprints—fit the person or making the person fit the thing. On these terms, the formal unity of the novel issues neither from the mimetic exactitude of Crusoe's descriptions of the world nor from protracted descriptions of inwardness, but rather from the rendering of the world from a subjective point of view. The question this chapter raises is how—and whether—that subjective perspective comes to be understood as human.

By locating Crusoe's first-person perspective in the genealogy of the non-human vantages proffered by the fable, the riddle, the microscope, and the artifice of perspective in painting, we can see how the novel operates as a device or apparatus that wrests us into line with Crusoe's point of view. Yet this vantage is every bit as fictive as those afforded in the previous chapters. While a common species identity may close the imaginative gap between the reader's and the character's perspectives, it is as impossible to know another human's inner experience as it is to know what it is like to be a bat or a louse or a bird. Notwithstanding its claims to realism, the novel offers us two things we can never know or experience in real life: what passes in another's mind and what the world is like when we are not there. In describing the world through Crusoe's eyes, the novel borrows techniques for imagining other (nonhuman) points of view to access Crusoe's first-person conscious-ness; in reporting on transactions occurring in our absence, it represents the world without us.

The projection of such virtual standpoints involves substantial imagina-tive labor. The realist novel's ultimate trick is to erase that labor by represent-ing its crafted eye-view as mimetic—as a copy of reality. As Michael McKeon astutely observes, *Robinson Crusoe*'s "astonishing descent to the subjective roots of objective and empirical reality has been turned so productively to the stabilizing of that reality that it can be treated as though it had never happened."[17] While *Robinson Crusoe* exposes the processes by which the novel fashions a human perspective on its world, it takes as a last step the forgetting of this hard work, so that Crusoe's subjective interpretation of the world can pass for an account of the world as it really is. We saw in the introduction that humans "realize" their abstractions, "speak[ing] of them in imitation of the way they speak of real objects."[18] Here the novel makes real, through fiction, the fiction that is humanity.

If our sense of the humanity of Crusoe's first-person perspective issues as much from the way he describes the world he encounters as it does from any direct representation of his subjectivity, *our* humanity is confirmed by the fact that we find his descriptions to be lifelike. We saw in Chapter 3 that humanity is retroactively defined by the likeness discovered by anthropomorphism (we come to understand what we look like when we see other entities crafted in "our" image). Here the human "eye-view" is retroactively grasped in the legibility of the realist text. Indeed, inasmuch as realism affirms a human perspective (in contrast with the estranging optics of the fable, the microscope, the riddle, the trompe l'oeil), the novel becomes a device for reproducing—indeed, reifying—a "human" eye-view through the immediacy with which the novelistic world seems intelligible. These modes of description, once designated as realistic, acquire the power to designate what counts as real. Novelistic realism not only accommodates an anthropocentric perspective but also, by representing that framework as natural or true, helps consolidate the abstract category of "humanity" into a fixed (rather than processual) form. The fact that Crusoe's Eurocentric eye comes to be denominated generically human is part of the colonizing project of the novel, as the emergence of a consolidated template locks other hierarchies in place. In putting the novel in proximity with the trompe l'oeil, the riddle, the fable, the microscopic world, we can, however, glimpse the erased labor that aligns the world we designate as realistic with what we stipulate to be human. Recognizing that labor, in turn, helps us grasp the ways that literature not only elicits humanity by interpellating its readers, but also works to reify the category, sanctioning one set of values—one version of the human—over all others.

Fitting Words (Detail, Description, Defoe)

Most discussions of things and animals in *Robinson Crusoe*—and there are many, variously taking up his cats, his dog, his parrot, his goats, his gold, his clothing, his tools, his pots, his raisins—proceed as if the identity of the object or animal is self-evident.[19] Yet entities in Crusoe's narrative—from the misshapen pots and his "Creature like a wild Cat" (41) to the chair of "a tolerable Shape, but never to please me" (54)—do not neatly fit into their own shapes; indeed, they often slide out of the categories that ostensibly contain them. Thus when Crusoe reports that he has made himself "a Squab or Couch, with the Skins of the Creatures, I had kill'd, and with other soft Things" or describes his goats as "a living Magazine of Flesh, Milk, Butter and Cheese" (111), the casual assimilation of animal and thing reminds us of the fragility of the barriers that distinguish one kind of being from another. The incorporation of "the Skins of the Creatures I had kill'd" into the catalog of "other soft Things," the characterization of the goats as a "living Magazine" of the "Flesh, Milk, Butter and Cheese" taken from their bodies, remind us of the way language may absorb or forget the origins of the usable object: a skin refashioned ceases to be primarily a skin and becomes a glove, or a goatskin glove, with its origins subordinated to an adjective, an attribute, an accidental trait.

Things move—or are transported by language—across the categories (natural and social, real and fabricated, animate and nonanimate) that uphold their ostensible difference. Woolf's pot "staring us full in the face" is strangely humanized,[20] while Crusoe himself frequently blurs the line between human and animal, whether in his famously anthropomorphized family of feline and canine surrogates or in his expressed relief at escaping both the "Hands of . . . Savages" and the "Hands of Lyons" (20). Crusoe's famous apostrophe to the money he rescues from the ship ("O thou Drug") addresses it as a living thing, which he chooses not to send "to the Bottom as a Creature whose Life is not worth saving" (43). If, as Bruno Latour has argued, the definition of modernity in terms of humanism "overlooks the simultaneous birth of 'nonhumanity'—things, or objects, or beasts,"[21] then the border between them would seem to be still under negotiation in the early eighteenth-century novel, as if, to borrow Latour's vocabulary, the modern settlement that theoretically sunders humanity from nonhumanity is indeed accompanied by the ongoing material production of hybrid entities that embody both. In this sense, the sundered world of heterogeneous elements that Lukács associates with the novel may help us retrace the emergence of the partitioned world that Latour associates with modernity.

Latour's modern constitution involves the simultaneous activities of "translation" (which creates "mixtures between entirely new types of beings, hybrids of nature and culture") and of "purification" (which creates "two entirely distinct ontological zones: that of human beings on the one hand; that of nonhumans on the other").[22] Inasmuch as descriptions are embroiled in classificatory and definitional projects that seek to align the empirical with the epistemological, they might be understood as engaged in "purification"; insofar as they simultaneously register the recalcitrance of things before the words designed to denominate them, they record continuous acts of "translation." The attempted separation and ongoing conjunction of subject and object, person and thing, human and animal that Latour associates with modernity is particularly apparent in an emerging literary form such as the novel. The novel is a useful place to look for the sorting of human, animal, and thing not only because its formal realism is perforce invested in the detailed and verisimilar recording of the empirical world but also because the novelty of its form makes it an important index of what happens when, as John Bender and Michael Marrinan put it, "the technology used to register descriptive features changes so dramatically that things previously invisible become newly visible."[23] Like the camera obscura or the microscope, the novel readjusts the thresholds of the perceptible; like these devices, it brings to light things that do not always conform to the categories available to receive them.

Recent scholarship has seen the proliferation of description in eighteenth-century natural history, philosophy, rhetoric, aesthetics, and literature as a symptom of the tensions between the empirical (real, particular, historical) and the ideal (abstract, universal, system-based). The shift from the seventeenth century's spare invocation of isolated things to the rich, contextualizing descriptions of later eighteenth-century novels, Cynthia Wall has argued, reflects the insufficiency of the common stock of familiar images to capture the heterogeneity of things in an era of burgeoning commerce. In Joanna Stalnaker's account of the centrality of Enlightenment natural history to literary description, the incapacity of the word to measure up to the thing and of language to capture the historically evanescent becomes the engine of epistemological transformation, as the unfinished nature of description becomes the impetus for further scientific exploration and generic experimentation. In their study of the diagram as a "working object," Bender and Marrinan likewise stress the ways descriptions compel readers to correlate parts and data into processes (a dynamic contrast with the fixed Albertian modes of single-point perspective discussed in Chapter 1). In eighteenth-century Europe, the welter of information and objects flooding in from all over the globe, coupled with the emergence of new disciplines of knowledge, transforms (manifold, sometimes contradictory) descriptive protocols, exemplified in the multiple entries—drawn from mathematics, natural history, and belles-lettres—for the word *description* offered in the *Encyclopédie*.[24] No unified field theory of description masters the world, which also means that no one point of view—anthropocentric or otherwise—can hold sway.

As we have seen in the previous chapters, the fact that a single entity might be rendered from multiple vantage points turns the very identity of a thing into an object of contention, making description one of the sites where the literary and political senses of the word *representation* converge. Drawing on the etymological link between *chose* and *cause* [*thing* and *cause*], Michel Serres argues that the settlement of "what a thing is" also decides its "cause" in both the natural and juridical-political senses of the word. A far cry from Woolf's serenely self-evident earthenware pot, the thing becomes a collective verdict in Serres's account, "as if objects themselves only existed in accordance with the debates of a legislative body or in the wake of a verdict pronounced by a jury. Language wishes that the world would derive only from it. At least so it says."[25] The very name conferred on an object is the outcome of a campaign to keep things firmly in the grasp of a particular language. The wish of language that "the world would derive from it" precipitates a mortal struggle to extinguish all that does not cleave to the word, a "philosophical imperialism," in Theodor Adorno's evocative expression, that "bewitche[s] what is heterogeneous to it."[26] Eighteenth-century descriptive practices simultaneously succumb to the "philosophical imperialism" of language and rebel against it, as they engage in Latour's work of "purification" while registering ongoing acts of "translation." In logic and rhetoric, in natural history, and in the novel, writers strive to devise modes of description able to accommodate the uncertain relation of real to ideal, concrete particular to abstract classification, incidental detail to essential trait. (Although the *dictée* of language usurps the place of the human jury or assembly in Serres's prose, he slyly undermines the fixed intent behind language's will to power: "at least so it says.")

To be sure, Defoe's characters often circumvent description altogether, simply dubbing objects X or Y. "*Things,*" as Wall points out, "*often stand in for description in early texts.*"[27] The objects to which Crusoe and Moll Flanders and Captain Singleton refer seem real because they are already familiar to modern readers, not because they are described to us in painstaking detail. *Robinson Crusoe*'s realism emerges not from lavish description but from the minimal references that summon objects before the reader's eyes by invoking rather than describing them. When Crusoe does not have a proper name ready to hand, he borrows one based on similitude: "two Fowls like Ducks," "a Sea Fowl or two, something like a brand Goose," "Hares, as I thought them to be" (53, 70, 80). Crusoe describes the world using analogies to known entities when he encounters creatures of uncertain kind: the cat-*like* creatures are analogously cats, or even, in the absence of a proper name, cats as catachreses. And when Crusoe drops the suffix—the cat-like creature subsequently becomes a cat—it seems like a form of antonomasia: a proper noun invited to stand for an entire category, a name borrowed to denominate the species in much the same way that a rake might be named a Lothario. The world Crusoe thereby builds—and in this it parallels the fictive world Defoe constructs—is here summoned into being and fashioned through nominalist language, as names are bestowed through an arbitrary christening and things take on a presumptive form by virtue of this primary baptism.

Words in this sense work exactly as if "everything fits into its own shape." On those occasions when things do not quite fit into their own shape, Crusoe recounts his endeavors to *make* them into the thing we have in mind, capturing the object en route to its conformity to his needs. Although Crusoe does not possess a godlike capacity to wield the logos ("let there be a pot"), his descriptions of making amount to a circuitous version of the demiurge ("and so it was, kind of, eventually"). His labors produce pallid but functional imitations of their originals: "I made me a Thing like a Hodd," he tells us (55). He moors his boat with "a Thing like an Anchor, but indeed which could not be call'd either Anchor or Grapling; however, it was the best I could make of its kind" and contrives a "three Corner'd ugly Thing, like what we call in *England*, a Shoulder of Mutton Sail" (126, 165). His is a world of jury-rigged approximations, both linguistic and material. His pots, his shoes, his houses are all good enough, usable if not consummately realized, in much the same way that his language is composed of good-enough words, words that offer a sense of objects without exhaustively or even mimetically rendering them, words that do the trick.

Crusoe placidly proceeds as if imperfect incarnations of English objects really were what he says they are—a process that silently assimilates the labor and know-how of others into his work.[28] Yet few of Crusoe's things live up to the grandiose names bestowed on them (his country house is no Chatsworth). Indeed, the form and the fiction of Crusoe's pot is summoned via a *withheld* name—"I cannot call them Jarrs" (88)—that simulates the object, both in the sense that this is a novel (so there is no real pot) and in the sense that the creation of a pot, any pot, involves a kind of fiction, a gap to be traversed between the idea and the thing, between the category (of jar or pot) and the empirical object (the large, ugly earthen things). Under such circumstances, naming becomes part of making both inasmuch as it designates the object to be approximated or realized and inasmuch as it describes the object in novelistic space.[29] If we think of description not simply as the fleshing out of an already known object but as a strategy for what Barbara Stafford calls "imaging the unseen," then description involves not only detail—the filling in of the outline of a preordained form—but also drawing an object into visibility, and even, potentially, *making* the object.[30] The etymological root of detail in the French *détailler*, to carve out a shape, likewise suggests the constituting labor it performs. The workings of language in the novel—its evocation of distant worlds through an appeal to the imagination—thus might be understood in terms not only of mimetic verisimilitude or aesthetic embellishment but also in terms of making, of *poeisis* as *techne*. That is, the novel bears the traces of what Rayna Kalas argues is an earlier Renaissance understanding of "poetic language as an instrument of figuration that partakes of worldly reality rather than as an artifact or concept that reflects reality by observing the mimetic conventions of pictorial representation."[31]

For although Defoe's descriptions at times deliver objects prêt-à-porter (ready for material or cognitive appropriation by a Watt-like self-possessed individual), still others offer us the phenomenological struggle to perceive or recognize what a thing is. Crusoe's objects are not invariably prefabricated entities, always already known and recognized, a fact that, as Ala Alryyes argues, should be understood in terms of empiricism's treatment of the senses. "Lockean empiricism is both cognitive and material. It seeks to clarify how the senses convey objects to the mind and how objects themselves—fruits, say, or land—become fit for apprehension, for both perception and possession."[32] Whereas Crusoe describes some objects "with an exactitude that makes them fit for possession," Alryyes notes, others are highlighted "as 'things' that make readers glimpse his narrators' struggle with rendering arduous experiences."[33] On these terms, Defoe's descriptions are not strictly mimetic.

Entities encountered by the senses are not already known objects relayed intact to the mind, but things or creatures that attain shape and meaning through sensory and descriptive processing. Thus when Crusoe enters a cave and encounters what will prove to be a dying goat, he initially apprehends "two broad shining Eyes of some Creature, whether Devil or Man" (128) and hears "a very loud Sigh, . . . follow'd by a broken Noise, *as if* of Words half-express'd" (129). The "broken Noise" that Crusoe strains to make into words offers up the raw unprocessed nature of experience before the imposition of an idea, the terror incited by what Addison evocatively calls "sounds that have no Ideas annexed to them."[34] Before experience has been named, digested, fitted to ideas, it is inchoate, knowable through fractured elements (eyes, a sigh, a broken noise), hesitant analogies ("as if") and speculative extrapolations ("Devil or Man"). Crusoe, John Richetti astutely argues, offers us "the unruly and actually incommunicable world of reality as experienced

. . . only by constantly giving up the attempt to describe it and rendering it in the solid sequences of orderly narrative. What we read is not simply the sequence but the sequence offering itself again and again as a partial description and evocation of the experience itself."[35] The novel *narrates* through description both encounters with the unintelligible—the battery of external impressions not yet assimilated to an idea or a word—and the reprocessing of these inchoate encounters into intelligible experience, exposing the work performed by description in shoehorning the recalcitrant raw material of the world into ideas or concepts.

The realism of *Robinson Crusoe*'s world emerges not from exhaustive, mimetically exact description (the perfection of Zeuxis's grapes) but from its rendering of the world from an individualized perspective. Defoe's characters, as George Starr puts it, "tell us directly rather little about themselves or their external world, but they create an illusion of both by projecting themselves upon their world in the act of perceiving it. . . . Character is revealed through response to the other, the external thing or event encountered; at the same time, the external thing or event is described less in objective terms, as it is in itself, than in subjective terms, as it is perceived by the narrator."[36] What we are given to see of the object—what Crusoe's narrative describes—constitutes much of what we get of Crusoe's subjectivity. The reality presented in *Robinson Crusoe* "is subjective rather than interior," as Leo Damrosch puts it in his gloss on Starr's essay. "So long as we imagine ourselves looking outward *with* Crusoe, we see what he sees and feel what he feels. . . . If we try to look *into* any of Defoe's characters we find ourselves baffled; when Crusoe, on seeing the footprint, speaks of being 'confused and out of myself,' we have no clear idea of what kind of self he has when he is in it."[37] The inner world of Robinson Crusoe is manifested largely through his description of things outside. *Who* Crusoe is becomes evident through *what* he describes. Character emerges through the subjective perception of objects rather than through the transparent depiction of inwardness.

Thus Crusoe's laborious conversion of the cannibals from "Thing[s] in human Shape" (112) into fellow human beings traces his shifting perception of what they are, while exposing the difficulty of making empirically encountered entities fit into the broader structures that render the world intelligible. Crusoe turns the cannibals from "Savage Wretches" (120) to "Monsters" and "Creatures" (122) to "barbarous Wretches" and "naked Savages" (123) and thence to "Men" and "People" (124) in a progressive redescription of their nature and proper class. His classification of the cannibals depends neither on their outward forms nor on an itemized catalog of traits associated with "man," like Locke's child ticking off his laundry list of human characteristics (described in the introduction). Instead, what determines the name assigned to the cannibals is Crusoe's subjective emotion (fear, rage, pity). While the philosophical categories that separate the world into humans and nonhumans presuppose an aloof and dispassionate observer able to sort neatly demarcated things into their clearly labeled pigeonholes, Crusoe's descriptive practice reveals classification to involve the rhetorical management of affect, a reminder—to return to the terms with which we began—that the "worlds of subject and object" are not "mutually alien" but mutually constitutive. The name *cannibal* sutures inner and outer worlds in a kind of fetishistic inversion that makes the object possess the trait (fearsomeness) produced by the feeling of the subject (fear).[38]

Crusoe's vocabulary thus reflects his *relations* with other beings rather than their membership in a preexisting class. Throughout the novel, as Keenleyside argues, the word *creature* serves as a "radically nonspecific category" that reveals human and animal alike to be governed by a shared "ontological determination effected by exposure to external force."[39] Crusoe famously characterizes Poll, his cats, and dog as part of his "Family" (108), and extends the pronoun "who," restricted to humans in eighteenth-century grammar manuals, to his animal companions: "my Poll, who began now to be a meer Domestick" (82); "my Dog, who was now grown very old and crazy" (108); "my Flock[,] . . . who were not so wild now as at first they might be supposed to be" (118).[40] The recognition of kinship does not prevent Crusoe from staking a proprietary claim over his fellow creatures. Indeed, his extension of the possessive to "my man Friday" erodes the boundary between human and animal from another direction.

Notwithstanding the capaciousness of his creaturely vocabulary, Crusoe draws lines between human and animal in practice, above all, around the question of who—and what—may be permissibly killed. The term "Murther," for example, is reserved for human beings. To be sure, he cannot "find it [in his] Heart to kill" (105) the kid he bred up tame, but he never describes the slaughter of goats, cats, even a parrot, as murder, and while Crusoe fears being devoured by beasts throughout, it is only when he contemplates the possible presence of "Savages" on the island that "murther" gets added to his list of worries (97). Significantly, Crusoe's famous foray into cultural relativism uses the relation the cannibals take to other creatures to determine whether they are murderers according to their own system of classification:

"They think it no more a crime to kill a Captive taken in War, than we to kill an Ox; nor to eat humane Flesh, than we do to eat Mutton. When I had consider'd this a little, it follow'd necessarily, that . . . these People were not Murtherers" (124). What distinguishes killing from murder is not the nature of the action but its object. As Locke puts it, "What greater Connexion in Nature, has the *Idea* of a Man, than the *Idea* of a Sheep with Killing, that this is made a particular Species of Action, signified by the word *Murther*, and the other not?"[41] Individual words harbor assumptions that create and police boundaries—boundaries that chiefly become visible when violated in practice.

The terminology we use to describe the world selectively registers traits that advance human purposes. Thus we single out the pointed tip of a knife, Locke notes, leaving out "the Figure and the Matter of the Weapon," in order "to make the distinct Species call'd *Stabbing*," as if the verb governs the noun. Language is no impersonal mirror of nature but reflects the desires and aims of the speakers: "The Mind searches not its Patterns in Nature, nor refers the *Ideas* it makes to the real existence of Things; but puts such together, as may best serve its own Purposes, without tying it self to a precise imitation of any thing that really exists." Grounded neither in the referential world ("Nature") nor in mimesis ("a precise imitation"), the mind's ideas are pieced together to accommodate "its own Purposes" rather than answering to the demands of what "really exists." What Locke describes as "the free choice of the Mind, pursuing its own ends" involves a selective recognition of properties, which means, in turn, that "others that have altogether as much union in Nature, are left loose."[42] While words purport to represent the objective world, they are the fruits of an anterior litigation that organizes language around human interests and intentions.

The details Crusoe includes in his descriptions likewise reflect principles of selection and omission that cater to human ends. Of the "*Iron Tree*" we learn that "its exceeding Hardness" makes it suitable material for a shovel (54); the abundance of "Orange, and Lemon, and Citron Trees" is notable because "very few [are] bearing any Fruit" (73). Plants without discoverable uses do not merit description: "There were divers other Plants," Crusoe notes, "which I had no Notion of, or Understanding about, and might perhaps have Vertues of their own, which I could not find out" (72). Crusoe leaves a blank where he draws a blank. Objects are incorporated into extended "how to" sequences that single out those affordances that enable things to meet Crusoe's needs. With the exception of occasional remarks on the luxurance of a vale or the beautiful "Figure" (77) into which his hedges grow, few descriptions are offered just for themselves. Even those moments in which Crusoe entertains a goat's-eye view get harnessed to human purposes. "I observ'd if they saw me in the Valleys, tho' they were on the Rocks, they would run away . . . but if they were feeding in the Valleys and I was upon the Rocks, they took no Notice of me, from whence I concluded, that by the Position of their Opticks, their Sight was so directed downward that they did not readily see Objects that were above them" (46). What matters to Crusoe is not what goats see per se but whether they see *him*. His projection of their perspective contributes not to cross-species communication (unsurprisingly in a survival novel) but to trapping his quarry.[43] After this, Crusoe shoots from above.

Crusoe's unvarying concern with human needs and interests aligns his descriptions with an anthropocentric framework. As Coleridge observes, had Defoe made Crusoe "find out qualities and uses in the before (to him) unknown plants of the island, discover a substitute for hops, for instance, or describe birds, etc.—many delightful pages and incidents might have enriched the book; but then Crusoe would cease to be the universal representative, the person for whom every reader could substitute himself. But now nothing is done, thought, or suffered, or desired, but what every man can imagine himself doing, thinking, feeling, or wishing for."[44] We can all identify with Crusoe's needs, and there is nothing inimitable in his practice. Anyone might carry out these plans and actions.[45] "By Reason and by making the most rational Judgment of things, every Man may be in time Master of every mechanic Art," Crusoe assures us. "Time and Necessity made me a compleat natural Mechanick . . . as I believe it would do any one else" (51, 53). Recapitulating in small Hooke's collective model of technological progress, *Robinson Crusoe* offers one man's single-handed reconstruction of human civilization. Yet if this narrative for Coleridge "calls forth the *whole* of my being," it is (perversely) because it acknowledges only those aspects of the world that answer to human needs. Its universality depends upon its human partiality. Tautological though it may sound, Crusoe is human because he sees from a human point of view—one that places the material world at his disposition as a means to anthropocentric ends.

These instrumental relations have a role to play in our sense of the novel's realism as well. As Margaret Cohen has argued, *Robinson Crusoe*, like other maritime novels, "measures plausibility by performance rather than mimesis," using "the successful accomplishment of a deed" in the arena "of practical action" as the gauge of the veracity Crusoe's account. What Cohen calls the "performability effect" anchors verisimilitude in efficacy or felicity: whether an action is or seems doable. Our willingness to credit the account of our desert island MacGyver, that is, stems from relations of cause and effect rather than a fixed mirroring of some external, referential reality (we may recall Hooke's depictions of the microscopic world, which depend not on a verifiable resemblance but on operability). And inasmuch as the realism of this "performability effect" depends on the practical subordination of the world to human ends, it consolidates the novel's anthropocentric framework.[46] We confirm Crusoe's humanity and affirm our own through our alignment with a common instrumental relation to the material world.

In imagining how we would do things, we implicitly associate ourselves with a human eye-view. Thus when Rousseau wishes Émile "to learn in detail everything one would have to know in such a case [of shipwreck], not through books but through things," he desires Émile "to identify himself with Robinson, to see himself dressed in skins, with a big hat and a broadsword—the whole grotesque paraphernalia of his appearance." Émile's entry into Crusoe the subject is through Crusoe's objects. To identify with another—to put ourselves in another's shoes or walk a mile or two in them—is to draw about us the outer carapace of another's body, to inhabit another's habits. For Rousseau, Émile has but to decant himself into the vessel of Crusoe's dress, clap on the hat and sword.[47]

Yet Rousseau's description takes as a given something laboriously constructed by the novel. The figure of Crusoe is not always already there: prêt-à-porter. While Crusoe's descriptions, as we have just seen, align bodily forms with their proper names, making the exotic world of the island intelligible to the human (English) eye, the material world does not always cooperate. Even as his descriptions must coax entities into their proper categories, so too must Crusoe's skins, shoes, and other accoutrements be tailored to fit his body. Things, as Philip Fisher writes in another context, would seem to "imply the human by existing like jigsaw pieces whose outer surfaces have meaning only when it is seen that they are designed to snap into position against the body."[48] Yet Crusoe's objects do not readily snap into place. If realism's affirmation of an anthropocentric vantage stems from its depiction of a material world subjected to human will, the recalcitrance of things to human intentions—the boat too unwieldy to move to the sea, the unpaired shoes that do not fit Crusoe's body—indicates that the failure or breakdown of these processes likewise has a role to play in producing the novel's reality effect. In the next section, I turn from the way novelistic description musters bodies into categories that accommodate a human eye-view to the ways it deals with those elements and objects that resist assimilation to Crusoe's mastering human form.

Crusoe *bien dans ses peaux*

Nowhere is the figure of Crusoe as an exemplary human being more fully realized than in the indelible image (see Figure 10) propagated by the frontispiece to the first English edition of the novel (some version of which appeared in almost every other edition throughout the eighteenth century).[49] The frontispiece does not depict an actual scene from the text. The shipwreck depicted at left occurs long before Crusoe's domestic enclosure of the island, depicted at right, while the serene weather in the foreground belies the tumultuous sea in the background. Here nature, water, sky, and ship become the backup singers for a diva subject planted at center stage. Crusoe's dominating figure seems to affirm what Michel Serres describes as the assumption that "we others, the masters and possessors of nature, are seated at the center of a system of things that gravitate around us, the navel of the universe."[50] Yet its depiction of a commanding, clearly delineated, free-standing man takes for granted something laboriously produced by the novel and by Crusoe within it, converting Crusoe from the text's work in progress into a fully realized form: a template for an Émile to copy.

The frontispiece depicts a theriomorphic figure, part human, part animal, a central body of goat with human hands and feet tacked on (rather like the footed pajamas children sometimes wear or a goat sporting human slippers).[51] Filched from beasts, his clothing betokens dependency as well as dominion, an autonomy secured through borrowings from other creatures. Skin and skins create a kind of ragged boundary between self and world, separating figure and ground, conferring on him a form, a discrete shape. Yet even in his casement of goatskins, within the novel Crusoe is never a neatly demarcated figure. His detailed descriptions of himself in his goatskin ensemble underscore the imperfect fit between his skin and skins:

> I had a great high shapeless Cap, made of a Goat's Skin. . . . I had
> a short Jacket of Goat-skin, the Skirts coming down to about the
> middle of my Thighs; and a Pair of open-knee'd Breeches of the
> same, the Breeches were made of the Skin of an old *He-goat*, whose

Clark & Pine Sc.

FIGURE 10. Frontispiece, in Daniel Defoe, *The Life and Strange Surprizing Adventures of Robinson Crusoe, of York, Mariner* (London: Printed for W. Taylor at the Ship in Pater-Noster-Row, 1719). HEW 2.3.6. Harry Elkins Widener Collection, Harvard University.

Hair hung down such a Length on either Side, that like *Pantaloons* it reach'd to the middle of my Legs. . . . I had on a broad Belt of Goat's-Skin dry'd, which I drew together with two Thongs of the same, instead of Buckles, and in a kind of Frog on either Side of this. . . . At my back I carry'd my Basket, on my Shoulder my Gun, and over my Head a great clumsy ugly Goat-Skin Umbrella. (108–9)

Crusoe's verbal self-portrait emphasizes the formlessness of the elements of his goatskin ensemble, a sartorial blazon that leaves us to piece together the parts into a morphological whole. Indeed, it is only because we *already* know what a man looks like that we can so readily assemble the sequential details that make up Crusoe's description into a man. "Without ecphrastic conventions," Elizabeth Fowler notes, "even the most realistic verbal description is more spatially deranged than any Picasso."[52]

Crusoe frames his self-description in the language of portraiture, inviting the reader in a present-tense address to "be pleas'd to take a Sketch of my Figure as follows," as if he were erecting a painter's easel before which viewers might station themselves (108). He locates the viewing eye of the reader-observer in a virtual point outside of the narrating self: "Had any one in *England* been to meet such a Man as I was, it must either have frighted them, or rais'd a great deal of Laughter; and as I frequently stood still to look at my self, I could not but smile at the Notion of my travelling through *Yorkshire* with such an Equipage, and in such a Dress" (108). The place-holding hypothetical "any one in *England*" becomes the mediating figure through which we encounter the interchangeable exemplary figure of Crusoe ("such a Man as I was") in a sequential displacement of both geography (from desert island to British isle) and temporality (from the past tense of "I was" to the present concurrent taking of the sketch). The view he offers of his goatskin-clad body cannot be mustered from within (a paradox made evident in Crusoe's odd account of self-displacement through immobility: "as I frequently stood still to look at my self"). If one threshold separating human being from animality or objecthood is grounded in the capacity to adopt perspectives not one's own, the novel here captures the ipseity of the human by inviting us to join Crusoe in imagining himself from the outside. Although Crusoe at such moments is split or double—simultaneously subject and object of his own apprehension—the image abstracted from the text and offered to us in the frontispiece allows us to put the figure of Crusoe "into its own shape" and see "that it fitted," to return to Wittgenstein's terms from the beginning of this chapter. The image of man extracted from the novel possesses a unity and coherence that subjects and objects within the novel often lack.

In Defoe's novel, skins are made into clothes and other serviceable objects—shoes, an umbrella—but they repeatedly fail to fulfill their charge, either because their origins, like so many epistemological and ethical upstarts, contradict the message (about the civility of the wearer, for example) that they are meant to carry or because they do not quite line up with their proper shape. The shoes Crusoe contrives out of skins, for example, never seem to live up to their name. Despite the fact that Crusoe eventually becomes "a tollerable good Taylor" (150), the approximation of an English shoe defeats him: "Stockings and Shoes I had none," he writes, "but had made me a Pair of somethings, I scarce know what to call them, like Buskins to flap over my Legs, and lace on either Side like Spatterdashes; but of a most barbarous Shape, as indeed were all the rest of my Cloaths" (108–9). Although the "barbarous Shape" of the "Pair of somethings" can be described through an analogy with European garments (Buskins and Spatterdashes), these shoe-like objects, these blank somethings, defeat language. It is not so much that the word fails to conjure the thing, as that the thing fails to conjure the word. These mock-ups or mockeries of shoes do not step into their proper form or name, although they fulfill the function of the shoe; they are not *quite* shoes, although they are used as such. The "Pair of somethings" do not fit into their own shape, as if—to return to the Wittgenstein epigraph—they have no blank imagined for them: "I scarce know what to call them," Crusoe confesses (109). Yet the very fact that they are a pair binds them to the mastering figure of man, that featherless biped capable of speech and reason.

If the "Pair of somethings" is intelligible by reference to the human form, what happens when that relation is severed, when the shoe circulates without the foot, or when the two halves of the pair are separated from each other? For if shoes may be detached from the human form, they may also be detached from each other. From the shipwreck, Crusoe tells us, there was not "one Soul sav'd but my self; for, as for them, I never saw them afterwards, or any Sign of them, except three of their Hats, one Cap, and two Shoes that were not Fellows" (35). These six items—three hats, one cap, two unmatched shoes—are the signs of something, someone, gone missing, the sole leftover of the sea's devouring. What motivates the detail of the shoes, the hats, the cap, is their relation to the bodies from which they have been torn, for Crusoe associates these shoes quite explicitly with lost souls (he does not imagine, for example, that they are the wreckage of a stray shoe shipment being transported from Brazil to the coast of Guinea). "No large words, no despair," as J. M. Coetzee puts it, "just hats and caps and shoes."[53]

In their banality, their seeming insignificance and lack of motivation, the hats, the cap, the shoes confer verisimilitude on Crusoe's performance as our recording angel, creating the illusion that there is an actual world out there, a setting of tempests and rolling waves that swallow up men and spew shoes, caps, and hats upon the shore. Whereas things in early novels, as Wall has argued, tend to materialize on an ad hoc basis—John Bunyan, like Harold with his purple crayon, draws a door for Christian when he needs one to pass through—the shoe here seems closer to one of Roland Barthes's scandalous, insignificant details, the superfluity that cannot be recuperated by the unifying structure.[54] It is, for Barthes, the item like the shoe—the part that remains unassimilated, the metonymy that refuses to become a synecdoche, a kind of detail abandoned by god—that becomes the element of description most tightly bound to the referential status of the text or at least to its capacity to create what Barthes terms its "reality effect."

Whereas the novel's anthropocentric framework (as we saw above) registers objects insofar as they are useful for humanity, Barthes's reality effect depends on the fact that things defy such assimilation. For Barthes, it is the sheer gratuity of the detail—its meaninglessness, its practical uselessness, its unassimilability to the symbolic and diegetic economy of the novel—that enables it to denote the real. More important for my purposes, the detail's resistance to the instrumental or communicative functions of language perversely exemplifies our distinctively human relation to language, for description, in Barthes' account, "appears as a kind of characteristic of the so-called higher [human] languages, to the apparently paradoxical degree that it is justified by no finality of action or of communication." Although bees possess a "predictive system of dances (in order to collect their food)," Barthes observes, "nothing in it approached a *description*."[55] Humans alone become invested in what exceeds their instrumental needs or ends. It is the presence of the insignificant detail, the gratuity of description, that distinguishes human language from the signs used by other creatures. Indeed, part of what individuates the beholder is the capacity to attend to those superfluous details that do not answer to biological urges shared by the entire species.

It is helpful in this context to recall the discussion in Chapter 1 of what draws the human or avian eye to the work of art. We saw there that Zeuxis's grapes are biological "carriers of significance" that lure the birds to the canvas, like the painted red dot at which herring-gull chicks peck. By contrast, the human is arrested by the stray detail—the shadow of a floating feather that has worked loose from the wing of a dead bird in Biltius's trompe l'oeil—and even seduced by what is not there at all—what lies behind Parrhasius's painted curtain. Whereas the herring gull's response to the red dot bespeaks membership in a species, Robinson Crusoe's hats, cap, and two unmatched shoes, like the stray feather, are of no biological or functional interest. The superfluous detail that signifies nothing answers to no imperative or purpose, and in its uselessness, it proclaims a human relation to the world.

In Defoe's novel as in Barthes's essay, the arbitrarily singled-out concrete particular produces the effect of the real, the impression of a referential touchdown, as the text alights on the comforting solidity of a thing. Despite the fact that Crusoe's hats, caps, and shoes are not described in any great detail, the choice of nouns, even shorn of adjectives, confers a striking degree of particularity on them. Although Crusoe omits specifying traits (the color of the shoes, the shape of the hats, the size of the cap), he distinguishes similar kinds of objects from each other, sorting hat from cap, the two shoes from each other. Whatever these things look like, they are not identical. Yet, for all the promise of solidity implicit in the material object, things in Crusoe's novel ghost other objects as well as other souls. The serene insularity of the shoe, for example, is undermined by the fact that it is described as missing something: its fellow.

Why does Crusoe bother to tell us that the two shoes were not fellows? Pairs imply a symmetrical doubling, an imposed organizing principle, a relation that corrals two objects into a set. "You don't say a pair of feet," as Derrida points out. "You say a pair of shoes and gloves."[56] Yet these shoes, like Crusoe and Friday, make for an odd couple that is not quite a pair. Shoes that do not match do not pose the same problem as clothing that does not match: the unmatched shoe moves beyond a question of aesthetic discordance (the garish collision of unpleasing colors, for example) to reorient the entire body.[57] The individual who wears unmatched shoes often limps and may even stumble. Indeed, unless one is an amputee, one shoe is worse than none for walking (it is for this reason that shoe departments serenely put out only one shoe without fear of them disappearing).[58] The fact that the shoes swept up on shore are not fellows renders them useless, in defiance of Crusoe's preoccupation with rendering anything and everything useful. In their uselessness, they become all the more materially present, acquiring something of the obduracy of Woolf's earthenware pot. That the shoe is missing both its partner and the foot that fills it creates a kind of double absence that brings its thingness to life.

I contended above that Crusoe's interest in use tailors the world to a human eye-view, one that recognizes things and other creatures to the extent that they comply with our needs. Here we see how the novel undercuts that anthropocentric framework, revealing the recalcitrance of the material world to our desires. Things, as Bill Brown and others have argued, become most present to us when they balk or stall out regular processes, deviating from their "natural" allotted function. What Brown calls "misuse value" frees objects such as Crusoe's shoes without fellows from "the systems to which they've been beholden,"[59] allowing them to be recognized as "things." If, as Derrida argues, pairing "rivets things to use, to 'normal' use," the unpaired shoe finds itself exposed to "a certain uselessness . . . a so-called perverse usage."[60] In the novel, this perverse usage is not that of Freud's fetishist; instead, the item that can be only imperfectly incorporated into a whole is a perversion of the detail—but it is a perversion that is useful to the novel precisely because, as Barthes argues, it *cannot* be fully integrated into the whole. For the purposes of formal realism, the unpaired shoe is *better* than the paired one. Like the speaking details in Barthes's essay—Flaubert's barometer and Michelet's knock on the door—the unpaired shoes (do these shoes have tongues?) "say nothing but this: *we are the real.*"[61]

That our examples of the realist detail are so often things like the barometer or the unpaired shoes means they already possess a discrete form, which enables us to circumvent the question of what picks them out as details in the first place. While the definite article that singles out *the* detail treats it as something identifiable, isolated, the reward of an attentive eye, the detail is not a preestablished element, always already defined as such. What makes a detail spring out to a narrator's (or reader's) consciousness is not entirely self-evident. "What happens in those privileged moments in which a detail makes itself seen?" Daniel Arasse asks in his fascinating study of the detail in early modern art.[62] Arasse distinguishes between the mimetic detail—an imitative particular, such as the fold of an eyelid or the wrinkle of a brow—and what might be called the idiosyncratic detail—a perturbation or disturbance within the whole that arrests the spectator: "a divergence or a resistance in relation to the whole of the painting" that captivates the viewer. This second form of detail, Arasse argues, reveals not only the potential command of the object over the subject—the fascination that compels us to approach a canvas to take a closer look, a kind of sovereignty of the detail—but also the action of the subject on the object, for it is the gaze of the observer—what Arasse calls the "point of view of the 'detailer'"—that picks out the detail in the first place.[63]

Novelistic realism draws on Arasse's mimetic detail to produce the impression of an empirical object, but it also capitalizes on the arbitrariness and the allure of the idiosyncratic detail to depict the experience of the empirical observing subject.[64] Not unlike the Rorschach blots analyzed by Peter Galison, details create a complex interplay between subject and object, "reaching . . . into the domain of the objective by their unformed, chance images and at the same time into the very core of private desires."[65] It is here that the novel's focalization through Crusoe's first person becomes important, for his singling out of the unpaired shoe particularizes the subject as much as the object. It is on these terms that the unpaired shoes turn out to say more than "*we are the real.*"

Part of what these shoes might say (were they to speak) might involve the reversible priority of subject over object: the question of whether the shoe has lost its owner or the owner has lost the shoe. When Derrida asks in *The Truth in Painting* how we should understand shoes—as "these convex objects which he has pulled off his feet—or these hollow objects from which he has withdrawn himself"[66]—he suggests that the demarcation of the wearer and the worn, the inside and the outside, is by no means as simple as it might seem, and this in turn draws into question the forms and outlines—the discrete form, the plenitude—of subject and object alike. Although the detail is meant to offer the promise of referentiality—the wholeness of a shoe, the solidity of a thing—it simultaneously undermines its discreteness by gesturing towards its own incompleteness. Without a wearer, without a companion, the orphaned shoe becomes *a detail that declares that it is missing some interior detail.* If the singularity of a thing, a detail, issues from the fact that something is missing, what does that missing element elicit from the reader or beholder that marks her as distinctively human?

I want to give an abbreviated answer to this question by placing the singularity of the unpaired shoe in relation with the single unpaired footprint that Crusoe famously encounters in the sand midway through the novel.[67] "It happen'd one Day," he tells us,

> about Noon going towards my Boat, I was exceedingly surpriz'd
> with the Print of a Man's naked Foot on the Shore, which was very

plain to be seen in the Sand: I stood like one Thunderstruck, or as
if I had seen an Apparition; I listen'd, I look'd round me, I could
hear nothing, nor see any Thing; I went up to a rising Ground to
look farther; I went up the Shore and down the Shore, but it was all
one, I could see no other Impression but that one, I went to it again
to see if there were any more, and to observe if it might not be my
Fancy; but there was no Room for that, for there was exactly the
very Print of a Foot, Toes, Heel, and every Part of a Foot; how it
came thither, I knew not, nor could in the least imagine. (112)

The opening words of the passage—"it happen'd one day"—circumvent the
question of *what* exactly happened: what is the event here? The encounter
with the footprint in the sand at first glance is *not* an event; it is the narration
of Crusoe's attempt at description that makes it into one. Rather than balking
narration, description here constitutes it: the world as perceived and
described reflects, acts on, even redefines, the narrating subject.

The fact that the lonely Crusoe feels fear not joy at the traces of others
stems, as many critics have observed, from the prospect of rival claimants to
his property and terror at the engulfing alterity of the figure of the cannibal;
the discovery of the footprint at the height of Crusoe's imagined dominion
shatters his sense of omnipotence. Yet the footprint also presents the blow to
human narcissism incurred by an encounter with the world without us—the
fact that a "thing seen," as Ann Banfield puts it in another context, "doesn't
need him to be there to be seen."[68] In the footprint, Crusoe meets with a
start his own absence: the world has continued to record the impress of other
creatures, indifferent to the fact that he is not there. What Banfield writes of
the photograph might be extended to this other kind of print: it "makes clear
that it is the continuing existence of things outside the mind which is disturbing to the individual and not their non-existence, a solipsism which absorbs
the whole world into a single subject's perspective being rather consoling."[69]
Indeed, the desire to protect this solipsism causes Crusoe to cling to the
possibility that the print is a product of his "Fancy."

Although every part of the footprint—"foot, toes, heel, and every Part
of a Foot"—is there, it, like the unpaired shoe, offers us a whole from which
something is missing. The impossibility of a single (unpaired) footprint with
no traces leading to it or away from it opens up a set of questions about the
making of an indexical sign: "How it came thither," Crusoe announces, "I

knew not, nor could in the least imagine." The fact that it is a print made by a bare foot indicates that it belongs to a member of the non-shoe-wearing public—it invites us to take a stab at classification—but, unlike the hoof-prints that Gulliver encounters in Houyhnhnmland, the footprint cannot be dismissed as the trace of another species: it must be either human or demonic. Crusoe's frenzied efforts to find an anterior force behind the print fail, although he notably does not look in the right place for such a cause: as the image from John Stockdale's 1790 edition shows (Figure 11), Crusoe scruti-nizes the print itself, the one place where the foot producing it cannot by definition be. While Crusoe is utterly absorbed by the footprint, the dog accompanying him seems arrested—what Heidegger or Agamben would term "captivated"—by the birds swooping low over the waves. The dog is indiffer-ent to the footprint—not even depicted as sniffing about for the residual scent of the man who presumably made it, and Crusoe likewise appears obliv-ious to the birds that capture the dog's interest.[70] The incorporation of Crusoe's canine companion into the Stockdale illustration underscores the ways Crusoe's absorption in the print betokens a uniquely human relation to the world: like Zeuxis, who seeks what is behind the painted curtain, Crusoe is invested in what is *not* there.

Crusoe himself moves to supply what is missing—to fill in the space of the print with his own foot. He decides, he tells us, that

> I should go down to the Shore again, and see this Print of a Foot, and measure it by my own, and see if there was any Similitude or Fitness, that I might be assur'd it was my own Foot: But when I came to the Place, *First*, It appear'd evidently to me, that when I laid up my Boat, I could not possibly be on Shore any where there about. *Secondly*, When I came to measure the Mark with my own Foot, I found my Foot not so large by a great deal; both these Things fill'd my Head with new Imaginations, and gave me the Vapours again, to the highest Degree; so that I shook with cold, like one in an Ague. (115)

In returning to the print, Crusoe seeks confirmation, through the refindabil-ity of an object in the external world, that the print of the foot is not, so to speak, all in his head. Crusoe measures his foot against the print in a quest for "Similitude or Fitness," a likeness or symmetry between his own form

FIGURE 11. Thomas Stothard, [Robinson Crusoe discovers the Print of a Man's Foot], in Daniel Defoe, *The Life and Strange Surprizing Adventures of Robinson Crusoe, of York, Mariner* (London: John Stockdale, 1790), opposite p. 194. *AC85.Al245.Zy790d, Houghton Library, Harvard University.

and the marks in the sand, the complement of convex foot and concave print. In effect, he endeavors to convert the footprint to a shoe, making the print fit the foot since he cannot make the foot fit the print. He hopes to find identity, to make what Wittgenstein, to return to the epigraph, describes as a useless proposition—the desire to make "a thing identical with itself"—an act that Wittgenstein nevertheless conjoins to a certain play of the imagination: "It is as if in imagination we put a thing into its own shape and saw that it fitted." Crusoe endeavors to cast the print into his own shape, but it does not fit: the footprint refuses the foot, denies the possibility of a complementary symmetry that would restore Crusoe to an unsundered world. And the failure of this fit produces another kind of fit, a fit of the "Vapours," converting Crusoe into a vessel for new phantasms: "Both these Things," he writes, "fill'd my Head with new Imaginations." The failure of the print to match the foot is psychically and physically disorienting: so shattering is this revelation that Crusoe's body shakes "with cold, like one in an ague."

What marks Crusoe's humanity is not so much that Crusoe possesses a foot like the one imprinted on the sand ("foot, toes, heel, and every Part of a Foot") but that he endeavors to find himself in the print. In *The Open: Man and Animal*, Giorgio Agamben quotes a letter by the eighteenth-century natural historian Linnaeus: " 'Just as the shoemaker sticks to his last, I must remain in my workshop and consider man and his body as a naturalist, who hardly knows a single distinguishing mark which separates man from the apes, save for the fact that the latter have an empty space between their canines and their other teeth.' " Ossified into a differential trait, a seemingly trivial detail—here the empty space between canines and other teeth—is supposed (but fails) to define inclusion in or exclusion from the category of the human. The impoverished categories devised to denominate man in philosophical writings and natural histories—even in novels—exposes the inadequacy of words to wield the matter of the world. The distinction between human and animal, Agamben argues, ultimately resides for Linnaeus neither in the possession of specific traits, nor in a particular essence: "Man has no specific identity other than the *ability* to recognize himself."[71] The separation of the human from the nonhuman resides, that is, in the capacity to engage in a play of the imagination that casts not a thing, but a human being, into its own shape and skin to see that it fits.

The endeavor to fit a foot to a print, a human to its form, implies, of course, a separation between the two. We may recall Lukács's contention that the novel can only come into being when the organic totality of epic gives way, such that a part of the world—an individual within it—can become "enclosed within itself" and "find itself as an interiority." Crusoe's failure to fit his foot into the print reminds us that the world of the novel is no organic totality. The effort to overcome the alien nature of the world and to accommodate it to a human form requires immense labor, even as that labor helps produce the interiority that Lukács says must "find itself." We have seen Crusoe's unflagging efforts to make the world fit together. Yet his attempts to find himself "as an interiority" do not produce an unmediated description of his inner experience (as if his mind exists as something that can be objectively described); instead, it yields a jarring reconstruction of his panic-stricken passage across the island, in which his ability to sort inside from outside—empirical things from mental fictions—has broken down, even in Crusoe's retroactive account:

> After innumerable fluttering Thoughts, like a Man perfectly con-
> fus'd and out of my self, I came Home to my Fortification, not
> feeling, as we say, the Ground I went on, but terrify'd to the last
> Degree, looking behind me at every two or three Steps, mistaking
> every Bush and Tree, and fancying every Stump at a Distance to be
> a Man; nor is it possible to describe how many various Shapes
> affrighted imagination represented Things to me in, how many wild
> Ideas were found every Moment in my Fancy, and what strange
> unaccountable Whimsies came into my Thoughts by the Way. (112)

The senses cease to be reliable emissaries: the eye encounters distorted forms and the ground loses its solidity. When Crusoe describes himself as "a Man perfectly confus'd and out of my self," the ungrammatical conjoining of the indefinite article ("a Man") and the personal possessive ("my self") doubles down on this dispossession. While no "Man" is lodged in Crusoe's "self," the figure of man stalks him in the outside world. Like one of Giambattista Vico's fearful primitives, Crusoe materializes his terror as anthropomorphic shapes, refashioning bushes and trees into the guise of men.

While the epistemological dislocation produced by Crusoe's encounter with the footprint distorts his perception of outward things, the mind itself escapes representation. The passive voice—the wild ideas "found . . . in my Fancy," the "Whimsies that came into my Thoughts"—makes him simultaneously subject and object of mental forces that cannot quite be pinned

down. He offers personifications of his consciousness (it is "affrighted imagination" that "represented Things to me"), but notes that it is not "possible
to describe" the number and variety of his fancies. We get the fact of inner
experience—the "innumerable fluttering Thoughts" and "many wild
Ideas"—without the content. Here, as in his sketch of himself in his goatskin
ensemble, Crusoe invites us to join him in what seems like a strangely exteriorized point of view in relation both to his own figure and to his own mind,
a displaced vantage that suggests that the optic or eye-view from which the
novelistic world is described may not be, strictly speaking, lodged securely
within the self. [72] Crusoe treats his own consciousness as something to which
he has limited access, as elusive as the consciousness of another being.

The doubled consciousness that marks Crusoe's estrangement from himself reflects the peculiar artifice of the novel, which, as Dorrit Cohn has
argued, offers the immediate experience of what we can never know in real
life: what passes in another's mind. Cohn quotes Proust on the impossible
knowledge afforded by novelistic narration: "'A real person, profoundly as
we may sympathize with him, is in a great measure perceptible only through
our senses, that is to say, he remains opaque, offers a dead weight which our
sensibilities have no strength to lift. . . . The novelist's happy discovery was
to think of substituting for those opaque sections, impenetrable by the
human spirit, their equivalent in immaterial sections, things, that is, which
the spirit can assimilate to itself.'"[73] Inasmuch as we only have empirical
access to the outward tokens of reason, of emotion, of thought, the elaboration of novelistic character is a kind of extended Viconian anthropomorphism: the projection of what we imagine to be a human likeness onto the
scrim of our own ignorance. The commonality of species may enable us to
sympathize more readily with the narration of human consciousness, but we
cannot *know* what it is like to be another person any more than we can know
what it is like to be a bird or a bat. Indeed, Crusoe's description of his
confused thoughts suggests that we can never entirely capture what passes in
our own minds either.[74] While the substitution of a linguistic "equivalent"
for those "opaque sections, impenetrable by the human spirit," promises to
fill in the blanks, Defoe's novel keeps returning us not just to wholes that are
missing parts and shoes that lack their fellows but to an individual who
cannot offer a full account of his own experience.

I have argued throughout this book that art and literature define humanity through enacted capacities and that the withholding of a fixed template
of "man" in these "fictions without humanity" is part of what keeps the

category of the human open. While we imaginatively enter into the *processes* by which Crusoe endeavors to make sense of the world, his disjointed descriptions of his own consciousness produce no consolidated whole with which to identify, no neatly demarcated figure of "man" to be elevated as a template. Crusoe understood as Coleridge's "representative of humanity," or seen as the indelible figure bestriding the landscape in the famous frontispiece, is something readers *extract* from the novel that is not fully realized within it (which is not to say that Crusoe himself does not try to foreclose the category or to exalt himself above other men, including Friday, Xury, and the savages).[75] In the final section of this chapter, I want to think about the vantage from which the provisional, partial descriptions offered throughout the novel can yield this sense of Crusoe as a representative figure of man. From what prospect, imaginary or virtual, can the disparate elements that make up the novel be unified into a whole—and is that prospect human?

The Novel and the World Without Us

I want to return in closing to the epigraphs from Woolf and Wittgenstein with which this chapter began and reconsider them in light of the implied wholes and missing parts, unpaired shoes and solitary footprint, examined above. This chapter has addressed the descriptive labor involved in yoking discrete elements into the semblance of unity, in making things *fit*: fit into Woolf's harmonious fictive universe; fit into the cookie-cutter fulfillment of the identity or shape suggested by a word (for Wittgenstein); fit—or fail to fit—into the complementary relations that reattach stray objects—shoes, footprints—to the human body. The leashed violence through which Defoe's earthenware pot subdues all before it, "roping the universe into harmony" in Woolf's words, finds a counterpart in the dictatorial imperative that Wittgenstein's "thing identical with itself" realize its own shape. While the novel reflects the ways order may be alternately imposed on or imposed by things, it also grapples with the possibility that people do not quite belong to that order: Woolf's earthenware pot opposes, even dwarfs, "man in all his sublimity"; Wittgenstein's spot that does not know its own edges betrays the fruitlessness of our self-fulfilling logical propositions; two feet cannot be paired in the way the accessories of shoe and glove may be, for things achieve a perfection of symmetry that humans cannot attain. A ruthlessly ordered universe banishes humans, not things, to the island of misfit toys.

It is of course precisely the failure to fit that, for Lukács, drives the novel's quest to forge a provisional unity out of the "mutually alien worlds of subject and object."[76] The moments in which *Robinson Crusoe* veers toward what Lukács describes as a kind of bad infinity—in which "the discretely heterogeneous mass of isolated persons, non-sensuous structures and meaningless events" threatens the coherence of the whole—opens up the troubling possibility that one may be left with parts that cannot be fully assimilated into a whole, skins that do not fit, prints that defy attribution, and shoes that are missing their fellows. For Lukács, the novel "overcomes its 'bad' infinity by recourse to the biographical form," threading the arbitrary circumstance or random detail into the narrative history of the individual; the unity of the novelistic world comes from the synthesizing subject.[77] Studies of the object often return to the subject, and here too what knits vagrant details together—makes the shoe fit—seems to be the consciousness of an individual, be it a character or a reader.

Yet what of Woolf's earthenware pot, with which we began? If, for Lukács, the unity of *Robinson Crusoe* would issue from the individual, for Woolf, it issues from the thing. I have always found Woolf's remarks on *Crusoe* puzzling, despite the frequency with which they crop up as epigraphs, and I want to conclude with some speculations, perhaps far-fetched, on what her cryptic but evocative reflections suggest in the context of my argument. Woolf's earthenware pot, "staring us full in the face," ropes the universe into harmony from a perspective unaffiliated with an individual subject; it records what Ann Banfield, quoting Bertrand Russell, calls " 'sensibilia' ": " 'the appearance that things present in places where there are no minds to perceive them.' "[78] In Banfield's account, scientific instruments and free indirect discourse both offer impersonal descriptions of the world from perspectives that are not lodged in human beings, proffering not "objective, centerless statements" but rather statements that are "impersonal yet subjective," "subjective yet subjectless," that (like the footprint before its discovery) "render the appearances of things to no one."[79] Seen from this point of view, Woolf's earthenware pot suggests that the novel strives to "describe the world seen without a self," as Woolf put it elsewhere.[80] What if we considered the novel on Banfield's terms as a machine for producing a virtual perspective not necessarily anchored in a particular subject and under no particular obligation to be human?

At first glance it seems truly ridiculous to suggest that *Robinson Crusoe*—a first-person narrative steeped in the tradition of spiritual autobiography—

presents a description of "the world seen without a self." And yet the innumerable devices that register what David Marshall calls *Robinson Crusoe*'s "compulsive autobiographical acts"—the "accounts, journals, calendars, self-inscriptions, names called out by disembodied voices, and repeated representations and reflections of the self"—relentlessly pry the narrative from Crusoe's subjective stranglehold.[81] The multiplication of accounts and of media—as well as the division of Crusoe into once and future narrators—converts the subject Crusoe into the object of description, recording the experiences undergone by "my self" through devices and perspectives not fully his own. For all the centrality given to the subject in accounts of *Robinson Crusoe*, the perspective offered does not entirely collate with the individual or with the human.

If we enfold the reader into this account, we might think about the novel in relation to the model of description presented in Bender and Marrinan's *Culture of Diagram*. The diagram, which offers "a proliferation of manifestly selective packets of dissimilar data correlated in an explicitly process-oriented array that has some of the attributes of a representation but is situated in the world like an object," embroils its user in the active recombination, synthesis, extrapolation, and instrumentalization of the verbal and visual artifacts it presents.[82] Even as "diagrams incite a correlation of sensory data with the mental schema of lived experience that emulates the way we explore objects in the world," so too do novels (and other literary genres) serve as machinery that generate schema: knowledge structures that organize and interpret experience and meaning.[83] Like things, diagrams "do not privilege a single vantage point, but are viewed or handled or manipulated in many different ways"; unlike pictorial representations done according to Albertian perspective, they do not "converge in a single vantage point or entity that might be called a viewer."[84] The reading or viewing subject is not the cynosure of the diagram; instead the diagram, with its multiple points of entry, its multitude of possible uses, embroils its user in an ongoing negotiation of perspective and activity, a kind of bricolage that creates a dynamic and plural relation of part to whole. One does not need to engage in the bibliomancy of Gabriel Betteredge in Wilkie Collins's *The Moonstone*, who has "worn out six stout *Robinson Crusoes* with hard work in my service," to recognize that the novel is capable of operating to a surprising extent as a diagrammatic object receptive to "mimetic simulations."[85]

John Bender calls the novel "apparitional" in that it "produces a coherent linguistic version of the real that never has been, is, or will be"; it creates a virtual reality possessed of the organic wholeness that the contingency of the lived empirical world cannot possess. Realism, Bender argues, uses "means other than the direct, sensory apprehension of the real in order to project a reality"; it is through "surrogate projection" that media such as the novel create "the illusion of sharing the first-hand experience of others."[86] One way—not the only way—that this coherence can be produced is through the mediation of a nonhuman virtual perspective that wrests the embattled subject from the clutches of a cruelly playful universe. That is, although what grips us about Crusoe's adventures is precisely the vicissitudes of his fortunes and his resourcefulness in dealing with them, what allows us to weave it all into a meaningful unity issues from the "coherent linguistic version of the real" offered by the novel, a coherence that—pace Lukács—does not necessarily have to issue from the subjective unity of the novelistic hero.

The solidity of Woolf's earthenware pot promises a world more durable than the evocations of fallible mortal witnesses, but in offering that durability it "exacts" a perspective that differs from the strictly human. What the novel gives us, in other words, is an intimation of our capacity to imagine the world from a place that is not already colonized by subjectivity (our own or someone else's)—from the place of a character, perhaps, but also possibly from the place of a thing. In giving us an eerie glimpse of what happens when we are not in the room, the novel creates the ability to apprehend the world from the perspective of Woolf's pot or to find ourselves in the hollow of the footprint. In the process, it reminds us that we (if not with Crusoe, then through him) possess the ability to imagine the world without making ourselves its cynosure, to imagine the world without us. And what if it is this capacity to grasp the world from the place of a thing—to find fitting a shape so utterly not one's own—that makes a person human?

Coda

I began this book with a discussion of the elusive nature of humanity as an abstraction—a unifying fiction extracted from an unruly mass of individual men and women—and have focused throughout on the ongoing efforts by writers, artists, scientists, and philosophers to disaggregate the human from the creaturely and material nature with which it is inextricably intertwined. I have argued that humanity is elaborated less through its likeness to a fixed figure than through performances elicited by literature and works of art: the exercise of capacities (reason, speech) that distinguish humans from animals, machines, mere things. Although these texts for the most part represent humanity as a work in progress and seek to avoid elevating a fixed template of the human, what is mined from them is often less supple, something closer to the figure of Crusoe as depicted in the frontispiece, lording it over the landscape—an ossified model of humanity used to justify the exploitation of those who do not cleave to its ideal form.

While the works analyzed in this book refine (or reify) the reader's sense of human particularity on an individual level, they do not necessarily yield an understanding of humanity as a common species, both in the sense that the category in practice does not embrace all who should fall into its purview and in the sense that we do not comprehend the agency of humanity as a collective, cumulative force that acts in and on the world. The question I want to raise in closing involves the way our conception of ourselves as a consolidated group is extracted less from the relations we deliberately take to things and other creatures than from the occasional glimpse of the effects that our conjoined actions have on their existence and well-being. If we began with the human as a proleptic object—a subject called into being through predicates not yet locked in place—we conclude with the retroactive constitution of humanity through the representation and acknowledgment of its own deeds and misdeeds. We grasp our identity as a species by apprehending the stamp of human power on the world.

The Enlightenment, as Max Horkheimer and Theodor Adorno famously showed, was the era in which an ascendant humanity sought to know itself through the maximization of its instrumental powers—a realization of the humanity of one part of the species that depended upon the subjection and exploitation of another. It was, however, only with the advent of nuclear weapons able to annihilate the entire species, Hannah Arendt contends, that humanity truly became one in its shared vulnerability.[1] More recently, the historians Michael Geyer and George Bright have argued that the task of world history in a global age is "to make transparent the lineaments of power, underpinned by information, that compress humanity into a single human-kind." Globalization, they claim, means that "humanity . . . is no longer a universalizing image or a normative construct of what some civilization or some intellectuals would want the people of this earth to be. Neither is this humanity any longer a mere species or a natural condition. For the first time, we as human beings collectively constitute ourselves and, hence, are responsible for ourselves."[2] While my argument would take issue with Geyer and Bright's description of humanity as an autonomous self-constituting force, I want to draw on their claim—shared by Adorno, Horkheimer, and Arendt—that the power that humanity as a whole exerts over the globe rede-fines both what humanity is and the means through which humanity may come to know itself. It is the scale of humanity's mark on the world—a scale that exceeds the compass of any one individual's agency—that makes visible our activities and existence as a species.

The abstract and collective fiction of humanity on these terms becomes visible retroactively, through what it has wrought: " 'The doer' is merely a fiction added to the deed," as Nietzsche famously asserted in *The Genealogy of Morals*.[3] In what sense is humanity such a superadded fiction, and what deeds yield a sense of such a doer? In Nietzsche's account, the doing precedes and determines the designation of the doer, while the subject is conjured to serve as the agent of the deed for which she or he will be held accountable. On these terms, we derive actors from actions, causes from effects, becoming "conscious of ourselves," Judith Butler writes, "only after certain injuries have been inflicted . . . [and someone] asks us whether we might be that cause."[4] If, at the beginning of this book, I claimed that humanity is generated through what Rancière calls the "predicates of a non-existent being"—an aspirational model that yields, among other things, the possibility of human rights for those excluded from the political domain—here we encounter the negative version of a subject back-formed from predicates, in which being called to account for what we as a species have done refashions what we as human beings are.[5]

At a moment in which global capitalism and climate change are leaving indelible marks on the planet, our sense of humanity is gleaned less from the immediate imagining of our fellow human creatures than from the dispiriting recognition of our collective capacity to produce immense, unintended, catastrophic effects. Global warming makes humanity as an agent visible in the estranged form of environmental events that are, as Amitav Ghosh puts it, "the mysterious work of our own hands returning to haunt us in unthinkable shapes and forms."[6] If climate change means, as Dipesh Chakrabarty contends, that "humans are a force of nature in the geological sense," this self-recognition occurs—here as elsewhere in this book—through the objectification of our own practices in a nonhuman form.[7]

The anthropomorphisms and personifications analyzed in the previous chapters may impose a human face or subjective unity upon the otherwise inchoate forces that animate the world, but even these tropes and figures cannot traverse the immense gap between our empirical experience and the outsized effects of the cumulative actions of humanity as a whole. Inasmuch as "we can only intellectually comprehend or infer the existence of the human species but never experience it as such," as Chakrabarty observes, our collective inability to fathom the immensity of our impact on the planet may issue from the difficulty we have in grasping the nature of the "humanity" of which we are a part.[8] If we began with César Chesneau Dumarsais's assertion that "*humanity* does not exist; that is, there is no being that is *humanity*," we end with Chakrabarty's claim that humanity understood as a geological agent points us "to a figure of the universal that escapes our capacity to experience the world," for there is "no phenomenology of us as a species."[9] While the sequential adoption of nonhuman perspectives traced in this book enacts a distinctively human capacity to apprehend the agencies and interests of other creatures and objects in the world, it offers only a glimpse of the massive collective power humanity itself blindly wields.

The reciprocal dependency of human and nonhuman at the heart of this book has not left both parties on equal footing, and the indexical marks of humanity's footprint on earth summon not, as with Crusoe, the forlorn sense that the world persists in our absence but the bleak recognition that very little is exempt from our touch. If fictions without humanity at first glance offer up a world in which our likeness has no visible place, it is perhaps because we so persistently elect to misread who and what we are. On these terms, the quest for anthropomorphic traces in other sorts of beings may be not just the narcissistic projection of a human semblance onto the nonhuman world but a step toward recognizing and taking responsibility for what we are doing and what we have done.

NOTES

INTRODUCTION

1. John Locke, *An Essay Concerning Human Understanding*, ed. Peter Nidditch (Oxford: Clarendon, 1979), 3.6.§27, 454. In quotations from early printed sources, spelling, typography, and punctuation have been kept as close as possible to the originals, although the letters *u*, *v*, *w*, *i*, and *j* have been modernized.

2. Ephraim Chambers, *Cyclopaedia, or, an Universal Dictionary of Arts and Sciences*, 5 vols. (London: W. Strahan et al., 1779), vol. 2.29, s.v. "Definition of the thing, or real definition."

3. Bruno Latour, *We Have Never Been Modern*, trans. Catherine Porter (Cambridge, MA: Harvard University Press, 1993), 13.

4. Georg Lukács, *The Theory of the Novel*, trans. Anna Bostock (Cambridge, MA: MIT Press, 1971), 74–75.

5. Bernard Mandeville, *Fable of the Bees*, 2 vols. (Indianapolis: Liberty Fund, 1988), 1.127; Jonathan Swift, "A Beautiful Young Nymph Going to Bed," in *Poems of Jonathan Swift*, ed. Harold Williams, 3 vols. (Oxford: Oxford University Press, 1958), 581–83.

6. Cary Wolfe, *Animal Rites: American Culture, the Discourse of Species, and Posthumanist Theory* (Chicago: University of Chicago Press, 2003), 1.

7. See Susan Maslan, "The Antihuman: Man and Citizen Before the Declaration of the Rights of Man," *South Atlantic Quarterly* 103, no. 2/3 (2004): 357–74.

8. Raymond Williams, *Keywords: A Vocabulary of Culture and Society* (Oxford: Oxford University Press, 1985), 149. The *Oxford English Dictionary* derives *humanity* from the French *humanité* and the Latin *humanitas*, as "characteristic of human nature, human form," with post-classical Latin adding *mankind* in the late second century, the human nature of Christ in the fifth century, and literary scholarship in the sixteenth. *OED Online*, Oxford University Press, July 2018, www.oed.com/view/Entry/89280, s.v. humanity (n.).

9. "Il y a des hom[m]es, mais *l'humanité* n'est point, c'est-à-dire, qu'il n'y a point un être qui soit *l'humanité*." César Chesneau Dumarsais, *Les tropes de Dumarsais, avec un commentaire raisonné . . . par M. Fontanier*, ed. Pierre Fontanier, 2 vols. (Paris: Belin-Le-Prieur, 1818), 1.332.

10. Étienne Bonnot de Condillac, *Essay on the Origin of Human Knowledge*, trans. and ed. Hans Aarsleff (Cambridge: Cambridge University Press, 2001), 98. Jean-Henri-Samuel Formey, "definition (logique)," in Denis Diderot and Jean le Rond d'Alembert, eds., *Encyclopédie, ou dictionnaire raisonné des sciences, des arts et des métiers, etc.* University of Chicago: ARTFL Encyclopédie Project (Autumn 2017 Edition), ed. Robert Morrissey and Glenn Roe, http://encyclopedie.uchicago.edu/, 4.747.

11. Alexander Cook, Ned Curthoys, and Shino Konishi, "The Science and Politics of Humanity in the Eighteenth Century: An Introduction," in *Representing Humanity in the Age of Enlightenment*, ed. Cook, Curthoys, and Konishi (London: Pickering and Chatto, 2013), 1.

12. Cook, Curthoys, and Konishi, "Science and Politics of Humanity," 3.

13. A comprehensive survey is impossible here, given the wealth of recent work in both areas. On eighteenth-century things, thing theory, and materialist philosophy, see Barbara Benedict, Mark Blackwell, Elizabeth Kowaleski-Wallace, Jonathan Kramnick, Jonathan Lamb, Christina Lupton, Deidre Lynch, Sandra Macpherson, Julie Park, Wolfram Schmidgen, Sean Silver, and Cynthia Wall. On eighteenth-century animal studies, see Laura Brown, Sarah Cohen, Lucinda Cole, Diana Donald, Heather Keenleyside, Christine Kenyon-Jones, Donna Landry, Tobias Menely, Richard Nash, Frank Palmeri, David Perkins, Louise Robbins, Ingrid Tague, and Keith Thomas. I address this scholarship in greater detail in the individual chapters.

14. Laurie Shannon, *The Accommodated Animal: Cosmopolity in Shakespearean Locales* (Chicago: University of Chicago Press, 2013), 5. For other work on animals in early modern England, see, among others, Julia Reinhard Lupton, *Thinking with Shakespeare: Essays on Politics and Life* (Chicago: University of Chicago Press, 2011) and Erica Fudge, *Perceiving Animals: Humans and Beasts in Early Modern English Culture* (New York: St. Martin's Press, 2000) and Fudge, *Brutal Reasoning: Animals, Rationality, and Humanity in Early Modern England* (Ithaca: Cornell University Press, 2006).

15. Festa, *Sentimental Figures of Empire in Eighteenth-Century Britain and France* (Baltimore: Johns Hopkins University Press, 2006).

16. Hannah Arendt, *The Origins of Totalitarianism*, rev. ed. (New York: Harcourt Brace Jovanovich, 1994), 297.

17. Throughout the book I use the pronoun *we*, often interchangeably with a presumptive humanity. While this usage may imply a preestablished, circumscribed community (humans vs. animals and things, us vs. them), my claim is that this plural first-person emerges *from* the processes of reading: that is, the humanity of the readers—and hence their participation in a collective "we"—is *produced* through the device of the text or work of art. Inasmuch as the texts I consider belong to oral and visual traditions, my argument does not make literacy a prerequisite for human status.

18. Descartes offers a version of the Turing test in the *Discourse on the Method* and in a 1638 letter to Reneri for Pollot. See *Discourse on the Method*, trans. Robert Stoothoff, in *The Philosophical Writings of Descartes: Vol. I*, ed. John Cottingham et al. (Cambridge: Cambridge University Press, 1985), 139–40; *The Correspondence*, trans. John Cottingham et al., in *The Philosophical Writings of Descartes: Vol. III* (Cambridge: Cambridge University Press, 1991), 99–100. For reasons of length, a more extensive discussion of seventeenth-century philosophy has been omitted. While Descartes's notorious characterization of animals as bête-machines has been thoroughly addressed by many critics, it is also worth noting that the cogito arrives unescorted by a species qualifier: "I do not yet have a sufficient understanding of what this 'I' is," Descartes writes, "that now necessarily exists." Descartes uses the famous beeswax to distinguish human from animal, transmuting its physical properties beyond recognition so that its "perception now requires a human mind." *Meditations on First Philosophy*, trans. John Cottingham, in *The Philosophical Writings of Descartes: Vol. II* (Cambridge: Cambridge University Press, 1984), 17, 22; *Méditations métaphysiques*, ed. Jean-Marie Beyssade (Paris: Garnier-Flammarion, 1979), 81, 93.

19. Jacques Derrida, "The Animal That Therefore I Am (More to Follow)," in *The Animal That Therefore I Am*, trans. David Wills, ed. Marie-Louise Mallet (New York: Fordham University Press, 2008), 11.

20. Thomas Hobbes, *On the Citizen* [*De cive*], ed. Richard Tuck and Michael Silverthorne (Cambridge: Cambridge University Press, 1998), 3.

21. The thing that refuses to become an object, Robin Bernstein argues, "demands that people confront it on its own terms," forcing "a person into an awareness of the self in material relation to the thing." Things in Bernstein's account liberate people from the culturally bound scripts that bind them to normative activities: they "script meaningful bodily movements, and these citational movements think the otherwise unthinkable." Yet the thing that refuses to become an object may also bar the subject from other forms of participation. Bernstein, "Dances with Things: Material Culture and the Performance of Race," *Social Text* 27, no. 4 (2009): 69, 69–70, 70. For a recent insightful feminist reading of things, see Elizabeth Kowaleski-Wallace, "The Things Things Don't Say: *The Rape of the Lock*, Vitalism, and New Materialism," *The Eighteenth Century: Theory and Interpretation* 59, no. 1 (2018): 105–22.

22. Jean de La Bruyère, *Les Caractères* [1689], in *Oeuvres completes,* ed. Julien Benda, Bibliothèque de la Pléiade (Paris: Gallimard, 1978), 333; Jonathan Swift, *Gulliver's Travels,* ed. Albert Rivero (New York: Norton, 2002), 195.

23. Robert Hooke, *Micrographia: or, Some Physiological Descriptions of Minute Bodies Made by Magnifying Glasses* (London: Jo. Martyn, 1665), sig. a.

24. On the "thing-character" of the world, see Arendt, *The Human Condition* (New York: Doubleday Anchor, 1959), 81–3.

25. Lucinda Cole et al., "Speciesism, Identity Politics, and Ecocriticism: A Conversation with Humanists and Posthumanists," *The Eighteenth Century: Theory and Interpretation* 52, no. 1 (2011): 98.

26. Lorraine Daston, "Intelligences: Angelic, Animal, Human," in *Thinking with Animals: New Perspectives on Anthropomorphism,* ed. Lorraine Daston and Gregg Mitman (New York: Columbia University Press, 2005), 40.

27. John Ogilby, *Fables of Aesop, Paraphras'd in Verse and Adorn'd with Sculptures* (London: Thomas Warren, 1651), frontispiece.

28. John Frow, *Character and Person* (Oxford: Oxford University Press, 2016), 41.

29. Michel de Montaigne, "Apology for Raymond Sebond," in *The Complete Essays of Montaigne,* trans. Donald Frame (Stanford, CA: Stanford University Press, 1965), 342.

30. Dorrit Cohn, *Transparent Minds: Narrative Modes for Presenting Consciousness in Fiction* (Princeton, NJ: Princeton University Press, 1984), 5–6.

31. See S. Watanabe, J. Sakamoto, and M. Wakita, "Pigeon's Discrimination of Paintings by Monet and Picasso," *Journal of the Experimental Analysis of Behavior* 63 (1995): 165–74. Cited in Frans de Waal, *The Ape and the Sushi Master: Cultural Reflections of a Primatologist* (New York: Basic, 2001), 162–63.

32. Siep Stuurman, *The Invention of Humanity: Equality and Cultural Difference in World History* (Cambridge, MA: Harvard University Press, 2017).

33. John Abernethy, *Discourses Concerning the Being and Natural Perfections of God,* 2 vols. Dublin: A. Reilly, 1742), 1.130.

34. Shannon, *The Accommodated Animal,* 34; Latour, *We Have Never Been Modern,* trans. Porter, 142–45.

35. Frank Trentmann, "Materiality in the Future of History: Things, Practices, and Politics," *Journal of British Studies* 48 (2009): 284, 292.

36. Theodore Walker, Jr., "African-American Resources for a More Inclusive Liberation Theology," in *This Sacred Earth: Religion, Nature, Environment,* ed. Roger Gottlieb (New York:

Routledge, 1996), 311. See also Kimberly Ruffin, *Black on Earth: African American Ecoliterary Traditions* (Athens: University of Georgia Press, 2010).

37. Richard Grusin, "Introduction," in *The Nonhuman Turn*, ed. Grusin (Minneapolis: University of Minnesota Press, 2015), xviii.

38. Joseph Addison, *Spectator* 519 (October 25, 1712), in *The Spectator*, ed. Donald Bond, 5 vols. (Oxford: Clarendon, 1965), 4.349; Olaudah Equiano, *The Interesting Narrative of the Life of Olaudah Equiano*, ed. Werner Sollors (New York: Norton, 2000), 137.

39. Samera Esmeir, "On Making Dehumanization Possible," *PMLA* 121, no. 5 (2006): 1550. On the ways "Africans in the Atlantic diaspora gained power through their recognition and exploitation of human and parahuman beings' relations with nonhuman forms," see Monique Allewaert, *Ariel's Ecology: Plantations, Personhood, and Colonialism in the American Tropics* (Minneapolis: University of Minnesota Press, 2013), 7. As Joshua Brandon Bennett argues, "black authors [have] cultivated a poetics of persistence and interspecies empathy, a literary tradition in which nonhuman . . . life forms are acting up and out in ways we might not expect or yet have a language for." Bennett, " 'Being Property Once Myself': In Pursuit of the Animal in Twentieth-Century African American Literature" (PhD dissertation, Princeton University, 2016), 2.

40. G. W. F. Hegel, *Aesthetics: Lectures on Fine Art*, trans. T. M. Knox, 2 vols. (Oxford: Clarendon, 1975), 1.387.

41. Dumarsais, *Les tropes de Dumarsais*, 1.71.

42. Ephraim Chambers, *Cyclopaedia: or, an Universal Dictionary of Arts and Sciences*, 2 vols. (London: James and John Knapton et al., 1728), vol. 1, s.v. humanity.

43. Samuel Johnson, *A Dictionary of the English Language*, 2nd ed., 2 vols. (London: W. Strahan, 1755–56), vol. 1, s.v. humanity. The third entry is "Benevolence; tenderness," and the fourth is "Philology." *Man* is defined as "1. Human being. 2. Not a woman. 3. Not a boy. 4. A servant; an attendant." Only in the tenth entry does the animal surface: "Not a beast."

44. Derrida, "The Animal That Therefore I Am," 47.

45. Barbara Johnson, "A Hound, a Bay Horse, and a Turtle Dove: Obscurity in *Walden*," in *A World of Difference* (Baltimore: Johns Hopkins University Press, 1987), 53.

46. Thomas Hobbes, *Human Nature*, in *The Elements of Law, Natural and Politic: Part 1, Human Nature, Part 2, De Corpore Politico*, ed. J. C. A. Gaskin (Oxford: Oxford University Press, 1994), 36.

47. See, for example, Condillac, *Essay on the Origin of Human Knowledge*, 1.5.§4, 93; David Hume, *Treatise of Human Nature*, 2nd ed., ed. L. A. Selby-Bigge, revised ed., P. H. Nidditch (Oxford: Clarendon, 1980), 20.

48. Locke, *Essay Concerning Human Understanding*, 3.3.§7, 411.

49. George Berkeley, *Principles of Human Knowledge/Three Dialogues*, ed. Roger Woolhouse (New York: Penguin, 1988), introduction, §10, 41; see also 40–42.

50. Rosi Braidotti, *The Posthuman* (Cambridge: Polity, 2013), 26.

51. While we indisputably know "we have in us something that thinks," Locke notes, we "must content our selves in the Ignorance of what kind of *Being* it is" (4.3.§6, 543). The fact that our own consciousness eludes knowledge and representation makes our speculations on the minds of others even more specious, Locke argues, in a passage that takes on both the Cartesian cogito and the bête-machine: "They must needs have a penetrating sight, who can certainly see, that I think, when I cannot perceive it my self; and when I declare, that I do not; and yet can see, that Dogs or Elephants do not think, when they give all the demonstration of it imaginable, except only telling us, that they do so" (2.1.§19, 115–16).

52. Condillac, *Essay on the Origin of Human Knowledge*, 1.5.§8, 96.

53. Cicero, *Sest.*, 91–92, qtd. in Richard Baumann, *Human Rights in Ancient Rome* (New York: Routledge, 2012), 47. Christian Høgel, *The Human and the Humane: Humanity as Argument from Cicero to Erasmus* (Göttingen, Germany: V & R Academic, 2015); Daniel Heller-Roazen, *The Enemy of All: Piracy and the Law of Nations* (Cambridge, MA: MIT Press, 2009), chap. 13, 147–61.

54. Martin Heidegger, "Letter on 'Humanism,'" trans. Frank A. Capuzzi, in *Basic Writings*, ed. David F. Krell (New York: Harper & Row, 1977), 189–242; on the perdurability of works in stabilizing human life, see Arendt, *The Human Condition*.

55. Maslan, "The Antihuman," 360.

56. Hannah Arendt, *On Revolution* (New York: Penguin, 1965), 107.

57. Hannah Arendt, *Origins of Totalitarianism*, 300. For Agamben's reading, see *Homo Sacer: Sovereign Power and Bare Life*, trans. Daniel Heller-Roazen (Stanford, CA: Stanford University Press, 1998), esp. 126–35. As Alastair Hunt observes, it is possible to argue that "for Arendt human rights are best viewed as a form of animal rights, because they conceive of human beings possessing rights in their naked life." Hunt, "Rightlessness: The Perplexities of Human Rights," *CR: The New Centennial Review* 11, no. 2 (Fall 2011): 128.

58. Thomas Hobbes, *Leviathan*, ed. Richard Tuck (Cambridge: Cambridge University Press, 1996), 111. Owing to length constraints, I have omitted discussions of animals, machines, and personhood in Hobbes and Descartes. On Hobbes, see Jacques Derrida, *The Beast and the Sovereign, Vol. 1*, trans. Geoffrey Bennington (Chicago: University of Chicago Press, 2009), 24–31; on Descartes, see Derrida, "'But as for me, who am I (following)?',"" *The Animal That Therefore I Am*, trans. David Wills, ed. Marie-Louise Mallet (New York: Fordham University Press, 2008), 69–87.

59. Thomas Blount, *Glossographia Anglicana nova* (London: D. Brown, 1707), s.v. humanity. The word does not appear in seventeenth-century editions of the *Glossographia*. Henry Cockeram's 1623 *English Dictionarie* defines *humanitie* as "Curtesie" and *humane* as "Gentle, pertaining to a man." *The English Dictionarie; or, An Interpreter of Hard English Words* (London: Edmund Weaver, 1623), s.v. humanitie, humane. John Kersey's 1702 *New English Dictionary* offers "Humane, *belonging to Man, also courteous, civil, obliging*"; "A Humanist, *one that is vers'd in* humane *learning*"; and "Humanity, Humane *nature; liberal; knowledge, learning, or courtesie.*" Kersey, *A New English Dictionary* (London: Henry Bonwicke, 1702). In the 1731 third edition of Kersey's *Dictionary*, "Mildness" has been added to the list of adjectives, as has the verb "To Humanize," defined as "*to civilize and make tractable.*"

60. Lynn Festa, "Humanity Without Feathers," *Humanity: An International Journal of Human Rights, Humanitarianism, and Development* 1, no. 1 (2010): 3–27.

61. Sir William Dawes, *Self-Love the Great Cause of Bad Times* (London: Thomas Speed, 1701), 9; qtd. in R. S. Crane, "Suggestions Towards a Genealogy of the 'Man of Feeling,'" *ELH* 1, no. 3 (1934): 225.

62. Indeed, the very trait that consolidates the category for Dawes produces a dehiscence that splits it apart, as the separation of "pity and kindness . . . from humane Nature" thrusts those who fail to feel from the class of humankind. As James Steintrager argues, the "movement of the mark of humanity from reason to pity" authorizes the demonization of those who lack compassion as inhuman. Steintrager, *Cruel Delight: Enlightenment Culture and the Inhuman* (Bloomington: Indiana University Press, 2004), 43.

63. On pets, see Paul Friedland, "Friends for Dinner: The Early Modern Roots of Modern Carnivorous Sensibilities," *History of the Present* 1, no. 1 (2011): 84–112; Srinivas Aravamudan, *Tropicopolitans: Colonialism and Agency, 1688–1804* (Durham, NC: Duke University Press,

1999), 29–70; Ingrid Tague, *Animal Companions: Pets and Social Change in Eighteenth-Century Britain* (University Park: Penn State University Press, 2015).

64. Tobias Menely, *The Animal Claim: Sensibility and the Creaturely Voice* (Chicago: University of Chicago Press, 2015), 1, 15. Sensibility, Menely argues, returns us to the animal claim as an unassimilable and irreducible passionate kernel—"an unintegrated origin and never fully actualized surplus of meaning that precedes the signifier itself"—that persists in the face of our emergence from the state of nature into a "symbolic order, and . . . a model of community [understood] as necessarily human" (5, 4).

65. Lynn Hunt, *Inventing Human Rights: A History* (New York: W. W. Norton, 2007); Thomas Laqueur, "Bodies, Details, and the Humanitarian Narrative," in *The New Cultural History*, ed. Lynn Hunt (Berkeley: University of California Press, 1989), 176–204; Joseph Slaughter, *Human Rights, Inc.: The World Novel, Narrative Form, and International Law* (New York: Fordham University Press, 2007); Dan Edelstein, "Enlightenment Rights Talk," *Journal of Modern History* 86, no. 3 (2014): 530–65; James Dawes, "Human Rights in Literary Studies," *Human Rights Quarterly* 31, no. 2 (2009): 394–409.

66. For a survey of such critiques, see Zachary Manfredi, "Recent Histories and Uncertain Futures: Contemporary Critiques of International Human Rights and Humanitarianism," *Qui Parle: Critical Humanities and Social Sciences* 22, no. 1 (2013): 3–32. See also Esmeir, "On Making Dehumanization Possible"; Talal Asad, "Redeeming the 'Human' Through Human Rights," *Formations of the Secular: Christianity, Islam, Modernity* (Stanford, CA: Stanford University Press, 2003), 127–58.

67. Reinhart Koselleck, "The Historical-Political Semantics of Asymmetric Counterconcepts," in *Futures Past: On the Semantics of Historical Time*, trans. Keith Tribe (New York: Columbia University Press, 2004), 181–82, 184. See also Dan Edelstein, *The Terror of Natural Right: Republicanism, the Cult of Nature, and the French Revolution* (Chicago: University of Chicago Press, 2009).

68. Karl Schmitt, *The Concept of the Political,* trans. George Schwab (Chicago: University of Chicago Press, 1996), 54.

69. Jacques Rancière, "Who Is the Subject of the Rights of Man?" *South Atlantic Quarterly* 103, no. 2/3 (2004): 305.

70. Costas Douzinas, *Human Rights and Empire: The Political Philosophy of Cosmopolitanism* (Oxford: Routledge, 2007), 55.

71. Claude Lefort, "Politics and Human Rights," in *The Political Forms of Modern Society: Bureaucracy, Democracy, Totalitarianism*, ed. John B. Thompson (Cambridge, MA: MIT Press, 1986), 257, 258.

72. Étienne Balibar, "'Rights of Man' and 'Rights of the Citizen': The Modern Dialectic of Equality and Freedom," *Masses, Classes, Ideas: Studies on Politics and Philosophy Before and After Marx*, trans. James Swenson (New York: Routedge, 1991), 49; Alastair Hunt, "The Rights of the Infinite," *Qui Parle* 19, no. 2 (2011): 236.

73. Étienne Balibar, "Citizen Subject," trans. James Swenson, in *Who Comes After the Subject?* ed. Eduardo Cadava, Peter Connor, and Jean-Luc Nancy (New York: Routledge, 1991), 50.

74. Rancière, "Who Is the Subject of the Rights of Man?" 303.

75. Peter de Bolla, *The Architecture of Concepts: The Historical Formation of Human Rights* (New York: Fordham University Press, 2013), 265.

76. Jacques Rancière, "Ten Theses on Politics," trans. Rachel Bowlby and Davide Panagia, *Theory and Event* 5, no. 3 (2001): thesis 7, §20.

77. Arendt, *Human Condition*, 12.

78. The texts analyzed below invite readers to imagine the world from a point of view not their own; indeed, some go a step further, withholding or dissevering the possessive that attaches an eye-view to a particular individual or species and offering the eerie detachment that Sharon Cameron describes as impersonality: "a penetration through or a falling outside of the boundary of the human particular" that "disrupts elementary categories we suppose to be fundamental to specifying human distinctiveness." Cameron, *Impersonality: Seven Essays* (Chicago: University of Chicago Press, 2007), ix.

79. Wolfe, *Animal Rites*, 8.

80. See Festa, "Humanity Without Feathers."

81. Saidiya Hartman, *Scenes of Subjection: Terror, Slavery, and Self-Making in Nineteenth-Century America* (New York: Oxford University Press, 1997), 5, 6.

82. See Allewaert, *Ariel's Ecology*; Bennett, " 'Being Property Once Myself.' "

83. Wynter, "Unsettling the Coloniality of Being/Power/Truth/Freedom: Towards the Human, After Man, Its Overrepresentation—An Argument," *CR: The New Centennial Review* 3, no. 3 (2003): 260, 266. Wynter's seminal account of the intertwining of racism and humanism, modernity and coloniality, has inspired important recent work on the question of the human, including Alexander Weheliye's *Habeas Viscus: Racializing Assemblages, Biopolitics, and Black Feminist Theories of the Human* (Durham, NC: Duke University Press, 2014).

84. Stuurman, *Invention of Humanity*, 260. On this progressive model of history, see Dipesh Chakrabarty, *Provincializing Europe: Postcolonial Thought and Imperial Difference* (Princeton, NJ: Princeton University Press, 2000), 8.

85. Judith Butler, *Frames of War: When Is Life Grievable?* (London: Verso, 2009), 76–77. I am not alone in wishing to keep humanity as a resource. Pheng Cheah, for example, concludes his fiercely critical analysis of the way human rights discourses seek to "humanize" global capitalism by affirming that humanity's failure to transcend this instrumentality nevertheless does not strip it of all value: "to say that humanity and its freedoms are product-effects of forces that precede and exceed the *anthrōpos* does not mean that humanity is a myth or a mere ideological abstraction. These humanity effects are concretely real and efficacious and can be progressive or enabling." Cheah, "Humanity in the Field of Instrumentality," *PMLA* 121, no. 5 (2006): 1556. See also Wynter, "Unsettling the Coloniality of Being/ Power/ Truth/ Freedom."

86. See Jane Bennett, *Vibrant Matter: A Political Ecology of Things* (Durham, NC: Duke University Press, 2010); Rob Nixon, *Slow Violence and the Environmentalism of the Poor* (Cambridge, MA: Harvard University Press, 2013); Ursula Heise, *Sense of Place and Sense of Planet: The Environmental Imagination of the Global* (Oxford: Oxford University Press, 2008); and Latour, *We Have Never Been Modern*.

CHAPTER I

1. Martin Heidegger, "The Origin of the Work of Art," in *Poetry, Language, Thought*, trans. Albert Hofstadter (New York: Harper and Row, 1971), 19.

2. W. J. T. Mitchell, *What Do Pictures Want? The Lives and Loves of Images* (Chicago: University of Chicago Press, 2005).

3. *An Essay on Laughter* (London: T. Davies, 1769), 73.

4. Guido Panciroli, *The History of Many Memorable Things in Use Among the Ancients, but Now Lost*, 2 vols. (London: A. Ward, 1727), 2.333.

5. Panciroli, *History*, 2.333; Pliny, *Natural History: Vol. 9, Books 33–35*, 10 vols., trans. H. Rackham, Loeb Classical Library (Cambridge, MA: Harvard University Press, 1952), 35.36.§65; 309; on Vitellesco, see Constance Classen, "Museum Manners: The Sensory Life of the Early Museum," *Journal of Social History* 40, no. 4 (2007): 901. Thanks to James Delbourgo for this reference and to Françoise Lavocat for drawing my attention to the numerous humans deceived by art.

6. Pliny, *Natural History*, 9.35.36.§65–§67, 309–11. Pliny's comeback begins in the Renaissance. See Sarah Blake McHam, *Pliny and the Artistic Culture of the Italian Renaissance: The Legacy of the* Natural History (New Haven, CT: Yale University Press, 2013). For other versions of the anecdote, see André Félibien, *Entretiens sur les vies et sur les ouvrages des plus excellens peintres anciens et modernes*, 5 vols. (Paris: Pierre Le Petit, 1666), 1.79–80; Pierre Bayle, *A General Dictionary, Historical and Critical*, trans. Jean Peter Bernard et al., 10 vols. (London: James Bettenham, 1741), 10.278–79, s.v. Zeuxis; Bayle, *Dictionnaire historique et critique* [1697], 5th ed., 4 vols. (Amsterdam: P. Brunel, 1740), 4.550–51, s.v. Zeuxis.

7. Norman Bryson, *Vision and Painting: The Logic of the Gaze* (New Haven, CT: Yale University Press, 1983), 4. As Bryson points out, "the Essential Copy, if it were ever achieved, would possess no stylistic features," since the perfect "simulacrum would at last have purged away all traces of the productive process" (7). For a critique of this evolutionary model with special attention to Zeuxis's grapes, see Stephen Bann, *The True Vine: On Visual Representation and the Western Tradition* (Cambridge: Cambridge University Press, 1989), esp. pp. 27–37.

8. Seneca the Orator, qtd. in *Recueil Milliet: Textes grecs et latins relatifs à l'histoire de la peinture ancienne: t. 1*, trans. and ed. Adolphe Reinach (Paris: C. Klincksieck, 1921), 213 (my translation). Pliny also tells this second version in the *Natural History*, 9.35.36.§66, 311. For additional early modern references, see Anne-Marie Lecoq, " 'Tromper les yeux,' disent-ils: XIVe–XVIe siècle," *Le trompe l'oeil de l'antiquité au XXe siècle*, ed. Patrick Mauriès (Paris: Gallimard, 1996), 67; Leonard Barkan, "The Heritage of Zeuxis: Painting, Rhetoric, and History," in *Antiquity and Its Interpreters*, ed. Alina Payne, Ann Kuttner, and Rebeka Smick (Cambridge: Cambridge University Press, 2000), 99–109; Creighton E. Gilbert, "Grapes, Curtains, Human Beings: The Theory of Missed Mimesis," in *Künstlerischer Austausch—Artistic Exchange: Akten des XXVIII. Internationalen Kongresses für Kunstgeschichte, Berlin, 15.–20. Juli 1992*, ed. Thomas W. Gaehtgens, 3 vols. (Berlin: Akademie Verlag, 1993), 2.413–22.

9. Norman Bryson, *Looking at the Overlooked: Four Essays on Still Life Painting* (Cambridge, MA: Harvard University Press, 1990), 31, 32.

10. On the frame, see Rayna Kalas, *Frame, Glass, Verse: The Technology of Poetic Invention in the English Renaissance* (Ithaca, NY: Cornell University Press, 2007); and David Marshall, *The Frame of Art: Fictions of Aesthetic Experience, 1750–1815* (Baltimore: Johns Hopkins University Press, 2005).

11. On metalepsis, see Gérard Genette, "De la figure à la fiction," in *Métalepses: Entorses au pacte de la représentation*, ed. John Pier and Jean-Marie Schaeffer (Paris: Éditions de l'École des Hautes Études en Sciences Sociales, 2005), 21–35.

12. Bann, *True Vine*, 35.

13. Thomas Hickey, *Storia della pittura e la scultura; scritta in Italiano ed Inglese da Tomaso Icchi* [The History of Ancient Painting and Sculpture; Written in Italian and English] (Calcutta: Stuart and Cooper, 1788), 29.

14. Bryson, *Looking at the Overlooked*, 36.

15. Jacques Lacan, "What Is a Picture?" in *The Four Fundamental Concepts of Psycho-Analysis*, trans. Alan Sheridan (New York: Norton, 1981), 112.

16. Barbara Maria Stafford, *Artful Science: Enlightenment Entertainment and the Eclipse of Visual Education* (Cambridge, MA: MIT Press, 1994).

17. See Olaf Koester, "Cornelius Norbertus Gijsbrechts—an Introduction," in *Illusions: Gijsbrechts Royal Master of Deception*, ed. Olaf Koester and Celeste Brusati (Copenhagen: Statens Museum for Kunst, 1999), 23ff.

18. See Celeste Brusati, "Honorable Deceptions and Dubious Distinctions: Self-Imagery in Trompe-l'Oeil," in Koester and Brusati, *Illusions*, 49–73. On curtains in Dutch art, see Thijs Weststeijn, *The Visible World: Samuel Van Hoogstraten's Art Theory and the Legitimation of Painting in the Dutch Golden Age,* trans. Beverley Jackson and Lynne Richards (Amsterdam: Amsterdam University Press, 2008), 152; Victor Stoichita, *The Self-Aware Image: An Insight into Early Modern Meta-Painting*, trans. Anne-Marie Glasheen (Cambridge: Cambridge University Press, 1997), 60–62.

19. Fatma Yalcin, "Van Hoogstraten's Success in Britain," in *The Universal Art of Samuel Van Hoogstraten (1627–1678): Painter, Writer, and Courtier,* ed. Thijs Weststeijn (Amsterdam: Amsterdam University Press, 2013), 161–81; Dror Wahrman, *Mr. Collier's Letter Racks: A Tale of Art and Illusion at the Threshold of the Information Age* (Oxford: Oxford University Press, 2012).

20. Abraham Cowley, *The Works of Mr. Abraham Cowley,* 12th ed., 3 vols. (London: Benj. Motte, 1721), 2.559.

21. On the connection between Cowley's and Bacon's description of his own method in *The New Organon*, see Achsah Guibbory, "Imitation and Originality: Cowley and Bacon's Vision of Progress," *SEL* 29, no. 1 (1989): 104.

22. Cowley, *Works*, 2.559–60.

23. See André Félibien, preface, *Conférences de l'Académie royale de peinture et de sculpture, pendant l'année 1667* (Paris: F. Léonard, 1668), n.p.

24. Kate Tunstall, "Text, Image, Intertext: Diderot, Chardin and Pliny," in *Interdisciplinarity: Qu'est-ce que les Lumières? La reconnaissance au dix-huitième siècle* ed. G. J. Mallinson, Studies on Voltaire and the Eighteenth Century 2006:12 (Oxford: Voltaire Foundation, 2006), 346.

25. Elizabeth Mansfield, *Too Beautiful to Picture: Zeuxis, Myth, and Mimesis* (Minneapolis: University of Minnesota Press, 2007), esp. 57–74.

26. William Aglionby, *Choice Observations upon the Art of Painting* (London: R. King, 1719), 18.

27. Charles Perrault, *Parallèle des anciens et des modernes,* nouvelle édition, 4 vols. (Paris: Jean Baptiste Coignard, 1693), 1.137, 1.138.

28. Charles Perrault, *Le siècle de Louis le Grand* [1687], in *Oeuvres choisies de Charles Perrault*, ed. Collin de Plancy (Paris: Brissot-Thivars, 1826), 297. Later writers use the anecdote to mock the affectation of virtuosity: "The testimony of animals, in taking works of art for realities, is of a more powerful kind than that of men," since "neither horses, dogs, nor birds, are biassed with pretended connoisseurship, but are affected according to the true appearance of the object." Hickey, *Storia della pittura e la scultura antica*, 31.

29. Perrault, *Le siècle de Louis le Grand,* 297.

30. From Perrault, *Parallèle,* 1.137. Translation by Christopher Miller from *Art in Theory, 1648–1815: An Anthology of Changing Ideas*, ed. Charles Harrison, Paul Wood, and Jason Gaiger (Oxford: Blackwell, 2000), 56.

31. Giorgio Agamben, *The Open: Man and Animal,* trans. Kevin Attell (Stanford, CA: Stanford University Press, 2004), 41.

32. Jakob von Uexküll, *A Foray into the Worlds of Animals and Humans,* trans. Joseph D. O'Neil (Minneapolis: University of Minnesota Press, 2010). On the tick see 50–52.

33. Martin Heidegger, *The Fundamental Concepts of Metaphysics: World, Finitude, Solitude*, trans. William McNeill and Nicholas Walker (Bloomington: Indiana University Press, 1995), 248. See also Agamben, *The Open*, 53.

34. Lacan, "What Is a Picture?" 111, 111, 112.

35. Ernst Gombrich, "Meditations on a Hobby Horse, or the Roots of Artistic Form," in *Art Theory and Criticism: An Anthology of Formalist, Avant-Garde, Contextualist and Post-Modernist Thought*, ed. Sally Everett (Jefferson, NC: McFarland, 1991), 47. Gombrich rejected some of these stances in his later work. See W. J. T. Mitchell, "Illusion: Looking at Animals Looking," in *Picture Theory: Essays on Verbal and Visual Representation* (Chicago: University of Chicago Press, 1994), 334–35, 340–42.

36. Ernst Gombrich, *Art and Illusion: A Study in the Psychology of Pictorial Representation* (Princeton, NJ: Princeton University Press, 2000), 99.

37. Gombrich, "Meditations on a Hobby Horse," 47.

38. Walter Benjamin, "The Cultural History of Toys," trans. Rodney Livingstone, *Selected Writings, Vol. 2: 1927–1934*, ed. Michael W. Jennings, et al. (Cambridge, MA: Belknap, 1999), 115.

39. Lacan, "The Line and Light," in *The Four Fundamental Concepts of Psycho-Analysis*, trans. Alan Sheridan (New York: Norton, 1981), 100.

40. Bayle, *General Dictionary*, 10.359–60; Bayle, *Dictionnaire historique et critique*, 4.595. Bayle refers here to the Venus of Cnidus (or Knidos). See Françoise Lavocat, *La Syrinx au bûcher: Pan et les satyres à la Renaissance et à l'âge baroque* (Geneva: Droz, 2005), 290n51.

41. Jacques Derrida, "But as for Me, Who Am I (Following)?" in *The Animal That Therefore I Am*, ed. Marie-Louise Mallet, trans. David Wills (New York: Fordham University Press, 2008), 59. John Ray and Francis Willughby fleetingly acknowledge the bird's response to its mirrored image in their contention that the bluebird flies "at men[']s Eyes, because seeing in them, as in a Looking-glass, its own image, it is affected with a desire of its like, and thinks to joyn it self in company with it." Ray and Willughby, *The Ornithology of Francis Willughby* (London: John Martyn, 1678), 192. That the bird recognizes itself hints at the possibility of reflexivity or self-knowledge.

42. Bayle is an outlier in ascribing this capacity to animals. See, e.g., Zachary Mayne, *Two Dissertations Concerning Sense, and the Imagination* (London: J. Tonson, 1728), 46.

43. Bayle, *General Dictionary*, 10.360n; *Dictionnaire historique et critique*, 4.595n. Bayle here is quoting an earlier critique of the tale by Lancelot de Perouse.

44. Robert Hooke, "Lectures on Light," in *The Posthumous Works of Robert Hooke*, ed. Richard Waller (London: Sam. Smith and Benj. Walford, 1705), 134.

45. Jacques-Henri Bernardin de Saint Pierre, *Études de la nature*, qtd. in Joanna Stalnaker, *The Unfinished Enlightenment: Description in the Age of the Encyclopedia* (Ithaca, NY: Cornell University Press, 2010), 80–81.

46. Stalnaker, *Unfinished Enlightenment*, 81.

47. Oliver Goldsmith, *An History of the Earth, and Animated Nature*, 8 vols. (London: J. Nourse, 1774), 5.10. For modern work on bird vision, see Olga F. Lazareva, Toru Shimizu, and Edward Wasserman, eds., *How Animals See the World: Comparative Behavior, Biology, and Evolution of Vision* (Oxford: Oxford University Press, 2012).

48. Goldsmith, *An History of the Earth*, 5.2.

49. Thomas Willis, *The Anatomy of the Brain*, in *The Remaining Medical Works of That Famous and Renowned Physician Dr. Thomas Willis*, trans. Samuel Pordage (London: T. Dring, 1681), 76. Chapter 5 addresses bird brains. Thanks to Frank Boyle for this reference.

50. Nehemiah Grew argues the opposite. The bird possesses a "Phancy, . . . so disposed, as to conceive a Cleer and Perfect Draught of her Nest. . . . For which purpose, . . . the

Chambers of the Optique Nerves . . . are in all Birds, made very large. Not to give them a Quicker Sight, . . . But to be the means, of their conceiving a Stronger Phancy of Visible Things." Grew, *Cosmologia Sacra: Or a Discourse of the Universe as It Is the Creature and Kingdom of God* (London: W. Rogers, 1701), 42.

51. Ray and Willughby, *Ornithology*, 6, sig. A2lr. See Paul Lawrence Farber, *Discovering Birds: The Emergence of Ornithology as a Scientific Discipline, 1760–1850* (Baltimore: Johns Hopkins University Press, 1997).

52. Ray and Willughby, *Ornithology*, 31, 33, 34.

53. This question lies at the heart of Derrida's critique of Lacan's denial of the animal's ability to "*pretend to pretend* or to *erase its traces.*" While the animal may engage in deception, it lacks the reflexive power that "is *conscious* of deceiving by pretending to pretend." Derrida, "And Say the Animal Responded?" in *The Animal That Therefore I Am*, 120, 128. These distinctions help differentiate animal camouflage or mimicry—itself a mid-nineteenth-century discovery—from human forms of imitation. See Peter Forbes, *Dazzled and Deceived: Mimicry and Camouflage* (New Haven, CT: Yale University Press, 2009).

54. Ray and Willughby, *Ornithology*, 34. See also Nicholas Cox, *The Gentleman's Recreation*, 6th ed. (London: N.C., 1721), 231–32; and *A New Universal History of Arts and Sciences*, 2 vols. (London: J. Coote, 1759), 1.523.

55. Alfred Gell, "Vogel's Net: Traps as Artworks and Artworks as Traps," *Journal of Material Culture* 1, no. 1 (1996): 27, 29.

56. Diana Donald, *Picturing Animals in Britain, 1750–1850* (New Haven, CT: Yale University Press, 2007), 37.

57. John Ray, *Wisdom of God* [1691] (London: W. Innys, 1743), 261; William Derham, *Physico-Theology: or, a Demonstration of the Being and Attributes of God*, 2nd ed. (London: W. Innys, 1714), 91. See also Henry More, *An Antidote Against Atheism, or, an Appeal to the Naturall Faculties of the Minde of Man* (London: J. Flesher, 1655), 140.

58. Uexküll, *Foray into the Worlds*, 50.

59. Joanna Picciotto, "Milton and the People," in *Milton in the Long Restoration*, ed. Blair Hoxby and Ann Baynes Coiro (Oxford: Oxford University Press, 2016), 486.

60. Picciotto, "Milton and the People," 491, 499. See, e.g., George Edwards, *A Natural History of Birds*, 4 vols. (London: for the author, 1743), 1.viii.

61. René Descartes, "Optics," trans. John Cottingham, Robert Stoothoff, and Dugald Murdoch, in *The Philosophical Writings of Descartes: Vol. 1* (Cambridge: Cambridge University Press, 1985), 166.

62. Since the universal laws of optics operate identically irrespective of species, natural historians such as Robert Hooke (to whom we turn in Chapter 2) calculated the scope, scale, and angle of vision from the refraction of rays into the differently shaped and sized eyes of various species, subordinating species difference to the automatic functioning of the organ. Hooke, "Lectures on Light," 135; see also 125–28.

63. Ofer Gal and Raz Chen-Morris, *Baroque Science* (Chicago: University of Chicago Press, 2013), 15, 16. Thanks to Roger Shank for this reference.

64. Stoichita, *Self-Aware Image*, 155.

65. Gassendi, in the fifth objection to the *Meditations*, uses the eye's blindness to itself to respond to Descartes's expressed perplexity about this "puzzling 'I'": "As to how it is possible for you to understand something that is foreign to you better than you understand yourself, I answer that the same thing happens in the case of the eye, which sees other things but does

not see itself." Descartes, *Meditations on First Philosophy*, trans. John Cottingham, in *The Philosophical Writings of Descartes: Vol. 2* (Cambridge: Cambridge University Press, 1984), 20, 187.

66. Descartes, "Letter to Plempius for Fromondus," October 3, 1637, in *The Correspondence*, trans. John Cottingham et al., in *The Philosophical Writings of Descartes: Vol. 3* (Cambridge: Cambridge University Press, 1991), 61–62.

67. As Gal and Chen-Morris note, optics "is not an attempt to get the objects as they are, but vision as it is"; it offers "the naked, optical phenomenon that is the retinal image before it is processed by the higher faculties." It tells us nothing about perception and nothing about the object perceived. Gal and Chen-Morris, *Baroque Science*, 29.

68. Descartes, "Optics," 167.

69. See Philip Steadman, *Vermeer's Camera: Uncovering the Truth Behind the Masterpiece* (Oxford: Oxford University Press, 2002); and Wolfgang Lefèvre, ed., *Inside the Camera Obscura: Optics and Art Under the Spell of the Projected Image* (Berlin: Preprint of the Max Planck Institute for the History of Science, 2007), especially the essays by Carsten Wirth and Karin Groen.

70. Svetlana Alpers, *The Art of Describing: Dutch Art in the Seventeenth Century* (Chicago: University of Chicago Press, 1984), 37.

71. Celeste Brusati, "Perspectives in Flux: Viewing Dutch Pictures in Real Time," *Art History* 35, no. 5 (2012): 922, 913.

72. See Adrian Johns, *The Nature of the Book: Print and Knowledge in the Making* (Chicago: University of Chicago Press, 1998), 391; Ernst Gombrich, "Standards of Truth: The Arrested Image and the Moving Eye," *Critical Inquiry* 7, no. 2 (1980): 237–73; Jonathan Crary, *Techniques of the Observer: On Vision and Modernity in the Nineteenth Century* (Cambridge, MA: MIT Press, 1992). By creating a coherence of vision that does not in fact exist, Lyle Massey argues, the artificial stability of perspective helps prop up the unity of the (Cartesian) subject. Once the body is "reinserted into the history and theory of perspective," however, the metaphorical equivalence between the perspectival eye and the first-person "I" collapses. Massey, *Picturing Space, Displacing Bodies: Anamorphosis in Early Modern Theories of Perspective* (University Park: Penn State University Press, 2007), 2.

73. Martin Kemp, *The Science of Art: Optical Themes in Western Art from Brunelleschi to Seurat* (New Haven, CT: Yale University Press, 1992), 165.

74. James Elkins identifies at least ten models of perspective current in the Renaissance. See Elkins, *The Poetics of Perspective* (Ithaca, NY: Cornell University Press, 1994). For fuller accounts of perspective than are possible here, see Hubert Damisch, *The Origin of Perspective*, trans. John Goodman (Cambridge, MA: MIT Press, 1995); Bryson, *Vision and Painting*; and Michel Foucault, *The Order of Things: An Archaeology of the Human Sciences* (New York: Vintage, 1994).

75. Erwin Panofsky, *Perspective as Symbolic Form* (New York: Zone, 1996), 67. It is easy to overstate the dominance of Albertian perspective. Panofsky himself acknowledges that "the exact perspectival construction of completely irregular structures, above all the human or animal body, hardly ever entered into day-to-day practice" (138n61).

76. Alpers, *Art of Describing*, 41, xix, xix, 41.

77. Brusati, "Perspectives in Flux," 917.

78. Brusati, "Perspectives in Flux," 911, 910–11, 911.

79. Joanna Woodall, "Laying the Table: The Procedures of Still Life," *Art History* 35, no. 5 (2012): 992.

80. Hanneke Grootenboer, *The Rhetoric of Perspective: Realism and Illusionism in Seventeenth-Century Dutch Still-Life Painting* (Chicago: University of Chicago Press, 2005), 9.

81. Grootenboer, *Rhetoric of Perspective*, 79.

82. See Grootenboer, *Rhetoric of Perspective*, 46. On inventories, see Celeste Brusati, "Honorable Deceptions and Dubious Distinctions: Self-Imagery in Trompe l'Oeil," in Koester and Brusati, *Illusions*, 54.

83. Bryson, *Looking at the Overlooked*, 61–63.

84. Gerard de Lairesse, *The Art of Painting* [1707], trans. John Frederick Fritsch (London: printed for the author, 1738), 548.

85. I am relying here on Grootenboer's use of Merleau-Ponty in her analysis of still life. See *Rhetoric of Perspective*, 35–42.

86. Grootenboer, *Rhetoric of Perspective*, 77, 80.

87. Roland Barthes, "The World as Object," trans. Richard Howard, in *The Barthes Reader*, ed. Susan Sontag (New York: Hill and Wang, 1987), 63. See also Simon Schama, *The Embarrassment of Riches: An Interpretation of Dutch Culture in the Golden Age* (New York: Vintage, 1997); and Julie Hochstrasser, *Still Life and Trade in the Dutch Golden Age* (New Haven, CT: Yale University Press, 2007).

88. Jean Baudrillard, "The Trompe l'Oeil," in *Calligram: Essays in New Art History from France*, ed. Norman Bryson (Cambridge: Cambridge University Press, 1988), 56.

89. Grootenboer, *Rhetoric of Perspective*, 54.

90. A "two-edged sword," perspective "creates distance between human beings and things, . . . but then in turn it abolishes this distance by, in a sense, drawing this world of things, an autonomous world confronting the individual, into the eye." Panofsky, *Perspective as Symbolic Form*, 67.

91. Our visual field is organized by what Lacan calls the "gaze," which structures what we see but to which we are blind. See Lacan, *Four Fundamental Concepts*, 67–119.

92. Bryson, *Looking at the Overlooked*, 65.

93. Feagin, "Presentation and Representation," *Journal of Aesthetics and Art Criticism* 56, no. 3 (1998): 237, 236.

94. Diderot's encounter with Chardin's still-life paintings involves a *fort-da* play of retreat and return, distance and nearness: "Approach, and everything becomes blurry, flattens out, and disappears; move away, everything recreates and reproduces itself." Denis Diderot, "Salon de 1763," in *Oeuvres esthétiques*, ed. Paul Vernière (Paris: Garnier, 1968), 484; see also 491, 493.

95. Barbara Johnson, *Persons and Things* (Cambridge, MA: Harvard University Press, 2008), 57, 57–58. Loving a form is not the same as loving a thing, although Johnson sees the unified body represented in the mirror stage as thinglike: "What happens in the mirror stage is the conflating of libidinal investments with beautiful forms: the fantasmatic and the aesthetic are henceforth the 'reality' of the self. And the definition of 'person' would then be: the repeated experience of *failing to become a thing*" (59).

96. Jacqueline Lichtenstein, *The Eloquence of Color: Rhetoric and Painting in the French Classical Age*, trans. Emily McVarish (Berkeley: University of California Press, 1993), 170, 169.

97. On optical illusions and seventeenth-century science, see Stafford, *Artful Science*; on the early eighteenth-century media revolution, see Wahrman, *Mr. Collier's Letter Racks*; on postrevolutionary citizenship, see Wendy Bellion, *Citizen Spectator: Art, Illusion, and Visual Perception in Early National America* (Chapel Hill: University of North Carolina Press, 2011); on nineteenth-century con games, see Paul Staiti, "Illusionism, Trompe l'Oeil, and the Perils of Viewership," in *William Harnett*, ed. Doreen Bolger, Marc Simpson, and John Wilmerding (New York: Metropolitan Museum of Art, 1992), 31–47; and Michael Leja, *Looking Askance:*

Skepticism and American Art from Eakins to Duchamp (Berkeley: University of California Press, 2004), 125–52. Thanks to Jane Sharp for these references.

98. Mitchell, "Illusion: Looking at Animals Looking," 339. As Michael Taussig observes of the famous RCA logo of a dog crouched before the ear-trumpet of a phonograph, quizzically attentive to a recording of "His Master's Voice," "the technology of reproduction triumphs over the dog but needs the dog's validation." Taussig, *Mimesis and Alterity: A Particular History of the Senses* (New York: Routledge, 1992), 224.

99. Nathaniel Wolloch, "Dead Animals and the Beast-Machine: Seventeenth-Century Netherlandish Paintings of Dead Animals, as Anti-Cartesian Statements," *Art History* 22 (1999): 718. See Scott Sullivan, *The Dutch Gamepiece* (Totowa, NJ: Rowman & Allanheld, 1984).

100. On the influence of Jan Baptist Weenix and William van Aelst, see Marrigje Rikken, *Melchior d'Hondecoeter: Bird Painter* (Amsterdam: Rijksmuseum, 2008), 11–14.

101. On bird sounds, see Jacob Smith, *Eco-sonic Media* (Berkeley: University of California Press, 2015), 42–79. I thank Judith Zeitlin for this reference.

102. Gell, "Vogel's Net," 27.

103. Perrault is, as usual, derisive. Perrault, *Parallèle*, 1.136–37.

104. Antoine Joseph Dezallier d'Argenville, *Supplément à l'abrégé de la vie des plus fameux peintres, troisième partie* (Paris: de Bure, 1752), 225; Simon-Philippe Mazière de Monville, *Vie de Pierre Mignard, premier peintre du roi* (Amsterdam: aux dépens de la compagnie, 1731), 24. Marin distinguishes between these two trompe l'oeil paintings: whereas Mignard's painted cat lures the canine eye to something present in the image itself (like the bird's captivation by painted grapes or even by a red dot), the birds "seek to pass through the wall towards the depths that painting has magically opened up[,] . . . the spring of the trap being the neutralization of the plane of the wall." Marin, "Le trompe-l'oeil, un comble de la peinture," in *L'effet trompe-l'oeil dans l'art et la psychanalyse*, ed. Raymond Court (Paris: Dunod, 1988), 80.

105. On the trompe l'oeil in the context of seventeenth-century theories of representation, see Marin, "Le trompe-l'oeil," 75–92.

106. Baudrillard, "Trompe l'Oeil," 56–57.

107. Grootenboer, *Rhetoric of Perspective*, 48.

108. Koester and Brusati, *Illusions*, cat. 47, 248.

109. Lacan, "What Is a Picture?" 112.

110. Bryson, *Looking at the Overlooked*, 143.

111. Stoichita, *Self-Aware Image*, 273–74.

112. Samuel Pepys, entry of April 11, 1669, in *Diary of Samuel Pepys*, ed. Robert Latham and William Matthews, 11 vols. (Berkeley: University of California Press, 2000), 9.515. He singles out "the drops of Dew hanging on the leaves" as a particularly compelling detail.

113. Lacan, "What Is a Picture?" 107.

114. Charles Murtagh Peterson, "Beautiful Painted Lies: Deception and Illusionistic Painting in the Seventeenth Century" (PhD dissertation, University of California, Santa Barbara, 2012), 39.

115. Olaf Koester, *Painted Illusions: The Art of Cornelis Gijsbrechts* (London: National Gallery, 2000), cat. 11, 36.

116. Peterson, "Beautiful Painted Lies," 38.

117. Denis Cosgrove, "Prospect, Perspective and the Evolution of the Landscape Idea," *Transactions of the Institute of British Geographers* 10 (1985): 51. See also Cosgrove, *Apollo's Eye: A Cartographic Genealogy of the Earth in the Western Imagination* (Baltimore: Johns Hopkins

University Press, 2001); and Juergen Schulz, "Jacopo de' Barberi's View of Venice: Map Making, City Views, and Moralized Geography Before the Year 1500," *Art Bulletin* 60, no. 3 (1978): 425–74.

118. Lucia Nuti, "The Perspective Plan in the Sixteenth Century: The Invention of a Representational Language," *Art Bulletin* 76, no. 1 (1994): 109.

119. For a characteristic definition, see *The Artist's Repository and Drawing Magazine*, 5 vols. (London: T. Williams, 1784–94), 3.29. Early references to the "bird's-eye view" crop up in discussions of balloon travel, where they vaunt its military potential. Late-century writers are often more interested in what that vantage point erases. On the landscape, see John Barrell, *English Literature in History, 1730–1780: An Equal, Wide Survey* (London: Hutchinson, 1983), 51–109.

120. Alpers, *Art of Describing*, 141, 138, 138.

121. Latour is quoting William Mills Ivins here. Bruno Latour, "Visualization and Cognition: Thinking with Eyes and Hands," *Knowledge and Society: Studies in the Sociology of Culture Past and Present* 6 (1986): 7.

122. Georges Louis Leclerc, comte de Buffon, *Histoire naturelle des oiseaux: t. 1* (Paris: Imprimerie Royale, 1770), 14; Buffon, *The Natural History of Birds*, 9 vols. (London: A. Strahan and T. Cadell, 1793), 1.6–7.

123. Buffon, *Histoire naturelle: t. 1*, 14; Buffon, *Natural History*, 1.7.

124. Malton, *An Appendix, or, Second Part to the Complete Treatise on Perspective* (London: for the author, 1800), 29.

125. F. L. d'Escherny, *Les lacunes de la philosophie*, 1783; qtd. in David Bates, "Cartographic Aberrations: Epistemology and Order in the Encyclopedic Map," in *Using the* Encyclopédie: *Ways of Knowing, Ways of Reading*, ed. Daniel Brewer and Julie Candler Hayes (Oxford: Voltaire Foundation, 2002), 10. See also Daniel Brewer, *The Discourse of Enlightenment in Eighteenth-Century France* (Cambridge: Cambridge University Press, 1993).

126. Anne-Lise François, "'O Happy Living Things': Frankenfoods and the Bounds of Wordsworthian Natural Piety," *Diacritics* 33, no. 2 (2003): 50.

127. Thanks to Daniel Brewer for his illuminating comments on this point.

CHAPTER 2

Epigraph: Karl Marx, "Economic and Philosophic Manuscripts of 1844," in *The Marx-Engels Reader*, 2nd ed., ed. Robert C. Tucker (New York: Norton, 1978), 89.

1. Richard Waller, "Life of Hooke," in *The Posthumous Works of Robert Hooke*, ed. Richard Waller (London: Sam. Smith and Benj. Walford, 1705), xxvi.

2. This lack—and the capacity to instrumentalize things to compensate for it—is often singled out as the defining trait of humanity. As Jean-François Lyotard puts it, "If humans are born human, as cats are born cats, . . . it would not be . . . possible to educate them. That children have to be educated . . . proceeds from the fact that they are not completely led by nature, not programmed. . . . What shall we call human in humans, the initial misery of their childhood, or their capacity to acquire a 'second nature'?" Lyotard, *The Inhuman: Reflections on Time*, trans. Geoffrey Bennington and Rachel Bowlby (Stanford, CA: Stanford University Press, 1991), 3. On the Renaissance history of human insufficiency, see Laurie Shannon, *The Accommodated Animal: Cosmopolity in Shakespearean Locales* (Chicago: University of Chicago Press, 2013), 127–73.

3. Pliny, *Natural History: Vol. 2, Books 3–7*, Loeb Classical Library, 10 vols., trans. H. Rackham (Cambridge, MA: Harvard University Press, 1942), 7.1.§2, 507.

4. Robert Hooke, *Micrographia: or, Some Physiological Descriptions of Minute Bodies Made by Magnifying Glasses* (London: Jo. Martyn, 1665), sig. a.

5. See Michael Hunter and Simon Schaffer, "Introduction," *Robert Hooke: New Studies*, ed. Hunter and Schaffer (Woodbridge, UK: Boydell, 1989), 1–6; Lisa Jardine, *The Curious Life of Robert Hooke: The Man Who Measured London* (New York: HarperCollins, 2005); Allan Chapman, *England's Leonardo: Robert Hooke and the Seventeenth-Century Scientific Revolution* (Bristol, UK: Institute of Physics Publishing, 2005).

6. Stephen Pumfrey, "Ideas Above His Station: A Social Study of Hooke's Curatorship of Experiments," *Journal of the History of Science* 29 (1991): 1. On the Royal Society, see Michael Hunter, *Establishing the New Science: The Experience of the Early Royal Society* (Woodbridge, UK: Boydell, 1989); and *Science and Society in Restoration England* (Cambridge: Cambridge University Press, 1981).

7. Steven Shapin, "Who Was Robert Hooke?" in Hunter and Schaffer, *Robert Hooke: New Studies*, 265.

8. Hooke, *Micrographia*, sig. bv; Steven Shapin, "Pump and Circumstance: Robert Boyle's Literary Technology," *Social Studies of Science* 14, no. 4 (1984): 495. See Hooke, *Micrographia*: "*The* Arts *of life have been too long* imprison'd *in the dark shops of Mechanicks themselves, & there* hindred from growth, *either by ignorance, or self-interest*" (sig. gv).

9. Thomas Birch, *History of the Royal Society*, 4 vols. (London: A. Millar, 1756), 1.490–91. On the Royal Society's commission, see John Harwood, "Rhetoric and Graphics in *Micrographia*," in Hunter and Schaffer, *Robert Hooke: New Studies*, 122–34.

10. See Robert Hooke, "A General Scheme, or Idea of the Present State of Natural Philosophy, and Wherein It Is Deficient," in *The Posthumous Works of Robert Hooke*, ed. Richard Waller (London: Sam. Smith and Benj. Walford, 1705), 34. Hereafter abbreviated GS parenthetically in the text. Scholars date the "true method" to roughly 1664–66. On the dating, see Harwood, "Rhetoric and Graphics in *Micrographia*," 137n43.

11. J. A. Bennett, "Robert Hooke as Mechanic and Natural Philosopher," *Notes and Records of the Royal Society of London* 35 (1980): 43.

12. Antonio Pérez-Ramos, *Francis Bacon's Idea of Science and the Maker's Knowledge Tradition* (Oxford: Clarendon, 1988), 48. As "the capacity to reproduce nature's effects became a sort of touchstone upon which claims to knowledge would have to be tested," as William Eamon puts it, "the new philosophy made how-to knowledge a criterion of truth," drawing heavily on alchemy, natural magic, and the "Book of Secrets" tradition. Eamon, *Science and the Secrets of Nature: Books of Secrets in Medieval and Early Modern Culture* (Princeton, NJ: Princeton University Press, 1994), 10. See also W. R. Newman, *Atoms and Alchemy: Chymistry and the Experimental Origins of the Scientific Revolution* (Chicago: University of Chicago Press, 2006).

13. Bennett, "Robert Hooke as Mechanic and Natural Philosopher," 44. See also Bennett, "Hooke's Instruments for Astronomy and Navigation," in Hunter and Schaffer, *Robert Hooke: New Studies*, 21–32. Instruments "determine theory, because instruments determine what is possible, and what is possible determines to a large extent what can be thought." Thomas Hankins and Robert J. Silverman, *Instruments and the Imagination* (Princeton, NJ: Princeton University Press, 1995), 5.

14. On this division of labor, see Pamela H. Smith, *The Body of the Artisan: Art and Experience in the Scientific Revolution* (Chicago: University of Chicago Press, 2004); Hannah

Arendt, *The Human Condition* (New York: Doubleday Anchor, 1959); Jacques Rancière, *The Philosopher and His Poor*, trans. John Drury, Corinne Oster, and Andrew Parker, ed. Andrew Parker (Durham, NC: Duke University Press, 2004); Paola Bertucci, *Artisanal Enlightenment: Science and the Mechanical Arts in Old Regime France* (New Haven, CT: Yale University Press, 2017).

15. Joanna Picciotto, *Labors of Innocence in Early Modern England* (Cambridge, MA: Harvard University Press, 2010), 138–39, 139.

16. "BOSWELL. 'I think Dr. Franklin's definition of *Man* a good one—'A tool-making animal.' JOHNSON. 'But many a man never made a tool; and suppose a man without arms, he could not make a tool.'" James Boswell, *Boswell's Life of Johnson,* ed. George Birkbeck Hill, 6 vols. (Oxford: Clarendon, 1887), 3.245.

17. Hooke, *Micrographia*, sig. b2r. See Francis Bacon, "Aphorisms," in *The New Organon*, ed. Fulton H. Anderson (New York: Macmillan, 1960), 39.

18. We say we "see through" a device when we understand the instrument to be an extension of the senses offering access to what is "really" there; we "look at" an instrument's output when we understand the data to be produced by the device. Hankins and Silverman, *Instruments and the Imagination*, 11.

19. Hooke, "Of Comets," in *Posthumous Works*, ed. Waller, 152. See Ofer Gal and Raz Chen-Morris, "Empiricism Without the Senses: How the Instrument Replaced the Eye," in *The Body as Object and Instrument of Knowledge: Embodied Empiricism in Early Modern Science*, ed. Charles Wolfe and Ofer Gal (Dordrecht, Netherlands: Springer, 2010), 121–47.

20. Jessica Wolfe, *Humanism, Machinery, and Renaissance Literature* (Cambridge: Cambridge University Press, 2004), 114.

21. Sean Silver, *The Mind Is a Collection: Case Studies in Eighteenth-Century Thought* (Philadelphia: University of Pennsylvania Press, 2015), 122. See also Silver, "Hooke, Latour, and the History of Extended Cognition," *The Eighteenth Century: Theory and Interpretation* 57, no. 2 (2016): 197–215. On the connection of manual and intellectual labor, see Lissa Roberts, Simon Schaffer, and Peter Dear, eds., *The Mindful Hand: Inquiry and Invention from the Late Renaissance to Early Industrialisation* (Amsterdam: Royal Netherlands Academy of Arts and Sciences, 2007).

22. Wolfe, *Humanism, Machinery, and Renaissance Literature*, 5. On ambivalence about instruments in conjunction with empiricism and the emergence of aesthetics, see Michael McKeon, "The Dramatic Aesthetic and the Model of Scientific Method, 1600–1800," *Eighteenth-Century Novel* 6–7 (2009), esp. 208–15.

23. Johnson's "instrument" also embraces legal contracts, music-making devices, and "tool[s] used for any work or purpose." Johnson, *Dictionary of the English Language*, 2nd ed., 2 vols. (London: W. Strahan, 1755–56), s.v., instrument, agency. See Liba Taub, "Introduction: Reengaging with Instruments," *Isis* 102, no. 4 (2011): 691–94.

24. See Georges Canguilhem, *A Vital Rationalist: Selected Writings from Georges Canguilhem*, ed. François Delaporte, trans. Arthur Goldhammer (New York: Zone, 1994), 291.

25. See Simon Schaffer, "Regeneration: The Body of Natural Philosophers in Restoration England," in *Science Incarnate: Historical Embodiments of Natural Knowledge,* ed. Christopher Lawrence and Steven Shapin (Chicago: University of Chicago Press, 1998), 84. The credibility of experimental results depended on the trust accorded to the operator, the witnesses, and the instrument itself (which could conveniently be blamed for a bad result). See also Steven Shapin and Simon Schaffer, *Leviathan and the Air Pump: Hobbes, Boyle, and the Experimental Life* (Princeton, NJ: Princeton University Press, 1985), 77.

26. Sigmund Freud, *Civilization and Its Discontents*, trans. James Strachey (New York: Norton, 1961), 41, 43.

27. Joseph Glanvill, *The Vanity of Dogmatizing* (London: E. C. for Henry Eversden, 1661), 27. John Locke echoes Glanvill: "The Understanding, like the Eye, whilst it makes us see, and perceive all other Things, takes no notice of it self." See Locke, *Essay Concerning Human Understanding*, ed. Peter Nidditch (Oxford: Clarendon, 1979), 1.1.§1, 43.

28. Even the human aspiration to convert sensory data into higher forms of knowledge might be deemed a perversion of the original ends for which our organs were designed: "The greatest Design indeed of the Organs of Sense," Hooke notes, "seems to have been for some other Use than for the acquiring of this kind of Knowledge, and to have been a very great Affinity with the Senses of other Animals" (GS, 8).

29. Hooke, *Micrographia*, sig. e. See also sig. b2v. On Hooke's faith in his successors, see J. A. Bennett, "Hooke's Instruments," in *London's Leonardo: The Life and Work of Robert Hooke* (Oxford: Oxford University Press, 2003), 63.

30. Bernard Stiegler, *Technics and Time, 1: The Fault of Epimetheus*, trans. Richard Beardsworth and George Collins (Stanford, CA: Stanford University Press, 1998), 137, 134.

31. André Leroi-Gourhan, *Gesture and Speech*, trans. Anna Bostock Berger (Cambridge, MA: MIT Press, 1993), 26.

32. Stiegler, *Technics and Time*, 141, 154.

33. Leroi-Gourhan, *Gesture and Speech*, 235.

34. Arendt, *Human Condition*, 9; on Bacon's *opera*, see Pérez-Ramos, *Francis Bacon's Idea of Science*, 135–49.

35. Arendt, *Human Condition*, 19.

36. Waller, "Life of Hooke," xxvii.

37. Hooke, *Micrographia*, sig. a. Hooke, Catherine Wilson observes, "is not seriously proposing the microscope as a means of secular salvation or release from original sin, but only countering the arguments of religious pessimists who employ skepticism under the guise of piety to depreciate research, and of the genuinely pious who see nature as forbidden territory." Wilson, *The Invisible World: Early Modern Philosophy and the Invention of the Microscope* (Princeton, NJ: Princeton University Press, 1995), 67.

38. Nick Wilding, "Graphic Technologies," in *Robert Hooke: Tercentennial Studies*, ed. Michael Cooper and Michael Hunter (Aldershot, UK: Ashgate, 2006), 123.

39. Alan Jacobs, "Naming of the Animals," in *A Dictionary of Biblical Tradition in English Literature*, ed. David Lyle Jeffrey (Grand Rapids, MI: William B. Eerdmans, 1992), 537–38. The microscope affords a glimpse of things "so small as not yet to have had any names," offering a whole new world to be christened: "Who knows but *Adam* might from some such contemplation, give names to all creatures? If at least his names had any significancy in them of the creature's nature on which he impos'd it. . . . And who knows, but the Creator may, in those characters, have written and engraven many of his mysterious designs and counsels" (Hooke, *Micrographia*, 80, 154). The bestowing of a name becomes an act of reading, not too far distant from the riddling activity to which we turn in the next chapter.

40. Glanvill, *Vanity of Dogmatizing*, 5. See also Robert South's 1662 sermon, "Man Was Made in God's Image," in *Sermons Preached upon Several Occasions* (Oxford: H. Hall, 1679), 128.

41. Henry Power, *Experimental Philosophy* (London: T. Roycroft, 1664), preface, n.p.

42. Robert Hooke, *Animadversions on the First Part of the Machina Coelestis of . . . Johannes Hevelius* (London: by T. R. for John Martyn, 1674), 9.

43. Peter Harrison, *The Fall of Man and the Foundations of Science* (Cambridge: Cambridge University Press, 2007).

44. Picciotto, *Labors of Innocence*, 2.

45. "*As at first, mankind* fell *by* tasting *of the forbidden Tree of Knowledge, so we, their Posterity, may be in part* restor'd *by the same way, not only by* beholding *and* contemplating, *but by* tasting *too those fruits of Natural knowledge, that were never yet forbidden*" (Hooke, *Micrographia*, sig. b2r–b2v). One must not only look (behold) but *do* (taste). Hooke's redemption of original sin involves a repetition with a difference, as the same quest for knowledge produces not a fall but a restoration. The strange temporal oscillation between past and future implied by "never yet forbidden" intimates the possibility that technological advancements may spawn new interdictions, as innovation exceeds the proper limits of humankind.

46. Anthony à Wood, *Athenae Oxonienses: An Exact History of All the Writers and Bishops Who Have Had Their Education in the . . . University of Oxford*, 2 vols. (London: R. Knaplock, 1721), 2.1039.

47. David Wills, *Prosthesis* (Stanford, CA: Stanford University Press, 1995), 27. The medical meaning of the term emerges in the late seventeenth century (218).

48. Barbara Johnson, *Persons and Things* (Cambridge, MA: Harvard University Press, 2008), 89.

49. David Wills, *Matchbook: Essays in Deconstruction* (Stanford, CA: Stanford University Press, 2005), 184.

50. Sarah Jain, "The Prosthetic Imagination: Enabling and Disabling the Prosthesis Trope," *Science, Technology, and Human Values* 24, no. 1 (1999): 44, 32.

51. Wilding, "Graphic Technologies," 124.

52. Hooke, *Animadversions*, 29.

53. See Lorraine Daston and Peter Galison, *Objectivity* (New York: Zone, 2010).

54. Ann Banfield, "Describing the Unobserved: Events Grouped Around an Empty Centre," in *The Linguistics of Writing: Arguments Between Language and Writing*, ed. Nigel Fabb et al. (New York: Methuen, 1987), 265.

55. See Daniel Tiffany, *Toy Medium: Materialism and Modern Lyric* (Berkeley: University of California Press, 2000), 160. Since only one person at a time can look through a microscope, no corrective eye can temper subjective or instrumental distortions in keeping with New Scientific protocols of collective witnessing. Whereas demonstrations of the air pump showed viewers "both the process and the product," the *Micrographia* offered "only the product of his [Hooke's] observations." Michael Aaron Dennis, "Graphic Understanding: Instruments and Interpretation in Robert Hooke's *Micrographia*," *Science in Context* 3, no. 2 (1989): 319.

56. Antonie van Leeuwenhoek, quoted in Wilson, *Invisible World*, 223.

57. Helen Thompson, *Fictional Matter: Empiricism, Corpuscles, and the Novel* (Philadelphia: University of Pennsylvania Press, 2017), 3.

58. For readings of this plate, see Barbara Stafford, *Body Criticism: Imaging the Unseen in Enlightenment Art and Medicine* (Cambridge, MA: MIT Press, 1993), 352–56; Adrian Johns, *The Nature of the Book: Print and Knowledge in the Making* (Chicago: University of Chicago Press, 1998), 430–31; Matthew Hunter, *Wicked Intelligence: Visual Art and the Science of Experiment in Restoration London* (Chicago: University of Chicago Press, 2013), 36–38; Silver, *The Mind Is a Collection*, 114–24. On the realism that emerges out of "graphic detail" and the *energeia* of Hooke's images, see Mary Baine Campbell, *Wonder and Science: Imagining Worlds in Early Modern Europe* (Ithaca, NY: Cornell University Press, 2004), 185ff; and Frédérique Ait-Touati, *Fictions of the Cosmos: Science and Literature in the Seventeenth Century*, trans. Susan Emanuel (Chicago: University of Chicago Press, 2011), 149ff.

59. Catherine Wilson, "Visual Surface and Visual Symbol: The Microscope and the Occult in Early Modern Science," *Journal of the History of Ideas* 49, no. 1 (1988): 101.

60. David Summers, *Real Spaces: World Art History and the Rise of Western Modernism* (London: Phaidon, 2003), 317.

61. Bruno Latour, "Drawing Things Together," in *Representation in Scientific Practice,* ed. Michael Lynch and Steve Woolgar (Cambridge, MA: MIT Press, 1992), 27, 26, 27.

62. Stafford, *Body Criticism,* 351. See Marian Fournier, *The Fabric of Life: Microscopy in the Seventeenth Century* (Baltimore: Johns Hopkins University Press, 1996); Marc J. Ratcliff, *The Quest for the Invisible: Microscopy in the Enlightenment* (Burlington, VT: Ashgate, 2009).

63. As Bruno Latour has argued, those elements that are "kept constant from one representation to the next" determine "what counts as an essence or a substance." Eventually, the representation morphs "into the *thing itself.*" Latour, "How to Be Iconophilic in Art, Science, and Religion?" in *Picturing Science, Producing Art,* ed. Caroline A. Jones and Peter Galison (New York: Routledge, 1998), 427.

64. Karen Barad, *Meeting the Universe Halfway: Quantum Physics and the Entanglement of Matter and Meaning* (Durham, NC: Duke University Press, 2007), 140.

65. Hunter, *Wicked Intelligence,* 42–43, 43.

66. Hunter, *Wicked Intelligence,* 42. On the cork, see Hooke, *Micrographia,* 114.

67. Margaret Cohen, *The Novel and the Sea* (Princeton, NJ: Princeton University Press, 2010), 72, 8.

68. Cohen, *Novel and the Sea,* 73, 8, 8. Cohen revises Barthes's reality effect, where the real is signified by the insignificant denotation—the detail's lack of motivation. By contrast, the detail in maritime fiction—and in Hooke's *Micrographia*—persuades because it is enfolded into procedures or actions in which the relation of cause to effect makes sense.

69. Abigail Zitin, "Thinking Like an Artist: Hogarth, Diderot, and the Aesthetics of Technique," *Eighteenth-Century Studies* 46, no. 4 (2013): 556.

70. Foucault, *The Order of Things: An Archaeology of the Human Sciences* (New York: Vintage, 1994).

71. Waller, "Life of Hooke," iv; Hunter, *Wicked Intelligence,* 81. For the vivisection experiment, see Birch, *History,* 1.485–86; and Henry Oldenburg, *The Correspondence of Henry Oldenburg, Vol. II: 1664–65,* ed. A. R. Hall and M. B. Hall (Madison: University of Wisconsin Press, 1966), 296–97.

72. See Bennett, "Robert Hooke as Mechanic and Natural Philosopher," 37.

73. Hooke, *Animadversions,* 44, 44–45.

74. Pérez-Ramos, *Francis Bacon's Idea of Science,* 159.

75. Robert Hooke, *Lampas: Or, Descriptions of Some Mechanical Improvements of Lamps and Waterpoises* (London: John Martyn, 1677), 34. This is a long-standing debate. See Keith Hutchison, "What Happened to Occult Qualities in the Scientific Revolution?" *Isis* 73 (1982): 233–53; Ron Millen, "The Manifestation of Occult Qualities in the Scientific Revolution," in *Religion, Science, and Worldview,* ed. Margaret J. Osler and Paul Lawrence Farber (Cambridge: Cambridge University Press, 1985), 185–216; John Henry, "Robert Hooke, The Incongruous Mechanist," in Hunter and Schaffer, *Robert Hooke: New Studies,* 149–80; Mark Ehrlich, "Mechanism and Activity in the Scientific Revolution: The Case of Robert Hooke," *Annals of Science* 52, no. 2 (1995): 127–51; Wilson, "Visual Surface and Visual Symbol."

76. Hooke, *Lampas,* 34.

77. Ian Hacking, *Representing and Intervening: Introductory Topics in the Philosophy of Natural Science* (Cambridge: Cambridge University Press, 1983), 263, 146.

78. Charles S. Peirce, "Logic as Semiotic: The Theory of Signs," in *The Philosophical Writings of Peirce*, ed. Justus Buchler (New York: Dover, 1955), 102.

79. Peirce, "Logic as Semiotic," 109. Hooke's understanding of the eye as a camera obscura involves photographic indexicality *avant la lettre*. The eye, Hooke writes, has "a distinct Point within it self, for every distinct Point without it self in the Universe"; it "becomes as it were a Hand, by which the Brain feels, and touches the Objects." Robert Hooke, "Lectures on Light," in Waller, *Posthumous Works*, 121, 124. See John Yolton, "As in a Looking Glass: Perceptual Acquaintance in Eighteenth-Century Britain," *Journal of the History of Ideas* 40 (1979): 212; and Silver, *The Mind Is a Collection*, 56–66.

80. Mary Ann Doane, "The Indexical and the Concept of Medium Specificity," *differences* 18, no. 1 (2007): 133.

81. Mary Ann Doane, "Indexicality: Trace and Sign," *differences* 18, no. 1 (2007): 4.

82. Charles Peirce, "An Elementary Account of the Logic of Relatives," in *Writings of Charles S. Peirce: Vol. 5, 1884–1886*, ed. Christian Kloesel (Bloomington: Indiana University Press, 1993), 379.

83. Terrence Deacon, *The Symbolic Species: The Co-Evolution of Language and the Brain* (New York: Norton, 1998); and Eduardo Kohn, *How Forests Think: Toward an Anthropology Beyond the Human* (Berkeley: University of California Press, 2013). On human language as issuing from the intertwining of "'actual,' prelinguistic indexicality" and "a symbolic, virtual indexicality in play as soon as one speaks," see Brian Rotman, "Ghost Effects," *differences* 18, no. 1 (2007): 60.

84. Webb Keane, "Semiotics and the Social Analysis of Material Things," *Language and Communication* 23 (2003): 419.

85. Joseph Addison, *Spectator* 519 (October 25, 1712), in *The Spectator*, ed. Donald Bond, 5 vols. (Oxford: Clarendon, 1965), 4.346.

86. Stafford, *Body Criticism*, 341. See Kevis Goodman's illuminating discussion of these questions in *Georgic Modernity and British Romanticism: Poetry and the Mediation of History* (Cambridge: Cambridge University Press, 2008), especially 11–13, 22–24, 40–56.

87. Cary Wolfe, "Introduction: Bring the Noise: *The Parasite* and the Multiple Genealogies of Posthumanism," in Michel Serres, *The Parasite*, trans. Lawrence R. Schehr (Minneapolis: University of Minnesota Press, 2007), xii.

88. Margaret Cavendish, "Further Observations upon Experimental Philosophy," in Cavendish, *Observations upon Experimental Philosophy*, ed. Eileen O'Neill (Cambridge: Cambridge University Press, 2001), 201–2.

89. "The Louse, in Imitation of the Flea," in *A Book to Help the Young and Gay, To Pass the Tedious Hours Away* (London: A. Pope, ca. 1750), 120.

90. Oliver Goldsmith, *An History of the Earth, and Animated Nature*, 8 vols. (London: J. Nourse, 1774), 7.270. Other vermin poach human food; the louse uses humans for food. Mary Fissell, "Imagining Vermin in Early Modern England," *History Workshop Journal* 47 (1999): 1–29.

91. Joseph Addison, *Tatler* 229 (September 26, 1710), in *The Tatler*, ed. Donald Bond, 3 vols. (Oxford: Clarendon, 1987), 3.186–87. See Janice Neri, *The Insect and the Image* (Minneapolis: University of Minnesota Press, 2011).

92. See Lucinda Cole, *Imperfect Creatures: Vermin, Literature, and the Sciences of Life, 1600–1740* (Ann Arbor: University of Michigan Press, 2016).

93. Cynthia Wall, *The Prose of Things: Transformations of Description in the Eighteenth Century* (Chicago: University of Chicago Press, 2006), 76.

94. Thomas Sprat, *The History of the Royal Society* (London: J. Martyn, 1667), 62. On rhetoric and the New Science, see Brian Vickers, "The Royal Society and English Prose Style: A Reassessment," in *Rhetoric and the Pursuit of Truth: Language Change in the Seventeenth and Eighteenth Centuries* (Los Angeles: William Andrews Clark Memorial Library, 1985), 3–76; and Richard W. F. Kroll, *The Material Word: Literate Culture in the Restoration and Early Eighteenth Century* (Baltimore: Johns Hopkins University Press, 1991).

95. Ebenezer Sibly, *Magazine of Natural History* (*An Universal System of Natural History*), 14 vols. (London: for the proprietor, 1794–1808), 13.21.

96. Letter from Swammerdam to Thévenot, April 1678, qtd. in Peter Harrison, *The Bible, Protestantism, and the Rise of Natural Science* (Cambridge: Cambridge University Press, 2009), 174. Courtney Weiss Smith locates Hooke's practice in the tradition of the occasional meditation, arguing that Hooke uses analogy "to move from particulars to the 'applications' that they prompt," placing "objects in complex patterns of meaning that stretch from plants to God and from the practical to the moral" and that gradually "slide from rhetorical gambits into epistemological tools and ontological facts." Courtney Weiss Smith, *Empiricist Devotions: Science, Religion, and Poetry in Early Eighteenth-Century England* (Charlottesville: University of Virginia Press, 2016), 64.

97. On the physico-theological redemption of the insect, see Harrison, *Bible, Protestantism*, 172–76; and Sawday, *Engines of the Imagination: Renaissance Culture and the Rise of the Machine* (New York: Routledge, 2007), 224–27.

98. Laurence Sterne, *The Life and Opinions of Tristram Shandy*, ed. Melvyn New and Joan New (New York: Penguin, 1978), 3.34, 181. The parasite's digestion of the host's body blurs the line between human and louse, as does the persistent belief that lice were spawned from sweat.

99. Serres, *The Parasite*, 7.

100. Margaret Cavendish, *The Description of a New World, Called the Blazing World*, in *Political Writings*, ed. Susan James (Cambridge: Cambridge University Press, 2003), 5.

101. Cavendish, *Observations upon Experimental Philosophy*, 52.

102. Cavendish, *Observations upon Experimental Philosophy*, 52, 52, 136.

103. Cavendish, *Blazing World*, 30.

104. Birch, *History*, 3.364–65.

105. Thomas Kirke junior to Thomas Kirke senior, Mar. 9, 1703, qtd. in Michael Hunter, "Hooke's Possessions at His Death: A Hitherto Unknown Inventory," in Hunter and Schaffer, *Robert Hooke: New Studies*, 290. "Whether lousy or otherwise, Hooke died and was wrapped in his academic gown, to be sent to his Maker as he had lived: a scholar." Chapman, *England's Leonardo*, 257.

106. Serres, *The Parasite*, 11.

CHAPTER 3

1. Giambattista Vico, *The New Science of Giambattista Vico*, trans. Thomas Goddard Bergin and Max Harold Fisch (Ithaca, NY: Cornell University Press, 1948), 129.

2. On defamiliarization or *ostraniene*, see Viktor Shklovsky, "Art as Device," in *Theory of Prose*, trans. Benjamin Sher (Elmwood Park, IL: Dalkey Archive Press, 1990), 1–14; see also Carlo Ginzburg, "Making Things Strange: The Prehistory of a Literary Device," *Representations* 56 (1996): 8–28.

3. Michel Serres, *Genesis*, trans. Genevieve James (Ann Arbor: University of Michigan Press, 1997), 4.

4. Charles Hutton, *The Ladies Diary, or Woman's Almanack for the Year of Our Lord 1790* (London: Company of Stationers, 1790), 27; *Reading Made Quite Easy and Diverting* (London: by all the booksellers, 1784), 164.

5. We have recourse to anthropomorphism, Barbara Johnson notes, "at those points where the infinite regress of language is most threatening," which perhaps explains why so many catachreses are anthropomorphisms. Johnson, *Persons and Things* (Cambridge, MA: Harvard University Press, 2008), 199.

6. James Paxson, *The Poetics of Personification* (Cambridge: Cambridge University Press, 1994).

7. Lorraine Daston, "Intelligences: Angelic, Animal, Human," in *Thinking with Animals: New Perspectives on Anthropomorphism,* ed. Lorraine Daston and Gregg Mitman (New York: Columbia University Press, 2005), 39.

8. Jane Bennett, *Vibrant Matter: A Political Ecology of Things* (Durham, NC: Duke University Press, 2010), xvi.

9. Walter Benjamin, "Doctrine of the Similar," trans. Michael Jennings, in *Walter Benjamin: Selected Writings, Vol. 2: 1927–1934*, ed. Michael W. Jennings et al. (Cambridge, MA: Belknap, 1999), 697.

10. I follow Daniel Tiffany in borrowing the term "riddle-creature" from Craig Williamson, "Introduction," *A Feast of Creatures: Anglo-Saxon Riddle-Songs*, trans. and ed. Williamson (Philadelphia: University of Pennsylvania Press, 2011), 6.

11. Benjamin, "Doctrine of the Similar," 694.

12. Daston, "Intelligences," 40.

13. Robert Hooke, "Dr. Hook's Discourse Concerning Telescopes and Microscopes," in *Philosophical Experiments and Observations of the Late Eminent Dr. Robert Hooke* (London: W. and J. Innys, 1726), 261.

14. On riddles and women, see Mary Chadwick, "'The Most Dangerous Talent': Riddles as Feminine Pastime," in *Women, Popular Culture, and the Eighteenth Century*, ed. Tiffany Potter (Toronto: University of Toronto Press, 2012), 185–201. On riddles' popularity, see William F. Shortz, "British Word Puzzles (1700–1800)," *Wordways* 6, no. 3 (1973): 131–38.

15. On riddles across cultures, see Archer Taylor, "The Riddle," *California Folklore Quarterly* 2 (1943): 129–47; on the enigma from the classical period through the Renaissance, see Eleanor Cook, *Enigmas and Riddles in Literature* (Cambridge: Cambridge University Press, 2006). I thank Judith Zeitlin for sharing her unpublished work on riddles in the Chinese literary tradition, "The Ghosts of Things," with me.

16. On it-narratives, see Mark Blackwell, ed., *The Secret Lives of Things: Animals, Objects, and It-Narratives in Eighteenth-Century England* (Lewisburg, PA: Bucknell University Press, 2007); and Jonathan Lamb, *The Things Things Say* (Princeton, NJ: Princeton University Press, 2011).

17. Joseph Priestley, *A Course of Lectures on Oratory and Criticism* (London: J. Johnson, 1777), 201.

18. Jacques Derrida, "Shibboleth: For Paul Celan," trans. Joshua Wilner, in *Word Traces: Readings of Paul Celan*, ed. Aris Fioretos (Baltimore: Johns Hopkins University Press, 1994), 35.

19. Daniel Tiffany, *Infidel Poetics: Riddles, Nightlife, Substance* (Chicago: University of Chicago Press, 2009), 11, 12. See Roger Caillois, "Riddles and Images," trans. Jeffrey Mehlman,

Yale French Studies 41 (1968): 148–58. For a criticism of Caillois on riddles, see Roger D. Abra-hams, "The Literary Study of the Riddle," *Texas Studies in Literature and Language* 14, no. 1 (1972): 177–97.

20. John Frow, *Genre* (New York: Routledge, 2006), 40.

21. Frances Ferguson, "Jane Austen, *Emma*, and the Impact of Form," *MLQ* 61, no. 1 (2000): 176–77.

22. Andrew Welsh, *Roots of Lyric: Primitive Poetry and Modern Poetics* (Princeton, NJ: Princeton University Press, 1978), 25. Benjamin argues that the myth of Adam bestowing names on the beasts "is intended as a repudiation of the mythical view that names are riddles that have to be guessed," and thus designed to guarantee the decipherable correspondence between word and thing. Benjamin, "Riddle and Mystery," trans. Rodney Livingstone, in *Selected Writings, Vol. I: 1913–1926*, ed. Marcus Bullock and Michael W. Jennings (Cambridge, MA: Belknap, 1996), 268.

23. Daniel Heller-Roazen, *Dark Tongues: The Art of Rogues and Riddles* (New York: Zone, 2013), 68.

24. Samuel Johnson's description of metaphysical conceit as "a combination of dissimilar images, or discovery of occult resemblances in things apparently unlike," offers, as Andrew Welsh notes, a pretty good definition of a riddle, though Johnson's characterization of this immixture as the "most heterogeneous ideas . . . yoked by violence together" repudiates such violations of the conceptual grid of the already known. Johnson, "Life of Cowley," in *The Lives of the Poets: A Selection*, ed. Roger Lonsdale (Oxford: Oxford University Press, 2006), 16; Welsh, *Roots of Lyric*, 40.

25. Northrop Frye, *Spiritus Mundi: Essays on Literature, Myth, and Society* (Bloomington: Indiana University Press, 1976), 137.

26. Aristotle, *The Art of Rhetoric*, trans. John Henry Freese, Loeb Classical Library (Cambridge, MA: Harvard University Press, 2000), 3.2.§12, 359. Part of what makes the riddle agreeable is that "the mind seems to say, 'How true it is! but I missed it'" (*Rhetoric* 3.11.§6, 409). We have here shades of the dynamic in the discussion of the trompe l'oeil in Chapter 1, where the beholder returns to see what the eye missed.

27. Taylor, "The Riddle," 130. On these contradictions, see Robert A. Georges and Alan Dundes, "Toward a Structural Definition of the Riddle," *Journal of American Folklore*, 76, no. 300 (1963): 111–18.

28. The potato riddle is from Archer Taylor, *English Riddles from Oral Tradition* (New York: Octagon, 1977), 95; the louse riddle is from *The Triumph of Wit: and Compleat Cant-Book* (Dublin: Richard Cross, 1767), 174, 174–75.

29. Taylor, *English Riddles from Oral Tradition*, 12.

30. Welsh, *Roots of Lyric*, 32.

31. See Michel Serres, *The Parasite*, trans. Lawrence Schehr (Minneapolis: University of Minnesota Press, 2007), esp. 51–55.

32. Theodor Adorno, *Negative Dialectics*, trans. E. B. Ashton (New York: Continuum, 1973), 5.

33. Aristotle, *De Poetica*, trans. Ingram Bywater, in *The Basic Works of Aristotle*, ed. Richard McKeon (New York: Random, 1941), 1458a27–29, 1478.

34. Frye, *Spiritus Mundi*, 147.

35. Benjamin, "Riddle and Mystery," 268. Riddles "appear where there is an emphatic intention to elevate an artifact or an event that seems to contain nothing at all, or nothing out of the ordinary, to the plane of symbolic significance" (267).

36. Tiffany, *Infidel Poetics*, 42.

37. Jonathan Swift, *The Poems of Jonathan Swift*, ed. Harold Williams, 3 vols. (Oxford: Oxford University Press, 1958), 915–16, lines 1–8.

38. Northrop Frye, *Anatomy of Criticism* (Princeton, NJ: Princeton University Press, 1971), 280.

39. What differentiates the weapon and the tool, as Elaine Scarry has argued, "is not the object itself but the surface on which they fall. . . . The hand that pounds a human face is a weapon and the hand that pounds the dough for bread . . . is a tool." Scarry, *The Body in Pain: The Making and Unmaking of the World* (New York: Oxford University Press, 1985), 173.

40. Luke Powers, "Tests for True Wit: Jonathan Swift's Pen and Ink Riddles," *South Central Review* 7, no. 4 (1990): 49.

41. Tiffany, *Infidel Poetics*, 41–42.

42. Paul de Man, "Anthropomorphism and Trope in the Lyric," in *The Rhetoric of Romanticism* (New York: Columbia University Press, 1984): 241.

43. See Johnson, *Persons and Things*, 188–207.

44. Elli Köngäs Maranda, "Riddles and Riddling: An Introduction," *Journal of American Folklore* 89, no. 352 (1976): 131. See also Maranda, "The Logic of Riddles," in *Structural Analysis of Oral Tradition*, ed. Pierre Maranda and Elli Köngäs Maranda (Philadelphia: University of Pennsylvania Press, 1971), 189–232.

45. Paul de Man, "The Epistemology of Metaphor," *Critical Inquiry* 5, no. 1 (1978): 19.

46. Enigma 39, in *The Diarian Miscellany: Consisting of All the Useful and Entertaining Parts, Both Mathematical and Poetical, Extracted from the Ladies' Diary*, ed. Charles Hutton, 5 vols. (London: G. Robinson and R. Baldwin, 1775), 4.385.

47. *Miscellanea curiosæ: or, Entertainments for the Ingenious of Both Sexes* (York, UK: Tho. Gent, 1734), 13–14.

48. *Diarian Miscellany*, 5.71, 4.385.

49. *Diarian Miscellany*, 5.71.

50. Frederick Engels, "The Part Played by Labour in the Transition from Ape to Man" [1876], in *Karl Marx and Frederick Engels: Selected Works in One Volume* (Moscow: Progress, 1977), 355.

51. Enigma II, *The Polite Companion; or, Wit-a-la-Mode* (London: G. Kearsly, 1760), 120.

52. Benjamin, "On the Mimetic Faculty," in *Reflections*, ed. Peter Demetz, trans. Edmund Jephcott (New York: Schocken, 1978), 333.

53. What distinguishes Benjamin's model from Vico's assertion that "man makes things out of himself and becomes them by transforming himself into them" is the temporality: for Vico, the transformation happens *after* we have anthropomorphized nature, whereas for Benjamin, likeness becomes a drive for our own self-alteration. Vico, *New Science*, 130.

54. Benjamin, "Doctrine of the Similar," 698.

55. Swift, *Poems of Jonathan Swift*, 936–37, ll. 1–4.

56. Swift, *Poems of Jonathan Swift*, 919–20, ll. 1–2.

57. Swift, *Poems of Jonathan Swift*, 920–21, ll. 10, 12.

58. Geoffrey Hartman, "Language from the Point of View of Literature," in *Beyond Formalism: Literary Essays, 1958–1970* (New Haven, CT: Yale University Press, 1970), 347.

59. Mikhail Bakhtin, "Discourse in the Novel," in *The Dialogic Imagination: Four Essays*, ed. Michael Holquist, trans. Caryl Emerson and Michael Holquist (Austin: University of Texas Press, 1981), 293.

60. Richard Steele, *Spectator* 504 (October 8, 1712), in *The Spectator*, ed. Donald Bond, 5 vols. (Oxford: Clarendon, 1965), 4.288.

61. *Spectator* 59 (May 8, 1711), 1.249.

62. *Spectator* 61 (May 10, 1711), 1.263. Addison's test of wit—"The only way therefore to try a Piece of Wit is to translate it into a different Language, if it bears the Test you may pronounce it true; but if it vanishes in the Experiment, you may conclude it to have been a Punn" (*Spectator* 61, 1.263)—renders the pun a vaporous form incapable of withstanding the trials of an experimental science: wit, by contrast, is a kind of elemental substance—a universal form—that lingers even after linguistic metamorphoses.

63. Alexander Pope, "God's Revenge Against Punning," in *The History of John Bull: And Poems on Several Occasions, by Dr. Jonathan Swift*, ed. John Arbuthnot (London: D. Midwinter and A. Tonson, 1750), 218.

64. Walter Redfern, *Puns: More Senses Than One* (New York: Basil Blackwell, 1985), 14. On the cultural and political valences of the pun, see Simon Alderson, "The Augustan Attack on the Pun," *Eighteenth-Century Life* 20, no. 3 (1996): 1–19.

65. Jonathan Culler, "The Call of the Phoneme: Introduction," in *On Puns: The Foundation of Letters*, ed. Culler (Oxford: Basil Blackwell, 1988), 16.

66. Derek Attridge, "Unpacking the Portmanteau, or, Who's Afraid of *Finnegans Wake?*" in Culler, *On Puns,* 140.

67. Swift, *Poems of Jonathan Swift*, 929, ll. 1–2, 4.

68. Samuel Beckett, *Murphy* (New York: Grove, 1957), 65.

69. "For is it not most certain, that all learned Disputes are rather about Sounds than Sense? . . . Are not the Disputations of Philosophers about Words, and all their pompous Distinctions only so many Unravelings of double Meanings? . . . So great is the Excellence of this Art, so diffusive its Influence, that when I go into a Library I say to my self, *What Volumes of Punns do I behold!*" *The Guardian* 36 (April 22, 1714), in *The Guardian*, 2 vols. (London: J. Tonson, 1714), 1.207–8.

70. Addison, *Spectator* 61 (May 10, 1711), 1.259.

71. Culler, "Call of the Phoneme," 15.

72. Neil Saccamano, "Wit's Breaks," in *Body and Text in the Eighteenth Century*, ed. Veronica Kelly and Dorothea von Mücke (Stanford, CA: Stanford University Press, 1994), 46, 57.

73. Saccamano, "Wit's Breaks," 57.

74. Swift, *Poems of Jonathan Swift*, 930–31, ll. 1–2, 3, 4.

75. Michel Butor, "Bricolage: An Interview with Michel Butor," trans. Noah Guynn, *Yale French Studies* 84 (1994): 19.

76. Thanks to Ala Alryyes for this point.

77. Swift, "A Rebus Written by a Lady, on the Rev. D---n S-----t. With his Answer," in *Poems of Jonathan Swift*, 716.

78. Swift, *Poems of Jonathan Swift*, 933, ll. 13–16.

79. Daniel Tiffany, "Lyric Substance: On Riddles, Materialism, and Poetic Obscurity," in *Things*, ed. Bill Brown (Chicago: University of Chicago Press, 2004), 73.

80. Frye, *Anatomy of Criticism*, 81.

81. Dorrit Cohn, *Transparent Minds: Narrative Modes for Presenting Consciousness in Fiction* (Princeton, NJ: Princeton University Press, 1984), 5–6.

82. Jean-Pons-Victor Lecoutz de Lévizac, *A Theoretical and Practical Grammar of the French Tongue* (London: Baylis, 1799), 71.

83. Emile Benveniste, *Problems in General Linguistics*, trans. Mary Elizabeth Meek (Coral Gables, FL: University of Miami Press, 1971), 218, 219.

84. William Ward, *An Essay on Grammar, as It May Be Applied to the English Language* (London: Robert Horsfield, 1765), 349, 126. The "Pronoun Personal *it* is used in English only to represent an inanimate and irrational thing, and to distinguish it from a rational creature in the Third Person Singular." M. Guelfi Borzacchini, *The Parisian Master* (Bath: R. Cruttwell, 1789), 59.

85. James Elphinston, *Principles of the English Language Digested*, 2 vols. (London: James Bettenham, 1765), 1.247.

86. Benveniste, *Problems in General Linguistics*, 198.

87. The third person is "exactly the non-person, which possesses as its sign the absence of that which specifically qualifies the 'I' and the 'you.' Because it does not imply any person, it can take any subject whatsoever or no subject, and this subject, expressed or not, is never posited as a 'person.'" Benveniste, *Problems in General Linguistics*, 200. On the political possibilities of the third person as that which "cannot be circumscribed within a specific subject" and thus escapes the "dialogical regime of interlocution" that fixes *I* and *you*, see Roberto Esposito, *The Third Person: Politics of Life and Philosophy of the Impersonal*, trans. Zakiya Hanafi (Cambridge: Polity, 2012), 15.

88. Johnson, *Persons and Things*, 9. The I-you postulates the possibility of response (precisely what is denied the animal, in Derrida's account.)

89. César Chesneau Dumarsais, "Lettre d'une jeune demoiselle à l'auteur des *Vrais principes de la langue française*," in *Oeuvres de Du Marsais*, 7 vols. (Paris: De l'Imprimerie de Pougin, 1797), 3.333. The "jeune demoiselle" is Dumarsais; the author to whom the letter is addressed is the abbé Girard, author of the 1747 text referenced in the title. As a "shifter" (whose referents need to supplied each time it is used), the "I" is both empty and possessed of the immediate, existential relation to the present speaking situation associated with index (as we saw in Chapter 2). Like Dumarsais, Peirce claims that "a noun is an imperfect substitute for a pronoun." Charles Peirce, *Collected Papers of Charles Sanders Peirce: Vol 2, Elements of Logic*, ed. Charles Hartshorne and Paul Weiss (Cambridge, MA: Harvard University Press, 1960), 163n.

90. Swift, *Poems of Jonathan Swift*, 3.931, ll. 1–4.

91. John Locke, *An Essay Concerning Human Understanding*, ed. Peter H. Nidditch (Oxford: Claredon, 1979), 2.27.§9, 335.

92. See *Amusing Recreations; or a Collection of Charades and Riddles on Political Characters, Dedicated to Lady Onslow by Mrs. Pilkington* (London: Vernor and Hood, 1798).

93. Claude Lévi-Strauss, *The Savage Mind*, trans. John Weightman and Doreen Weightman (Chicago: University of Chicago Press, 1966), 215. My discussion here is indebted to Frances Ferguson, "Canons, Poetics, and Social Value: Jeremy Bentham and How to Do Things with People," *MLQ* 110, no. 5 (1995): 1148–64.

94. "Personality, n. and adj.," *OED Online*, Oxford University Press, July 2018, www.oed.com/view/Entry/141486. Accessed 9 September 2018. The term is also commonly used as a legal category: a suit in personality is "brought against the right Person." John Harris, *Lexicon Technicum: or, an Universal English Dictionary of Arts and Sciences,* 5th ed., 2 vols. (London: J. Walthoe et al., 1736), vol. 2, s.v. personality. It also means a personal attack on an individual: "This was a pitiful personality, calculated to depreciate the character of a gentleman." Robert Anderson, *The Life of Tobias Smollett* (London: J. Mundell, 1796), 13. Finally, it refers to the physical beauty of an individual ("as to *personality*; hast thou any doubt, that thy

strong-muscled bony face was as much admired by thy mother, as if it had been the face of a Lovelace?" Samuel Richardson, *Clarissa*, 7 vols. (London: S. Richardson, 1748), 6.5.

95. Raymond Williams, *Keywords: A Vocabulary of Culture and Society*, rev. ed., (Oxford: Oxford University Press, 1985), 235 (s.v. personality).

96. Theodor Adorno, "Gloss on Personality," in *Critical Models: Interventions and Catchwords*, trans. Henry W. Pickford (New York: Columbia University Press, 1998), 162. Adorno laments the modern derogation from Kant's definition of personality as "the freedom and independence from the mechanism of nature regarded as a capacity of a being subject to special laws (pure practical laws given by its own reason)." Immanuel Kant, *Critique of Practical Reason*, trans. Lewis White Beck, 3rd ed. (New York: Macmillan, 1993), 90.

97. Ferguson, "Canons, Poetics, and Social Value," 1157.

98. Lévi-Strauss, *Savage Mind*, 214.

99. Ferguson, "Canons, Poetics, and Social Value," 1159.

100. See Swift, *Poems of Jonathan Swift*, 3.924–25, ll. 1–2.

101. As Barbara Johnson has argued in a slightly different context, "A difference *between* opposing forces presupposes that the entities in conflict be knowable. A difference *within* one of the entities in question is precisely what problematizes the very *idea* of an entity in the first place." Johnson, "Melville's Fist: The Execution of *Billy Budd*," *Studies in Romanticism* 18, no. 4 (1979): 596.

102. Carol Houlihan Flynn, *The Body in Swift and Defoe* (Cambridge: Cambridge University Press, 1990), 40.

103. Heather Keenleyside, "Personification for the People: On James Thomson's *The Seasons*," *ELH* 76, no. 2 (2009): 447–72.

104. Johnson, *Persons and Things*, 196.

105. Johnson, *Persons and Things*, 207.

106. Johnson, "Melville's Fist," 599.

107. Henry James, *The Golden Bowl*, ed. Virginia Llewellyn Smith (Oxford: Oxford University Press, 1988), 90.

108. Daston, "Intelligences," 40.

109. Johnson, *Persons and Things*, 207.

CHAPTER 4

1. Francis Bacon, "Of Vain-Glory" [1625], in *The Major Works*, ed. Brian Vickers (Oxford: Oxford University Press, 2008), 443.

2. John Ogilby, *Fables of Aesop, Paraphras'd in Verse and Adorn'd with Sculptures* (London: Thomas Warren, 1651), frontispiece. Whereas Ogilby insists that the fable would make men lesser beasts, Jonathan Swift in *The Beasts' Confession to the Priest* [1732] accuses Aesop of "libeling the *Four-foot* race" and making "Beasts . . . *degen'rate* into Men." Swift, *Poems of Jonathan Swift*, ed. Harold Williams, 3 vols. (Oxford: Oxford University Press, 1958), 607, 608, l. 202, 220.

3. Giorgio Agamben, *The Open: Man and Animal*, trans. Kevin Attell (Stanford, CA: Stanford University Press, 2004), 16.

4. On vermin, see Lucinda Cole, *Imperfect Creatures: Vermin, Literature, and the Sciences of Life, 1600–1740* (Ann Arbor: University of Michigan Press, 2016).

5. Thomas Hobbes singles out vainglory—the distinction of the self from others—as chief among the elements that distinguish human and animal: "In the first place, men compete for honour and dignity, animals do not." Hobbes, *On the Citizen* (*De Cive*), ed. Richard Tuck and Michael Silverthorne (Cambridge: Cambridge University Press, 1998), 71. Vainglory involves "the fiction . . . of actions done by ourselves, which were never done," as exemplified "in the fable by the fly sitting on the axletree." Hobbes, *The Elements of Law, Natural and Political: Part 1, Human Nature, Part 2, De Corpore Politico*, ed. J. C. A. Gaskin (Oxford: Oxford University Press, 1994), 50–51. On Hobbes's vainglory, see Victoria Kahn, "Hobbes, Romance, and the Fiction of Mimesis," *Political Theory* 29, no. 1 (2001): 4–29; Jonathan Lamb, *The Things Things Say* (Princeton, NJ: Princeton University Press, 2011), 10–11.

6. Francis Barlow, *Aesop's Fables with His Life: in English, French and Latin* (London: William Godbid, 1666), 39.

7. Barlow, *Aesop's Fables*, 2; Roger L'Estrange, *Fables of Aesop and Other Eminent Mythologists* (London: R. Sare et al., 1692), 1.

8. Barlow, *Aesop's Fables*, 1.

9. Antoine Houdar de la Motte, *One Hundred New Court Fables*, trans. Mr. Samber (London: E. Curll, 1721), 57–58; La Motte, *Fables nouvelles*, 3rd ed. (Paris: Gregoire Dupuis, 1719), 44. French pages cited below in brackets following English reference.

10. Barlow, *Aesop's Fables*, 2.

11. John Locke, *An Essay Concerning Human Understanding*, ed. Peter Nidditch (Oxford: Clarendon, 1979), 4.4.§16, 572. See also 3.11.§20, 519.

12. Paul de Man, "The Epistemology of Metaphor," *Critical Inquiry* 5, no. 1 (1978): 19.

13. Locke, *Essay Concerning Human Understanding*, 3.6.§27, 455.

14. Ephraim Chambers, *Cyclopaedia: or, an Universal Dictionary of Arts and Sciences*, 2 vols. (London: James and John Knapton et al, 1728), vol. 1, s.v. humanity.

15. Locke, *Essay Concerning Human Understanding*, 4.8.§3, 610.

16. Agamben, *The Open*, 26.

17. Phillip Sloan, "The Gaze of Natural History," in *Inventing Human Science*, ed. Christopher Fox, Roy Porter, and Robert Wokler (Berkeley: University of California Press, 1995), 122–26; Roxann Wheeler, *The Complexion of Race: Categories of Difference in Eighteenth-Century British Culture* (Philadelphia: University of Pennsylvania Press, 2000); Andrew Curran, *The Anatomy of Blackness: Science and Slavery in an Age of Enlightenment* (Baltimore: Johns Hopkins University Press, 2011).

18. Annabel Patterson, *Fables of Power: Aesopian Writing and Political History* (Durham, NC: Duke University Press, 1991), 1.

19. Peter Travis, "Aesop's Symposium of Animal Tongues," *Postmedieval: A Journal of Medieval Cultural Studies* 2, no. 1 (2011): 36.

20. On "thickening" lines to create this possibility, see Jacques Derrida, "The Animal That Therefore I Am (More to Follow)," in *The Animal That Therefore I Am*, trans. David Wills, ed. Marie-Louise Mallet (New York: Fordham University Press, 2008), 29.

21. Agamben contrasts the "anthropological machine of the moderns," which "functions by excluding as not (yet) human an already human being from itself, that is, by animalizing the human, by isolating the nonhuman within the human," with an earlier model in which the "machine" turns the non-man (the primate, the primitive, the savage child) into a human by including what was outside. Agamben, *The Open*, 37, 37, 38.

22. On the use of fable by the de la Courts, see Arthur Weststeijn, *Commercial Republicanism in the Dutch Golden Age: The Political Thought of Johan and Pieter de la Court* (Leiden:

Brill, 2012), 114–40; on Mandeville, see E. J. Hundert, *The Enlightenment's* Fable: *Bernard Mandeville and the Discovery of Society* (Cambridge: Cambridge University Press, 1994), 24–25.

23. William Law, *Remarks upon a Late Book, Entituled,* The Fable of the Bees (London: Will and John Innys, 1724), 2.

24. Patterson, *Fables of Power*, 52. The fable enters English print history in the fifteenth century with the work of John Lydgate, the Scotsman Robert Henryson, and Caxton's 1484 translation of Aesop.

25. See Lev Loseff, *On the Beneficence of Censorship: Aesopian Language in Modern Russian Literature*, trans. Jane Bobko (Munich: Otto Sagner, 1984). Thanks to Jane Sharp for this reference. See Kenneth McKenzie, "Italian Fables of the Eighteenth Century," *Italica* 12, no. 2 (1935): 39–44; Arthur Weststeijn, "The Power of 'Pliant Stuff': Fables and Frankness in Seventeenth-Century Dutch Republicanism," *Journal of the History of Ideas* 72, no. 1 (2011): 1–27.

26. The oral form of the fable and the multiple hands involved in composing, translating, adapting it across millennia, made it a ductile form. Pierre Bayle turns Aesop into a kind of dummy corporation shielding modern authors from liability for their own libelous or blasphemous provocations. Bayle, *A General Dictionary, Historical and Critical*, trans. Jean Peter Bernard, 10 vols. (London: James Bettenham, 1734), s.v. Aesop, 1.305; Bayle, *Dictionnaire historique et critique* [1697], 5th ed., 4 vols. (Amsterdam: P. Brunel, 1740), s.v. Esope, 2.404. See also Richard Bentley's 1697 exposé of the anachronistic attributions of fables to Aesop, *A Dissertation upon the Epistles of Phalaris . . . and the Fables of Aesop* (London: J. Leake, 1697).

27. David Lee Rubin, *A Pact with Silence: Art and Thought in the Fables of La Fontaine* (Columbus: Ohio State University Press, 1991). Jean-Charles Darmon, *Philosophie épicurienne et littérature au XVII' siècle en France: Études sur Gassendi, Cyrano, La Fontaine, Saint-Évremond* (Paris: Presses Universitaires de France, 1998).

28. Roland Barthes, *Mythologies*, trans. Annette Lavers (New York: Hill and Wang, 1972), 116.

29. English antipathy toward French absolutism meant that La Fontaine never attained immense popularity. Mark Loveridge, *A History of Augustan Fable* (Cambridge: Cambridge University Press, 1998), 163. Jayne Elizabeth Lewis argues that English writers were invested in a self-consciously national version of the fable. Lewis, *The English Fable: Aesop and Literary Culture, 1651–1740* (Cambridge: Cambridge University Press, 1996), 19.

30. See Tomoko Hanazaki, "A New Parliament of Birds: Aesop, Fiction, and Jacobite Rhetoric," *Eighteenth-Century Studies* 27, no. 2 (1993–94): 235–54; Stephen Daniel, "Political and Philosophical Uses of Fables in Eighteenth-Century England," *The Eighteenth Century: Theory and Interpretation* 23, no. 2 (1982): 151–71.

31. Although Croxall's version was reissued at least eighteen times in the eighteenth century and ten in the nineteenth, with two separate illustrated editions, L'Estrange never went out of print for more than a few years. See Line Cottegnies, " 'The Art of Schooling Mankind': The Uses of the Fable in Roger L'Estrange's *Aesop's Fables* (1692)," in *Roger L'Estrange and the Making of Restoration Culture*, ed. Anne Dunan-Page and Beth Lynch (Aldershot, UK: Ashgate, 2008), 131–48; on Croxall, see Patterson, *Fables of Power*, 143–46.

32. François Fénelon, *Traité de l'éducation des filles*, in *Oeuvres*, ed. Jacques Le Brun, 2 vols., Bibliothèque de la Pléiade (Paris: Gallimard, 1983), 1.118–19; John Locke, *Some Thoughts Concerning Education* (London: A. and J. Churchill, 1693), 183–84.

33. L'Estrange, *Fables of Aesop*, preface, sig. Av.

34. Samuel Croxall, *Fables of Aesop and Others*, 2nd ed. (London: J. Tonson, 1724), preface.

35. Charles and Mary Anne Lamb, *The Letters of Charles and Mary Anne Lamb,* ed. Edwin W. Marrs Jr., 3 vols. (Ithaca, NY: Cornell University Press, 1976), 2.81–82. See Christine Kenyon-Jones, *Kindred Brutes: Animals in Romantic-Period Writing* (Burlington, VT: Ashgate, 2001), 51–78.

36. Children "are not born in this full state of *Equality*, though they are born to it." John Locke, *Two Treatises of Government*, ed. Peter Laslett (Cambridge: Cambridge University Press, 2003), §55, 304.

37. Heather Keenleyside, *Animals and Other People: Literary Forms and Living Beings in the Long Eighteenth Century* (Philadelphia: University of Pennsylvania Press, 2016), 176.

38. La Motte, *One Hundred New Court Fables*, 14 [French 14].

39. Jean-François Marmontel, *Encyclopédie, ou dictionnaire raisonné des sciences, des arts et des métiers, etc.*, eds. Denis Diderot and Jean le Rond d'Alembert. University of Chicago: ARTFL Encyclopédie Project (Autumn 2017 Edition), Robert Morrissey and Glenn Roe (eds), http://encyclopedie.uchicago.edu/, s.v. fable apologue, 6.346.

40. Charles Batteux, *Les principes de la littérature*, 6 vols. (Avignon: Chambeau, 1809), 2.15–16, 2.16.

41. L'Estrange, *Fables of Aesop*, preface, sig. Br–Bv.

42. Rousseau, *L'Émile*, ed. Charles Witz, in *Oeuvres complètes*, ed. Bernard Gagnebin and Marcel Raymond, 6 vols., Bibliothèque de la Pléiade (Paris: Gallimard, 1969), 4.541. For Locke, the pleasure children take in fables leads them to things worthier of study; for Rousseau, the fable flatters the child into a pleasurable overestimation of his own understanding. On the complexity of the fable's pedagogy, see Frances Ferguson, "Reading Morals: Locke and Rousseau," *Representations* 6 (1984): 66–84.

43. L'Estrange, *Fables of Aesop*, preface, sig. B2r.

44. Dumarsais, *Les tropes de Dumarsais, avec un commentaire raisonné . . . par M. Fontanier*, ed. Pierre Fontanier, 2 vols. (Paris: Belin-Le-Prieur, 1818), 185.

45. James Beattie, "On Fable and Romance," in *Dissertations Moral and Critical* (London: W. Strahan, 1783), 505.

46. Lewis, *The English Fable*, 7–8.

47. John Dennis, qtd. in Thomas Noel, *Theories of the Fable in the Eighteenth Century* (New York: Columbia University Press, 1975), 21.

48. La Motte, *One Hundred New Court Fables*, 24 [French 20].

49. Robert Dodsley, "An Essay on Fable," in *Select Fables of Esop and Other Fabulists* (Birmingham: John Baskerville, 1761), lxii, lxi.

50. Geoffrey Bennington, *Sententiousness and the Novel: Laying Down the Law in Eighteenth-Century French Fiction* (Cambridge: Cambridge University Press, 1985), 55.

51. Edme-François Mallet, *Encyclopédie*, s.v. apologue, 1.532.

52. Dodsley, "Essay on Fable," lx. On fable as riddle, see G. W. F. Hegel: "Aesop does not dare to recite his doctrines openly but can only make them understood hidden as it were in a riddle which at the same time is always being solved. In the slave, prose begins." Hegel, *Aesthetics: Lectures on Fine Art*, trans. T. M. Knox, 2 vols. (Oxford: Clarendon, 1975), 1.387.

53. Jean-François Marmontel, *Encyclopédie*, s.v. Fable, 6.348.

54. Louis Marin, *Food for Thought*, trans. Mette Hjort (Baltimore: Johns Hopkins University Press, 1997), 61.

55. John Gay, "The Man and the Flea," in *John Gay: Poetry and Prose*, ed. Vinton A. Dearing, 2 vols. (Oxford: Clarendon, 1974), 367–68.

56. Dearing, "Commentary: *Fables*, 1727," in *John Gay: Poetry and Prose*, ed. Dearing, 619.

57. Gay, "The Man and the Flea," ll. 1–2.

58. Loveridge, *History of Augustan Fable*, 240, 241.

59. Michel Serres, *The Parasite*, trans. Lawrence R. Schehr (Minneapolis: University of Minnesota Press, 2007), 24.

60. Gay, "The Man and the Flea," ll. 3–6.

61. Paul de Man, "Semiology and Rhetoric," *Diacritics* 3, no. 3 (1973): 29.

62. Print no. 2843 in Frederic George Stephens and M. Dorothy George, *Catalogue of Prints and Drawings in the British Museum, Division I. Political and Personal Satires,* 11 vols. in 12 parts (London: Chiswick, 1877), III.i.633–34.

63. Samuel Johnson, "Life of Gay," in *The Lives of the Poets: A Selection*, ed. Roger Lonsdale (Oxford: Oxford University Press, 2006), 236.

64. *Spectator* 512 (October 17, 1712), in *The Spectator*, ed. Donald Bond, 5 vols. (Oxford: Clarendon, 1965), 4.318.

65. Keenan, *Fables of Responsibility: Aberrations and Predicaments in Ethics and Politics* (Stanford, CA: Stanford University Press, 2007), 1, 2, 3.

66. Jacques Derrida, *The Beast and the Sovereign: Vol. I*, trans. Geoffrey Bennington (Chicago: University of Chicago Press, 2009), 108, 109.

67. Gotthold Ephraim Lessing, "Essay on Fable," in *Fables and Epigrams* (London: John and H. L. Hunt, 1825), 106.

68. Hegel, *Aesthetics*, 1.384.

69. Patterson, *Fables of Power*, 15–16.

70. M. Richer, *Fables nouvelles, mises en vers* (Paris: Étienne Ganeau, 1729), 10.

71. Marin, *Food for Thought*, 74.

72. John Ogilby, "Of the Rustick and the Flea," in *Aesopicks: or, a Second Collection of Fables* (London: printed by the author, 1675), 95–98.

73. Thomas Hobbes, *Leviathan*, ed. Richard Tuck (Cambridge: Cambridge University Press, 1996), 91.

74. Instantiating the etymological connection of hospitality and hostility, the flea is excepted from the right of "the absolute, unknown, anonymous other" to "absolute hospitality" that Derrida finds in Kant's essay on *Perpetual Peace*. That Kant identifies this as a "human right" raises the question of "what can be said of, or indeed can one speak of, hospitality toward the non-human." Apparently, the Flea has not read Kant. Jacques Derrida, *Of Hospitality*, trans. Rachel Bowlby (Stanford, CA: Stanford University Press, 2000), 25. Derrida, "Hostipitality," trans. Barry Stocker with Forbes Morlock, *Angelaki* 5, no. 3 (2000): 4.

75. Judith Butler, *Frames of War: When Is Life Grievable?* (London: Verso, 2009), 2.

76. Ogilby, "Of the Rustick and the Flea," 95.

77. Samuel Johnson, *A Dictionary of the English Language*, 2nd ed., 2 vols. (London, 1755–56), vol. 1, s.v. fiction.

78. Ogilby, "Of the Rustick and the Flea," 97.

79. L'Estrange, *Fables of Aesop*, 127.

80. Laurence Sterne, *The Life and Opinions of Tristram Shandy*, ed. Melvyn New and Joan New (New York: Penguin, 1978), 2.12.91.

81. L'Estrange, *Fables of Aesop*, 127.

82. Aesop, *Aesop's Fables, with Their Morals*, 16th ed. (London: J. Phillips, H. Rhodes, and J. Taylor, 1706), 264.

83. Aesop, *A New Translation of Aesop's Fables, Adorn'd with Cutts . . . with Reflections . . . by J. J. Gent* (London: Tho. Tebb, 1708), 236–37. All three morals are couched in the passive voice: whereas the fable's story personifies agency in characters, the principles extracted are abstract, impersonal, detached from specific actors.

84. Lewis, *The English Fable*, 82.

85. John Ray, *A Compleat Collection of English Proverbs*, 3rd ed. (London: J. Hughs, 1737), 117. See also Thomas Fuller, *Gnomologia: Adages and Proverbs* (Dublin: S. Powell, 1733), 49; John Trusler, *Proverbs Exemplified* (London: printed for the author, 1790), 138.

86. Aesop, *Aesop's Fables, with Their Morals*, 265.

87. Aesop *The Fables of Aesop, with the Moral Reflections of Monsieur Baudoin* (London: Tho. Leigh and Dan. Midwinter, 1704), 198–99.

88. Butler, *Frames of War*, 1.

89. Joseph Priestley, *A Course of Lectures on Oratory and Criticism* (London: J. Johnson, 1777), 254.

90. Steven Knapp, *Personification and the Sublime* (Cambridge, MA: Harvard University Press, 1985), 2.

91. See Hugh Raffles, "Jews, Lice, and History," *Public Culture* 19, no. 3 (2007): 521–66; see also Clapperton Chakanetsa Mavhunga, "Vermin Beings: On Pestiferous Animals and Human Game," *Social Text* 29, no. 1 (2011): 151–176.

92. Priestley, *Lectures on Oratory and Criticism*, 249.

93. La Fontaine, "L'homme et la puce," Bk. 8, Fable 5, in *Oeuvres complètes*, 2 vols., ed. Jean-Pierre Collinet, Bibliothèque de la Pléiade (Paris: Gallimard, 1991), 1.298, ll. 13–14. My translation here.

94. La Fontaine, "L'homme et la puce," 1.298, ll. 1–2.

95. Eyal Weizman, "Material Proportionality," in *The State of Things*, ed. Marta Kuzma, Pable Lafuente, and Peter Osborne (London: Koenig, 2012), 143.

96. Charles Hinnant, *The Poetry of Anne Finch: An Essay in Interpretation* (Newark: University of Delaware Press, 1994), 178.

97. Henry Home, Lord Kames, *Elements of Criticism*, 3 vols. (Edinburgh: A. Kincaid and J. Bell, 1762), 1.191–92.

98. Miguel Tamen, "Kinds of Persons, Kinds of Rights, Kinds of Bodies," *Cardozo Studies in Law and Literature* 10, no. 1 (1998): 4. Tamen is elaborating on a point made in Oliver Wendell Holmes's 1881 *The Common Law*.

99. Kames, *Elements of Criticism*, 3.81–82.

100. Anne Kingsmill Finch, Countess of Winchilsea, "The Man Bitten by Fleas," *Miscellany: Poems on Several Occasions* (London: John Barber, 1713), 223–26.

101. Hannah Arendt, *The Human Condition* (New York: Doubleday Anchor, 1959), 169.

102. Finch, "The Man Bitten by Fleas," 226.

103. Anne-Lise François, "'O Happy Living Things': Frankenfoods and the Bounds of Wordsworthian Natural Piety," *Diacritics* 33, no. 2 (2003): 67.

104. Kames, *Elements of Criticism,* 3.240, 3.241.

105. Diana Donald, *Picturing Animals in Britain, 1750–1850* (New Haven, CT: Yale University Press, 2007), 114.

106. See, e.g., La Fontaine, "Discours à Mme de La Sablière," in *Oeuvres complètes*, ed. Collinet, 1.383–87. On anthropomorphism in fable illustration, see Donald, *Picturing Animals,*

esp. 115–19; Sarah Cohen, "Animal Performance in Oudry's Illustrations to the Fables of La Fontaine," *Studies in Eighteenth-Century Culture* 39 (2010): 35–76.

107. Frank Palmeri, "The Autocritique of Fables," in *Humans and Other Animals in Eighteenth-Century British Culture: Representation, Hybridity, Ethics*, ed. Palmeri (Aldershot, UK: Ashgate, 2006), 83–100.

108. *Encyclopédie*, s.v. apologue, 1.533.

109. Warton, *An Essay on the Genius and Writings of Pope*, 4th ed., 2 vols. (London: J. Dodsley, 1782), 2.251–52.

110. Beattie, "On Fable and Romance," 507.

111. Bruce Boehrer, *Animal Characters: Nonhuman Beings in Early Modern Literature* (Philadelphia: University of Pennsylvania Press, 2010), 9, 5, 9.

112. René Le Bossu, *Traité du poëme épique* (Paris: Michel le Petit, 1675), 130, 52–53. See Aristotle, *De poetica*, trans. Ingram Bywater, in *The Basic Works of Aristotle*, ed. Richard McKeon (New York: Random House, 1941), §1450b, p. 1461.

113. Le Bossu, *Traité du poëme épique*, 131.

114. Charles Batteux, *Les beaux arts réduits à un même principe* (Paris: Durand, 1746), 238.

115. Propp, *Morphology of the Folktale*, trans. Lawrence Scott (Austin: University of Texas Press, 2011), 21. Because the actant embraces extra-human and extra-subjective entities not normally treated as agents, it offers a more capacious understanding of the forces that act in the world, and for this reason, Bruno Latour's Actor-Network-Theory has conscripted the term. See Latour, *Reassembling the Social: An Introduction to Actor-Network-Theory* (Oxford: Oxford University Press, 2007).

116. La Motte, *One Hundred New Court Fables*, 38 [French 30–31].

117. Dodsley, "An Essay on Fable," lxxi.

118. La Motte, *One Hundred New Court Fables*, 14 [French 13].

119. Johann Gottfried Herder, "On Image, Poetry, and Fable" [1787], in *Selected Writings on Aesthetics*, trans. and ed. Gregory Moore (Princeton, NJ: Princeton University Press, 2006), 367.

120. Thomas Reid, *Essay on the Active Powers of Man* (Edinburgh: John Bell, 1788), 282, 281. Thanks to Evelyn Brooks Higginbotham for this reference.

121. See Vicesimus Knox, *Winter Evenings: or, Lucubrations on Life and Letters*, 2 vols. (London: Charles Dilly, 1790), 1.439.

122. *Spectator* 183 (September 29, 1711), in *The Spectator*, ed. Bond, 2.220.

123. Barbara Johnson, *Persons and Things* (Cambridge, MA: Harvard University Press, 2008), 206–7.

124. Herder, "On Image, Poetry, and Fable," 370, 369.

125. Herder, "On Image, Poetry, and Fable," 370.

126. Herder, "On Image, Poetry, and Fable," 370.

127. Michael Taussig, *Mimesis and Alterity: A Particular History of the Senses* (New York: Routledge, 1992), 16.

128. Marmontel, *Encyclopédie*, s.v. fable apologue, 6.348.

129. La Motte, *One Hundred New Court Fables*, 37–38 [French 30].

130. Richer, *Fables nouvelles*, 11.

131. Paul de Man, "Conclusions: Walter Benjamin's 'The Task of the Translator'," in *The Resistance to Theory* (Minneapolis: University of Minnesota Press, 1986), 90.

132. La Motte, *One Hundred New Court Fables*, 25 [French 21].

133. David Hume, *Natural History of Religion*, in *Essays and Treatises on Several Subjects*, 4 vols. (London: A. Millar, 1760), 4.266–67.

134. Jane Bennett, *Vibrant Matter: A Political Ecology of Things* (Durham, NC: Duke University Press, 2010), xvi.

135. Bruno Latour, *We Have Never Been Modern*, trans. Catherine Porter (Cambridge, MA: Harvard University Press, 1993), 137.

136. Lorraine Daston, "Intelligences: Angelic, Animal, Human," in *Thinking with Animals: New Perspectives on Anthropomorphism*, ed. Lorraine Daston and Gregg Mitman (New York: Columbia University Press, 2006), 51.

CHAPTER 5

Epigraphs: Virginia Woolf, *The Second Common Reader*, ed. Andrew McNeillie (New York: Harcourt, 1986), 54, 58; Ludwig Wittgenstein, *Philosophical Investigations*, 3rd ed., trans. G. E. M. Anscombe (Upper Saddle River, NJ: Prentice-Hall, 1958), 84e–85e.

1. Wittgenstein, *Philosophical Investigations*, 84e.

2. See Deidre Lynch, *The Economy of Character: Novels, Market Culture, and the Business of Inner Meaning* (Chicago: University of Chicago Press, 1998); Bruce Boehrer, *Animal Characters: Nonhuman Beings in Early Modern Literature* (Philadelphia: University of Pennsylvania Press, 2010); Jonathan Lamb, *The Things Things Say* (Princeton, NJ: Princeton University Press, 2011); Heather Keenleyside, *Animals and Other People: Literary Forms and Living Beings in the Long Eighteenth Century* (Philadelphia: University of Pennsylvania Press, 2016).

3. On Crusoe as homo economicus, see, e.g., Karl Marx, *Capital*, trans. Ben Fowkes, 3 vols. (New York: Vintage, 1977), 1.169–70; and Ian Watt, *The Rise of the Novel: Studies in Defoe, Richardson and Fielding* (Berkeley: University of California Press, 1957). As man of nature, see Rousseau, *L'Émile* [1762], ed. Charles Witz, in *Oeuvres complètes*, ed. Bernard Gagnebin and Marcel Raymond, 6 vols. (Paris: Gallimard, 1969), 4.455; Maximilian Novak, *Defoe and the Nature of Man* (Oxford: Oxford University Press, 1963). On spiritual autobiography, see G. A. Starr, *Defoe and Spiritual Autobiography* (Princeton, NJ: Princeton University Press, 1965); Starr, *Defoe and Casuistry* (Princeton, NJ: Princeton University Press, 1971); Leopold Damrosch Jr., *God's Plots and Man's Stories* (Chicago: University of Chicago Press, 1985), 187–212. On the dialectical relation between these accounts, see Michael McKeon, *Origins of the English Novel, 1600–1740* (Baltimore: Johns Hopkins University Press, 1987), esp. 315–37. For a postcolonial reading, see Peter Hulme, *Colonial Encounters: Europe and the Native Caribbean, 1492–1797* (London: Methuen, 1986); and Roxann Wheeler, *The Complexion of Race: Categories of Difference in Eighteenth-Century British Culture* (Philadelphia: University of Pennsylvania Press, 2000).

4. Coleridge, [Crusoe as Representative of Humanity], in Daniel Defoe, *Robinson Crusoe*, ed. Michael Shinagel, 2nd ed. (New York: Norton, 1994), 268. All citations from *Robinson Crusoe* will be made parenthetically in the text.

5. Watt, *Rise of the Novel*, 62.

6. Keenleyside, *Animals and Other People*, 64.

7. Poe, [Defoe's Faculty of Identification], in Defoe, *Robinson Crusoe*, 270.

8. On the excessive clarity and simplicity of the objects selected to discuss the nature of things in philosophy, see John Frow, "A Pebble, a Camera, a Man Who Turns into a Telephone Pole," *Things*, ed. Bill Brown (Chicago: University of Chicago Press, 2004), 353; Bruno Latour,

"Why Has Critique Run out of Steam: From Matters of Fact to Matters of Concern," in Brown, *Things*, 159.

9. An earlier version of this chapter discusses classification in greater detail. See Lynn Festa, "Crusoe's Island of Misfit Things," *The Eighteenth Century: Theory and Interpretation* 52, no. 3–4 (2011): 449–52.

10. Judith Butler, *Bodies That Matter: On the Discursive Limits of "Sex"* (New York: Routledge, 1993), 69.

11. See Lukács, "Narrate or Describe? A Preliminary Discussion of Naturalism and Formalism," in *Writer and Critic and Other Essays*, ed. and trans. Arthur Kahn (London: Merlin, 1970), 110–48. See also Philippe Hamon, "Rhetorical Status of the Descriptive," trans. Patricia Baudoin, *Yale French Studies* 61 (1981): 1–26.

12. Cynthia Wall, *The Prose of Things: Transformations of Description in the Eighteenth Century* (Chicago: University of Chicago Press, 2006), 10.

13. Joanna Stalnaker, *The Unfinished Enlightenment: Description in the Age of the Encyclopedia* (Ithaca, NY: Cornell University Press, 2010), 103.

14. Georg Lukács, *Theory of the Novel*, trans. Anna Bostock (Cambridge, MA: MIT Press, 1971), 56, 56, 84.

15. Lukács, *Theory of the Novel*, 66, 66, 66, 75.

16. Lukács, *Theory of the Novel*, 75. For Lukács, description is not the means of overcoming the division of subject and object but a symptom of that division, generated by the "dehumanization of social life [and] the general debasement of humanity" under capitalism. Descriptive style reveals the loss of a "narrative interrelationship between objects and their function in concrete human experiences." Lukács notably excepts *Robinson Crusoe* from this rule. Rather than reflecting the nigh-complete dissociation of subject from object, Defoe grapples with the intensity of their association. Lukács, "Narrate or Describe?" 127, 131.

17. McKeon, *Origins of the English Novel*, 337.

18. Dumarsais, *Les tropes de Dumarsais, avec un commentaire raisonné . . . par M. Fontanier*, ed. Pierre Fontanier, 2 vols. (Paris: Belin-Le-Prieur, 1818), 1.71.

19. On the clothes, see Wheeler, *Complexion of Race*, 72–73; on the parrots, see Eric Jager, "The Parrot's Voice: Language and Self in *Robinson Crusoe*," *Eighteenth-Century Studies* 21, no. 3 (1988): 316–33; on the cats, see Rajani Sudan, *Fair Exotics: Xenophobic Subjects in English Literature, 1720–1850* (Philadelphia: University of Pennsylvania Press, 2002), 1–6; on the rats, see Lucinda Cole, *Imperfect Creatures: Vermin, Literature, and the Sciences of Life, 1600–1740* (Ann Arbor: University of Michigan Press, 2016), 143–71; on the pots, see Lydia H. Liu, "Robinson Crusoe's Earthenware Pot," *Critical Inquiry* 25, no. 4 (1999): 728–57; on the goats, see Richard Nash, *Wild Enlightenment: The Borders of Human Identity in the Eighteenth Century* (Charlottesville: University of Virginia Press, 2003), 83–84, 87–89, 94–95, 99; on the raisins, see Wall, *Prose of Things*, 108–13; on Crusoe's appropriation of the island, see Wolfram Schmidgen, *Eighteenth-Century Fiction and the Law of Property* (Cambridge: Cambridge University Press, 2002), 32–62.

20. Woolf, *Second Common Reader*, 54. Woolf does not register the theological significance or emblematic status of the pots. The pot shadows the figure of man as clay in God's hands (Isaiah 45.9; 64.8; 2 Cor. 4.7; Jer. 18.6; Romans 9.21): "As we are all the Clay in the Hand of the Potter," Crusoe writes, "no Vessel could say to him, Why hast thou form'd me thus?" (Defoe, *Robinson Crusoe*, 152). Man is simultaneously speaking subject and object fashioned by divine hands.

21. Bruno Latour, *We Have Never Been Modern*, trans. Catherine Porter (Cambridge, MA: MIT Press, 1993), 13.

22. Latour, *We Have Never Been Modern*, 10–11.

23. John Bender and Michael Marrinan, "Introduction," in *Regimes of Description: In the Archive of the Eighteenth Century*, ed. Bender and Marrinan (Stanford, CA: Stanford University Press, 2005), 4.

24. Wall, *Prose of Things*; Stalnaker, *Unfinished Enlightenment*; John Bender and Michael Marrinan, *The Culture of Diagram* (Stanford, CA: Stanford University Press, 2010). There are multiple entries on "description" in the *Encyclopédie*, by Louis-Jean-Marie Daubenton (natural history); Jean le Rond D'Alembert (geometry); and Edme-François Mallet with an addition by Louis de Jaucourt (belles-lettres). *Encyclopédie, ou dictionnaire raisonné des sciences, des arts et des métiers, etc.*, ed. Denis Diderot and Jean le Rond d'Alembert. University of Chicago: ARTFL Encyclopédie Project (Autumn 2017 Edition), Robert Morrissey and Glenn Roe (eds.), http://encyclopedie.uchicago.edu/, 4.878–79, s.v., description.

25. Michel Serres, *Statues: Le second livre des fondations* (Paris: Flammarion, 1987), 110–11.

26. Theodor Adorno, *Negative Dialectics*, trans. E. B. Ashton (New York: Continuum, 2000), 191, 194. A novel is not a philosophical treatise, and what Serres sees as language's desire to dictate (to) the world is a far cry from the ebullient heteroglossia associated with the novel by Mikhail Bakhtin—although the two accounts share a notion of language as a site of contestation in which rival voices joust and commingle. Understood in the context of Serres's claims (and of the broader systematizing impulse in eighteenth-century logic and natural history), the novel's multiple Bakhtinian languages give voice to the also-rans: the other possible names, causes, things, experiences, banished by the lofty edicts of Adorno's "philosophical imperialism." Even where the novel, on the level of content, shows how categories are thematically applied or worked out (slotting prefabricated entities into their designated pigeonholes), it presents, on the level of form, the heterogeneity that spills beyond that order.

27. Wall, *The Prose of Things*, 2.

28. As Lydia Liu has shown, Crusoe's description of the earthenware pot's accidental fabrication proffers as independent discovery the advanced technology involved in making Chinese porcelain, long sought by the West. The autonomy of the object produces and guarantees the autonomy of the subject, as the self-sufficiency of the pot underwrites the fantasy of human (or rather English) self-sufficiency—returning us to Hooke's account of technology in Chapter 2. Liu, "Robinson Crusoe's Earthenware Pot," 728–57.

29. Thanks to Henry Turner for this point.

30. Barbara Stafford, *Body Criticism: Imaging the Unseen in Enlightenment Art and Medicine* (Cambridge, MA: MIT Press, 1993).

31. Rayna Kalas, *Frame, Glass, Verse: The Technology of Poetic Invention in the English Renaissance* (Ithaca, NY: Cornell University Press, 2007), 1. See also Richard W. F. Kroll, *The Material Word: Literate Culture in the Restoration and Early Eighteenth Century* (Baltimore: Johns Hopkins University Press, 1991).

32. Ala Alryyes, "Description, the Novel, and the Senses," *Senses and Society* 1, no. 1 (2006): 57. Like Alryyes, Wolfram Schmidgen sees Crusoe's description as a form of mental apprehension that facilitates material appropriation, as the repetitive narratives of endless upkeep and patrolling secure the permanence of his claim to property. Schmidgen, *Eighteenth-Century Fiction and the Law of Property*, 39.

33. Alryyes, "Description, the Novel, and the Senses," 58.

34. *Spectator* 416 (June 27, 1712), in *The Spectator*, ed. Donald Bond, 5 vols. (Oxford: Clarendon, 1965), 3.559.

35. John J. Richetti, *Defoe's Narratives: Situations and Structures* (Oxford: Oxford University Press, 1975), 36.

36. George Starr, "Defoe's Prose Style: 1. The Language of Interpretation," *Modern Philology* 71, no. 3 (1974): 280.

37. Damrosch, *God's Plots and Man's Stories*, 195.

38. Crusoe's renaming of the cannibals anticipates Rousseau's description of the reworking of "giants" into "men" in the *Essay on the Origin of Language*. Fear initially leads Rousseau's primitive to name the men he encounters giants; once experience reveals that they are "neither larger nor stronger than himself," he invents the proper name *man*. Jean-Jacques Rousseau, *Essai sur l'origine des langues,* ed. Jean Starobinski, in *Oeuvres complètes*, ed. Bernard Gagnebin and Marcel Raymond, 6 vols., Bibliothèque de la Pléiade (Paris: Gallimard, 1995), 5.381. As Paul de Man argues, calling other men giants "displaces the referential meaning from an outward, visible property to an 'inward' feeling. The coinage of the word 'giant' simply means 'I am afraid.'. . . The statement may be in error, but it is not a lie. It 'expresses' the inner experience correctly." De Man, "Metaphor (Second Discourse)," in *Allegories of Reading: Figural Language in Rousseau, Nietzsche, Rilke, and Proust* (New Haven, CT: Yale University Press, 1979), 150, 151.

39. Keenleyside, *Animals and Other People*, 18, 66.

40. See, e.g., John Ash, *The New and Complete Dictionary of the English Language,* 2nd ed., 2 vols. (London: Vernor and Hood, 1795), 1.17–18. The ontological and sociological assumptions nested in seemingly casual word choices surface in the disputed examples: whether it should be God "who" or "*which* art in Heaven," or the poet William Cowper's degrading insistence that "the man *that* dresses me" is colloquially more acceptable than the grammatically correct "who." John Bentick, *The Spelling and Explanatory Dictionary of the English Language* (London: Thomas Carnan, 1786), xxvi; Cowper, *Letters and Prose Writings of William Cowper: Vol. 2, 1782–1786*, ed. James King and Charles Ryskamp (Oxford: Clarendon, 1981), 372.

41. John Locke, *An Essay Concerning Human Understanding*, ed. Peter Nidditch (Oxford: Clarendon, 1979), 3.5.§6, 430.

42. John Locke, *An Essay Concerning Human Understanding*, 3.5.§6, 431.

43. Crusoe's use of bird carcasses to protect his crops involves a slightly more complicated cross-species psychic projection. Having shot three birds for preying on his shoots of corn, Crusoe serves "them, as we serve notorious Thieves in *England*, (*viz.*) [I] Hang'd them in Chains for a Terror to others; it is impossible to imagine almost, that this should have such an Effect, as it had; . . . I could never see a Bird near the Place as long as my Scare-Crows hung there" (85). That the scarecrows *are* literal crows (not a human effigy) means that the birds not only recognize their own likeness in the rotting carcasses but also project beyond their present state to a future punishment—shades here of Zeuxis's birds and Bayle's horse in Chapter 1.

44. Coleridge, [Crusoe as Representative of Humanity], in Defoe, *Robinson Crusoe*, 268.

45. The murderous inventiveness of his inexhaustible plots to destroy the cannibals points to the existence of a mode of Bataillian wasteful expenditure even within Crusoe's often relentlessly utilitarian world.

46. Margaret Cohen, *The Novel and the Sea* (Princeton, NJ: Princeton University Press, 2010), 11, 72.

47. Pat Rogers, ed., *Defoe: The Critical Heritage* (London: Routledge, 1972), 53. (Original in *L'Emile*, 4.455.)

48. Philip Fisher, *Making and Effacing Art: Modern American Art in a Culture of Museums* (Cambridge, MA: Harvard University Press, 1997), 243.

49. David Blewett, *The Illustration of Robinson Crusoe, 1719–1920* (Gerrards Cross, UK: Colin Smythe, 1995).

50. Michel Serres, "The Natural Contract," trans. Felicia McCarren, *Critical Inquiry* 19, no. 1 (1992): 7.

51. The image confirms, as Keenleyside also argues, that Crusoe "is what he always is, which is what a goat also is: a creature." Yet inasmuch as goats do not flay men and make outfits from their skin, the frontispiece reaffirms human difference. Keenleyside, *Animals and Other People*, 90.

52. Elizabeth Fowler, *Literary Character: The Human Figure in Early English Writing* (Ithaca, NY: Cornell University Press, 2003), 69. On the tension between poetry's sequential exposition and the supposedly instantaneous vision of the whole offered in painting, see Gotthold Ephraim Lessing's *Laocöon* [1766], trans. Ellen Frothingham (New York: Farrar, Straus and Giroux, 1969), 102–3; and Alex Potts, "Disparities Between Part and Whole in the Description of Works of Art," in Bender and Marrinan, *Regimes of Description*, 136.

53. J. M. Coetzee, *Elizabeth Costello* (New York: Penguin, 2003), 4.

54. Wall, *Prose of Things*, 10.

55. Barthes, "The Reality Effect," in Barthes, *The Rustle of Language,* trans. Richard Howard (Oxford: Blackwell, 1986), 143.

56. Jacques Derrida, *The Truth in Painting*, trans. Geoffrey Bennington and Ian McLeod (Chicago: University of Chicago Press, 1987), 264.

57. Shoes were still at the time often fabricated as "straights," with no distinction between left and right; the pair would thus not possess the asymmetrical complementarity of a modern pair of shoes. See Giorgio Riello, *A Foot in the Past: Consumers, Producers and Footwear in the Long Eighteenth Century* (Oxford: Oxford University Press, 2006).

58. On unpaired shoes and gloves, see Peter Stallybrass and Ann Rosalind Jones, "Fetishizing the Glove in Renaissance Europe," in Brown, *Things*, 174–92.

59. Bill Brown, "How to Do Things with Things (a Toy Story)," *Critical Inquiry* 24 (1998): 953.

60. Derrida, *Truth in Painting*, 332–33, 333.

61. Barthes, "Reality Effect," 148. It is difficult, however, for things to say "we are the real" and nothing more. In literary texts, even unpaired shoes that have been wrested from "normal" use cannot be mere, literal things: their very uselessness becomes their literary utility. Read exclusively in terms of the reality effect, novelistic things lose their specificity and materiality; they become nonmimetic. As Elaine Freedgood puts it, "Even the use value of most novelistic objects has largely been an abstraction: things are reified as markers of a real in which they can participate only generically." The realist detail cannot avoid being conscripted into the symbolic economy of the text. Freedgood, *The Ideas in Things: Fugitive Meaning in the Victorian Novel* (Chicago: University of Chicago Press, 2006), 10.

62. Daniel Arasse, *Le détail: Pour une histoire rapprochée de la peinture* (Paris: Flammarion, 1996), 7.

63. Arasse, *Le détail*, 6–7, 12.

64. The idiosyncratic detail is akin to Barthes's *punctum*: "this prick, this mark made by a pointed instrument . . . that accident which pricks me (but also bruises me, is poignant to me)." Barthes, *Camera Lucida: Reflections on Photography,* trans. Richard Howard (New York: Hill & Wang, 1982), 26, 27. The punctum for Barthes is often a "detail, *i.e.*, a partial object."

Hence, to give examples of *punctum* is, in a certain fashion, to *give myself up*" (43). Notably the punctum escapes the easy denomination of a thing that fits into a word: "What I can name cannot really prick me" (51).

65. Peter Galison, "Image of Self," in *Things That Talk: Object Lessons from Art and Science*, ed. Lorraine Daston (New York: Zone, 2004), 293.

66. Derrida, *The Truth in Painting*, 260.

67. On the variety of readings to which the footprint has been subjected, see Robert Folkenflik, "*Robinson Crusoe* and the Semiotic Crisis of the Eighteenth Century," in *Defoe's Footprints: Essays in Honour of Maximillian E. Novak*, ed. Robert Maniquis and Carl Fisher (Toronto: University of Toronto Press, 2009), 98–125.

68. Ann Banfield, "L'imparfait de l'objectif: The Imperfect of the Object Glass," *Camera Obscura* 24, no. 3 (1990): 81.

69. Banfield, "L'imparfait de l'objectif," 79.

70. Like the dog in John Constable's *Hay Wain* as analyzed by William Galperin, the dog in John Stockdale's image "militate[s] against the aesthetics of absorption in replacing human contemplation with animal distraction," tagging the possibility that "viewer *and* painter [may be] consigned . . . to invisibility." Like Constable's painting, Stockdale's image elevates us to a vantage that preserves our "exteriority to things," underscoring our double relation to the novel—steeped in Crusoe's eye-view and aware of the impossibility of our presence on the desert island with him. Galperin, *The Return of the Visible in British Romanticism* (Baltimore: Johns Hopkins University Press, 1993), 92, 93.

71. Qtd. in Giorgio Agamben, *The Open: Man and Animal*, trans. Kevin Attell (Stanford, CA: Stanford University Press, 2004), 24, 26.

72. Crusoe's doubling of consciousness occurs elsewhere in the novel as well. To give intelligible form to the unruly forces of experience, Richetti argues, Crusoe must separate "the self from circumstances in order to master them by co-operating with their flow. It is no accident that Crusoe begins to speak . . . as if he operated on himself as well, as if he had a self which dealt in various ways with another part of himself . . . [and] the other self that is negated is like the potentially destructive world of tides and winds that surround him." Richetti, *Defoe's Narratives*, 40.

73. Dorrit Cohn, *Transparent Minds: Narrative Modes for Presenting Consciousness in Fiction* (Princeton, NJ: Princeton University Press, 1984), 4.

74. Steven Shaviro takes up these questions in relation to Thomas Nagel and Wittgenstein. "The bat's inner experience is inaccessible to me; but this is so in much the same way (albeit to a far greater extent) that any other person's inner experience is inaccessible to me. It is even similar to the way that *my own* inner experience is in fact also inaccessible to me." Shaviro, "Consequences of Panpsychism," in *The Nonhuman Turn*, ed. Richard Grusin (Minneapolis: University of Minnesota Press, 2015), 26.

75. The scene that Crusoe interprets as a sign of his dominion over Friday is literally destabilizing. Friday, Crusoe tells us, "laid his Head upon the Ground, and taking me by the Foot, set my Foot upon his Head," a pantomime that Crusoe famously construes to be a "token of swearing to be my Slave for ever" (147). The anxious repetition of the scene several pages later indicates the fragility of Crusoe's claim, but it is also worth noting that Friday's seizure of Crusoe's foot leaves the upright body off-balance.

76. Lukács, *Theory of the Novel*, 75.

77. Lukács, *Theory of the Novel*, 81.

78. Banfield, "L'imparfait de l'objectif," 71.

79. Banfield, "L'imparfait de l'objectif," 77, 78, 77, 77.

80. Virginia Woolf, *The Waves* (Harmondsworth, UK: Penguin, 1951), 247; also qtd. in Banfield, "L'imparfait de l'objectif," 74. Other chapters of this book have explored similarly impersonal perspectives: the abstract geometric projection of the bird's-eye view; Hooke's autonomous instruments, recording data in the absence of a human percipient; the cryptic self-descriptions of the riddle creature; the suspended position of the fable reader, poised between example and moral in search of a lesson. In all of these cases, humanity is solicited not through a structure of identification but through the provisional occupation of an impersonal, non-human eye-view.

81. David Marshall, "Autobiographical Acts in *Robinson Crusoe*," *ELH* 71, no. 4 (2004): 917.

82. Bender and Marrinan, *Culture of Diagram*, 7.

83. Bender and Marrinan, *Culture of Diagram*, 21. On schemas, see Paula Backscheider, "Literary Culture as Immediate Reality," in *Blackwell Companion to the Eighteenth-Century English Novel and Culture,* ed. Backscheider and Catherine Ingrassia (Malden, MA: Wiley-Blackwell, 2006), 505.

84. Bender and Marrinan, *Culture of Diagram*, 13, 72.

85. Wilkie Collins, *The Moonstone*, ed. John Sutherland, 2nd ed. (Oxford: Oxford University Press, 2000), 9; Bender and Marrinan, *Culture of Diagram*, 23. Indeed, understood as a quest for "meaning without intention, and even without responsibility," bibliomancy suggests the allure of a form of meaning-making that resides not in the subject but in the object. John W. DuBois, "Meaning Without Intentions: Lessons from Divination," in *Responsibility and Evidence in Oral Discourse*, ed. Jane H. Hill and Judith T. Irvine (Cambridge: Cambridge University Press, 1993), 48.

86. Bender, "The Novel as Modern Myth," in Maniquis and Fisher, *Defoe's Footprints*, 233, 232, 234.

CODA

1. Max Horkheimer and Theodor Adorno, *Dialectic of Enlightenment*, trans. John Cumming (New York: Continuum, 2002); Hannah Arendt, *The Human Condition* (New York: Doubleday Anchor, 1959).

2. Michael Geyer and Charles Bright, "World History in a Global Age," *American Historical Review* 100, no. 4 (1995): 1060.

3. Friedrich Nietzsche, *On the Genealogy of Morals*, trans. Walter Kaufmann (New York: Vintage, 1969), 45.

4. Judith Butler, *Giving an Account of Oneself* (New York: Fordham University Press, 2005), 10. Butler emphasizes the ongoingness of *the doing* over its retroactive containment in the English translation of *das Tun* as "the deed," in ways that resonate with this book's emphasis on the processual constitution of humanity. Butler, *Excitable Speech: A Politics of the Performative* (New York: Routledge, 1997), 45. The scale of global warming makes it difficult to contemplate as a circumscribed effect (a "deed") for which we may be held accountable. This is perhaps why Alan Weisman, rather than describing humanity's planetary depredations, offers instead a speculative account of what would happen if the entire species suddenly vanished from the earth, tracing the rapidity with which the elements would reclaim the urban landscape of New York City. If, as we saw in Chapter 5, the novel invites us to imagine what the world is like

when we are not there, Weisman's thought experiment asks us to envision the world without us altogether, exposing the vast amount of energy expended to hold nature at bay in crafting a built environment to our needs. The fiction without humanity of this book's title should thus be considered in relation to the literal fiction without humanity explored in Weisman's *The World Without Us* (New York: Picador, 2008).

5. Rancière, "Who is the Subject of the Rights of Man?" *South Atlantic Quarterly* 103, no. 2/3 (2004), 303. The first-person plural "we" conscripts those human beings who have been neither the chief culprits not the beneficiaries of global warming into the collective that will suffer its effects. In the context of global warming, the inclusion of all populations in the class of humanity seems like inviting people to a party when it is time to clean up.

6. Ghosh, *The Great Derangement: Climate Change and the Unthinkable* (New York: Penguin, 2016), 32.

7. Chakrabarty, "Climate of History," *Critical Inquiry* 35 (2009): 207.

8. Chakrabarty, "Climate of History," 220. Because we cannot experience ourselves as the geological agent that we have as a species become, we inhabit a kind of environmental trompe l'oeil in which the mind cannot overrule the senses, in which what we *know* to be true cannot master the perception of everyday "reality".

9. Dumarsais, *Les tropes de Dumarsais, avec un commentaire raisonné . . . par M. Fontanier,* ed. Pierre Fontanier, 2 vols. (Paris: Belin-Le-Prieur, 1818), 1.332; Chakrabarty, "Climate of History," 222.

BIBLIOGRAPHY

PRIMARY SOURCES

Abernethy, John. *Discourses Concerning the Being and Natural Perfections of God.* 2 vols. Dublin: A. Reilly, 1742.

Addison, Joseph, and Richard Steele. *The Spectator.* Edited by Donald Bond. 5 vols. Oxford: Clarendon, 1965.

———. *The Tatler.* Edited by Donald Bond. 3 vols. Oxford: Clarendon, 1987.

Aesop. *Aesop's Fables, with Their Morals.* 16th ed. London: J. Phillips, H. Rhodes and J. Taylor, 1706.

———. *The Fables of Aesop, with the Moral Reflections of Monsieur Baudoin.* London: Tho. Leigh and Dan. Midwinter, 1704.

———. *A New Translation of Aesop's Fables, Adorn'd with Cutts . . . with Reflections . . . by J. J. Gent.* London: Tho. Tebb, 1708.

Aglionby, William. *Choice Observations upon the Art of Painting.* London: R. King, 1719.

Amusing Recreations; or a Collection of Charades and Riddles on Political Characters, Dedicated to Lady Onslow by Mrs. Pilkington. London: Vernor and Hood, 1798.

Anderson, Robert. *The Life of Tobias Smollett.* London: J. Mundell, 1796.

Aristotle. *The Art of Rhetoric.* Translated by John Henry Freese. Loeb Classical Library. Cambridge, MA: Harvard University Press, 2000.

———. *De poetica.* Translated by Ingram Bywater. In *The Basic Works of Aristotle*, edited by Richard McKeon, 1455–87. New York: Random, 1941.

The Artist's Repository and Drawing Magazine. 5 vols. London: T. Williams, 1784–94.

Ash, John. *The New and Complete Dictionary of the English Language.* 2nd ed. 2 vols. London: Vernor and Hood, 1795.

Bacon, Francis. *The New Organon.* Edited by Fulton H. Anderson. New York: Macmillan, 1960.

———. "Of Vain-Glory." [1625]. In *The Major Works*, edited by Brian Vickers, 443–45. Oxford: Oxford University Press, 2008.

Barlow, Francis. *Aesop's Fables with His Life: In English, French and Latin.* London: William Godbid, 1666.

Batteux, Charles. *Les beaux arts reduits à un même principe.* Paris: Durand, 1746.

———. *Les principes de la littérature.* 6 vols. Avignon: Chambeau, 1809.

Bayle, Pierre. *Dictionnaire historique et critique.* [1697]. 5th ed. 4 vols. Amsterdam: P. Brunel, 1740.

———. *A General Dictionary, Historical and Critical.* Translated by Jean Peter Bernard et al. 10 vols. London: James Bettenham, 1734–41.

Beattie, James. "On Fable and Romance." In *Dissertations Moral and Critical,* 505–74. London: W. Strahan, 1783.

Bentick, John. *The Spelling and Explanatory Dictionary of the English Language.* London: Thomas Carnan, 1786.

Bentley, Richard. *A Dissertation upon the Epistles of Phalaris . . . and the Fables of Aesop.* London: J. Leake, 1697.

Berkeley, George. *Principles of Human Knowledge/Three Dialogues.* Edited by Roger Woolhouse. New York: Penguin, 1988.

Birch, Thomas. *History of the Royal Society.* 4 vols. London: A. Millar, 1756–57.

Blount, Thomas. *Glossographia anglicana nova.* London: D. Brown, 1707.

A Book to Help the Young and Gay, to Pass the Tedious Hours Away. London: A. Pope, c. 1750.

Borzacchini, M. Guelfi. *The Parisian Master.* Bath: R. Cruttwell, 1789.

Boswell, James. *Boswell's Life of Johnson.* Edited by George Birkbeck Hill. 6 vols. Oxford: Clarendon, 1887.

Buffon, Georges Louis Leclerc, comte de. *Histoire naturelle des oiseaux, tome 1.* Paris: Imprimerie Royale, 1770.

———. *The Natural History of Birds.* 9 vols. London: A. Strahan and T. Cadell, 1793.

Cavendish, Margaret. *The Description of a New World, Called the Blazing World.* In *Political Writings,* edited by Susan James, 1–109. Cambridge: Cambridge University Press, 2003.

———. *Observations upon Experimental Philosophy.* Edited by Eileen O'Neill. Cambridge: Cambridge University Press, 2001.

Chambers, Ephraim. *Cyclopaedia: or, an Universal Dictionary of Arts and Sciences.* 2 vols. London: James and John Knapton et al., 1728.

———. *Cyclopaedia: or, an Universal Dictionary of Arts and Sciences.* 5 vols. London: W. Strahan et al., 1778–88.

Cockeram, Henry. *The English Dictionarie; or, an Interpreter of Hard English Words.* London: Edmund Weaver, 1623.

Condillac, Etienne Bonnot de. *Essay on the Origin of Human Knowledge.* Translated and edited by Hans Aarsleff. Cambridge: Cambridge University Press, 2001.

Cowley, Abraham. *The Works of Mr. Abraham Cowley.* 12th ed. 3 vols. London: Benj. Motte, 1721.

Cowper, William. *Letters and Prose Writings of William Cowper.* Edited by James King and Charles Ryskamp. 5 vols. Oxford: Clarendon, 1979–86.

Cox, Nicholas. *The Gentleman's Recreation.* 6th ed. London: N.C., 1721.

Croxall, Samuel. *Fables of Aesop and Others.* 2nd ed. London: J. Tonson, 1724.

Dawes, Sir William. *Self-Love, the Great Cause of Bad Times.* London: Thomas Speed, 1701.

De la Court, Pieter. *Fables Moral and Political, with Large Explications,* 2 vols. London: n.p., 1703.

Defoe, Daniel. *Robinson Crusoe.* 2nd ed. Edited by Michael Shinagel. New York: Norton, 1994.

Derham, William. *Physico-Theology: or, a Demonstration of the Being and Attributes of God.* 2nd ed. London: W. Innys, 1714.

Descartes, René. *The Correspondence.* In *The Philosophical Writings of Descartes: Vol. 3,* translated by John Cottingham et al. Cambridge: Cambridge University Press, 1991.

———. *Discourse on the Method.* In *The Philosophical Writings of Descartes: Vol. 1,* translated by Robert Stoothoff, 109–51. Cambridge: Cambridge University Press, 1985.

————. *Meditations on First Philosophy.* In *The Philosophical Writings of Descartes: Vol. 2*, translated by John Cottingham, 1–62. Cambridge: Cambridge University Press, 1984.

————. *Méditations métaphysiques.* Edited by Jean-Marie Beyssade. Paris: Garnier-Flammarion, 1979.

————. "Optics." In *The Philosophical Writings of Descartes: Vol. 1*, translated by John Cottingham, Robert Stoothoff, and Dugald Murdoch, 152–75. Cambridge: Cambridge University Press, 1985.

Dezallier d'Argenville, Antoine Joseph. *Supplément à l'abrégé de la vie des plus fameux peintres, troisième partie.* Paris: de Bure, 1752.

The Diarian Miscellany: Consisting of All the Useful and Entertaining Parts, Both Mathematical and Poetical, Extracted from the Ladies' Diary. Edited by Charles Hutton. 5 vols. London: G. Robinson and R. Baldwin, 1775.

Dictionnaire de l'Académie Française. ARTFL Project, University of Chicago. https://artfl-project.uchicago.edu/content/dictionnaires-dautrefois.

Diderot, Denis. *Oeuvres esthétiques.* Edited by Paul Vernière. Paris: Garnier, 1968.

Dodsley, Robert. "An Essay on Fable." In *Select Fables of Esop and Other Fabulists*, lvii–lxxviii. Birmingham, UK: John Baskerville, 1761.

Dumarsais, César Chesneau. "Lettre d'une jeune demoiselle à l'auteur des *Vrais principes de la langue française.*" In *Oeuvres de Du Marsais*, 3.299–336. 7 vols. Paris: De l'Imprimerie de Pougin, 1797.

————. *Les tropes de Dumarsais, avec un commentaire raisonné . . . par M. Fontanier.* Edited by Pierre Fontanier. 2 vols. Paris: Belin-Le-Prieur, 1818.

Edwards, George. *Natural History of Birds.* 4 vols. London: for the author, 1743.

Elphinston, James. *Principles of the English Language Digested.* 2 vols. London: James Bettenham, 1765.

Encyclopédie, ou dictionnaire raisonné des sciences, des arts et des métiers, etc. Edited by Denis Diderot and Jean le Rond d'Alembert. University of Chicago: ARTFL Encyclopédie Project, Autumn 2017 Edition. Edited by Robert Morrissey and Glenn Roe. http://encyclopedie.uchicago.edu/.

Equiano, Olaudah. *The Interesting Narrative of the Life of Olaudah Equiano.* Edited by Werner Sollors. New York: Norton, 2000.

An Essay on Laughter. London: T. Davies, 1769.

Félibien, André. *Conférences de l'Académie royale de peinture et de sculpture, pendant l'année 1667.* Paris: F. Léonard, 1668.

————. *Entretiens sur les vies et sur les ouvrages des plus excellens peintres anciens et modernes.* 5 vols. Paris: Pierre Le Petit, 1666.

Fénelon, François. *Traité de l'éducation des filles.* In *Oeuvres*, edited by Jacques Le Brun, 1.91–171. 2 vols. Bibliothèque de la Pléiade. Paris: Gallimard, 1983.

Finch, Anne Kingsmill, Countess of Winchilsea. *Miscellany: Poems on Several Occasions.* London: John Barber, 1713.

Fuller, Thomas. *Gnomologia: Adages and Proverbs.* Dublin: S. Powell, 1733.

Gay, John. *John Gay: Poetry and Prose.* Edited by Vinton A. Dearing. 2 vols. Oxford: Clarendon, 1974.

Glanvill, Joseph. *The Vanity of Dogmatizing.* London: by E. C. for Henry Eversden, 1661.

Goldsmith, Oliver. *An History of the Earth, and Animated Nature.* 8 vols. London: J. Nourse, 1774.

Grew, Nehemiah. *Cosmologia Sacra: or a Discourse of the Universe as It Is the Creature and Kingdom of God*. London: W. Rogers, 1701.

The Guardian, 2 vols. London: J. Tonson, 1714.

Harris, John. *Lexicon Technicum: or, an Universal English Dictionary of Arts and Sciences*. 5th ed. 2 vols. London: J. Walthoe et al., 1736.

Herder, Johann Gottfried. "On Image, Poetry, and Fable." [1787]. In *Selected Writings on Aesthetics*, translated and edited by Gregory Moore, 357–82. Princeton, NJ: Princeton University Press, 2006.

Hickey, Thomas. *Storia della pittura e la scultura; scritta in Italiano ed Inglese da Tomaso Icchi* [The History of Ancient Painting and Sculpture; Written in Italian and English]. Calcutta: Stuart and Cooper, 1788.

Hobbes, Thomas. *The Elements of Law, Natural and Political: Part 1, Human Nature, Part 2, De Corpore Politico*. Edited by J. C. A. Gaskin. Oxford: Oxford University Press, 1994.

———. *Leviathan*. Edited by Richard Tuck. Cambridge: Cambridge University Press, 1996.

———. *On the Citizen* [*De cive*]. Edited by Richard Tuck and Michael Silverthorne. Cambridge: Cambridge University Press, 1998.

Hooke, Robert. *Animadversions on the First Part of the Machina Coelestis of the Honourable, Learned, and Deservedly Famous Astronomer Johannes Hevelius*. London: T. R. for John Martyn, 1674.

———. "Dr. Hook's Discourse Concerning Telescopes and Microscopes." In *Philosophical Experiments and Observations of the Late Eminent Dr. Robert Hooke*, 257–68. London: W. and J. Innys, 1726.

———. "A General Scheme, or Idea of the Present State of Natural Philosophy, and Wherein It Is Deficient." In *The Posthumous Works of Robert Hooke,* edited by Richard Waller, 3–70. London: Sam. Smith and Benj. Walford, 1705.

———. *Lampas: or, Descriptions of Some Mechanical Improvements of Lamps and Waterpoises*. London: John Martyn, 1677.

———. "Lectures on Light." In *The Posthumous Works of Robert Hooke*, edited by Richard Waller, 71–148. London: Sam. Smith and Benj. Walford, 1705.

———. *Micrographia: or, Some Physiological Descriptions of Minute Bodies Made by Magnifying Glasses*. London: Jo. Martyn, 1665.

———. "Of Comets." In *Posthumous Works*, edited by Richard Waller, 149–90. London: Sam. Smith and Benj. Walford, 1705.

Hume, David. *Natural History of Religion*. In *Essays and Treatises on Several Subjects*, 4.253–352. 4 vols. London: A. Millar, 1760.

———. *Treatise of Human Nature*. 2nd ed, edited by L. A. Selby-Bigge, revised edition by P. H. Nidditch. Oxford: Clarendon, 1980.

Hutton, Charles. *The Ladies Diary, or Woman's Almanack for the Year of Our Lord 1790*. London: Company of Stationers, 1790.

Johnson, Samuel. *A Dictionary of the English Language*. 2nd ed. 2 vols. London: W. Strahan, 1755–56.

———. "Life of Cowley." In *The Lives of the Poets: A Selection*, edited by Roger Lonsdale, 5–53. Oxford: Oxford University Press, 2006.

———. "Life of Gay." In *The Lives of the Poets: A Selection*, edited by Roger Lonsdale, 229–37. Oxford: Oxford University Press, 2006.

Kames, Henry Home, Lord. *Elements of Criticism*. 3 vols. Edinburgh: A. Kincaid and J. Bell, 1762.

Kant, Immanuel. *Critique of Practical Reason.* 3rd ed. Translated by Lewis White Beck. New York: Macmillan, 1993.

Kersey, John. *A New English Dictionary.* London: Henry Bonwicke, 1702.

———. *A New English Dictionary.* 3rd ed. London: Robert Knaplock, 1731.

Knox, Vicesimus. *Winter Evenings: or, Lucubrations on Life and Letters.* 2 vols. London: Charles Dilly, 1790.

La Bruyère, Jean de. *Les Caractères.* In *Oeuvres completes,* edited by Julien Benda, 59–478. Bibliothèque de la Pléiade. Paris: Gallimard, 1978.

La Fontaine, Jean de. *Oeuvres complètes.* Edited by Jean-Pierre Collinet. 2 vols. Bibliothèque de la Pléiade. Paris: Gallimard, 1991.

La Motte, Antoine Houdar de. *Fables nouvelles.* 3rd ed. Paris: Gregoire Dupuis, 1719.

———. *One Hundred New Court Fables.* Translated by Mr. Samber. London: E. Curll, 1721.

Lairesse, Gerard de. *The Art of Painting.* [1707]. Translated by John Frederick Fritsch. London: printed for the author, 1738.

Lamb, Charles, and Mary Anne Lamb. *The Letters of Charles and Mary Anne Lamb.* Edited by Edwin W. Marrs Jr. 3 vols. Ithaca, NY: Cornell University Press, 1976.

Law, William. *Remarks upon a Late Book, Entituled,* The Fable of the Bees. London: Will. and John Innys, 1724.

Le Bossu, René. *Traité du poëme épique.* Paris: Michel le Petit, 1675.

Lessing, Gotthold Ephraim. "Essay on Fable." In *Fables and Epigrams,* 65–143. London: John and H. L. Hunt, 1825.

———. *Laocöon.* Translated by Ellen Frothingham. New York: Farrar, Straus and Giroux, 1969.

L'Estrange, Roger. *Fables of Aesop and Other Eminent Mythologists.* London: R. Sare et al., 1692.

Lévizac, Jean-Pons-Victor Lecoutz de. *A Theoretical and Practical Grammar of the French Tongue.* London: Baylis, 1799.

Locke, John. *An Essay Concerning Human Understanding.* Edited by Peter Nidditch. Oxford: Clarendon, 1979.

———. *Some Thoughts Concerning Education.* London: A. and J. Churchill, 1693.

———. *Two Treatises of Government.* Edited by Peter Laslett. Cambridge: Cambridge University Press, 2003.

Malton, Thomas. *An Appendix, or, Second Part to the Complete Treatise on Perspective.* London: for the author, 1800.

Mandeville, Bernard. *Aesop Dress'd, or, A Collection of Fables Writ in Familiar Verse.* London: Richard Wellington, 1704.

———. *Fable of the Bees.* 2 vols. Indianapolis: Liberty Fund, 1988.

———. *The Grumbling Hive: or, Knaves Turn'd Honest.* London: n.p., 1705.

———. *Some Fables After the Easie and Familiar Method of Monsieur de la Fontaine.* London: n.p., 1703.

Mayne, Zachary. *Two Dissertations Concerning Sense, and the Imagination.* London: J. Tonson, 1728.

Mazière de Monville, Simon-Philippe. *Vie de Pierre Mignard, premier peintre du roi.* Amsterdam: aux dépens de la compagnie, 1731.

Miscellaneae Curiosae: or, Entertainments for the Ingenious of Both Sexes. York, UK: Tho. Gent, 1734–35.

Montaigne, Michel de. "Apology for Raymond Sebond." In *The Complete Essays of Montaigne,* translated by Donald Frame, 318–457. Stanford, CA: Stanford University Press, 1965.

More, Henry. *An Antidote Against Atheism, or, an Appeal to the Naturall Faculties of the Minde of Man*. London: J. Flesher, 1655.

A New Universal History of Arts and Sciences. 2 vols. London: J. Coote, 1759.

Ogilby, John. *Aesopicks: or, a Second Collection of Fables*. London: printed by the author, 1675.

———. *Fables of Aesop, Paraphras'd in Verse and Adorn'd with Sculptures*. London: Thomas Warren, 1651.

Oldenburg, Henry. *The Correspondence of Henry Oldenburg, Vol. 2: 1664–65*. Edited by A. R. Hall and M. B. Hall. Madison: University of Wisconsin Press, 1966.

Oxford English Dictionary Online. Oxford University Press, July 2018.

Panciroli, Guido. *The History of Many Memorable Things in Use Among the Ancients, but Now Lost*. 2 vols. London: A. Ward, 1727.

Pepys, Samuel. *Diary of Samuel Pepys*. Edited by Robert Latham and William Matthews. 11 vols. Berkeley: University of California Press, 2000.

Perrault, Charles. *Parallèle des anciens et des modernes*. Nouvelle edition. 4 vols. Paris: Jean Baptiste Coignard, 1693.

———. *Le siècle de Louis le Grand*. [1687]. In *Oeuvres choisies de Charles Perrault*, edited by Collin de Plancy, 290–308. Paris: Brissot-Thivars, 1826.

Pliny. *Natural History*. Translated by H. Rackham. 10 vols. Loeb Classical Library. Cambridge, MA: Harvard University Press, 1938–1962.

The Polite Companion; or, Wit-a-la-Mode. London: G. Kearsly, 1760.

Pope, Alexander. "God's Revenge Against Punning." In *The History of John Bull. And Poems on Several Occasions, by Dr. Jonathan Swift*, edited by John Arbuthnot, 217–19. London: D. Midwinter and A. Tonson, 1750.

Power, Henry. *Experimental Philosophy*. London: T. Roycroft, 1664.

Priestley, Joseph. *A Course of Lectures on Oratory and Criticism*. London: J. Johnson, 1777.

Ray, John. *A Compleat Collection of English Proverbs*. 3rd ed. London: J. Hughs, 1737.

———. *Wisdom of God*. [1691]. London: W. Innys, 1743.

Ray, John and Francis Willughby. *The Ornithology of Francis Willughby*. London: John Martyn, 1678.

Reading Made Quite Easy and Diverting. London: by all the booksellers, 1784.

Reid, Thomas. *Essays on the Active Powers of Man*. Edinburgh: John Bell, 1788.

Richardson, Samuel. *Clarissa*. 7 vols. London: S. Richardson, 1748.

Richer, M. *Fables nouvelles, mises en vers*. Paris: Étienne Ganeau, 1729.

Rousseau, Jean-Jacques. *Essai sur l'origine des langues*. Edited by Jean Starobinski. In *Oeuvres complètes*, edited by Bernard Gagnebin and Marcel Raymond, 5.375–429. 6 vols. Bibliothèque de la Pléiade. Paris: Gallimard, 1995.

———. *L'Émile*. Edited by Charles Witz. In *Oeuvres completes*, edited by Bernard Gagnebin and Marcel Raymond, vol. 4. 6 vols. Bibliothèque de la Pléiade. Paris: Gallimard, 1969.

Sibly, Ebenezer. *Magazine of Natural History* (*An Universal System of Natural History*). 14 vols. London: for the proprietor, 1794–1808.

South, Robert. "Man Was Made in God's Image." In *Sermons Preached upon Several Occasions*, 117–54. Oxford: H. Hall, 1679.

Sprat, Thomas. *The History of the Royal Society*. London: J. Martyn, 1667.

Sterne, Laurence. *The Life and Opinions of Tristram Shandy*. Edited by Melvyn New and Joan New. New York: Penguin, 1978.

Swift, Jonathan. *Gulliver's Travels*. Edited by Albert Rivero. New York: Norton, 2002.

————. *The Poems of Jonathan Swift*. Edited by Harold Williams. 3 vols. Oxford: Oxford University Press, 1958.

The Triumph of Wit: and Compleat Cant-Book. Dublin: Richard Cross, 1767.

Trusler, John. *Proverbs Exemplified*. London: printed for the author, 1790.

Vico, Giambattista. *The New Science of Giambattista Vico*. Translated by Thomas Goddard Bergin and Max Harold Fisch. Ithaca, NY: Cornell University Press, 1948.

Waller, Richard. "Life of Hooke." In *The Posthumous Works of Robert Hooke*, edited by Richard Waller, i–xxviii. London: Sam. Smith and Benj. Walford, 1705.

Ward, William. *An Essay on Grammar, as It May Be Applied to the English Language*. London: Robert Horsfield, 1765.

Warton, Joseph. *An Essay on the Genius and Writings of Pope*. 4th ed. 2 vols. London: J. Dodsley, 1782.

Willis, Thomas. *The Anatomy of the Brain*. In *The Remaining Medical Works of That Famous and Renowned Physician Dr. Thomas Willis*, trans. Samuel Pordage, 55–136. London: T. Dring, 1681.

Wood, Anthony à. *Athenae Oxonienses: An Exact History of All the Writers and Bishops Who Have Had Their Education in the . . . University of Oxford*. 2 vols. London: R. Knaplock, 1721.

SECONDARY SOURCES

Abrahams, Roger D. "The Literary Study of the Riddle." *Texas Studies in Literature and Language* 14, no. 1 (1972): 177–97.

Adorno, Theodor. "Gloss on Personality." In *Critical Models: Interventions and Catchwords*, translated by Henry W. Pickford, 161–66. New York: Columbia University Press, 1998.

————. *Negative Dialectics*. Translated by E. B. Ashton. New York: Continuum, 2000.

Agamben, Giorgio. *Homo Sacer: Sovereign Power and Bare Life*. Translated by Daniel Heller-Roazen. Stanford, CA: Stanford University Press, 1998.

————. *The Open: Man and Animal*. Translated by Kevin Attell. Stanford, CA: Stanford University Press, 2004.

Ait-Touati, Frédérique. *Fictions of the Cosmos: Science and Literature in the Seventeenth Century*. Translated by Susan Emanuel. Chicago: University of Chicago Press, 2011.

Alderson, Simon. "The Augustan Attack on the Pun." *Eighteenth-Century Life* 20, no. 3 (1996): 1–19.

Allewaert, Monique. *Ariel's Ecology: Plantations, Personhood, and Colonialism in the American Tropics*. Minneapolis: University of Minnesota Press, 2013.

Alpers, Svetlana. *The Art of Describing: Dutch Art in the Seventeenth Century*. Chicago: University of Chicago Press, 1984.

Alryyes, Ala. "Description, the Novel, and the Senses." *Senses and Society* 1, no. 1 (2006): 53–70.

Arasse, Daniel. *Le détail: Pour une histoire rapprochée de la peinture*. Paris: Flammarion, 1996.

Aravamudan, Srinivas. *Tropicopolitans: Colonialism and Agency, 1688–1804*. Durham, NC: Duke University Press, 1999.

Arendt, Hannah. *The Human Condition*. New York: Doubleday Anchor, 1959.

————. *On Revolution*. New York: Penguin, 1965.

————. *The Origins of Totalitarianism*. Rev. ed. New York: Harcourt Brace Jovanovich, 1994.

Asad, Talal. "Redeeming the 'Human' Through Human Rights." In *Formations of the Secular: Christianity, Islam, Modernity*, 127–158. Stanford, CA: Stanford University Press, 2003.

Attridge, Derek. "Unpacking the Portmanteau, or, Who's Afraid of *Finnegans Wake?*" In *On Puns: The Foundation of Letters*, edited by Jonathan Culler, 140–55. Oxford: Basil Blackwell, 1988.

Backscheider, Paula. "Literary Culture as Immediate Reality." In *Blackwell Companion to the Eighteenth-Century English Novel and Culture*, edited by Paula Backscheider and Catherine Ingrassia, 504–38. Malden, MA: Wiley-Blackwell, 2006.

Bakhtin, Mikhail. *The Dialogic Imagination: Four Essays*. Edited by Michael Holquist. Translated by Caryl Emerson and Michael Holquist. Austin: University of Texas Press, 1981.

Balibar, Étienne. "Citizen Subject." Translated by James Swenson. In *Who Comes After the Subject?* edited by Eduardo Cadava, Peter Connor, and Jean-Luc Nancy, 33–57. New York: Routledge, 1991.

———. "'Rights of Man' and 'Rights of the Citizen': The Modern Dialectic of Equality and Freedom." In *Masses, Classes, Ideas: Studies on Politics and Philosophy Before and After Marx*, translated by James Swenson, 39–59. New York: Routledge, 1991.

Banfield, Ann. "Describing the Unobserved: Events Grouped Around an Empty Centre." In *The Linguistics of Writing: Arguments Between Language and Writing*, edited by Nigel Fabb, Derek Attridge, Alan Durant, and Colin MacCabe, 265–85. New York: Methuen, 1987.

———. "'L'imparfait de l'objectif': The Imperfect of the Object Glass." *Camera Obscura* 24, no. 3 (1990): 64–87.

Bann, Stephen. *The True Vine: On Visual Representation and the Western Tradition*. Cambridge: Cambridge University Press, 1989.

Barad, Karen. *Meeting the Universe Halfway: Quantum Physics and the Entanglement of Matter and Meaning*. Durham, NC: Duke University Press, 2007.

Barkan, Leonard. "The Heritage of Zeuxis: Painting, Rhetoric, and History." In *Antiquity and Its Interpreters*, edited by Alina Payne, Ann Kuttner, and Rebeka Smick, 99–109. Cambridge: Cambridge University Press, 2000.

Barrell, John. *English Literature in History, 1730–1780: An Equal, Wide Survey*. London: Hutchinson, 1983.

Barthes, Roland. *Camera Lucida: Reflections on Photography*. Translated by Richard Howard. New York: Hill and Wang, 1982.

———. *Mythologies*. Translated by Annette Lavers. New York: Hill and Wang, 1972.

———. "The Reality Effect." In Barthes, *The Rustle of Language*, translated by Richard Howard, 141–48. Oxford: Blackwell, 1986.

———. "The World as Object." In *The Barthes Reader*, edited by Susan Sontag, translated by Richard Howard, 62–73. New York: Hill and Wang, 1987.

Bates, David. "Cartographic Aberrations: Epistemology and Order in the Encyclopedic Map." In *Using the* Encyclopédie: *Ways of Knowing, Ways of Reading*, edited by Daniel Brewer and Julie Candler Hayes, 1–20. Oxford: Voltaire Foundation, 2002.

Baudrillard, Jean. "The Trompe l'Oeil." In *Calligram: Essays in New Art History from France*, edited by Norman Bryson, 53–62. Cambridge: Cambridge University Press, 1988.

Baumann, Richard. *Human Rights in Ancient Rome*. New York: Routledge, 2012.

Beckett, Samuel. *Murphy*. New York: Grove, 1957.

Bellion, Wendy. *Citizen Spectator: Art, Illusion, and Visual Perception in Early National America*. Chapel Hill: University of North Carolina Press, 2011.

Bender, John. "The Novel as Modern Myth." In *Defoe's Footprints: Essays in Honour of Maximillian E. Novak*, edited by Robert Maniquis and Carl Fisher, 223–37. Toronto: University of Toronto Press, 2009.

Bender, John, and Michael Marrinan. *The Culture of Diagram*. Stanford, CA: Stanford University Press, 2010.

———. "Introduction." In *Regimes of Description: In the Archive of the Eighteenth Century*, edited by Bender and Marrinan, 1–7. Stanford CA: Stanford University Press, 2005.

Benedict, Barbara. *Curiosity: A Cultural History of Early Modern Inquiry*. Chicago: University of Chicago Press, 2001.

———. "Encounters with the Object: Advertisements, Time, and Literary Discourse in the Early Eighteenth-Century Thing-Poem." *Eighteenth-Century Studies* 4, no. 2 (2006): 193–207.

Benjamin, Walter. "The Cultural History of Toys." Translated by Rodney Livingstone. In *Selected Writings, Vol. 2: 1927–1934*, edited by Michael W. Jennings et al., 113–16. Cambridge, MA: Belknap, 1999.

———. "Doctrine of the Similar." Translated by Michael Jennings. In *Walter Benjamin: Selected Writings, Vol. 2: 1927–1934*, edited by Michael W. Jennings et al., 694–98. Cambridge, MA: Belknap, 1999.

———. "On the Mimetic Faculty." In *Reflections*, translated by Edmund Jephcott, edited by Peter Demetz, 333–36. New York: Schocken, 1978.

———. "Riddle and Mystery." Translated by Rodney Livingstone. In *Selected Writings, Vol. 1: 1913–1926*, edited by Marcus Bullock and Michael W. Jennings, 267–68. Cambridge, MA: Belknap, 1996.

Bennett, J. A. "Hooke's Instruments." In *London's Leonardo: The Life and Work of Robert Hooke*, 63–104. Oxford: Oxford University Press, 2003.

———. "Hooke's Instruments for Astronomy and Navigation." In *Robert Hooke: New Studies*, edited by Michael Hunter and Simon Schaffer, 21–32. Woodbridge, UK: Boydell, 1989.

———. "Robert Hooke as Mechanic and Natural Philosopher." *Notes and Records of the Royal Society of London* 35 (1980): 33–47.

Bennett, Jane. *Vibrant Matter: A Political Ecology of Things*. Durham, NC: Duke University Press, 2010.

Bennett, Joshua Brandon. "'Being Property Once Myself': In Pursuit of the Animal in Twentieth-Century African American Literature." PhD Dissertation, Princeton University, 2016.

Bennington, Geoffrey. *Sententiousness and the Novel: Laying Down the Law in Eighteenth-Century French Fiction*. Cambridge: Cambridge University Press, 1985.

Benveniste, Emile. *Problems in General Linguistics*. Translated by Mary Elizabeth Meek. Coral Gables, FL: University of Miami Press, 1971.

Bernstein, Robin. "Dances with Things: Material Culture and the Performance of Race." *Social Text* 27, no. 4 (2009): 67–94.

Bertucci, Paola. *Artisanal Enlightenment: Science and the Mechanical Arts in Old Regime France*. New Haven, CT: Yale University Press, 2017.

Blackwell, Mark, ed. "The People Things Make: Locke's *Essay Concerning Human Understanding* and the Properties of the Self." *Studies in Eighteenth-Century Culture* 35 (2006): 77–94.

———. *The Secret Lives of Things: Animals, Objects, and It-Narratives in Eighteenth-Century England*. Lewisburg, PA: Bucknell University Press, 2007.

Blewett, David. *The Illustration of Robinson Crusoe, 1719–1920.* Gerrards Cross, UK: Colin Smythe, 1995.

Boehrer, Bruce. *Animal Characters: Nonhuman Beings in Early Modern Literature.* Philadelphia: University of Pennsylvania Press, 2010.

Braidotti, Rosi. *The Posthuman.* Cambridge: Polity, 2013.

Brewer, Daniel. *The Discourse of Enlightenment in Eighteenth-Century France.* Cambridge: Cambridge University Press, 1993.

Brown, Bill. "How to Do Things with Things (a Toy Story)." *Critical Inquiry* 24 (1998): 935–64.

Brown, Laura. *Homeless Dogs and Melancholy Apes: Humans and Other Animals in the Modern Literary Imagination.* Ithaca, NY: Cornell University Press, 2010.

Brusati, Celeste. "Honorable Deceptions and Dubious Distinctions: Self-Imagery in Trompe-l'Oeil." In *Illusions: Gijsbrechts Royal Master of Deception,* edited by Olaf Koester and Celeste Brusati, 49–73. Copenhagen: Statens Museum for Kunst, 1999.

———. "Perspectives in Flux: Viewing Dutch Pictures in Real Time." *Art History* 35, no. 5 (2012): 908–33.

Bryson, Norman. *Looking at the Overlooked: Four Essays on Still Life Painting.* Cambridge, MA: Harvard University Press, 1990.

———. *Vision and Painting: The Logic of the Gaze.* New Haven, CT: Yale University Press, 1983.

Butler, Judith. *Bodies That Matter: On the Discursive Limits of "Sex."* New York: Routledge, 1993.

———. *Excitable Speech: A Politics of the Performative.* New York: Routledge, 1997.

———. *Frames of War: When Is Life Grievable?* London: Verso, 2009.

———. *Giving an Account of Oneself.* New York: Fordham University Press, 2005.

Butor, Michel. "Bricolage: An Interview with Michel Butor." Translated by Noah Guynn. *Yale French Studies* 84 (1994): 17–26.

Caillois, Roger. "Riddles and Images." Translated by Jeffrey Mehlman. *Yale French Studies* 41 (1968): 148–58.

Cameron, Sharon. *Impersonality: Seven Essays.* Chicago: University of Chicago Press, 2007.

Campbell, Mary Baine. *Wonder and Science: Imagining Worlds in Early Modern Europe.* Ithaca, NY: Cornell University Press, 2004.

Canguilhem, Georges. *A Vital Rationalist: Selected Writings from Georges Canguilhem.* Edited by François Delaporte. Translated by Arthur Goldhammer. New York: Zone, 1994.

Carey, Daniel. *Locke, Shaftesbury, and Hutcheson: Contesting Diversity in the Enlightenment and Beyond.* Cambridge: Cambridge University Press, 2009.

Cassirer, Ernst. *Philosophy of the Enlightenment.* Princeton, NJ: Princeton University Press, 1979.

Chadwick, Mary. "'The Most Dangerous Talent': Riddles as Feminine Pastime." In *Women, Popular Culture, and the Eighteenth Century,* edited by Tiffany Potter, 185–201. Toronto: University of Toronto Press, 2012.

Chakrabarty, Dipesh. "Climate of History." *Critical Inquiry* 35 (2009): 197–222.

———. *Provincializing Europe: Postcolonial Thought and Imperial Difference.* Princeton, NJ: Princeton University Press, 2000.

Chapman, Allan. *England's Leonardo: Robert Hooke and the Seventeenth-Century Scientific Revolution.* Bristol, UK: Institute of Physics Publishing, 2005.

Cheah, Pheng. "Humanity in the Field of Instrumentality." *PMLA* 121, no. 5 (2006): 1552–1557.

Classen, Constance. "Museum Manners: The Sensory Life of the Early Museum." *Journal of Social History* 40, no. 4 (2007): 895–914.

Coetzee, J. M. *Elizabeth Costello.* New York: Penguin, 2003.

Cohen, Margaret. *The Novel and the Sea.* Princeton, NJ: Princeton University Press, 2010.

Cohen, Sarah. "Animal Performance in Oudry's Illustrations to the Fables of La Fontaine." *Studies in Eighteenth-Century Culture* 39 (2010): 35–76.

Cohn, Dorrit. *Transparent Minds: Narrative Modes for Presenting Consciousness.* Princeton, NJ: Princeton University Press, 1984.

Cole, Lucinda. *Imperfect Creatures: Vermin, Literature, and the Sciences of Life, 1600–1740.* Ann Arbor: University of Michigan Press, 2016.

Cole, Lucinda, et al. "Speciesism, Identity Politics, and Ecocriticism: A Conversation with Humanists and Posthumanists." *The Eighteenth Century: Theory and Interpretation* 52, no. 1 (2011): 87–106.

Collins, Wilkie. *The Moonstone.* 2nd ed. Edited by John Sutherland. Oxford: Oxford University Press, 2000.

Cook, Alexander, Ned Curthoys, and Shino Konishi. "The Science and Politics of Humanity in the Eighteenth Century: An Introduction." In *Representing Humanity in the Age of Enlightenment,* edited by Cook, Curthoys, and Konishi, 1–14. London: Pickering and Chatto, 2013.

Cook, Eleanor. *Enigmas and Riddles in Literature.* Cambridge: Cambridge University Press, 2006.

Cosgrove, Denis. *Apollo's Eye: A Cartographic Genealogy of the Earth in the Western Imagination.* Baltimore: Johns Hopkins University Press, 2001.

———. "Prospect, Perspective and the Evolution of the Landscape Idea." *Transactions of the Institute of British Geographers* 10 (1985): 45–62.

Cottegnies, Line. "'The Art of Schooling Mankind': The Uses of the Fable in Roger L'Estrange's *Aesop's Fables* (1692)." In *Roger L'Estrange and the Making of Restoration Culture,* edited by Anne Dunan-Page and Beth Lynch, 131–48. Aldershot, UK: Ashgate, 2008.

Crane, R. S. "Suggestions Towards a Genealogy of the 'Man of Feeling.'" *ELH* 1, no. 3 (1934): 205–30.

Crary, Jonathan. *Techniques of the Observer: On Vision and Modernity in the Nineteenth Century.* Cambridge, MA: MIT Press, 1992.

Culler, Jonathan. "The Call of the Phoneme: Introduction." In *On Puns: The Foundation of Letters,* edited by Culler, 1–16. Oxford: Basil Blackwell, 1988.

Curran, Andrew. *The Anatomy of Blackness: Science and Slavery in an Age of Enlightenment.* Baltimore: Johns Hopkins University Press, 2011.

Damisch, Hubert. *The Origin of Perspective.* Translated by John Goodman. MIT Press, 1995. Cambridge, MA.

Damrosch, Leopold Jr. *God's Plots and Man's Stories.* Chicago: University of Chicago Press, 1985.

Daniel, Stephen. "Political and Philosophical Uses of Fables in Eighteenth-Century England." *The Eighteenth Century: Theory and Interpretation* 23, no. 2 (1982): 151–71.

Darmon, Jean-Charles. *Philosophie épicurienne et littérature au XVII siècle en France: Études sur Gassendi, Cyrano, La Fontaine, Saint-Évremond.* Paris: Presses Universitaires de France, 1998.

Daston, Lorraine. "Intelligences: Angelic, Animal, Human." In *Thinking with Animals: New Perspectives on Anthropomorphism,* edited by Lorraine Daston and Gregg Mitman, 37–58. New York: Columbia University Press, 2005.

Daston, Lorraine, and Peter Galison. *Objectivity*. New York: Zone, 2010.

Dawes, James. "Human Rights in Literary Studies." *Human Rights Quarterly* 31, no. 2 (2009): 394–409.

Deacon, Terrence. *The Symbolic Species: The Co-Evolution of Language and the Brain*. New York: Norton, 1998

de Bolla, Peter. *The Architecture of Concepts: The Historical Formation of Human Rights*. New York: Fordham University Press, 2013.

Deleuze, Gilles, and Félix Guattari. *A Thousand Plateaus: Capitalism and Schizophrenia*. Translated by Brian Massumi. Minneapolis: University of Minnesota Press, 1987.

De Man, Paul. "Anthropomorphism and Trope in the Lyric." In *The Rhetoric of Romanticism*, 239–62. New York: Columbia University Press, 1984.

———. "Conclusions: Walter Benjamin's 'The Task of the Translator.'" In *The Resistance to Theory*, 73–105. Minneapolis: University of Minnesota, 1986.

———. "The Epistemology of Metaphor." *Critical Inquiry* 5, no. 1 (1978): 13–30.

———. "Metaphor (Second Discourse)." In *Allegories of Reading: Figural Language in Rousseau, Nietzsche, Rilke, and Proust*, 135–69. New Haven, CT: Yale University Press, 1979.

———. "Semiology and Rhetoric." *Diacritics* 3, no. 3 (1973): 27–33.

Dennis, Michael Aaron. "Graphic Understanding: Instruments and Interpretation in Robert Hooke's *Micrographia*." *Science in Context* 3 (1989): 309–64.

Derrida, Jacques. *The Animal That Therefore I Am*. Translated by David Wills. Edited by Marie-Louise Mallet. New York: Fordham University Press, 2008.

———. *The Beast and the Sovereign: Vol. 1*. Translated by Geoffrey Bennington. Chicago: University of Chicago Press, 2009.

———. "Hostipitality." Translated by Barry Stocker with Forbes Morlock. *Angelaki* 5, no. 3 (2000): 3–18.

———. *Of Hospitality*. Translated by Rachel Bowlby. Stanford, CA: Stanford University Press, 2000.

———. "Shibboleth: For Paul Celan." Translated by Joshua Wilner. In *Word Traces: Readings of Paul Celan*, edited by Aris Fioretos, 3–72. Baltimore: Johns Hopkins University Press, 1994.

———. *The Truth in Painting*. Translated by Geoffrey Bennington and Ian McLeod. Chicago: University of Chicago Press, 1987.

de Waal, Frans. *The Ape and the Sushi Master: Cultural Reflections by a Primatologist*. New York: Basic, 2001.

Doane, Mary Ann. "The Indexical and the Concept of Medium Specificity." *differences* 18, no. 1 (2007): 128–52.

———. "Indexicality: Trace and Sign." *differences* 18, no. 1 (2007): 1–7.

Donald, Diana. *Picturing Animals in Britain, 1750–1850*. New Haven, CT: Yale University Press, 2007.

Douzinas, Costas. *Human Rights and Empire: The Political Philosophy of Cosmopolitanism*. Oxford: Routledge, 2007.

DuBois, John W. "Meaning Without Intentions: Lessons from Divination." In *Responsibility and Evidence in Oral Discourse*, edited by Jane H. Hill and Judith T. Irvine, 48–71. Cambridge: Cambridge University Press, 1993.

Eamon, William. *Science and the Secrets of Nature: Books of Secrets in Medieval and Early Modern Culture*. Princeton, NJ: Princeton University Press, 1994.

Edelstein, Dan. "Enlightenment Rights Talk." *Journal of Modern History* 86, no. 3 (2014): 530–65.

———. *The Terror of Natural Right: Republicanism, the Cult of Nature, and the French Revolution.* Chicago: University of Chicago Press, 2009.

Ehrlich, Mark. "Mechanism and Activity in the Scientific Revolution: The Case of Robert Hooke." *Annals of Science* 52, no. 2 (1995): 127–51.

Elkins, James. *The Poetics of Perspective.* Ithaca, NY: Cornell University Press, 1994.

Engels, Frederick. "The Part Played by Labour in the Transition from Ape to Man." [1876]. In *Karl Marx and Frederick Engels: Selected Works in One Volume,* 354–64. Moscow: Progress, 1977.

Esmeir, Samera. "On Making Dehumanization Possible." *PMLA* 121, no. 5 (2006): 1544–1551.

Esposito, Roberto. *The Third Person: Politics of Life and Philosophy of the Impersonal.* Translated by Zakiya Hanafi. Cambridge: Polity, 2012.

Farber, Paul Lawrence. *Discovering Birds: The Emergence of Ornithology as a Scientific Discipline, 1760–1850.* Baltimore: Johns Hopkins University Press, 1997.

Feagin, Susan. "Presentation and Representation." *Journal of Aesthetics and Art Criticism* 56, no. 3 (1998): 234–40.

Ferguson, Frances. "Canons, Poetics, and Social Value: Jeremy Bentham and How to Do Things with People." *MLQ* 110, no. 5 (1995): 1148–64.

———. "Jane Austen, *Emma,* and the Impact of Form." *MLQ* 61, no. 1 (2000): 157–80.

———. "Reading Morals: Locke and Rousseau." *Representations* 6 (1984): 66–84.

Festa, Lynn. "Crusoe's Island of Misfit Things." *The Eighteenth Century: Theory and Interpretation* 52, no. 3–4 (2011): 443–71.

———. "Humanity Without Feathers." *Humanity: An International Journal of Human Rights, Humanitarianism, and Development* 1, no. 1 (2010): 3–27.

———. *Sentimental Figures of Empire in Eighteenth-Century Britain and France.* Baltimore: Johns Hopkins University Press, 2006.

Fisher, Philip. *Making and Effacing Art: Modern American Art in a Culture of Museums.* Cambridge, MA: Harvard University Press, 1997.

Fissell, Mary. "Imagining Vermin in Early Modern England." *History Workshop Journal* 47 (1999): 1–29.

Flynn, Carol Houlihan. *The Body in Swift and Defoe.* Cambridge: Cambridge University Press, 1990.

Folkenflik, Robert. "*Robinson Crusoe* and the Semiotic Crisis of the Eighteenth Century." In *Defoe's Footprints: Essays in Honour of Maximillian E. Novak,* edited by Robert Maniquis and Carl Fisher, 98–125. Toronto: University of Toronto Press, 2009.

Forbes, Peter. *Dazzled and Deceived: Mimicry and Camouflage.* New Haven, CT: Yale University Press, 2009.

Foucault, Michel. *The Order of Things: An Archaeology of the Human Sciences.* New York: Vintage, 1994.

Fournier, Marian. *The Fabric of Life: Microscopy in the Seventeenth Century.* Baltimore: Johns Hopkins University Press, 1996.

Fowler, Elizabeth. *Literary Character: The Human Figure in Early English Writing.* Ithaca, NY: Cornell University Press, 2003.

François, Anne-Lise. "'O Happy Living Things': Frankenfoods and the Bounds of Wordsworthian Natural Piety." *Diacritics* 33, no. 2 (2003): 42–70.

Freedgood, Elaine. *The Ideas in Things: Fugitive Meaning in the Victorian Novel.* Chicago: University of Chicago Press, 2006.

Freud, Sigmund. *Civilization and Its Discontents.* Translated by James Strachey. New York: Norton, 1961.

Friedland, Paul. "Friends for Dinner: The Early Modern Roots of Modern Carnivorous Sensibilities." *History of the Present* 1, no. 1 (2011): 84–112.

Frow, John. *Character and Person.* Oxford: Oxford University Press, 2016.

———. *Genre.* New York: Routledge, 2006.

———. "A Pebble, a Camera, a Man Who Turns into a Telephone Pole." In *Things*, edited by Bill Brown, 346–61. Chicago: University of Chicago Press, 2004.

Frye, Northrop. *Anatomy of Criticism.* Princeton, NJ: Princeton University Press, 1971.

———. *Spiritus Mundi: Essays on Literature, Myth, and Society.* Bloomington: Indiana University Press, 1976.

Fudge, Erica. *Brutal Reasoning: Animals, Rationality, and Humanity in Early Modern England.* Ithaca, NY: Cornell University Press, 2006.

———. *Perceiving Animals: Humans and Beasts in Early Modern English Culture.* New York: St. Martin's Press, 2000.

Gal, Ofer, and Raz Chen-Morris. *Baroque Science.* Chicago: University of Chicago Press, 2013.

———. "Empiricism Without the Senses: How the Instrument Replaced the Eye." In *The Body as Object and Instrument of Knowledge: Embodied Empiricism in Early Modern Science*, edited by Charles Wolfe and Ofer Gal, 121–47. Dordrecht, Netherlands: Springer, 2010.

Galison, Peter. "Image of Self." In *Things That Talk: Object Lessons from Art and Science*, edited by Lorraine Daston, 257–94. New York: Zone, 2004.

Galperin, William. *The Return of the Visible in British Romanticism.* Baltimore: Johns Hopkins University Press, 1993.

Gay, Peter. *The Enlightenment.* 2 vols. New York: Norton, 1995.

Gell, Alfred. "Vogel's Net: Traps as Artworks and Artworks as Traps." *Journal of Material Culture* 1, no. 1 (1996): 15–38.

Genette, Gérard. "De la figure à la fiction." In *Métalepses: Entorses au pacte de la representation*, edited by John Pier and Jean-Marie Schaeffer, 21–35. Paris: Éditions de l'École des Hautes Études en Sciences Sociales, 2005.

Georges, Robert A., and Alan Dundes. "Toward a Structural Definition of the Riddle." *Journal of American Folklore* 76, no. 300 (1963): 111–18.

Geyer, Michael, and Charles Bright. "World History in a Global Age." *American Historical Review* 100, no. 4 (1995): 1034–50.

Ghosh, Amitav. *The Great Derangement: Climate Change and the Unthinkable.* New York: Penguin, 2016.

Gilbert, Creighton E. "Grapes, Curtains, Human Beings: The Theory of Missed Mimesis." In *Künstlerischer Austausch—Artistic Exchange: Akten des XXVIII. Internationalen Kongresses für Kunstgeschichte, Berlin, 15.–20. Juli 1992*, edited by Thomas W. Gaehtgens, 413–22. 3 vols. Berlin: Akademie Verlag, 1993.

Ginzburg, Carlo. "Making Things Strange: The Prehistory of a Literary Device." *Representations* 56 (1996): 8–28.

Gombrich, Ernst. *Art and Illusion: A Study in the Psychology of Pictorial Representation.* Princeton, NJ: Princeton University Press, 2000.

———. "Meditations on a Hobby Horse, or the Roots of Artistic Form." In *Art Theory and Criticism: An Anthology of Formalist, Avant-Garde, Contextualist and Post-Modern Thought*, edited by Sally Everett, 41–54. Jefferson, NC: McFarland, 1991.

———. "Standards of Truth: The Arrested Image and the Moving Eye." *Critical Inquiry* 7, no. 2 (1980): 237–73.

Goodman, Kevis. *Georgic Modernity and British Romanticism: Poetry and the Mediation of History.* Cambridge: Cambridge University Press, 2008.

Grootenboer, Hanneke. *The Rhetoric of Perspective: Realism and Illusionism in Seventeenth-Century Dutch Still-Life Painting.* Chicago: University of Chicago Press, 2005.

Grusin, Richard. "Introduction." In *The Nonhuman Turn*, edited by Richard Grusin, vii–xxix. Minneapolis: University of Minnesota Press, 2015.

Guibbory, Achsah. "Imitation and Originality: Cowley and Bacon's Vision of Progress." *SEL* 29, no. 1 (1989): 99–120.

Hacking, Ian. *Representing and Intervening: Introductory Topics in the Philosophy of Natural Science.* Cambridge: Cambridge University Press, 1983.

Hamon, Philippe. "Rhetorical Status of the Descriptive." Translated by Patricia Baudoin. *Yale French Studies* 61 (1981): 1–26.

Hanazaki, Tomoko. "A New Parliament of Birds: Aesop, Fiction, and Jacobite Rhetoric." *Eighteenth-Century Studies* 27, no. 2 (1993–94): 235–54.

Hankins, Thomas L., and Robert J. Silverman. *Instruments and the Imagination.* Princeton, NJ: Princeton University Press, 1995.

Haraway, Donna. *The Companion Species Manifesto: Dogs, People, and Significant Otherness.* Chicago: Prickly Paradigm, 2003.

———. "A Cyborg Manifesto: Science, Technology, and Socialist-Feminism in the Late Twentieth Century." In *Simians, Cyborgs, and Women*, 149–81. New York: Routledge, 1990.

Harrison, Charles, Paul Wood, and Jason Gaiger, eds. *Art in Theory, 1648–1815: An Anthology of Changing Ideas.* Oxford: Blackwell, 2000.

Harrison, Peter. *The Bible, Protestantism, and the Rise of Natural Science.* Cambridge: Cambridge University Press, 2009.

———. *The Fall of Man and the Foundations of Science.* Cambridge: Cambridge University Press, 2007.

Hartman, Geoffrey. "Language from the Point of View of Literature." In *Beyond Formalism: Literary Essays, 1958–1970*, 337–55. New Haven, CT: Yale University Press, 1970.

Hartman, Saidiya. *Scenes of Subjection: Terror, Slavery, and Self-Making in Nineteenth-Century America.* New York: Oxford University Press, 1997.

Harwood, John. "Rhetoric and Graphics in *Micrographia*." In *Robert Hooke: New Studies*, edited by Michael Hunter and Simon Schaffer, 119–47. Woodbridge, UK: Boydell, 1989.

Hegel, G. W. F. *Aesthetics: Lectures on Fine Art.* Translated by T. M. Knox. 2 vols. Oxford: Clarendon, 1975.

Heidegger, Martin. *The Fundamental Concepts of Metaphysics: World, Finitude, Solitude.* Translated by William McNeill and Nicholas Walker. Bloomington: Indiana University Press, 1995.

———. "Letter on 'Humanism.'" Translated by Frank A. Capuzzi. In *Basic Writings*, edited by David F. Krell, 189–242. New York: Harper and Row, 1977.

———. "The Origin of the Work of Art." In *Poetry, Language, Thought*, translated by Albert Hofstadter, 15–87. New York: Harper and Row, 1971.

Heise, Ursula. *Sense of Place and Sense of Planet: The Environmental Imagination of the Global.* Oxford: Oxford University Press, 2008.

Heller-Roazen, Daniel. *Dark Tongues: The Art of Rogues and Riddles.* New York: Zone, 2013.

———. *The Enemy of All: Piracy and the Law of Nations.* Cambridge, MA: MIT Press, 2009.

Henry, John. "Robert Hooke, The Incongruous Mechanist." In *Robert Hooke: New Studies*, edited by Michael Hunter and Simon Schaffer, 149–80. Woodbridge, UK: Boydell, 1989.

Hinnant, Charles. *The Poetry of Anne Finch: An Essay in Interpretation*. Newark: University of Delaware Press, 1994.

Hochstrasser, Julie. *Still Life and Trade in the Dutch Golden Age*. New Haven, CT: Yale University Press, 2007.

Høgel, Christian. *The Human and the Humane: Humanity as Argument from Cicero to Erasmus*. Göttingen, Germany: V & R Academic, 2015.

Horkheimer, Max, and Theodor Adorno. *Dialectic of Enlightenment*. Translated by John Cumming. New York: Continuum, 2002.

Hulme, Peter. *Colonial Encounters: Europe and the Native Caribbean, 1492–1797*. London: Methuen, 1986.

Hundert, E. J. *The Enlightenment's Fable: Bernard Mandeville and the Discovery of Society*. Cambridge: Cambridge University Press, 1994.

Hunt, Alastair. "Rightlessness: The Perplexities of Human Rights." *CR: The New Centennial Review* 11, no. 2 (Fall 2011): 115–42.

———. "The Rights of the Infinite." *Qui Parle* 19, no. 2 (2011): 223–51.

Hunt, Lynn. *Inventing Human Rights: A History*. New York: Norton, 2007.

Hunter, Matthew. *Wicked Intelligence: Visual Art and the Science of Experiment in Restoration London*. Chicago: University of Chicago Press, 2013.

Hunter, Michael. *Establishing the New Science: The Experience of the Early Royal Society*. Woodbridge, UK: Boydell, 1989.

———. "Hooke's Possessions at His Death: A Hitherto Unknown Inventory." In *Robert Hooke: New Studies*, edited by Michael Hunter and Simon Schaffer, 287–94. Woodbridge, UK: Boydell, 1989.

———. *Science and Society in Restoration England*. Cambridge: Cambridge University Press, 1981.

Hunter, Michael, and Simon Schaffer. "Introduction." In *Robert Hooke: New Studies*, edited by Michael Hunter and Simon Schaffer, 1–6. Woodbridge, UK: Boydell, 1989.

Hutchison, Keith. "What Happened to Occult Qualities in the Scientific Revolution?" *Isis* 73 (1982): 233–53.

Jacobs, Alan. "Naming of the Animals." In *A Dictionary of Biblical Tradition in English Literature*, edited by David Lyle Jeffrey, 537–38. Grand Rapids, MI: William B. Eerdmans, 1992.

Jager, Eric. "The Parrot's Voice: Language and Self in *Robinson Crusoe*." *Eighteenth-Century Studies* 21, no. 3 (1988): 316–33.

Jain, Sarah. "The Prosthetic Imagination: Enabling and Disabling the Prosthesis Trope." *Science, Technology, and Human Values* 24, no. 1 (1999): 31–54.

James, Henry. *The Golden Bowl*. Edited by Virginia Llewellyn Smith. Oxford: Oxford University Press, 1988.

Jardine, Lisa. *The Curious Life of Robert Hooke: The Man Who Measured London*. New York: HarperCollins, 2005.

Johns, Adrian. *The Nature of the Book: Print and Knowledge in the Making*. Chicago: University of Chicago Press, 1998.

Johnson, Barbara. "A Hound, a Bay Horse, and a Turtle Dove: Obscurity in *Walden*." In *A World of Difference*, 49–56. Baltimore: Johns Hopkins University Press, 1987.

———. "Melville's Fist: The Execution of *Billy Budd*." *Studies in Romanticism* 18, no. 4 (1979): 567–99.

———. *Persons and Things*. Cambridge, MA: Harvard University Press, 2008.

Kahn, Victoria. "Hobbes, Romance, and the Fiction of Mimesis." *Political Theory* 29, no. 1 (2001): 4–29.

Kalas, Rayna. *Frame, Glass, Verse: The Technology of Poetic Invention in the English Renaissance*. Ithaca, NY: Cornell University Press, 2007.

Keane, Webb. "Semiotics and the Social Analysis of Material Things." *Language and Communication* 23 (2003): 409–25.

Keenan, Thomas. *Fables of Responsibility: Aberrations and Predicaments in Ethics and Politics*. Stanford, CA: Stanford University Press, 2007.

Keenleyside, Heather. *Animals and Other People: Literary Forms and Living Beings in the Long Eighteenth Century*. Philadelphia: University of Pennsylvania Press, 2016.

———. "Personification for the People: On James Thomson's *The Seasons*." *ELH* 76, no. 2 (2009): 447–72.

Kemp, Martin. *The Science of Art: Optical Themes in Western Art from Brunelleschi to Seurat*. New Haven, CT: Yale University Press, 1992.

Kenyon-Jones, Christine. *Kindred Brutes: Animals in Romantic-Period Writing*. Burlington, VT: Ashgate, 2001.

Knapp, Steven. *Personification and the Sublime*. Cambridge, MA: Harvard University Press, 1985.

Koester, Olaf. "Cornelius Norbertus Gijsbrechts—an Introduction." In *Illusions: Gijsbrechts, Royal Master of Deception*, edited by Olaf Koester and Celeste Brusati, 13–47. Copenhagen: Statens Museum for Kunst, 1999.

———. *Painted Illusions: The Art of Cornelis Gijsbrechts*. London: National Gallery, 2000.

Koester, Olaf, and Celeste Brusati, eds. *Illusions: Gijsbrechts, Royal Master of Deception*. Copenhagen: Statens Museum for Kunst, 1999.

Kohn, Eduardo. *How Forests Think: Towards an Anthropology Beyond the Human*. Berkeley: University of California Press, 2013.

Koselleck, Reinhart. "The Historical-Political Semantics of Asymmetric Counterconcepts." In *Futures Past: On the Semantics of Historical Time*, translated by Keith Tribe, 155–91. New York: Columbia University Press, 2004.

Kowaleski-Wallace, Elizabeth. "The Things Things Don't Say: *The Rape of the Lock*, Vitalism, and New Materialsim." *The Eighteenth Century: Theory and Interpretation* 59, no. 1 (2018): 105–22.

Kramnick, Jonathan. *Actions and Objects from Richardson to Hobbes*. Stanford, CA: Stanford University Press, 2010.

Kroll, Richard W. F. *The Material Word: Literate Culture in the Restoration and Early Eighteenth Century*. Baltimore: Johns Hopkins University Press, 1991.

Lacan, Jacques. *The Four Fundamental Concepts of Psycho-Analysis*. Translated by Alan Sheridan. New York: Norton, 1981.

Lamb, Jonathan. *The Things Things Say*. Princeton, NJ: Princeton University Press, 2011.

Landry, Donna. *Noble Brutes: How Eastern Horses Transformed English Culture*. Baltimore: Johns Hopkins University Press, 2008.

Laqueur, Thomas. "Bodies, Details, and the Humanitarian Narrative." In *The New Cultural History*, edited by Lynn Hunt, 176–204. Berkeley: University of California Press, 1989.

Latour, Bruno. "Drawing Things Together." In *Representation in Scientific Practice*, edited by Michael Lynch and Steve Woolgar, 19–68. Cambridge, MA: MIT Press, 1992.

————. "How to Be Iconophilic in Art, Science, and Religion?" In *Picturing Science, Producing Art*, edited by Caroline A. Jones and Peter Galison, 418–40. New York: Routledge, 1998.

————. *Reassembling the Social: An Introduction to Actor-Network-Theory*. Oxford: Oxford University Press, 2007.

————. "Visualization and Cognition: Thinking with Eyes and Hands." *Knowledge and Society: Studies in the Sociology of Culture, Past and Present* 6 (1986): 1–40.

————. *We Have Never Been Modern*. Translated by Catherine Porter. Cambridge, MA: Harvard University Press, 1993.

————. "Why Has Critique Run Out of Steam: From Matters of Fact to Matters of Concern." In *Things*, edited by Bill Brown, 151–73. Chicago: University of Chicago Press, 2004.

Lavocat, Françoise. *La syrinx au bûcher: Pan et les satyrs à la Renaissance et à l'âge baroque*. Geneva: Droz, 2005.

Lazareva, Olga F., Toru Shimizu, and Edward Wasserman, eds. *How Animals See the World: Comparative Behavior, Biology, and Evolution of Vision*. Oxford: Oxford University Press, 2012.

Lecoq, Anne-Marie. "'Tromper les yeux,' disent-ils: XIVe–XVIe siècle." In *Le trompe l'oeil de l'antiquité au XXe siècle*, edited by Patrick Mauriès, 63–113. Paris: Gallimard, 1996.

Lefèvre, Wolfgang, ed. *Inside the Camera Obscura: Optics and Art Under the Spell of the Projected Image*. Berlin: Preprint of the Max Planck Institute for the History of Science, 2007.

Lefort, Claude. "Politics and Human Rights." In *The Political Forms of Modern Society: Bureaucracy, Democracy, Totalitarianism*, edited by John B. Thompson, 239–72. Cambridge, MA: MIT Press, 1986.

Leja, Michael. *Looking Askance: Skepticism and American Art from Eakins to Duchamp*. Berkeley: University of California Press, 2004.

Leroi-Gourhan, André. *Gesture and Speech*. Translated by Anna Bostock Berger. Cambridge, MA: MIT Press, 1993.

Lévi-Strauss, Claude. *The Savage Mind*. Translated by John Weightman and Doreen Weightman. Chicago: University of Chicago Press, 1966.

Lewis, Jayne Elizabeth. *The English Fable: Aesop and Literary Culture, 1651–1740*. Cambridge: Cambridge University Press, 1996.

Lichtenstein, Jacqueline. *The Eloquence of Color: Rhetoric and Painting in the French Classical Age*. Translated by Emily McVarish. Berkeley: University of California Press, 1993.

Liu, Lydia H. "Robinson Crusoe's Earthenware Pot." *Critical Inquiry* 25, no. 4 (1999): 728–57.

Loseff, Lev. *On the Beneficence of Censorship: Aesopian Language in Modern Russian Literature*. Translated by Jane Bobko. Munich: Otto Sagner, 1984.

Loveridge, Mark. *A History of Augustan Fable*. Cambridge: Cambridge University Press, 1998.

Lukács, Georg. "Narrate or Describe? A Preliminary Discussion of Naturalism and Formalism." In *Writer and Critic and Other Essays*, edited and translated by Arthur Kahn, 110–48. London: Merlin, 1970.

————. *The Theory of the Novel*. Translated by Anna Bostock. Cambridge, MA: MIT Press, 1971.

Lupton, Julia Reinhard. *Thinking with Shakespeare: Essays on Politics and Life*. Chicago: University of Chicago Press, 2011.

Lupton, Christina. *Knowing Books: The Consciousness of Mediation in Eighteenth-Century Britain*. Philadelphia: University of Pennsylvania Press, 2012.

Lynch, Deidre. *The Economy of Character: Novels, Market Culture, and the Business of Inner Meaning*. Chicago: University of Chicago Press, 1998.

Lyotard, Jean-François. *The Inhuman: Reflections on Time*. Translated by Geoffrey Bennington and Rachel Bowlby. Stanford, CA: Stanford University Press, 1991.

Macpherson, Sandra. *Harm's Way: Tragic Responsibility and the Novel Form*. Baltimore: Johns Hopkins University Press, 2009.

Manfredi, Zachary. "Recent Histories and Uncertain Futures: Contemporary Critiques of International Human Rights and Humanitarianism." *Qui Parle: Critical Humanities and Social Sciences* 22, no. 1 (2013): 3–32.

Mansfield, Elizabeth. *Too Beautiful to Picture: Zeuxis, Myth, and Mimesis*. Minneapolis: University of Minnesota Press, 2007.

Maranda, Elli Köngäs. "The Logic of Riddles." In *Structural Analysis of Oral Tradition*, edited by Pierre Maranda and Elli Köngäs Maranda, 189–232. Philadelphia: University of Pennsylvania Press, 1971.

———. "Riddles and Riddling: An Introduction." *Journal of American Folklore* 89, no. 352 (1976): 127–37.

Marin, Louis. *Food for Thought*. Translated by Mette Hjort. Baltimore: Johns Hopkins University Press, 1997.

———. "Le trompe-l'oeil, un comble de la peinture." In *L'effet trompe-l'oeil dans l'art et la psychanalyse*, edited by Raymond Court, 75–92. Paris: Dunod, 1988.

Marshall, David. "Autobiographical Acts in *Robinson Crusoe*." *ELH* 71, no. 4 (2004): 899–920.

———. *The Frame of Art: Fictions of Aesthetic Experience, 1750–1815*. Baltimore: Johns Hopkins University Press, 2005.

Marx, Karl. *Capital*. Translated by Ben Fowkes. 3 vols. New York: Vintage, 1977.

———. "Economic and Philosophic Manuscripts of 1844." In *The Marx-Engels Reader*, 2nd ed., edited by Robert C. Tucker, 66–125. New York: Norton, 1978.

Maslan, Susan. "The Antihuman: Man and Citizen Before the Declaration of the Rights of Man." *South Atlantic Quarterly* 103, no. 2/3 (2004): 357–74.

Massey, Lyle. *Picturing Space, Displacing Bodies: Anamorphosis in Early Modern Theories of Perspective*. University Park: Penn State University Press, 2007.

Mavhunga, Clapperton Chakanetsa. "Vermin Beings: On Pestiferous Animals and Human Game." *Social Text* 29, no. 1 (2011): 151–176.

McHam, Sarah Blake. *Pliny and the Artistic Culture of the Italian Renaissance: The Legacy of the Natural History*. New Haven, CT: Yale University Press, 2013.

McKenzie, Kenneth. "Italian Fables of the Eighteenth Century." *Italica* 12, no. 2 (1935): 39–44.

McKeon, Michael. "The Dramatic Aesthetic and the Model of Scientific Method in Britain, 1600–1800." *Eighteenth-Century Novel* 6–7 (2009): 197–259.

———. *The Origins of the English Novel: 1600–1740*. Baltimore: Johns Hopkins University Press, 1987.

Menely, Tobias. *The Animal Claim: Sensibility and the Creaturely Voice*. Chicago: University of Chicago Press, 2015.

Millen, Ron. "The Manifestation of Occult Qualities in the Scientific Revolution." In *Religion, Science, and Worldview*, edited by Margaret J. Osler and Paul Lawrence Farber, 185–216. Cambridge: Cambridge University Press, 1985.

Mitchell, W. J. T. "Illusion: Looking at Animals Looking." In *Picture Theory: Essays on Verbal and Visual Representation*, 329–44. Chicago: University of Chicago Press, 1994.

———. *What Do Pictures Want? The Lives and Loves of Images*. Chicago: University of Chicago Press, 2005.

Nash, Richard. *Wild Enlightenment: The Borders of Human Identity in the Eighteenth Century*. Charlottesville: University of Virginia Press, 2003.

Neri, Janice. *The Insect and the Image*. Minneapolis: University of Minnesota Press, 2011.

Newman, W. R. *Atoms and Alchemy: Chemistry and the Experimental Origins of the Scientific Revolution*. Chicago: University of Chicago Press, 2006.

Nietzsche, Friedrich. *On the Genealogy of Morals*. Translated by Walter Kaufmann. New York: Vintage, 1969.

Nixon, Rob. *Slow Violence and the Environmentalism of the Poor*. Cambridge, MA: Harvard University Press, 2013.

Noel, Thomas. *Theories of the Fable in the Eighteenth Century*. New York: Columbia University Press, 1975.

Novak, Maximilian. *Defoe and the Nature of Man*. Oxford: Oxford University Press, 1963.

Nussbaum, Felicity. *The Limits of the Human: Fictions of Anomaly, Race and Gender in the Long Eighteenth Century*. Cambridge: Cambridge University Press, 2003.

Nuti, Lucia. "The Perspective Plan in the Sixteenth Century: The Invention of a Representational Language." *Art Bulletin* 76, no. 1 (March 1994): 105–28.

Pagden, Anthony. *The Fall of Natural Man: The American Indian and the Origins of Comparative Ethnology*. Cambridge: Cambridge University Press, 1987.

Palmeri, Frank. "The Autocritique of Fables." In *Humans and Other Animals in Eighteenth-Century British Culture: Representation, Hybridity, Ethics*, edited by Frank Palmeri, 83–100. Aldershot, UK: Ashgate, 2006.

Panofsky, Erwin. *Perspective as Symbolic Form*. New York: Zone, 1996.

Park, Julie. *The Self and It: Novel Objects and Material Subjects in Eighteenth-Century England*. Stanford, CA: Stanford University Press, 2009.

Patterson, Annabel. *Fables of Power: Aesopian Writing and Political History*. Durham, NC: Duke University Press, 1991.

Paxson, James. *The Poetics of Personification*. Cambridge: Cambridge University Press, 1994.

Peirce, Charles S. *Collected Papers of Charles Sanders Peirce: Vol 2, Elements of Logic*. Edited by Charles Hartshorne and Paul Weiss. Cambridge, MA: Harvard University Press, 1960.

———. "An Elementary Account of the Logic of Relatives." In *Writings of Charles Peirce: Vol. 5, 1884–86*, edited by Christian Kloesel, 379–87. Bloomington: Indiana University Press, 1993.

———. "Logic as Semiotic: The Theory of Signs." In *The Philosophical Writings of Peirce*, edited by Justus Buchler, 98–119. New York: Dover, 1955.

Pérez-Ramos, Antonio. *Francis Bacon's Idea of Science and the Maker's Knowledge Tradition*. Oxford: Clarendon, 1988.

Perkins, David. *Romanticism and Animal Rights*. Cambridge: Cambridge University Press, 2003.

Peterson, Charles Murtagh. "Beautiful Painted Lies: Deception and Illusionistic Painting in the Seventeenth Century." PhD dissertation, University of California, Santa Barbara, 2012.

Picciotto, Joanna. *Labors of Innocence in Early Modern England*. Cambridge, MA: Harvard University Press, 2010.

———. "Milton and the People." In *Milton in the Long Restoration*, edited by Blair Hoxby and Ann Baynes Coiro, 483–502. Oxford: Oxford University Press, 2016.

Potts, Alex. "Disparities Between Part and Whole in the Description of Works of Art." In *Regimes of Description: In the Archive of the Eighteenth Century*, edited by John Bender and Michael Marrinan, 135–50. Stanford, CA: Stanford University Press, 2005.

Powers, Luke. "Tests for True Wit: Jonathan Swift's Pen and Ink Riddles." *South Central Review* 7, no. 4 (1990): 40–52.

Propp, Vladimir. *Morphology of the Folktale*. Translated by Lawrence Scott. Austin: University of Texas Press, 2011.

Pumfrey, Stephen. "Ideas Above His Station: A Social Study of Hooke's Curatorship of Experiments." *Journal of the History of Science* 29 (1991): 1–44.

Raffles, Hugh. "Jews, Lice, and History." *Public Culture* 19, no. 3 (2007): 521–66.

Rancière, Jacques. *The Philosopher and His Poor*. Translated by John Drury, Corinne Oster, and Andrew Parker. Edited by Andrew Parker. Durham, NC: Duke University Press, 2004.

———. "Ten Theses on Politics." Translated by Davide Panagia and Rachel Bowlby. *Theory and Event* 5, no. 3 (2001). https://muse.jhu.edu/ (accessed September 8, 2018).

———. "Ten Theses on Politics." In *Dissensus: On Politics and Aesthetics*, edited and translated by Steven Corcoran, 27–44. London: Bloomsbury Academic, 2010.

———. "Who Is the Subject of the Rights of Man?" *South Atlantic Quarterly* 103, no. 2/3 (2004): 297–310.

Ratcliff, Marc J. *The Quest for the Invisible: Microscopy in the Enlightenment*. Burlington, VT: Ashgate, 2009.

Recueil Milliet. Textes grecs et latins relatifs à l'histoire de la peinture ancienne: t. 1. Translated and edited by Adolphe Reinach. Paris: C. Klincksieck, 1921.

Redfern, Walter. *Puns: More Senses Than One*. New York: Basil Blackwell, 1985.

Richetti, John. *Defoe's Narratives: Situations and Structures*. Oxford: Oxford University Press, 1975.

Riello, Giorgio. *A Foot in the Past: Consumers, Producers and Footwear in the Long Eighteenth Century*. Oxford: Oxford University Press, 2006.

Rikken, Marrigje. *Melchior d'Hondecoeter: Bird Painter*. Amsterdam: Rijksmuseum, 2008.

Robbins, Louise E. *Elephant Slaves and Pampered Parrots: Exotic Animals in Eighteenth-Century Paris*. Baltimore: Johns Hopkins University Press, 2002.

Roberts, Lissa, Simon Schaffer, and Peter Dear, eds. *The Mindful Hand: Inquiry and Invention from the Late Renaissance to Early Industrialisation*. Amsterdam: Royal Netherlands Academy of Arts and Sciences, 2007.

Rogers, Pat, ed. *Defoe: The Critical Heritage*. London: Routledge, 1972.

Rotman, Brian. "Ghost Effects." *differences* 18, no. 1 (2007): 53–86.

Rubin, David Lee. *A Pact with Silence: Art and Thought in the Fables of La Fontaine*. Columbus: Ohio State University Press, 1991.

Ruffin, Kimberly. *Black on Earth: African American Ecoliterary Traditions*. Athens, GA: University of Georgia Press, 2010.

Saccamano, Neil. "Wit's Breaks." In *Body and Text in the Eighteenth Century*, edited by Veronica Kelly and Dorothea von Mucke, 45–67. Stanford, CA: Stanford University Press, 1994.

Sawday, Jonathan. *Engines of the Imagination: Renaissance Culture and the Rise of the Machine*. New York: Routledge, 2007.

Scarry, Elaine. *The Body in Pain: The Making and Unmaking of the World*. New York: Oxford University Press, 1985.

Schaffer, Simon. "Regeneration: The Body of Natural Philosophers in Restoration England." In *Science Incarnate: Historical Embodiments of Natural Knowledge*, edited by Christopher Lawrence and Steven Shapin, 83–120. Chicago: University of Chicago Press, 1998.

Schama, Simon. *The Embarrassment of Riches: An Interpretation of Dutch Culture in the Golden Age*. New York: Vintage, 1997.

Schmidgen, Wolfram. *Eighteenth-Century Fiction and the Law of Property*. Cambridge: Cambridge University Press, 2002.

Schmitt, Karl. *The Concept of the Political*. Translated by George Schwab. Chicago: University of Chicago Press, 1996.

Schulz, Juergen. "Jacopo de' Barberi's View of Venice: Map Making, City Views, and Moralized Geography Before the Year 1500." *Art Bulletin* 60, no. 3 (1978): 425–74.

Serres, Michel. *Genesis*. Translated by Genevieve James. Ann Arbor: University of Michigan Press, 1997.

———. "The Natural Contract." Translated by Felicia McCarren. *Critical Inquiry* 19, no. 1 (1992): 1–21.

———. *The Parasite*. Translated by Lawrence R. Schehr. Minneapolis: University of Minnesota Press, 2007.

———. *Statues: Le second live des fondations*. Paris: Flammarion, 1987.

Shannon, Laurie. *The Accommodated Animal: Cosmopolity in Shakespearean Locales*. Chicago: University of Chicago Press, 2013.

Shapin, Steven. "Pump and Circumstance: Robert Boyle's Literary Technology." *Social Studies of Science* 14, no. 4 (1984): 481–520.

———. "Who Was Robert Hooke?" In *Robert Hooke: New Studies*, edited by Michael Hunter and Simon Schaffer, 253–85. Woodbridge, UK: Boydell, 1989.

Shapin, Steven, and Simon Shaffer. *Leviathan and the Air Pump: Hobbes, Boyle, and the Experimental Life*. Princeton, NJ: Princeton University Press, 1985.

Shaviro, Steven. "Consequences of Panpsychism." In *The Nonhuman Turn*, edited by Richard Grusin, 19–44. Minneapolis: University of Minnesota Press, 2015.

Shklovsky, Viktor. "Art as Device." In *Theory of Prose*, translated by Benjamin Sher, 1–14. Elmwood Park, IL: Dalkey Archive, 1990.

Shortz, William F. "British Word Puzzles (1700–1800)." *Wordways* 6, no. 3 (1973): 131–38.

Silver, Sean. "Hooke, Latour, and the History of Extended Cognition." *The Eighteenth Century: Theory and Interpretation* 57, no. 2 (2016): 197–215.

———. *The Mind Is a Collection: Case Studies in Eighteenth-Century Thought*. Philadelphia: University of Pennsylvania Press, 2015.

Slaughter, Joseph. *Human Rights, Inc.: The World Novel, Narrative Form, and International Law*. New York: Fordham University Press, 2007.

Sloan, Phillip. "The Gaze of Natural History." In *Inventing Human Science*, edited by Christopher Fox, Roy Porter, and Robert Wokler, 112–51. Berkeley: University of California Press, 1995.

Smith, Courtney Weiss. *Empiricist Devotions: Science, Religion, and Poetry in Early Eighteenth-Century England*. Charlottesville: University of Virginia Press, 2016.

Smith, Jacob. *Eco-sonic Media*. Berkeley: University of California Press, 2015.

Smith, Pamela H. *The Body of the Artisan: Art and Experience in the Scientific Revolution*. Chicago: University of Chicago Press, 2004.

Stafford, Barbara Maria. *Artful Science: Enlightenment Entertainment and the Eclipse of Visual Education*. Cambridge, MA: MIT Press, 1994.

———. *Body Criticism: Imaging the Unseen in Enlightenment Art and Medicine*. Cambridge, MA: MIT Press, 1993.

Staiti, Paul. "Illusionism, Trompe l'Oeil, and the Perils of Viewership." In *William Harnett*, edited by Doreen Bolger, Marc Simpson, and John Wilmerding, 31–47. New York: Metropolitan Museum of Art, 1992.

Stallybrass, Peter, and Ann Rosalind Jones. "Fetishizing the Glove in Renaissance Europe." In *Things*, edited by Bill Brown, 174–92. Chicago: University of Chicago Press, 2004.

Stalnaker, Joanna. *The Unfinished Enlightenment: Description in the Age of the Encyclopedia.* Ithaca, NY: Cornell University Press, 2010.

Starr, G. A. *Defoe and Casuistry.* Princeton, NJ: Princeton University Press, 1971.

———. *Defoe and Spiritual Autobiography.* Princeton, NJ: Princeton University Press, 1965.

———. "Defoe's Prose Style: 1. The Language of Interpretation." *Modern Philology* 71, no. 3 (1974): 277–94.

Steadman, Philip. *Vermeer's Camera: Uncovering the Truth Behind the Masterpiece.* Oxford: Oxford University Press, 2002.

Steintrager, James. *Cruel Delight: Enlightenment Culture and the Inhuman.* Bloomington: Indiana University Press, 2004.

Stephens, Frederic George, and M. Dorothy George. *Catalogue of Prints and Drawings in the British Museum, Division I: Political and Personal Satires.* 11 vols. in 12 parts. London: Chiswick, 1870–1954.

Stiegler, Bernard. *Technics and Time, 1: The Fault of Epimetheus.* Translated by Richard Beardsworth and George Collins. Stanford, CA: Stanford University Press, 1998.

Stoichita, Victor. *The Self-Aware Image: An Insight into Early Modern Meta-Painting.* Translated by Anne-Marie Glasheen. Cambridge: Cambridge University Press, 1997.

Stuurman, Siep. *The Invention of Humanity: Equality and Cultural Difference in World History.* Cambridge, MA: Harvard University Press, 2017.

Sudan, Rajani. *Fair Exotics: Xenophobic Subjects in English Literature, 1720–1850.* Philadelphia: University of Pennsylvania Press, 2002.

Sullivan, Scott. *The Dutch Gamepiece.* Totowa, NJ: Rowman & Allanheld, 1984.

Summers, David. *Real Spaces: World Art History and the Rise of Western Modernism.* London: Phaidon, 2003.

Tague, Ingrid. *Animal Companions: Pets and Social Change in Eighteenth-Century Britain.* University Park: Penn State University Press, 2015.

———. "Companions, Servants, or Slaves: Considering Animals in Eighteenth-Century England." *Studies in Eighteenth-Century Culture* 39 (2010): 111–30.

Tamen, Miguel. "Kinds of Persons, Kinds of Rights, Kinds of Bodies." *Cardozo Studies in Law and Literature* 10, no. 1 (1998): 1–32.

Taub, Liba. "Introduction: Reengaging with Instruments." *Isis* 102, no. 4 (2011): 689–96.

Taussig, Michael. *Mimesis and Alterity: A Particular History of the Senses.* New York: Routledge, 1992.

Taylor, Archer. *English Riddles from Oral Tradition.* New York: Octagon, 1977.

———. "The Riddle." *California Folklore Quarterly* 2 (1943): 129–47.

Thomas, Keith. *Man and the Natural World: A History of the Modern Sensibility.* New York: Pantheon, 1983.

Thompson, Helen. *Fictional Matter: Empiricism, Corpuscles, and the Novel.* Philadelphia: University of Pennsylvania Press, 2017.

Tiffany, Daniel. *Infidel Poetics: Riddles, Nightlife, Substance.* Chicago: University of Chicago Press, 2009.

————. "Lyric Substance: On Riddles, Materialism, and Poetic Obscurity." In *Things*, edited by Bill Brown, 72–98. Chicago: University of Chicago Press, 2004.

————. *Toy Medium: Materialism and Modern Lyric.* Berkeley: University of California Press, 2000.

Travis, Peter. "Aesop's Symposium of Animal Tongues." *Postmedieval: A Journal of Medieval Cultural Studies* 2, no. 1 (2011): 33–49.

Trentmann, Frank. "Materiality in the Future of History: Things, Practices, and Politics." *Journal of British Studies* 48 (2009): 283–307.

Tunstall, Kate. "Text, Image, Intertext: Diderot, Chardin and Pliny." In *Interdisciplinarity: Qu'est-ce que les Lumières? La reconnaisssance au dix-huitième siècle*, edited by G. J. Mallinson, 345–57. Studies on Voltaire and the Eighteenth Century 2006:12. Oxford: Voltaire Foundation, 2006.

Uexküll, Jakob von. *A Foray into the Worlds of Animals and Humans.* Translated by Joseph D. O'Neil. Minneapolis: University of Minnesota Press, 2010.

Vickers, Brian. "The Royal Society and English Prose Style: A Reassessment." In *Rhetoric and the Pursuit of Truth: Language Change in the Seventeenth and Eighteenth Centuries*, by Vickers and Nancy S. Struever, 3–76. Los Angeles: William Andrews Clark Memorial Library, 1985.

Wahrman, Dror. *Mr. Collier's Letter Racks: A Tale of Art and Illusion at the Threshold of the Information Age.* Oxford: Oxford University Press, 2012.

Walker, Jr., Theodore. "African-American Resources for a More Inclusive Liberation Theology." In *This Sacred Earth: Religion, Nature, Environment*, edited by Roger Gottlieb, 309–316. New York: Routledge, 1996.

Wall, Cynthia. *The Prose of Things: Transformations of Description in the Eighteenth Century.* Chicago: University of Chicago Press, 2006.

Watanabe, S., J. Sakamoto, and M. Wakita. "Pigeon's Discrimination of Paintings by Monet and Picasso." *Journal of the Experimental Analysis of Behavior* 63 (1995): 165–74.

Watt, Ian. *The Rise of the Novel: Studies in Defoe, Richardson and Fielding.* Berkeley: University of California Press, 1957.

Weheliye, Alexander. *Habeas Viscus: Racializing Assemblages, Biopolitics, and Black Feminist Theories of the Human.* Durham, NC: Duke University Press, 2014.

Weisman, Alan. *The World Without Us.* New York: Picador, 2008.

Weizman, Eyal. "Material Proportionality." In *The State of Things*, edited by Marta Kuzma, Pable Lafuente, and Peter Osborne, 137–60. London: Koenig, 2012.

Wellmon, Chad. *Becoming Human: Romantic Anthropology and the Embodiment of Freedom.* University Park: Penn State University Press, 2010.

Welsh, Andrew. *Roots of Lyric: Primitive Poetry and Modern Poetics.* Princeton, NJ: Princeton University Press, 1978.

Weststeijn, Arthur. *Commercial Republicanism in the Dutch Golden Age: The Political Thought of Johan and Pieter de la Court.* Leiden: Brill, 2012.

————. "The Power of 'Pliant Stuff': Fables and Frankness in Seventeenth-Century Dutch Republicanism." *Journal of the History of Ideas* 72, no. 1 (2011): 1–27.

Weststeijn, Thijs. *The Visible World: Samuel Van Hoogstraten's Art Theory and the Legitimation of Painting in the Dutch Golden Age.* Translated by Beverley Jackson and Lynne Richards. Amsterdam: Amsterdam University Press, 2008.

Wheeler, Roxann. *The Complexion of Race: Categories of Difference in Eighteenth-Century British Culture.* Philadelphia: University of Pennsylvania Press, 2000.

Wilding, Nick. "Graphic Technologies." In *Robert Hooke: Tercentennial Studies*, edited by Michael Cooper and Michael Hunter, 123–34. Aldershot, UK: Ashgate, 2006.

Williams, Raymond. *Keywords: A Vocabulary of Culture and Society.* Rev. ed. Oxford: Oxford University Press, 1985.

Williamson, Craig. "Introduction." In *A Feast of Creatures: Anglo-Saxon Riddle-Songs*, translated and edited by Williamson, 3–56. Philadelphia: University of Pennsylvania Press, 2011.

Wills, David. *Matchbook: Essays in Deconstruction.* Stanford, CA: Stanford University Press, 2005.

———. *Prosthesis.* Stanford, CA: Stanford University Press, 1995.

Wilson, Catherine. *The Invisible World: Early Modern Philosophy and the Invention of the Microscope.* Princeton, NJ: Princeton University Press, 1995.

———. "Visual Surface and Visual Symbol: The Microscope and the Occult in Early Modern Science." *Journal of the History of Ideas* 49, no. 1 (1988): 85–108.

Wittgenstein, Ludwig. *Philosophical Investigations.* 3rd ed. Translated by G. E. M. Anscombe. Upper Saddle River, NJ: Prentice-Hall, 1958.

Wolfe, Cary. *Animal Rites: American Culture, the Discourse of Species, and Posthumanist Theory.* Chicago: University of Chicago Press, 2003.

———. "Introduction: Bring the Noise: *The Parasite* and the Multiple Genealogies of Posthumanism." In Michel Serres, *The Parasite*, xi–xxviii. Minneapolis: University of Minnesota Press, 2007.

Wolfe, Jessica. *Humanism, Machinery, and Renaissance Literature.* Cambridge: Cambridge University Press, 2004.

Wolloch, Nathaniel. "Dead Animals and the Beast-Machine: Seventeenth-Century Netherlandish Paintings of Dead Animals, as Anti-Cartesian Statements." *Art History* 22 (1999): 705–27.

Woodall, Joanna. "Laying the Table: The Procedures of Still Life." *Art History* 35, no. 5 (2012): 976–1003.

Woolf, Virginia. *The Second Common Reader.* Edited by Andrew McNeillie. New York: Harcourt, 1986.

———. *The Waves.* Harmondsworth, UK: Penguin, 1951.

Wynter, Sylvia. "Unsettling the Coloniality of Being/Power/Truth/Freedom: Towards the Human, After Man, Its Overrepresentation—An Argument." *CR: The New Centennial Review* 3, no. 3 (2003): 257–337.

Yalcin, Fatma. "Van Hoogstraten's Success in Britain." In *The Universal Art of Samuel Van Hoogstraten (1627–1678): Painter, Writer, and Courtier*, edited by Thijs Weststeijn, 161–81. Amsterdam: Amsterdam University Press, 2013.

Yolton, John. "As in a Looking Glass: Perceptual Acquaintance in Eighteenth-Century Britain." *Journal of the History of Ideas* 40 (1979): 207–34.

Zeitlin, Judith. "The Ghosts of Things." Unpublished Paper.

Zitin, Abigail. "Thinking Like an Artist: Hogarth, Diderot, and the Aesthetics of Technique." *Eighteenth-Century Studies* 46, no. 4 (2013): 555–70.

INDEX

abstraction, 14, 24–25, 239, 265n85, 297n61; and anthropomorphism, 167; and bird's-eye view, 40, 43, 81, 84; capacity for, 8–9, 21, 24–25; and Condillac, 27; and Defoe, 220; and description, 228, 229; and fables, 211–15, 217; and Hooke, 88, 89, 112; and humanity, 8–9; humanity as, 5, 22–24, 28, 32, 34, 36, 37, 40, 226, 255, 256; and maker's knowledge, 88, 89; and manual labor, 88, 89; and novelistic realism, 226; realization of, 21, 27, 28, 225; and retinal image, 61; and riddles, 136, 137, 138

actants, 122, 210–11, 292n115

actor network theory, 122, 292n115

Adam, 91, 95, 99–101, 132, 139, 164, 282n22. *See also* Eden; Fall

Adamic man, 212

Addison, Joseph, 20, 122, 124, 152–54, 194, 212, 231, 284n62

Adorno, Theodor, 141, 229, 256, 286n96, 295n26

Aesop, 18, 20, 174, 177, 183, 199, 210; *Aesop's Fables, with Their Morals* (1706), 201; and Bayle, 288n26; depictions of, 177, 179; as enslaved, 20, 177, 289n52; Kames on, 208; *A New Translation of Aesop's Fables* (1708), 201. *See also* Barlow, Francis; L'Estrange, Roger; Mandeville, Bernard de; Ogilby, John; Toland, John

aesthetics, 177, 179, 191, 271n95; and Cowley, 48; and Defoe, 242; description in, 228; and language in novel, 231; and "low" genres, 9, 20, 49, 71–72, 223

Agamben, Giorgio, 3, 6, 51, 175, 181, 246, 287n21; *The Open*, 248

Aglionby, William, 49

Alberti, Leon Battista, 42, 270n75; *Della pittura*, 81

Albertian perspective, 63, 64, 228, 253, 270n75

allegory, 75, 177, 208; and Cowley, 48; and Defoe, 220; and fables, 15, 183, 184, 186, 197, 209, 212; and Hooke's louse, 13, 124–26, 128–29; and Swift, 164

Alpers, Svetlana, *The Art of Describing*, 42, 62, 64, 81

Alryyes, Ala, 231

American Revolution, 6, 70

Ancients and Moderns, Quarrel of, 47, 49–50

animals, 2, 3, 7; and abstract thought vs. manual labor, 89; adaptation of to nature, 51, 58; capacities of, 95; Cartesian, 61, 114; and deception, 57, 74, 269n53; in Defoe, 220, 222–27, 233, 237, 239; Derrida on, 10, 22, 54, 214, 269n53; Descartes on, 61, 260n18, 262n51; and environment, 51, 58; and estranging viewpoints, 2, 35; in fables, 175, 185, 195, 197, 208; and Hooke, 86, 87, 95, 130; human dominion over, 58; humane treatment of, 20, 185; human inferiority to, 95; humans' self-recognition in, 181–82; identification with, 36; intersubjective relation with humans, 57; Lacan on, 51–52, 54, 69, 269n53; as machines, 54, 61, 209, 260n18, 262n51; and mimesis, 84; naturalistic representation of, 209; real vs. fabulous, 208–9; in riddles, 135, 138, 143, 148, 149; speaking, 209; and species adaptation, 98; studies of, 6–7, 9, 10; sufficiency of, 86; sympathetic rendering of consciousness of, 58; and things, 9; as tricked by art, 12, 42, 50, 53, 74; and trompe l'oeil, 78; visual experience of, 42. *See also* birds; creatures; humans vs. animals; life (animal); trap(s)

animism, 211–12

Anne, Queen of England, 184

250; and Locke, 24, 231; of others, 43; perceptual processing of, 61; and Swift, 163. *See also* cogito, Cartesian; knowledge; reason

mirror stage, 54, 69, 271n95

mise-en-abîme, 75

Mitchell, W. J. T., 70

modernity, 71; and colonialism, 37; and humanism, 227; and individual, 122; and Latour, 3, 227, 228

Monet, Claude, 17

Montaigne, Michel de, 16

moral: in fables, 183, 186–88, 195, 208, 212, 215; in Gay, 189, 191, 192, 194; in La Fontaine, 204; in L'Estrange, 200; and "The Man and the Flea," 196–97, 201, 202; in Ogilby, 199

morality/ethics: and Derrida, 195; in fables, 184, 186, 194–95, 211, 215, 216; lessons in, 8; and riddles, 144; and Swift, 144; and unrecognizable other, 195; and wolves, 14

moral sense philosophy, 7

More, Henry, 118

Nagel, Thomas, 298n74

name(s): in Defoe, 222, 229, 230, 236; and descriptions, 222; in fables, 210; and language, 229; pronouns as proper, 162; proper, 165; and riddles, 133, 139–42, 152, 164–65, 170

narcissism, 134, 174, 217, 245

Narcissus and Daphne, 146, 147

natural history, 3, 5, 8, 12, 18, 42, 175, 183; Bayle on, 55; and Buffon, 82–83; description in, 228, 229; and fables, 184

natural philosophy, 99–100, 211

natural theology, 57

nature: and Adam, 100; adaptation of animals to, 58; Bayle on, 54; and Defoe, 220; in fables, 175, 209, 211; and fiction, 82; and Hooke, 94, 96, 101, 104, 106, 110, 113–15, 117, 119, 126, 127; and humanity, 175; humanity as improving, 95, 96; humans as masters and possessors of, 237; humans vs., 255; instrumentalization of, 149; in L'Estrange, 199–200; machines of, 92, 93; and "The Man and the Flea," 201; and New Science, 139; and riddles, 149; and Swift, 143; and technology, 98; transformation of, 94. *See also* state of nature

needle, riddle about, 134, 141, 152

Netherlands, 67

New Science, 12, 18, 101, 125; and Adam, 139; centrality of experiments to, 88; and nature, 139; realism of, 15; and Swift, 129, 219; and tale of Zeuxis and Parrhasius, 47

newspaper, riddle about, 138

Newton, Isaac, 99

Nietzsche, Friedrich, 146, 168; *The Genealogy of Morals*, 256

nonhumans, 8–10, 17, 31; and Defoe, 219; estranging perspective of, 8, 21, 220; and fables, 175; identification with, 20; and riddles, 134–35, 141, 159, 160; rights of, 39; and Swift, 145, 170. *See also* humans vs. nonhumans

Northern European art, 15, 42, 47, 62, 64. *See also* painting(s)

novel(s), 3, 7, 18, 210, 219; as apparitional, 253–54; biographical form of, 252, 253; description in, 15, 228, 229; as diagrammatic object, 253; and empirical world, 254; enactment of humanity in, 9; and epic, 223–24, 248–49; and estranging perspective, 15–17, 224, 226; and fables, 184; heterogeneous elements of, 227; humanity in, 38; impossible knowledge afforded by, 17, 225, 250; and individual, 16; and individual particularity, 15; language in, 231; Lukács on, 3, 223–24, 252; mind of other in, 16; and nonhuman perspectives, 35, 36; and other human perspective, 16–17; and perspective, 15; perspective of things in, 254; and psychology, 16, 138; and reader, 15; and realism, 16, 17, 210, 225, 226, 228; relation of parts to whole in, 224–25; relation of subject to object in, 224; and riddles, 138; and schema, 253; subjective unity of hero of, 254; unity of world of, 223; virtual perspective in, 251, 252; and virtual reality, 16, 254; virtual standpoints in, 225; Woolf on, 252; and world seen without self, 252–53. *See also* description; fiction

nuclear weapons, 256

Nussbaum, Felicity, 6

object(s): and anthropomorphism, 149; and constitution of subjects, 137; and Cowley, 49; in Defoe, 221, 223, 229–32, 236, 237, 239–41, 242; and Locke, 231; relationships

220, 225, 232; linear, 42, 82; literary experiments with, 7, 219; manipulation of, 12, 15; multiple, 64, 66, 253; and Northern painting, 64; not human, 15, 252–54, 299n80; not subjective, 15, 252–54; and novel, 16–17, 219, 221, 225, 226; of other humans, 16–17, 239; and production of humanity, 17, 36, 49, 62, 80, 84, 85; as prosthetic, 62; and realism, 15, 18, 35, 42, 221, 226; and representation of human consciousness, 8, 16; single-point, 228; stability and unity of, 16, 63, 82, 108, 270n72; and still life, 65; and trompe l'oeil, 65, 68; uniformity in, 82; virtual, 43, 62, 83–85. *See also* eye(s); first person; gaze; human perspective/eye-view; points of view; second person; third person; virtual perspectives

Peterson, Charles Murtagh, 79–80

Phaedrus, 183

philosophy, 2, 5, 7, 89, 182, 183, 229; alchemical, 105; and art, 89; description in, 228; Enlightenment, 211; and fables, 184; and Hooke, 87–89

photography, 70

physico-theology, 42, 57–59, 126

Physiologus, 183

pianta prospectiva, 81

Picasso, Pablo, 17

Picciotto, Joanna, 58, 89, 100–101

Pilpay/Bidpai, 183

pin, riddle about, 141

Pitt, William, 164

Plato, 2

Pliny, 18, 40, 44, 51, 52, 86

Poe, Edgar Allan, 220

points of view, 8, 12; in Defoe, 16, 225, 250; and details, 244; and formal unity of novel, 16; and Hooke, 13, 65; of individual vs. species, 8, 63, 221, 225; of other creatures, 57–59, 143; pronouns as representative of, 160–62; and realism, 15; in riddles, 13, 136, 153; and still life, 65, 66; and trompe l'oeil, 15, 76. *See also* perspective(s)

political theory, 2, 184

politics, 5; and Cavendish, 130; and Enlightenment, 28; in fables, 9, 183, 185, 186, 196, 197; and Finch, 205; and Gay, 192; and humanity, 28, 31; and Kames, 206; and representation, 229; and rights-bearing subjects, 28–29, 31–35. *See also* social relations

polysemy, 152

Pope, Alexander, 153, 191; *The Rape of the Lock*, 18, 149

potato, riddle about, 141

Power, Henry, *Experimental Philosophy*, 100

Powers, Luke, 145

Praxiteles, Venus of Cnidos, 42–43

prelapsarian state, 91, 93, 95, 101, 103. *See also* Adam; Eden; Fall

Priestley, Joseph, 138, 203

primates, 181

progress, 93, 96, 99, 101, 103, 106

Prometheus, 95, 101, 117, 121, 129, 130

property, 3, 6, 7

Propp, Vladimir, *Morphology of the Folktale*, 210

prosopopoeia, 134

prosthetic(s): and Adam, 91, 101–2; and body, 9, 91, 102–4, 111; as exteriorized technologies, 97; and God, 93–95; and Hooke, 12, 86–87, 93–106, 122, 123, 129, 130, 163; and humanity, 91; and human vs. nonhuman, 102; perspective as, 62; and senses, 87, 93; and transformation of human capacities, 106. *See also* technology/technologies

Proust, Marcel, 250

proverbs, 183

psychology, 3, 4, 13, 16, 17

puns, 126, 148, 152–55

Rabelais, François, 202

race, 4, 20, 37, 177, 181

Rancière, Jacques, 6, 32–35, 256

Raphael, 49

Rawlsian veil of ignorance, 144

Ray, John, *Wisdom of God*, 58

Ray, John and Francis Willughby, *The Ornithology of Francis Willughby*, 57, 268n41

Ray, William, 126

reader(s)/reading, 8; and adoption of nonhuman viewpoints, 8, 13, 14, 31, 35–36, 265n78; animals as of signs, 121; as author, 194, 276n39; and Defoe, 220, 224–25, 236, 239, 251; and descriptions, 51, 228; and diagrams, 121, 228, 253; as educational, 185–87, 215–16; as enacting human capacities, 8, 19, 30, 136, 188, 191; of fables, 174, 175, 182–85, 212–13, 215–16; humanity produced through, 2, 8, 21, 85, 175, 181, 191, 194, 216, 260n17; and identification, 15, 21, 235, 236; and interpellation, 6, 9, 21, 40,

ACKNOWLEDGMENTS

The title of this book, *Fiction Without Humanity*, is belied by the many friends and colleagues who helped bring this particular fiction into existence. This project took far longer than I anticipated and the debts I have racked up over the years mean that these acknowledgments partake of the epic catalogue. I hope that the sincerity of my gratitude is not diluted by the extensive list of people to whom it is owed.

I began work on this project through the generous support of an American Council of Learned Societies Charles A. Ryskamp Research Fellowship, and much of the manuscript was drafted during a 2013–14 fellowship at the National Humanities Center in North Carolina. I am grateful to the director, Geoffrey Harpham, and the staff of the center, especially Cassie Mansfield and Don Solomon, for making it a productive year. I was fortunate to be in the midst of a wonderful group of fellows who provided both support and friendship. For commenting on drafts, suggesting references, and after-hours respite from work, I am grateful to Barbara Ambros, Luis Cárcamo-Huechante, Cindy Hahamovitch, Evelyn Brooks Higginbotham, Betsy Krause, Heather Hyde Minor, Andy Jewett, Michael Lurie, Charlie McGovern, Vernon Minor, Scott Nelson, Louise Rice, Holly Smith, and most especially Jolie Olcott, Jane Sharp, and Noël Sugimura.

Generous leave and research support from Rutgers University made it possible to complete the manuscript, for which I am deeply indebted. I have been most fortunate in my current and former field colleagues at Rutgers, Billy Galperin, Jonathan Kramnick, Colin Jager, Michael McKeon, and Abigail Zitin. Colleagues in the department—David Kurnick, Rebecca Walkowitz, Elin Diamond, Jonah Seigel, Meredith McGill, Ann Coiro, Brad Evans, Andrew Goldstone, Chris Iannini, Ann Jurecic, Stacy Klein, John Kuchich, Jeff Lawrence, Mukti Lakhi Mangharam, Carter Mathes, Sarah Novacich,

Stéphane Robolin, Evie Shockley, Michelle Stephens, Carolyn Williams, and Nancy Youcef—and beyond it—James Delbourgo, Jane Sharp, Judith Surkis, and Jimmy Swenson—have made the ten years since I joined the faculty at Rutgers both happy and intellectually enlivening ones. I had the good fortune of participating in the 2016–17 Center for Cultural Analysis seminar on "Arts and Aesthetics" organized by Billy Galperin and Henry Turner, and I am indebted both to them and to my fellow participants for a lively year. Finally, I am abidingly grateful for the generous help and unflagging cheer of Cheryl Robinson and Courtney Borack, and the thoughtful engagement of my students at Rutgers, especially those who enrolled in my graduate seminar "Enlightenment Fictions of the Human."

Work from this book has been presented at the annual meeting of the American Society for Eighteenth-Century Studies, as well as at talks and workshops at the University of California–Berkeley, the University of Chicago, the Columbia University Eighteenth-Century Seminar, Harvard University, the Huntington Library, Michigan State University, the University of Minnesota, the New York Eighteenth-Century Seminar, New York University, Ohio State University, the University of Pennsylvania, the University of Pittsburgh, Princeton University, Trinity College, Vanderbilt University, the University of Virginia, Washington University, Wesleyan University, and Yale University. I thank the sponsors of these forums and the audiences for their thoughtful and generous responses to the work. For ideas and questions that have often remained lodged in my brain for months—years—after, I am especially grateful to Ala Alryyes, Srinivas Aravamudan, Barbara Benedict, Scott Black, Katharina Boehm, Dan Brewer, David Brewer, Dan Carey, Tita Chico, Andy Curran, Frances Ferguson, Anne-Lise François, Elaine Freedgood, Jody Greene, Jill Heydt-Stevenson, Sonia Hofkosh, Scott Juengel, Heather Keenleyside, Jonathan Lamb, Françoise Lavocat, Wendy Lee, Jayne Lewis, Ruth Mack, Sandra Macpherson, Bob Markley, Felicity Nussbaum, Julie Park, Alexander Regier, Wolfram Schmidgen, J. B. Shank, Courtney Weiss Smith, Chloe Wigston Smith, John Stevenson, Alexis Tadié, Helen Thompson, Cindy Wall, and Dror Wahrman. Special thanks are due to Tina Lupton, Deidre Lynch, and Sean Silver for generous insights and readings that shaped my thinking about this project in ways large and small. At a pivotal moment in this project I spent several happy, sunny days talking "things" with Sophie Volpp, Judith Zeitlin, and Nick Paige in Berkeley. Various New York–area seminars and working groups have been a central part of my intellectual life for the past few years, and I am grateful to Andrew Clark, Al Coppola, Joanna Stalnaker, Kathy Lubey, Madeleine Dobie, Jeff Freedman, and Frank Boyle.

One happy lesson I have learned in the past few years is that the friends you make in graduate school are for life. Thanks to Suzie Verderber, Rayna Kalas, Gregg Flaxman, Amy Wyngaard, Jeremy Braddock, Juliette Cherbuliez, Chloe Hogg, Tili Boon Cuillé, Claire Goldstein, Sven-Erik Rose, and Dan White. I was fortunate to attend the University of Pennsylvania while Joan DeJean, John Richetti, Margreta de Grazia, Peter Stallybrass, Lynn Hunt, and Liliane Weissberg were on the faculty, and I continue to draw on all that they taught me. Oren Izenberg, Leah Price, Ann Rowland, and Sharmila Sen helped make my years at Harvard, where this book began, happy ones. Sue Lanser, Ruth Perry, Susan Staves, and Beth Kowaleski-Wallace provided a stimulating eighteenth-century enclave in Cambridge. At the University of Wisconsin, I was fortunate to have Lisa Cooper, Terry Kelly, Caroline Levine, Jacques Lezra, Howard Weinbrot, and Susanne Wofford as friends and colleagues.

I am most grateful to Jerry Singerman for his support in bringing this book to publication and to the two anonymous readers for their suggestions and criticisms. I thank Hannah Blake, Pat Wieland, and Noreen O'Connor-Abel for their care in seeing the manuscript through the copyediting and production process and Tom Broughton-Willett for indexing. Thanks to Kelly Roberts for her help in obtaining permissions. Generous support for the publication of this book was provided by the Rutgers English Department, for which I thank our chair Colin Jager and our humanities dean, Michelle Stephens. An earlier version of Chapter 5 was published in *The Eighteenth Century: Theory and Interpretation*. I am also grateful to the libraries at Rutgers University, New York University, and Columbia University.

A number of people have contributed to this work in ways that they may or may not see but that are perfectly clear to me. I thank Frances Bennett, Liz Canner, Maria Festa Carter, Wendy Chun, Greg Coleman, Rob Cummings, Katy Fogle, Linda Festa Griglun, Mark Hershnik, Sue Jones, Analia Kaufman, Elizabeth Kaufman, John Keene, Laura Kopp, Phoebe Minias, Paul Moorcroft, Anita Oliva, Lisa Randall, Denise Robbi, the Rozetts, Sally Stiffler, Liz Festa Twohig, Elizabeth Festa Watson, Diana Wylie, and Tina Zwarg. I was fortunate to have two amazing parents, Winnie and Adam Festa. And as always, I simply don't know what I would do without my sister, Patty, and my wonderful niece and nephew, Kate Barnett and Nick Barnett.

This is a book about fictions and abstractions, but there has been nothing abstract or fictive in the support I have received from my family, friends, and colleagues. Truly no one could have been luckier.